GHOST

The Inside Story of the CIA's
Secret Rendition Programme

PLANE

STEPHEN GREY

HURST & COMPANY, LONDON

First published in the United Kingdom in 2006
by C. Hurst & Co. (Publishers) Ltd.
41 Great Russell Street, London WC1B 3PL
© Stephen Grey, 2006
All rights reserved.
Printed in India

A catalogue record for this volume is available
at the British Library

ISBN–10 1-85065-850-1
ISBN–13 978-1-85065-850-4

CONTENTS

ILLUSTRATIONS

ACKNOWLEDGEMENTS

The outlines of the CIA's rendition programme have emerged not from any single piece of reporting by journalist, or single disclosure by a public official. Instead, details have come to light in a piece-meal fashion. Beat reporters like me who have followed this story have worked co-operatively — not in concert but by picking up pieces of the jigsaw puzzle disclosed by others, and then adding new pieces to the picture of what we know so far. Much more remains to be discovered.

In researching this book, and in previous articles I've written on rendition, I have therefore drawn extensively on the work of others, some of whom have helped me directly, and others whose work I have followed. Not even half of this story of renditions could have emerged without the ground-breaking and neutral reporting of journalists such as Dana Priest and Anthony Shadid among others at *The Washington Post*, Douglas Jehl and other national security writers at the *New York Times*, Andrew Higgins and others at the *Wall Street Journal*, and John Crewdson of *The Chicago Tribune*, none of whom I know personally.

My own research, conducted across the world over the last three years, would not have been possible without the generous support of different editors who have backed my investigations, and tolerated my meagre output. In no particular order, I would like to thank: Matt Purdy, investigations editor of the *New York Times*; Sean Ryan, foreign editor of the *Sunday Times*, and John Witherow, the paper's editor; Peter Wilby and John Kampfner, successive editors of the *New Statesman*; Ed Pilkington, until lately home editor of the *Guardian*; David Ross of BBC Radio's *File on Four* programme, and Peter Barron, editor of *Newsnight*.

In 2005 and 2006, I was particularly lucky to work alongside many of the *New York Times'* finest reporters, and would like to thank for their help and encouragement Don van Natta and Souad Mekhennet, who broke the Khaled el Masri story, Tim Golden of the investigative team, Scott Shane of the Washington bureau, Elaine Sciolino, bureau chief in Paris, Ian Fisher in Rome, and Ray Bonner, the Far-East correspondent. Margot Williams, the paper's investigative reporter and researcher, was a great inspiration. She broke key aspects of the story and gave very generously of her time to help me.

Other journalists to whom I owe particular thanks include: Fredrik Laurin, Joachim Dyfvermark and Sven Bergman, lately of Swedish Channel 4, for their ground-breaking work and cooperation, Jane Mayer of the *New Yorker*, who has led the field in Washington and kindly helped correct some of my errors, Jörg-Hendrik Brase of Germany's ZDF television, who discovered great details of the el-Masri rendition and kindly shared his material, the Danish radio reporter and Uzbekistan expert Michael Andersen, John Barry and Mark Hosenball of *Newsweek*, Graham Messick, a senior producer on *60 Minutes*. Also Mary Wilkinson, Peter Marshall, and David Lewis from the BBC; Ian Cobain from the *Guardian*; Holger Stark of *Spiegel* magazine; Hans Martin-Tillack of *Stern*, Paolo Biondani and Guido Olympia of *Corriere della Serra*, Volker Steinhoff from the NDR in Hamburg; Michelle Shepherd of the *Toronto Star*, Matías Vallés of the *Diario de Mallorca*; and Bob Drogin of the *Los Angeles Times*.

Moreover in reporting a sensitive topic like national security there are very many sources that I wish to thank publicly but cannot do so given that they would not appreciate being named.

In the course of the research, I've had the honour to meet many serving and former officers of America's Central Intelligence Agency (the CIA). Many of them will radically disagree with some of my interpretations and conclusions, but I thank those who have educated me about the Agency — and in particular debunked some of the myths that surround their work. A tool of the President, CIA operatives are frequently confronted, as they have been in the rendition story, with impossible decisions — imposed on them by their orders from above and complicated by the limited means at their disposal. Many of those I've met are men and women of great integrity and few of the decisions they have taken, even in moments of great crisis, were made without great thought. The rendition programme described in *Ghost Plane* was but one aspect of their work — and none of what is written here should imply a comment on their broader activities.

To avoid confusion, all those quoted by name were interviewed entirely for the record and no other quote or material in this book should be attributed to them. Likewise, none of those who spoke on terms of anonymity are cited or thanked here.

Among the dozens of people who I interviewed or who simply helped me with aspects of my research for this project or into the War on Terror generally, I would particularly like to thank: Maher Arar, Abdullah Almalki, Arild Aspøy, Sir Brian Barder, Robert Baer, the (ever courteous) CIA public affairs staff, Alastair Crooke, Jack Cloonan, Tom Cooper, Nicole Choueiry, Gordon Corera, Claudio Cordone, Steve Crawshaw, Roger Cressey, Jack Devine, Sue Davies, Andrew Drzemczewski, the Foreign Office news department, James Fees, Mandi Fahmy, Ford Fessenden, Anne FitzGerald, Rob Freer, the researchers of Cage-Prisoners.com, Burton Gerber, former Congressman Porter Goss, Manfred Gnjidic, Clare Grey, Eloise Grey, Rupert Grey, Clara Gutteridge, Stephen Hopper,

Adam Holloway MP, Henry Kaufman, Dr Brian Jones, Basil Jaber, Dr Mahanad al Kubaisi, Jamal Khashoggi, Niels and Ulf Kadritzke, Dayanti Karunaratne, Kjell Jönsson, Khaled el-Masri, Gavin MacFadyen, Craig Murray, Olivier Minkwitz, Barbara Olshansky, Janet McElligott, John Mcchesney, Uzi Mahnaimi, Olivier Minkwitz, Professor Joe Margulies, Ann Marsh, Renwick McLean, Philippe Madelin, Professor Alfred McCoy, Adrian Monck, Chris Mullin MP, Nizar Nayouf, Alex Neve, Christoph Nufer, Manfred Nowak, Professor Georg Nolte, Stephane Ojeda, Mark Pallis, Mark Perry, Kerry Pither, Dan Raleigh, Carne Ross, Wahab al Rawi, Mihai Radu, Farah Stockman, Helmut Schroeder, Walid Safour, Neil Sammonds, Michael Sheehan, Senator Richard Shelby, Michael Scheuer, Reda Seyam, Guenter Schirmer, Gavin Simpson, Adnan Siddiqui, Lina Sinjab, Stefan Smith, Clive Stafford Smith, Martin Staudinger, Yasser al-Sirri, Chris Stephens, Andrew Tyrie MP, Bob Tyrer, Jonathan Ungoed-Thomas, Ambassador Edward Walker, Cory Walker, Steven Watt, David and Justin Wickham, Sven Zimmermann.

Thanks to my friend Richard Miniter for giving me a home in Washington, DC, and generous introductions — and for putting my arguments to the test. And to the hospitality in Iraq of the fine men and women of the 7th UK Armoured Brigade (the Desert Rats), and others from the US and British military.

Thanks to John Goetz, the Berlin-based investigative TV producer, and my partner in crime of many years, for everything he contributed, including extensive research and interviews in Germany for this book.

Most of all I would like to thank my tireless and enthusiastic researcher, Christina Czapiewska, for everything she contributed, as well as Duncan Brown and Jerome Taylor for their many hours of further research. Thanks too to Alex Bygate, for his research and translation in Milan, to Hossam el-Hamalawy, lately of *the Los Angeles Times*, for his interviews and extensive research in Cairo, and to Katherine Hawkins who helped review the legal aspects of rendition.

Last but not least, thanks to Emma Parry and Robert Kirby for inspiring me to write this book, and to Michael Dwyer and Maria Petalidou at Hurst for their enthusiastic support.

As always, any errors of fact and conclusions are entirely my own, and none mentioned should be assumed to endorse anything I have written. Many who were kind enough to help me would analyse the rendition programme quite differently, and I thank them for their courtesy and, in many cases, a great, great deal of their time.

In such a wide and contested topic, errors of fact and judgement do arise, and I would be grateful to any reader who identifies any mistake to contact me, as well as anyone with further information on these matters. I can be contacted through the website www.ghostplane.net.

London, September 2006　　　　　　　　　　　　　　　　　　S.G.

THE PRINCIPAL ACTORS

Air America

The Ghost Planes — a Gulfstream V and a Boeing Business Jet, both operating from North Carolina

Jim Rhyne — former chief pilot of Air America, founder of "Aero Contractors Limited," a CIA company in North Carolina, killed in a flying accident in 2001

"Captain James Fairing" — a pilot of the CIA Boeing used in renditions

The Prisoners

Maher Arar — a Canadian wireless computer engineer

Binyam Mohamed — an Ethiopian student from London

Ahmed Agiza and Mohammed al-Zery — two Egyptian asylum-seekers in Sweden

Osama Nasr, known as "Abu Omar," — an Egyptian living in Milan

Khaled el-Masri —unemployed German car salesman

Ahmed al-Maati — Canadian truck driver

Abdullah Almalki — Canadian businessman

Manadel al-Jamadi — an alleged insurgent who died at Abu Ghraib, Iraq

The Enemy

Osama bin Laden (OBL)

Dr Ayman al-Zawahiri — head of Egyptian Islamic Jihad, deputy to bin Laden

Abu Musab al-Zarqawi — insurgent leader in Iraq; killed in an air strike, 7 June 2006

Khalid Sheikh Mohammed — chief architect of the September 11 plot

Abu Zubaydah — senior associate of OBL

The Agency

John M. Deutch — Director of CIA, 1995-6
George Tenet — Director of CIA, 1997-2004
Porter Goss — Director of CIA, 2004-6
Michael Scheuer — Head of CIA's Osama bin Laden unit, 1995-9
Cofer Black — Head of the CIA's Counter-Terrorist Centre, 1999-2002
Robert Seldon Lady — former CIA chief of station in Milan, accused of involvement in rendition of Abu Omar

The White House

William J. Clinton — President of the United States, 1993-2001
George W. Bush — President of the United States, 2001-
Samuel "Sandy" Berger — Deputy National Security Advisor, 1993-6; National Security Advisor, 1997-2001
Condoleezza Rice — National Security Advisor, 2001-5
Richard Clarke — Head of Counterterrorism Security Group (CSG) at National Security Council (NSC) 1992-2003 and NSC Terrorism "Czar," 1998-2000
Alberto Gonzales — White House Legal Counsel, 2001-5

The Pentagon

Donald Rumsfeld — Secretary of Defense, 2001-
Paul Wolfowitz — Deputy Secretary of Defense, 2001-5

The Department of Justice

John Ashcroft — Attorney General of the United States, 2001-5
Alberto Gonzales — Attorney General of the United States, 2005-
Larry Thompson — Deputy Attorney General, 2001-3
Jay S. Bybee — Assistant Attorney General, 2001-3
John Yoo — Deputy Assistant Attorney General in the Office of Legal Counsel, 2001-2003

State Department

Condoleezza Rice — Secretary of State, 2005-
General Colin Powell — Secretary of State, 2001-5
Edward Walker Jr. —Ambassador to Egypt, 1994-7
Michael Sheehan — Coordinator for Counterterrorism, 1998-2001

The Whistleblower

Craig Murray — British Ambassador to Uzbekistan, 2002-4

Canada

Canadian Security Intelligence Service (CSIS)
Royal Canadian Mounted Police (RCMP)
Franco Pillarella — Canadian Ambassador to Syria, 2000-3

Egypt

Hosni Mubarak — President, 1981-
Omar Suleiman — Head of Egyptian Intelligence, 1993-
Hassan el-Alfi — Interior Minister, 1993-7
General Habib el-Adly — Interior Minister, 1997-

Italy

Armando Spataro — Deputy Prosecutor of Milan
Bruno Megale — Head of DIGOS Police Anti-Terrorism Squad in Milan
Silvio Berlusconi — Prime Minister, 2001-6

Pakistan

General Pervez Musharraf — President, 1999-
Makhdoom Syed Faisal Saleh Hayat — Interior Minister, 2002-4

Syria

Bashar al-Assad — President , 2000-
General Hassan Khalil — Head of Military Intelligence, 2000-5
Colonel George Salloum — Head of Counter-Terrorism Investigations at the Palestine Branch

United Kingdom

Tony Blair — Prime Minister, 1997-
Jack Straw — Foreign Secretary, 2001-6

Uzbekistan

Islam Karimov — President, 1991-
Shavkat Mirziyaev — former Samarkand regional governor; Prime Minister, 2003-

INSIDE THE PALESTINE BRANCH, SYRIA

Seven prisoners languish in the cells of the Palestine branch, the interrogation jail of Syria's military intelligence in downtown Damascus. All have been sent to Syria by the United States and all are suspects in the War on Terror.

DAMASCUS, SYRIA
Tuesday, 17 December 2002

The Sheraton Hotel boasts of its location at the hub of an ancient city. It is built around an open courtyard. In between clusters of four-storey buildngs, a marble staircase descends as if through an amphiteatre, to a wide shimmering swimming pool that is surrounded by deck chairs and palm trees. You can see the pool from the Ikonos spy satellite, orbiting 420 miles above the earth. The hotel features not only local cuisine but The English Pub, Luigi's Italian pizza restaurant, and the Rumours Disco Bar night club, open till 3 a.m.

Leave behind the liveried doorman and sharp-suited businessmen and exit into the Orient. A cacophony of car and bus horns will greet you as you turn right into busy Omayad Square.

Take the right-hand exit, Addakhel Street, and go up the hill past the large headquarters of Syrian TV. At the next junction, which bridges an old railway track, turn right down Palestine Street. Then take the wide boulevard on your left. The street, you will notice, is now stangely deserted. On the right are three imposing buildings, with wooden and concrete watchtowers on their corners, guarded by soldiers and others in plain clothes. All carry machine guns. By the third building is an entrance with a black metal sliding gate and a sign in English "no photography."[1] With an "invitation" you could enter what is a large complex. Keep going, across a courtyard into a building on your right, go through an office (the prison manager's), into a corridor, and then turn left down a short flight of stairs to the basement. After this imaginary journey, you would now be in Syria's most feared interrogation centre, the "Palestine Branch".

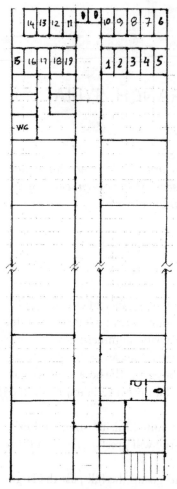

"The Grave"

Go further down the corridor past five large communal cells on either side. If the metal doors were open you would see men squatting on the concrete floors, and women and children in the final cell. Keep going, right to the end of the building and you'll come to a sort of T-junction. Ahead are two small toilets, and to your left and right is a mini-corridor where you will find a series of what look like monastic cells, five on each side of the passage, except in the far left corner, where one cell is missing and a door leads onwards to some forbidden room. This makes a total of nineteen little cells. As you stand at the T-junction, the cells are numbered anti-clockwise, beginning with cell no.1 on your immediate right and ending with cell no.19 on your immediate left.[2]

At this point, you'll notice the smell of uncleared toilets and the sweat of men crammed together. As you're a new visitor, it is likely you will go to an empty cell. The last cell, no.19, has recently been used for people coming in and out, so it's probably empty. As you're pushed through the door, you will see that, if you are of normal height and width, you can barely fit inside. The cell is three feet wide, six feet long and seven feet high.[3] Welcome to "The Grave", as this place is known to the inmates of a global network of prisons.

The Grave received its name because the cells are little larger than coffins. Pay close attention, because this is a key destination in the War on Terror. Admittedly, it is not where President George W. Bush would take visitors on a showpiece tour, and yet here in this dungeon, on this day, 17 December 2002, are at least seven prisoners who claim to have arrived courtesy of the United States.[4]

In charge of the centre is a man named George Salloum, an officer of Syrian military intelligence, dressed smartly in trousers, a golf shirt and a pair of leather shoes. He might seem an unlikely ally for the United States. By profession he is the head of interrogation of suspected terrorists at the Palestine Branch. In short, a torturer. The vice or virtue of his methods and whether, in the War on Terror, such methods may regrettably be necessary, will be examined later. But suffice for now to say Salloum extracts information, or at least confessions, by extreme force, both physical and psychological. The Palestine Branch is a house of confession.

In cell no. 2 is Maher Arar, a Canadian wireless technician who was deported to Syria from New York in a private American jet. As a teenage schoolboy he once had a part-time job folding towels at that Sheraton Hotel. But he left the country at the age of seventeen and never returned — till now. He will later be found innocent of all charges.[5] Every day, Maher is brought out of his cell to face Salloum and his team of interrogators. Among their worst methods is one known as the as the "German chair", so-called because it was said to have been taught to them by the Stasi, the East German secret service.[6] It has an empty metal frame with no backrest or seat and is used to stretch the prisoner's spine to near breaking point.

Maher is spared this worst torture. He is beaten on his back, his buttocks and his feet with a two-inch thick electric cable. Night and day, he hears around him the screams of other prisoners. But the worst of all is the rat-infested, tiny and solitary cell. He can barely stretch out in one direction. As a Muslim, he would like to pray towards Mecca, but no guard will tell him which direction that is. And, anyway, his body can only bend one way, forward towards the metal door.

There is no daylight coming into his cell, just a dim glow through a hole in the reinforced concrete ceiling. Crouching beneath, Maher tries to make out the words from his wife Monia back in Canada. In a letter she had promised "I will do whatever it takes to get you released." This was his only ray of hope. Maher tells the time by the meals that are brought to him. Once a week he is taken out to wash himself. He is held in the same cell for ten months. Later, an official inquiry would find his account of physical and mental torture to be truthful.[7]

Next door to Maher, in cell no.3, is a fellow Canadian called Abdullah Al-malki. Maher is accused of being a member of Al Qaeda, in part, because back in Ottawa, Maher was a friend of Abdullah's. Now, the two dare not exchange more than a whisper. Abdullah has been in his cell since May and he will remain there until August of the following year.[8] Like Maher he is accused of membership of Al Qaeda, and, like him, will be cleared of all such charges.

Another prisoner is Mohammed Haydar Zammar, a 42-year-old German businessman from Hamburg, a father of five. An enormous bear of a man, once described as having "arms like small tree trunks", before his capture he weighed more than twenty stone. Now he weighs considerably less. His cell, no.13, is shorter than his body length. From now on, for nearly two and a half years, he will be living in this cramped position. The only time he is taken from his cell again, say fellow inmates, is to be tortured.[9]

No public charges have been laid against Mohammed, but he is regarded by investigators as a key figure in the Al Qaeda cell that organised the strike on the Twin Towers — in short, one of the key suspects behind the September 11 attacks. But, two months after those crimes, rather than questioning Mohammed in America or Germany, he was picked up when he went on holiday in Morocco, just before he boarded a flight to return home. A secret report of the German government, which I obtained, confirmed he was questioned there by American agents and then flown on to Syria on 27 December, also at the request of the United States. While tortured by George Salloum's men, Mohammed had faced lists of questions sent directly by the CIA, the report confirmed. Mohammed's home country was complicit too in his treatment. The Germans tipped off the Americans about his travel to Morocco. They also sent lists of questions to Syria. And, just a month before this imaginary visit, officers from German intelligence and police came directly to interrogate him about his activities in Hamburg.[10]

Three other prisoners say the Americans brought them to the Palestine Branch. In cell no.5 is a man in his 30s called Abdel; in cell no. 8 is someone called Omar; and in cell no.12 is a teenager with a brother in Guantánamo.[11] The latter two were arrested on 28 March that year when a team of Pakistani and American agents stormed a Faisalabad compound being used by Abu Zubaydah, one of the alleged senior commanders of Al Qaeda. Fourteen people were in this building and the two prisoners say that each of those arrested was separated and sent to different countries. After their arrest, the prisoners say, they have both been brutally tortured. Omar says that Abu Zubaydah himself was treated the worst. In Pakistan, before their transfer, he was shown pictures of a bruised Abu Zubaydah and told: "If you don't talk, this is what will happen to you." Abdel Halim, a student also arrested in Pakistan, was on 14 May put with the other two on a US plane that brought all three to Damascus. I later found indications that the plane involved was a CIA-owned Gulfstream executive jet.[12] In Syria, the torture continued and Abdel Halim, in particular, seems to have got it worst. "He was treated really bad. He was brought down from the interrogation room wrapped in a blanket. He was brutally beaten and couldn't walk," remembers Abdullah, whose cell was two doors down.[13]

There are two more prisoners in this jail who were handed over by the United States. In cell no.17 is a prisoner called Barah; in cell no.7 is Bahaa, aged 29. Both say they were arrested in Pakistan and then interrogated by US agents before being handed over directly there to a team from Syrian intelligence.[14]

Of course, Syria's treatment of prisoners in this way is no secret. The United States, which considers Syria to be a state sponsor of terrorism,[15] has for many years detailed and criticised the country's human rights abuses. President Bush would condemn the regime for its "legacy of torture, oppression, misery, and ruin."[16] In 2003, the State Department, quoting human rights organisations and former prisoners, would describe torture methods as including:

administering electrical shocks; pulling out fingernails; forcing objects into the rectum; beating, sometimes while the victim is suspended from the ceiling; hyper-extending the spine; bending the detainees into the frame of a wheel and whipping exposed body parts; and using a chair that bends backwards to asphyxiate the victim or fracture the victim's spine.[17]

In January 2002, President Bush had declared an "Axis of Evil" consisting of Iran, Iraq and North Korea. In May, the US State Department added Syria as a candidate member of the list and called it a "rogue state" for seeking weapons of mass destruction.[18] But, in the War on Terror, many compromises were being made.

By the end of December 2002, Maher's interrogations had become less severe. There were no longer beatings with electric cables. This relative relaxation followed a series of visits by the Canadian consul that had begun on 23 October.[19] Despite this, Maher was still confined in his tiny cell and he experienced then his worst crisis. Three times, with his mind crowded with memories, he began screaming without control.

It was just at this time, when Maher thought he could stand no more, that President Bashar al-Assad, the leader of Syria, was visiting London on the first ever state visit by a President of Syria. In Bashar, the country had a 37-year-old leader who had been in power less than two years.[20] He had a British wife, Asma, a 27-year-old former banker, and, before being recalled to Damascus, al-Assad himself practised as a doctor in London for two years. Both the US and Britain were hoping to use Bashar to woo Syria out of its isolationist and hard-line policies. Prime Minister Tony Blair's mind, by now, was focused on winning the world's support for the forthcoming invasion of Iraq against Saddam Hussein.

At a news conference at 10 Downing Street, Blair gave a signal. The Syrian regime was on the right track. He spoke of the "continuing change and reform programme in Syria." There was no talk in public of human rights, no concern of how Syria might be treating terrorist suspects. The only pressure on Syria was to become tougher.

Bashar declared: "As for the issue of terrorism, Syria is known for its fight against terrorism for the last decade, and not just for the last few years. As a country that has the experience and rejects terrorism, we put our experience at the disposal of any country which seriously wants to fight terrorism."[21]

In the battle against terrorism, Britain was now prepared to set its differences aside with Syria — and with the United States. Just before the conference, in a Downing Street briefing room, Alastair Campbell, Blair's spokesman, was fending off repeated questions about a *New York Times* report that weekend. President Bush had signed an order, it said, to authorise the assassination, under defined circumstances, of senior Al Qaeda leaders. Journalists also asked Campbell if Britain was tolerating the use by the United States of torture. In response Campbell said he never commented on the security policies of other countries. It was a question "that should be directed to the American authorities." The questions continued but Campbell preferred not to elaborate.[22]

On the evening of Tuesday 17 December, President Bashar and his wife were welcomed to a banquet by the Lady Mayoress of London. Asma had proved a hit with the media. Scotland's *Daily Record* said her style had "earned comparisons with Jackie Kennedy and Princess Diana." On the menu was Gravadlax with Quail's Egg, followed by Canon of Lamb with Minted Béarnaise Sauce, Passion Fruit Soufflé Glacé or Tropical Fruit Salad. The wine on offer for the main course was a choice between Chateau Arnaud de Jacquemeau (1998) and Grand Cru St. Emilion; for dessert a Muscat de Beaumes de Venise was served to complement the soufflé, and Smith Woodhouse 1995 LBV Port followed.[23]

Meanwhile in Damascus, Maher was at his wit's end. By now he had already signed a false confession that he had trained at a camp in Afghanistan. He wondered what more he could say. "After the time went by," he remembered:

I got into a very, very desperate situation. I wanted to be out of that place at any cost, and that's when I realised, to be in that place, the psychological torture in that place is even worse than the beating, the torture. I was ready to accept anything. I was ready to accept a ten, twenty year sentence and say anything just to get to another place.[24]

The trouble for Maher was that he could not provide what the Syrians wanted most: useful information to pass back to the Americans. So his incarceration continued.

In the underground hell of the Palestine Branch, there were innocents like Maher. There were also those guilty of crimes, those who almost certainly were members of Al Qaeda. There are those who would say that, under torture, some useful intelligence might emerge. After all, the United States was to state that the Syrian government had provided information on terrorism that had "saved American lives".[25] So was this torture justified? Was the War on Terror too important to lose? And whose side were countries like Syria really on?

It is this dark side of the War on Terror, and its uncomfortable truths, that this book explores.

INTRODUCTION
NOT FOR THE SQUEAMISH

MONTEVIDEO
12 December 1965

Philip Agee, a CIA officer under diplomatic cover at the US Embassy in Uruguay, was with his Chief of Station, John Horton, at the headquarters of the city's Chief of Police, Col. Ventura Rodriguez, when he heard a strange low sound. As it became louder, he recognised it as the moan of a human voice. The moaning turned to screams.

One of the Uruguayan police officers, who were following a football game, had a transistor radio on. Rodriguez urged him to turn the volume up to drown out the noise, but to no avail.

It was a turning point for this young officer. He was listening to someone being tortured down the corridor. Agee suspected it was he who had supplied the name of this man to the Uruguayan authorities.

"Hearing that voice, whoever it was, made me feel terrified and helpless," recalled Agee, in his memoir, *Inside the Company*. "All I wanted to do was get away from that police headquarters. Why didn't Horton or I say anything to Rodriguez? We just sat there embarrassed and shocked ..."[1]

When he published his memoirs in 1975, Agee gave a perspective on what he saw as the harsh reality of what the CIA, during the Cold War, had become. Agee's anger led him to betray the Agency and his country. His book published the real names of hundreds of CIA officers operating undercover around the world. He was hounded by the US government.[2] A federal law was passed that would, in future, outlaw officers like Agee from revealing what they knew. President George H.W. Bush, a former head of the CIA himself, once said he would forgive many people in his life, but he would never forgive Philip Agee.[3] Despite his betrayals, Agee exposed a conflict at the heart of intelligence gathering. His story reminds us that when, after the terrorist attacks of 11 September 2001, the restrictions were lifted again on covert CIA warfare, the agency's officers were not evolving some new "thinking out of the box" experimental methods. They were dusting off the old manuals. The Romans and the British used to outsource their imperial tasks. And, during the Cold War, the out-sourcing of the CIA's difficult jobs had been just a matter of routine.

In theory, the CIA was set up with the main task of clandestine collection of intelligence. Its primary mission then was to recruit agents and steal information in enemy territory. Arising from its origins, the CIA also had another goal. In World War Two, the CIA's forerunner, the Office of Strategic Services (OSS), was tasked not only with finding spies but also with running paramilitary operations behind enemy lines. The supporting mission of the OSS and then CIA was therefore covert action. It was to engage in secret warfare against America's enemies. CIA officers were required not only passively to find out information, but also actively to intervene to disrupt and even destroy their quarry.[4]

During the Cold War, these two conflicting missions meant the CIA had to recruit two types of agents. Some agents could provide information about Communist activities. The others were more suited to taking action. For example, what the KGB called "agents of influence" might need to be recruited: those who could influence decision-making either directly (if he was a politician or a government official, for example) or indirectly (like a journalist willing to print propaganda in his newspaper). Or there might be a need for agents who could perform physical tasks, like burgling the office of a Soviet front organisation or even carrying out acts of violence. In the CIA, covert action required presidential approval — either for non-lethal activities like propaganda or lethal covert action, where a mission could mean the loss of lives. The latter orders from the President were and are known as "lethal findings".

Covert action could be dangerous. If an American intelligence officer was caught red-handed in an operation, he could be expelled or even arrested or killed. The officer's entire network and activities would then also be in danger, and his primary mission disrupted. For this reason, many conventional spy-masters in the CIA — those more interested in the old and difficult art of simply acquiring information — were always wary of those who advocated greater use of covert actions, regardless of how popular such actions might be to politicians whose knowledge of spying was gleaned from popular fiction. The obvious solution to this conflict was to out-source the covert action — to use proxies for American power. One of the key advantages of using proxies was "deniability": the ability of the United States to deny knowledge of an operation that either went wrong or became public, what the agency called a "flap". Another advantage was that the proxies were usually cheaper and better. They had local knowledge, required less training and could be disengaged after their mission was completed.

In Uruguay, Agee was an actor in such a classic relationship between a CIA case officer and his proxy for covert action. America was engaged in a global war against communism, just like the global war against terrorism. And instead of

CIA officers secretly arresting, questioning and imprisoning communist agitators, they used their proxies in the Montevideo police to carry out such actions. This relationship would officially be termed a "liaison" and might be justified as a two-way exchange. The police chief might not be a paid agent. He would be fed tidbits of information by the CIA to help him with his job. Whether paid or not, the problem with such a liaison was that it involved a loss of control. A CIA station chief like John Horton could not issue a direct order to Col. Rodriguez.[5] Horton might issue official or written guidance on how to interrogate a suspect without electric cattle prods. But, like it or not, the CIA knew full well the Uruguayan police questioned their suspects by torture. So, the consequence of the CIA passing names of communist suspects to Col. Rodriguez was that those individuals would soon be tortured.

When it comes to the secret history of covert action by the CIA, there has been much written in the fiction department. Its importance has often been completely overblown. The wild conspiracy theories of left-wing activists and novel writers have a close working relationship. Yet, as Henry Kissinger once deliciously remarked, "even the paranoid have enemies."[6] Some of the most fantastic stories do really turn out to be true.

The struggle against communism in central and southern America was one theatre for covert action. Assassination had generally been discouraged because usually it backfired. And yet there was an extensive attempt to recruit exiles to carry out assassinations against members of the Cuban regime, including the well-known attempts to kill President Fidel Castro with such ridiculous-sounding weapons as exploding sea shells.[7]

It was South East Asia amid increasingly desperate efforts to win supremacy against Communist forces in Vietnam, that saw the greatest post-war employment of covert action. In the late 1960s, the Phoenix Programme saw CIA operatives, mainly employed under temporary contract, organising the arrest and often assassination of thousands of those considered to be members or supporters of the Viet Cong insurgency in southern Vietnam.[8] South East Asia also witnessed the expansion of the CIA's proprietary airline, Air America, to become reportedly the largest commercial airline in the world and, to many, a symbol of the covert action programme.[9] The use of covert air transport went, in many ways, hand in hand with any type of covert direct action where CIA-trained paramilitaries were deployed. In Laos, Air America's primary and hugely-consuming role was the re-supply of a force of anti-communist guerrillas, known as the Meo. Their village bases in the hills were supplied and maintained by the CIA and these same bases were used to organise the opium trade. Though not involved in drug trafficking itself, the air operation sustained a force that guarded some of the world's most lucrative opium fields. The Meo were regarded as the lesser of two evils. But here again was a clear case of hypocrisy — of the sort that undermined the whole struggle against Communism. The Meo were being supported in a bid to prevent the spread of authoritarian anti-democratic rule. Yet the CIA's allies, the generals commanding its proxy armies, were not only anti-communists. They included criminals who helped spread drug addiction to the US Army in Vietnam and back to the US homeland.[10]

Of course, anyone who spent too long worrying about such moral dilemmas was hardly a useful asset to a covert action programme. Those executives who made policy would argue that, in the face of a real threat of Soviet subversion, the hypocrisy of US secret policies was justified. Just as their successors did in the modern-day War on Terror, they argued that a higher objective required the use, from time to time, of methods that might appear unpalatable.

A glimpse at some of the more extreme methods of covert action occasionally employed in the Cold War comes from a batch of de-classified CIA documents that can be read in the National Security Archive, at George Washington University in Washington, DC. They include the training papers used to prepare CIA agents to take part in "Operation PB Success", the 1954 coup authorised by President Eisenhower against the left-leaning (but democratically elected) president of Guatemala. Among the papers is a "Study of Assassination" that, after describing various justifications and methods for killing, concluded "assassination can seldom be employed with a clear conscience. Persons who are morally squeamish should not attempt it."[11] The same might be said of torture.

The pendulum swings, and the discovery of covert actions creates a backlash that puts those methods on hold, for a while.

By the mid-1970s, the CIA's ownership of Air America was an open secret. Much of its clandestine activity in South East Asia had been exposed to public scrutiny. President Nixon was revealed to have not only authorised the secret burglary of the Democrat headquarters at Watergate, but also to have been secretly bombing Cambodia. After he resigned, and the US began its pullout from Vietnam, there was briefly a sense that many of the secret tactics deployed in the war against Communism had been misguided.

As a Senate committee under Senator Frank Church began investigating the CIA's activities,[12] President Nixon's successor, President Ford issued instructions to the CIA that banned political assassinations.[13] Air America was wound up and a brake was put on the more aggressive end of covert action. When President Carter took office in 1977, the CIA was ordered to become a global advocate of human rights. CIA officers deployed in Central and South America, and at training schools in the US, were now advised to start teaching their police and intelligence liaisons that illegal arrests and torture were unacceptable. Many in the agency agreed with the switch of tactics. As Jack Devine, a former acting head of the agency's worldwide operations, told me: "It caused a bit of surprise with some of those we were dealing with; but it was a real and important turning point not just for the agency but for US policy in general." President Carter promoted human rights out of a genuine belief in their merits, said Devine, but the switch of policy also gave the United States a new ideological advantage. "Communism could be beaten because our ideas and our society were better. We didn't need to descend to their level."[14] That, ultimately, both then and after 9/11, became one of the strongest arguments against methods like torture.

In the late 1970s, President Brezhnev of the Soviet Union began an aggressive policy of deploying a new class of intermediate-range ballistic missile with nuclear heads, the SS-20. In response, the US under Ronald Reagan revived the Cold War with a vengeance.[15] Reagan also revived the CIA's covert action programme. In Central America, this included support for the Contra rebels against the Nicaraguan Sandinista government.

The most memorable covert action of the 1980s was the multi-billion dollar campaign to supply arms and cash to the mujahideen in Afghanistan fighting the Soviets. Here again the CIA was fighting the communists through their chosen proxy. CIA officers, unlike their counterparts in British and French intelligence, were not allowed to cross through the fabled Khyber Pass into Afghanistan, and though America's allies were often Islamic fundamentalists, this was a war which commanded support across the political spectrum. The US was not running an undercover war to topple a leftist regime, as in Nicaragua, or to prop up an unpopular dictatorship, as in south Vietnam. It was engaged in supporting a popular resistance against invasion. The Afghan War was probably the CIA's most successful covert action ever. It cost Soviet communism dearly, and was arguably a crucial factor in the entire collapse of the regime — one that sadly the CIA failed to predict.

When the Berlin Wall came down in 1989, it seemed to spell the end of covert action. Without an opponent like the Soviet Union, it was hard to justify not only the expense of such operations, but also the hypocrisy. As the Russians withdrew their support for their pet dictators around the world, the need to sanction extreme measures to counter-balance the Soviets was removed. To justify their continued existence, spy agencies like the CIA and Britain's MI6 began talking of how they might assist the war against drugs and organised crime or combat economic threats.

President Clinton, in his first term, saw little need for any kind of undercover work, let alone secret paramilitary operations. His first CIA chief, James Woolsey, secured not a single one-to-one meeting with the President in his entire two years at the agency. When a light plane crashed on the White House lawn, staff joked it was Woolsey trying to get in.[16] Veteran agency officials complained they were ordered to carry out a "scrub" from their payroll of any sources with even the slightest connection to human rights abuses.[17]

As new threats emerged, such as Osama bin Laden's Al Qaeda network and increased weapons proliferation, there were new demands placed on intelligence agencies. There was still optimism, however, that none of these new enemies represented anything like the kind of threat once posed by the Soviet Union during the Cold War. Although small-scale programmes were created to counter terrorist groups, and in particular bin Laden, there was no sense that the old days might return. From being a divisive institution of the Cold War, accused by the liberal left of being engaged in subversion against democratic leftists governments, the agency now appeared to have objectives that all might share.

Then, on 11 September 2001, Al Qaeda achieved what the Soviet Union never dared attempt. It struck a direct blow into the heart of American power, destroying the Twin Towers, damaging the Pentagon, and very nearly hitting the White House itself. It was the most devastating foreign attack on US soil since Pearl Harbor, but was organised not by a great military power like imperial Japan but by a small group of militants based in an out of the way place. Hard intelligence was at a premium.

Word soon spread that the game was back on. Vice-President Dick Cheney spoke of working "sort of [on] the dark side" and "spending time in the shadows."[18] In short, as Cofer Black, then head of the Counter-terrorism Centre at the CIA told Congress, after 9/11 "the gloves come off." In short, covert action was back in business.[19]

In the new bellicose atmosphere, there were many public commentators or politicians who urged no compromise in the methods required to defeat Islamic terrorism. While some were keen to emphasise the new nature of the threat, I was struck by the almost nostalgic excitement with which old Cold War warriors like Donald Rumsfeld could pick up the reins and return to how things were. In this frenzy, old military hands made the most aggressive statements. A former US army colonel, Alex Sands, for example, declared: "The whole point of using special operations is to fight terror with terror. Our guys are trained to do the things that traditionally the other guys have done: kidnap, hijack, infiltrate."[20] Yet it was perhaps the more liberal commentators who were most influential. They queued up to urge a new robust and "no holds barred" approach to combatting terrorism. Squeamishness or a liberal concern for human rights were to be things of the past.

As a reporter for the *Sunday Times*, working as the head of the paper's Insight team, I arrived in New York soon after September 11, and moved shortly onwards to Washington, DC for several weeks. The vindictive mood was palpable. I remember a t-shirt on sale in Maryland with a picture of a F16 plane and the slogan "Hijack this, ass-hole!"

After the invasion of Afghanistan and the arrest of hundreds of members of the Taliban and their foreign allies, Defense Secretary Rumsfeld soon announced the creation of a prison at Guantánamo Bay, Cuba, for what officials called the "the worst of the worst"[21] and without the protection of the Geneva Conventions. To many across the world, it seemed a dangerous precedent. These concerns were reinforced by pictures showing the terrorist suspects — to be known as "enemy combatants" or "detainees" not "prisoners" — trussed up and held in what appeared to be cages.

As I continued my reporting in Washington, I heard whispers there was something much bigger going on: a system of clandestine prisons that involved the incarceration of thousands of prisoners, not just the few hundred in Cuba. While the President spoke of spreading liberty across the world, CIA insiders referred to a return to the old days, of working hand-in-glove with some of the most repressive secret police in the world: regimes like Egypt and Uzbekistan that also happened to be the toughest opponents of Islamic extremism.

Administration officials referred to the CIA programmes as among the most top secret of activities. As a reporter without access to classified information, how could I hope to discover more? How would I penetrate this secret world to find out the truth behind these rumours?

Curiously, the first clue was to come from someone who would become important in this story. Sitting on a comfortable sofa on Capitol Hill in December 2001, I was interviewing a leading congressman, Representative Porter Goss. For the last five years, Goss had led the House's Intelligence Committee and he was complaining about how the CIA's operations had declined in effectiveness.[22] Goss was a believer in covert action. Far better, he told me, to have snatched a dictator like the Yugoslav President, Slobodan Milosevic, and haul him to The Hague to face a war crimes trial than to launch a war like President Clinton did and cause the death of many civilians. I asked him about Al Qaeda and whether the CIA could have kidnapped Osama bin Laden.

"It's called a rendition. Do you know that?," said Goss.

"No," I replied.

"Well, there is a polite way to take people out of action and bring them to some type of justice. It's generally referred to as a rendition."[23]

It was this man who, when director of the CIA, launched a campaign against those leaking information about the agency's classified programmes, set me on the trail of what is the subject of this book — the rendition programme of the CIA, a programme, as I shall explain in detail, of snatches and imprisonment that operated outside normal rules; and one that was protected almost always by a veil of secrecy.

The second clue came in early 2002, after Rumsfeld had opened the Guantánamo prison. I was talking to someone with close sources in the CIA. His advice was something of a riddle. "Start with what's public," he said. "Look at Guantánamo and look at the press releases. You'll see there are prisoners going in, and there are prisoners going out. Ask yourself what's happening to these people. Where they are going, and how are they are being transported?"[24] There were other clues too. Like the scattered reports from around the world of something else — the snatching of terrorist suspects by men wearing masks, and the presence always somewhere nearby of a mysterious private executive jet.[25] Were these the renditions that Goss had spoken about finally being put into effect? And was Air America back in use to do the transport?

Much later, when more pieces of the puzzle were in place, I remembered the work of Alexander Solzhenitsyn, the dissident writer. When he had described the Soviet Union's network of prison camps as a "Gulag Archipelago" he was portraying a parallel world that existed within physical reach of everyday life but yet could remain unseen to ordinary people. [26] After years of persecution, Solzhenitsyn described a jail system that he knew from first-hand experience which had swallowed millions of citizens into its entrails. At least a tenth of them never emerged alive.[27]

The modern world of prisons run by the United States and its allies in the War on Terror was far less extensive. As described in the next chapter, its inmates numbered thousands, not millions. And yet there were eerie parallels between what the Soviet Union had created and what we, in the West, were now constructing.

Solzhenitsyn's works were a gift to those engaged in the ideological struggle of the Cold War. He described Russia's darkest secrets and traced its errors back to the gloried founder of the Revolutionary State, Vladimir Illych Lenin. In this way he assaulted the very founders of the regime, offending those who tried to pin the evils of the Gulag on Stalin alone. And yet, as a relentless chronicle of human depravity, stretching to more than 1,900 pages, his three-part *Archipelago* was an uncomfortable and challenging journey for any reader, liberal or conservative. For like George Orwell, Solzhenitsyn described not only the evils of a totalitarian society but also explored what Orwell called the "double-think" that persuaded ordinary human beings to ignore the atrocities perpetrated in close their midst.

With the Cold War now over, it is this description of the Soviet system's surreal quality that still resonates. The Gulag was so very vast and extensive and yet still it could be hidden in people's minds. Ordinary citizens could persuade themselves that all was normal even as their next-door neighbours disappeared. Though all too real in its physical existence, for most in society the Gulag had a dreamlike, fantasy quality because it was a world that had yet to be experienced. In the preface to the first volume of the *Archipelago*, Solzhenitsyn wrote of it as an "amazing country" which "though scattered in an Archipelago geographically, was, in the psychological sense, fused into a continent — an almost invisible, almost imperceptible country inhabited by the Zek people."[28]

He continued:

And this Archipelago crisscrossed and patterned that other country within which it was located, like a gigantic patchwork, cutting into its cities, hovering over its streets. Yet there were many who did not even guess at its presence and many, many others who had heard something vague. And only those who had been there knew the whole truth.

How much more then "surreal", more apart from normal existence, was the network of prisons run after 9/11 by the US and its allies? How much easier too was the denial and the double-think when those who disappear into the modern gulag were, being mainly swarthy-skinned Arabs with a different culture, so different from most of us in the West? How much more reassuring were the words from our politicians that all was well?

Solzhenitsyn described a nightmare world that not only existed in parallel to normal life, but was in close physical proximity. Some of the "islands"of the archipelago were situated far away: in the wasteland permafrost of Siberia, for example, or the maritime archipelago in freezing seas north of Leningrad (now St Petersburg). Yet, much of the Gulag lay close at hand. In Soviet Russia, a prison might exist behind the walls of an un-marked house on an everyday shopping street and an unmarked van filled with "Zeks" might pass along that same street, un-noticed by normal citizens. At night, too, there could be strange transformations. By day, a railway station might be cheerfully filled with students and schoolchildren. Yet at night the platforms would echo with the harsh cries of armed guards as they pushed their prisoners onto cattle trucks. Normal humanity would be asleep and see nothing, not even in its dreams.[29]

In this Soviet world, a man might live most of his life and know nothing of this other world. Until perhaps, one day without warning, the knock would come on the door, and, in a moment, like Alice going through the Looking Glass he would disappear from normal society, perhaps forever. If he looked through the window of a secret van, labelled "Bread" on its exterior, he might see a landscape that seemed to him familiar. Behind its bars and denied all forms of communication and soon, perhaps, even denied hope, his dream life was now reversed. Normal existence was for him now a fantasy. The Gulag had become his normality.

The barriers that separate the dream world from normal life are a frequent theme explored in children's literature. For a child to sleep at night and walk tall by day, there needs to be a clear line between the true and make-believe. Just so that the child knows the goblins do not really trace his every step through the leafy forest. So time and again in children's stories, there is a concept of a portal that separates the two worlds. In C.S. Lewis' *The Lion, the Witch and the Wardrobe*, children enter the mythical Narnia by passing through the back of a wardrobe. Harry Potter's magical train to Hogwarts is caught by walking through what looks to ordinary mortals to be an ordinary wall.[30] Alice entered Wonderland by falling down a hole after she followed a rabbit wearing a waistcoat and examining a watch on a chain. As she fell down the hole, she seemed to travel for miles, perhaps even to the centre of the earth. But she could have been next door.

The modern prisoner, blindfolded, bound and shackled, is in a world as separate as Wonderland. Unlike Alice, he is more likely to be grabbed and tugged down the rabbit hole than seduced to enter. In the months ahead, he is cut off from radio and television. He can make no telephone calls or see any visitors, nor see a lawyer. The prisoner simply disappears. Like Alice he may travel for miles and miles, flown above the clouds on what seem like endless journeys to places that are never identified. Sometimes, he will have no conception at all of where he is.

And yet, just as Solzhenitsyn described in Russia, this Wonderland is not in some storybook, nor rarely in a far-flung desert, but instead it co-exists within a stone's throw of modern life.

As I took a sunset cruise from downtown Cairo up the Nile in a felucca sail boat in 2003, I might have spotted the watchtowers on the river bank. But I would not know the reality of life inside the Torah Prison that lay behind, or its feared inner sanctum, known as Al Aqrab, the Scorpion. A tourist would have no inkling of its secrets and its role as an ultimate, feared destination for prisoners captured or transported by the United States.[31]

In Morocco, visitors to the city zoo at Rabat might notice a nearby group of houses, surrounded by an ordinary-looking chain link fence and high trees. How could they have imagined the types of torture with razor blades or broken glass bottles that were perpetrated inside, not just on their own nationals but upon foreigners sent there from abroad?[32]

In the comfortable surroundings of Frankfurt Airport in Germany, the white Gulfstream executive jet, parked on the tarmac, betrayed nothing of its role for the CIA, or of its crew of American agents who wore boots and black masks and who transported prisoners, blindfolded and shackled, to these torture centres across the world.

When I examined this modern world of prisoners and terror suspects, the story of these airplanes grabbed me with special fascination. There was something discordant here that grated with the essential narrative of how the hard luck torture "victims" should be treated. When the Soviets loaded their Zeks to travel across the wastelands of Siberia, they put them into cold cattle trucks. When the US Army sent its prisoners to Guantánamo, they were trussed up with ropes and thrown into the cold and deafening holds of cargo planes. There seemed a certain appropriate symmetry. The CIA, however, was favouring something different. When the CIA transferred its prisoners, they were often placed in these large executive jets, with champagne coolers and in-flight movies. What was so important about these prisoners? Or could CIA agents not manage without an ice-bucket? The story seemed ever more fantastic, more surreal. The Canadian, Maher Arar, as I describe in Chapter 3, was snatched from a very ordinary place familiar to everyone: an ordinary terminal at New York's John F. Kennedy Airport. A few days later, there he was, sitting in a luxury Gulfstream business jet, staring at the clouds like some VIP jet-setter — even though his legs were shackled and he had no champagne.

It was this detail in the story, the use of these Gulfstream jets that stood out, and I began to think hard about it. In the end, it became clear that the airplanes were not only a surreal, bizarre detail. They were also a means to penetrate this secret world. These CIA planes were masquerading as normal civilian business jets. Yet to follow that path they would have to play by civilian rules, filing detailed flight plans for example and parking in highly-visible civilian airports. By tracking these flights I would have a clue to the precise movements of both the CIA and its prisoners. If Watergate was about "follow the money", the story of renditions was about "follow the planes". Or so it appeared.

What I and others discovered soon enough was that the CIA had created for itself a new version of the old Air America. After some months, I obtained flight logs of over twenty planes used by the CIA. In all, I had in my hands about 12,000 records of their movements. It was a ledger of global covert action. With this information, and with the help and research of others, I began to piece together a story of the CIA's new War on Terror, and of the new compromises that it was making.

At the centre of these movements, and of this story, was a 40-foot long luxury jet, painted white, with room for twelve passengers, a cruising speed of 400 knots and the fuel to fly about one quarter of the way round the world non-stop. Its base was the small town of Smithfield in Johnston County, North Carolina.

This account traces the history of America's programme of renditions through the journeys taken by this Gulfstream and other planes of the new Air America. It begins, in Part One, with the accounts of the prisoners who were on board. It examines the proof of the rendition journeys they described and of the torture they experienced.

In the course of my research I've interviewed CIA pilots who flew these men, CIA operations officers who held prisoners like these in their personal custody, CIA chiefs who planned the rendition programme, and White House officials who ordered and authorised the missions. These men and women told me that the rendition programme was vital — the "most important and most effective weapon that has been used in the War on Terror," according to one senior officer. But, because of its secrecy, this central policy of the US government had hardly been written about or evaluated in full detail.

Part Two of this book describes how I and others tracked down the programme and, based on interviews with those involved, I examine the history of the secret airline used for renditions and analyse the political reasons why renditions came to be used. Most of those involved in the programme claimed to me that torture was never the purpose of renditions. I believed them. Yet, almost to a man, they admitted that, when transferring prisoners to jails across the world, the CIA knew that the torture of these men was inevitable. Contrary to what was claimed later, the White House was fully informed. Those in charge knew the prisoner would be tortured.

After 9/11 the rendition system went much, much further. As I shall argue, it moved from a system where torture was incidental, to a system where interrogations and torture were actively out-sourced. Though it started as a means simply to return terrorist suspects to their home countries for trial (and is still publicly and falsely described like this, including by President Bush), the cases I outline showed a different pattern. The prisoners described in this book were not just "disappeared" and then returned to their home countries — they were sent on a journey through a network of jails, including to countries where they had never lived or had left decades earlier — and where they faced no allegations or suspicions. In many cases, prisoners arrived in such foreign jails with a list of questions to ask of them provided by Western intelligence. In other cases, such as in Afghanistan, the CIA established its own prisons on foreign soil. Local guards "prepared" the prisoners — and CIA contractors did the actual questioning.

Part Three is the story of the backlash against these renditions; of how, little by little, its secrets have been exposed — through public pressure after the outcry that began with photographs of abuse of prisoners in Iraq, through the activities of dissident diplomats and government officials, and through investigation by journalists, police and prosecutors in Europe. These inquiries, as I show, exposed not only the activities of the United States, but the complicity of many of those same European states. Under pressure, America's senior politicians and the CIA's leadership were finally forced to defend rendition publicly. They insisted the US "does not do torture." Yet as I show, such claims were falsehoods.

Torture is defined in law as the deliberate infliction by state officials of "severe pain, whether physical or mental." Such pain, the law defines, can be inflicted in a single act — like the use of electric shocks or a threat to kill someone's family. But torture, as defined, can also mean a pattern of treatment that, little by little, destroys the prisoner's mind. Dragged for months or even years from prison to prison, from country to country, with no hope of release, no hope of appearing in court or no hope of facing concrete charges, rendition for many became a tunnel with no light at the end. And for those held within its confines, the torture of rendition came not from the tactics of the interrogators. Those pains could be endured. Torture was the system itself. Ordered and authorised from the top of the White House, the rendition programme had become a torture programme.

PART ONE
DESTINATION TORTURE

1

THE MEN IN BLACK

Flightlog

Registration: **N379P**;
Type: **Gulfstream V**;
Operator: Premier Executive Transport, Massachusetts;
Date: **17 December 2001**

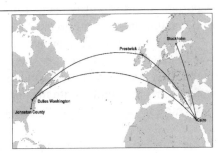

Flight plan:
Johnston County, NC (dep. 7.13 p.m.)
Dulles, Washington, DC

Dulles (dep. 9.15 p.m.)
Cairo (arr. 3.19 p.m.) 18 December

Cairo (dep. 4.43 p.m.)
Stockholm (arr. 8.43 p.m.)

Stockholm (dep. 9.48 p.m.)
Cairo (arr. 3.30 p.m.)

STOCKHOLM, SWEDEN
Bromma Airport, 18 December 2001, 8.20 p.m.

It was a dark and chilly night when the two cars pulled up within a few yards of an entrance door to the airport's small security office. The sky was clear, and with a breeze blowing from the southwest, the temperature hovered just above freezing. It was approaching the worst of the near-Arctic winter. The sun had set more than five hours ago.[1]

Paul Forell, a uniformed officer of the Border Police with twenty-five years experience, was already at his post inside, completing some paperwork. It was then that a group of plain-clothes detectives walked in, officers of the Swedish security police, known as SAPO. They said the deportation operation was getting underway. Ten minutes later, two Americans, dressed in suits, walked into Forell's office. Both were about thirty-five years old. They gave their first names and said they were from the US Embassy. They obviously knew the SAPO officers already, he recalled.[2]

As they were speaking, and just before 9 p.m., an American-registered Gulf-stream V jet was touching down on the 5,400-foot runway. Some of the SAPO officers went to meet the US plane and found onboard a security team of "seven or eight, among them a doctor and two Egyptian officials." In the cars parked outside Forell's police station, dressed in ordinary clothes but in handcuffs, were two other Egyptian citizens, both suspected terrorists under arrest and awaiting deportation. The "security team" from the plane reached the parked cars and, one at a time, brought the arrested men inside. Everything now went very fast.[3]

"I think there were four or five people who were around every suspect so it was at least twelve or fifteen persons in my little station. The first guy was coming in. They asked, 'what room can I use?' So I just showed them inside there [an inner room] and pointed with my finger." Forell described the agents as wearing black masks, with small holes that showed their eyes.[4]

In the crowded office with Forell were now several SAPO and other plain-clothes police officers, two Americans in suits, about eight agents in masks, and an interpreter too. What happened next would later cause a political crisis in Stockholm. The Americans were operating on Swedish soil and officially this was simply a Swedish deportation. But Forell watched as his SAPO colleagues allowed the US agents to take the prisoners, one by one, into the small, separate changing room to carry out what the Americans described as a "security check." According to a later inquiry, this security check included "a body search, their clothes were cut to pieces and placed in bags, their hair was thoroughly examined, as were their oral cavities and ears. In addition they were handcuffed and their ankles fettered. Each was then dressed in an overall and photographed. Finally loose hoods without holes for their eyes were placed over their heads."[5] Meanwhile, Forell stayed behind watching from the public premises. Later, one of the Egyptians reported that he had some kind of sedative that was administered by suppository. It left him drowsy.

Throughout, said Forell, the masked Americans had kept very quiet. "They were talking very, very swiftly. And quiet. So I couldn't understand what they were saying... And as I said before, they were acting very professional." Forell thought the whole incident very strange. "My Swedish colleagues, they didn't give me any information what the case was about. The only thing they were telling me was that two prisoners that are suspected for terrorists, and that's it."[6] He continued: "There was one thing I kept thinking of a little: it is a little extraordinary that we had not been contacted about the plane, because all aircraft that come from outside Schengen (the European passport-free zone) are to contact the police, and no one informed us that an American plane would land at Bromma."[7]

The two Egyptians prisoners were loaded onto the Gulfstream. Both were strapped down on mattresses at the rear. The plane finally took off into the dark moonless sky at 9.49 p.m.[8]

What happened that night at Bromma Airport had given Paul Forell and his colleagues a glimpse into a secret system of prisoner transfers. The "security team" involved was from the CIA. And in the following years, these men in black masks would be spotted again and again in locations across the world. In fact, a month before the Swedish case, a reporter in Pakistan had got wind of these men when they came to pick up another prisoner. "The entire operation was so mysterious that all persons involved in the operation, including US troops, were wearing masks," a source at Karachi airport told the reporter.[9]

In the Gambia, West Africa, a British resident was loaded on the same plane the following year and saw "big people in black balaclavas."[10] In Pakistan, another Londoner was put on a plane to Morocco by operatives "dressed in black, with masks, wearing what looked like Timberland boots."[11] In Macedonia, a German was handed over to a CIA team that consisted of "seven to eight men all dressed in black, with black gloves and wearing black masks. All you could see was their eyes."[12]

The means of transport of this security team was always a luxury business jet, often the Gulfstream used in Sweden. A glance at the records of the Federal Aviation Administration (FAA) would show the plane, with a registration N379P, belonged to a company in Dedham, Massachusetts called Premier Executive Transport Services. But this official ownership record was a sham, a cover story. Its real home was an airport in North Carolina, in a blue hanger, screened by pine trees, at the headquarters of a firm called Aero Contractors Limited. This was a front company that, as I found out, was directly run for the CIA itself. So what was going on in Sweden and all these cases?

SMITHFIELD, NORTH CAROLINA
Johnston County Airport, one night earlier

It was a warm and overcast night when the crew of the Gulfstream gathered for the first leg of their 16,400-mile trip.[13] Their first stop, as always, would be a safe in the company's office. Here they would pick up their passports and pilot's licences, all made out in false names. These men were among the country's finest aviators. They were prepared, at a drop of a hat, to fly a mission to almost anywhere, to land on a tiny strip in a jungle swamp, to take off uphill or downhill

N379P / © Konstantin von Wedelstaedt

in fearsome winds, and to brave enemy gunfire as they did so. Tonight's mission was not so hair-raising. But these men were CIA pilots, and so they travelled undercover.[14]

The Johnston County airport is in the town of Smithfield, a sleepy place less than an hour's drive out of the state capital of Raleigh. Probably its only claim to fame was when General Sherman stood outside the courthouse in April 1865 and heard news of the surrender of Robert E. Lee's Confederate armies at Appomattox.[15] On Sundays, when I visited, its streets resounded with Harley Davidsons heading for their local hang-out, the Last Resort Bar. Nothing here seemed to move very fast. Even the Harleys kept to the speed limit. But the small airport, surrounded by tobacco fields, pine forests and some small industries, was chosen by the CIA precisely because it was so quiet. It was also close to Fort Bragg, home to Special Forces, whose operators often joined the CIA's paramilitary missions.[16]

In the darkness that December evening, the Gulfstream was rolled out of its blue metal hanger. After final checks, the plane took off at 7.13 p.m. and headed north for the 30-minute flight to Washington, DC. It was at Dulles, the closest suitable airport to the CIA in Langley, Virginia, that the airmen picked up their first passengers. These were the men and women, including a doctor, from the Rendition Group. They had black masks stuffed into their bags. At 9.36 p.m. the Gulfstream took off from Dulles and set a course across the Atlantic. Its destination was Cairo, Egypt.

STOCKHOLM, SWEDEN
The Rosenbad Palace, 18 December, 11.45 a.m.

Göran Persson, the Prime Minister, was with his cabinet of ten in his official residence, across the lake from the country's parliament. They sat around a large oval table, considering an agenda of 48 items. All had to be completed by lunchtime.[17] Officially, at least, the decision to request American assistance had not been taken. But by now the CIA's Gulfstream was crossing the Mediterranean, already embarked on its mission on behalf of Sweden. Anna Lindh, the Foreign Minister, now asked the Cabinet to make a small but momentous decision: the rejection of a claim for asylum and immediate expulsion of the two Egyptian terror suspects under the Swedish Aliens Act.[18] The Cabinet was said to have taken less than a minute to grant their approval.[19] As soon as they were informed, immigration officials began completing their final paperwork. At 4 p.m., an official letter was posted by registered delivery to the two men's lawyers that announced their expulsion. The deportation operation, however, was already swinging into action.

Fifteen minutes walk from Persson's residence, an immigration lawyer was sitting at his desk in his downtown office. Kjell Jönsson was completing a rather ordinary day. At about 5pm, he was on the phone to one of his many clients, an asylum-seeker from Egypt named Mohammed al-Zery. He was speaking from his workplace, a café selling Middle-Eastern pastries in Stockholm's concrete suburb of Spänga. "Suddenly there was a voice interrupting our conversation," remembered Jönsson. "I heard someone say in Swedish: 'Hang up the telephone'. It was the police who had come to arrest him." It was the last time Jönsson would speak to his client for more than two years. Just a few minutes before al-Zery's arrest, the other Egyptian, Ahmed Agiza, was also picked up by the security police. He was at a bus stop in the town of Karlstad on his way back from Swedish language classes in Stockholm. The time of his arrest was 4.55 p.m.

Unknown to Jönsson, his client was a wanted man. Egypt had issued arrest warrants for both al-Zery and Agiza. The Swedish state had accepted that both were technically refugees, because both could expect to be persecuted if they returned to their home country. Even if that asylum claim were rejected, both men would normally have a right of appeal. Sweden, after all, was a liberal country. But SAPO had presented some additional secret information against the men that, under Swedish law, allowed normal judicial proceedings to be bypassed. Both, it was held, were members of an illegal terrorist organisation. In an unusual fashion, the Swedish Cabinet had functioned as both judge and jury. It was SAPO and the CIA now that would execute their guilty verdict. By the time Jönsson rang the ministry to check for news, he was told his client was already in Cairo. "I was given no hint about how this deportation was carried out," he said.

One hour before the arrests, the CIA plane had already taken off from Cairo. Its route now took it northwest across Europe. The CIA had picked up the two Egyptian officers. The idea was that, legally speaking, the two prisoners would never be in US custody. America, on this occasion, would just be a travel agency. For the return flight from Stockholm to Cairo, the team was augmented by a Swedish security officer and an interpreter. The CIA had originally said there was no room for any Swede but had later relented. The Swedes saw that the men's handcuffs, ankle chains and hoods were kept on for the entire flight. In his own notes, the Swedish officer recorded the men "were kept under observation for the entire time and the guards were changed every other hour. The doctor in the escort inspected them all the time [Agiza and al-Zery were probably given a tranquilliser by the doctor before take-off]." But the officer later said the note about the tranquilliser was a speculation. He did not see the dose being administered. Just after 3.30 a.m. local time the plane reached Cairo. It was met by Egyptian security officials and the prisoners were driven off in a transit van. The Swedes considered their work done.[20]

For the flight crew from North Carolina, it was off to a hotel for some rest. For the two arrested men it was off to visit Egyptian intelligence. The interrogations, they said later, began the same night and it would be five weeks before they received a visitor.

CAIRO, EGYPT
Lazoghly Square, October 2003

It was a sweltering day as I walked through downtown Cairo. It was here I had begun my investigations into rendition, and my destination was one of the city's most feared places. I had walked over from Egypt's Museum of Antiquities. Fifteen minutes later I reached a square compound with black-painted walls and white pillbox windows. There were fixed machine guns, on each corner. This jail building was the headquarters of Egyptian State Security (ESS), the internal secret police. It was also an interrogation centre. I had an appointment, I thought, with a secret policeman inside. I entered through the public entrance, passing through a metal detector, and sat in a waiting room. Around me there were family groups, chattering nervously. Some clutched photographs of their missing relatives. After about fifteen minutes an official came to send me away. There would be no comment today.

I had begun in Egypt because of what I'd heard: it was to Egypt that the United States was sending its prisoners. One source spoke of a secret prison, constructed by the US since 9/11, especially for their rendered prisoners. He heard it was in Upper Egypt, near the Aswan dam. I never confirmed that rumour. What I did find out were the basics — how exactly this country treated its own prisoners. I called the Egyptian Ministry of Information, the channel for all journalists' queries, and asked for an official interview with the security agencies. That request was declined but a helpful press officer suggested I speak to someone else, a lawyer named Montasser al-Zayat who represented many of the prisoners. Al-Zayat was an intriguing figure, part dissident and part government intermediary. He once knew Ayman al-Zawahiri, bin Laden's deputy. He also had helped negotiate the country's most important ceasefire — the ending of hostilities by the Gama'a al-Islamiya terrorist group. These were the people behind the Luxor Massacre.[21] Meeting me in his office, al-Zayat said he'd heard much about the Americans' transfer of prisoners. "We have heard of full airplanes arriving at night," he said, "but these prisoners are kept very, very isolated. It's really difficult to learn more." Cairo's government argued that terrorist suspects were dealt with according to the law and were brought to an open trial, albeit in a military not a civil court.

Before the prisoner came to court he had the chance to meet and discuss his treatment not only with a prosecutor but also with his own lawyer. But al-Zayat explained the government's trick. "When a prisoner is sent back to Egypt, he basically disappears for up to three months. That's when he is interrogated and tortured and when he is allowed no visitors. Only after that, when his wounds are healing, does he see the prosecutor and have visitors." Some, he explained, never reached that stage and simply remained disappeared. Later I visited other lawyers who confirmed these stories. Most had been imprisoned themselves at one time or another. They knew of these matters at first hand.[22]

The final destination for Islamist prisoners, most said, was generally a jail on the outskirts of the city known as Torah prison and its inner maximum security compound known as al-Aqrab, or The Scorpion. This was where Ahmed Agiza and Mohammed al-Zery were being held. One evening, I joined friends for a sunset cruise up the Nile. It was from this boat, as I sipped a glass of wine, that I first saw the prison's forbidding watchtowers. Within these walls had been held, at one time or other, some of the world's most infamous terrorists. The torture they received there, said many, had also helped inspire some of their most extreme ideas.[23] Journalists who approached much closer without permission could expect a quick invitation to a police cell.

By now, on this, my first trip to Cairo, the story of Agiza and al-Zery was well known, all of it apart from the involvement of the CIA. Ushered from the airport, I was to learn, they had been taken first to the offices of Egypt's General Intelligence Service (EGIS), its foreign intelligence service. Run since 1993 by General Omar Suleiman, a close friend of the West, this was the spy agency that had the closest links with America and the CIA.[24] From here they were transferred to Lazoghly Square, the headquarters of state security. They were shuttled between there and the agency's new annex in western Cairo for interrogation. Finally they made it to the Torah Prison, itself a feared place of detention and torture, but at least somewhere where they could at last receive visitors. Although Sweden had promised to visit the two prisoners and verify their treatment, it was only when the prisoners arrived in Torah that the country's diplomats got access to them, more than four weeks after their arrival. According to the two men, they were brutally treated from the outset. Jönsson, al-Zery's lawyer, said his client received horrific treatment for more than two months after he arrived: at the hands of Suleiman's intelligence agents, at state security, and finally in Torah prison. "Al-Zery was exposed to torture," said Jönsson. "He was kept in a very cold, very small cell and he was beaten. The most painful thing was the electrical torture that he was exposed to, where electrodes were put to all sensitive parts of his body many times — all under surveillance by a medical doctor."[25]

Interviewed later in Cairo, Agiza's mother, Hamida Shalibai, who visited her son in prison many times, described his account of his treatment: "When he arrived in Egypt, they took him, while hooded and handcuffed, to a building. He was led to an underground facility, going down a staircase. Then, they started interrogation, and torture. Whenever they would ask him a question, and he provided the answer, they wouldn't do anything. But as soon as he was asked a question, and he replied by 'don't know,' they would apply electric shocks to his body, and beat him. All of this was happening while he was naked. He was completely naked, without any clothes to cover his body! Not even underwear! He almost froze to death."[26]

Back in Sweden at the end of 2001, the deportation of the two Egyptians had been portrayed by the government as evidence of Sweden's support for the War on Terror, as indeed it was. Two days after the expulsion, the Associated Press (AP) headlined an article: "Swedish government repatriates two suspected terrorists." Gun-Britt Andersson, a foreign ministry official, declared: "We have clear evidence that they have had leading positions in organisations that have committed terrorist acts."[27] As the news broke in the US, one terrorism expert explained to the *Boston Globe* how the deportation signalled a shift in attitudes. "It's much more important than just between Egypt and Sweden," said Magnus Ranstorp, then director of the Centre for the Study of Terrorism and Political Violence at St Andrew's University. European countries "clearly understand that they are with the United States in fighting the terrorist menace and they know that they have to do so despite the fact that they may draw domestic political criticism," he said.[28]

As the Associated Press then reported, Agiza had been one of Egypt's most wanted. He had been sentenced to twenty-five years in jail in 1999 after being convicted in his absence by a military court. Egypt had accused Agiza of being a key member of Islamic Jihad, one of the regime's fiercest foes, and of helping plot the 1995 bomb attack on the Egyptian Embassy in Islamabad, Pakistan. He was also said to have once been close to Ayman al-Zawahiri, the former leader of Egypt's Islamic Jihad, and had even met bin Laden himself.[29]

In contrast to Agiza's known charge sheet, few were able to find much evidence of any accusations against al-Zery. Egypt was said to be preparing charges against him. It was not clear what they were.

I later interviewed an Egyptian activist in London who had a theory on why both the US and Sweden suddenly took an interest in al-Zery. On 23 October, fifty-six days before the Gulfstream came to Sweden, Yasser al-Sirri, an Egyptian dissident and campaigner for prisoners' rights, was arrested in London.[30] Scotland Yard questioned and charged al-Sirri over his alleged involvement in the murder of the Afghan Northern Alliance leader Ahmad Shah Massoud in a suicide bomb attack just before 11 September. Al-Sirri was later cleared of these charges. A judge described him as an "innocent fall guy."[31] But at the time of his October arrest, Scotland Yard had taken al-Sirri's computer hard drive and fax machine. The computer contained details of all the people he was in contact with. That information, he was told, was immediately shared with the US authorities. And among those contacts on al-Sirri's computer was an Egyptian in Sweden, Mohamed al-Zery.

"He asked me for help in many things. He wanted help with his asylum claim and he was even asking for help in finding a wife," said al-Sirri, interviewed in London. In the days that followed his arrest in London, al-Sirri discovered that up to a dozen people in his computer address book and among his files were arrested around the world. They included friends and relations in Egypt, Saudi Arabia, Yemen, Morocco and Sweden. Prior to his arrest, he later revealed, al-Zery had warned that an Egyptian secret agent had visited Sweden to spy on him. "He worked in a café. There was an Egyptian who found him there and followed him home and tried to speak to him. We later discovered he was a General in the Egyptian secret intelligence," said al-Sirri.[32]

As soon as the deportations were first revealed in Sweden, there was criticism from human rights activists. Amnesty International warned the men were "at grave risk of torture."[33] In the months ahead there was to be relentless campaign against the Swedish government over the decision, still ongoing when I visited Cairo in October 2003. But one thing had not yet been made public: the involvement of American agents, and the US Gulfstream jet.

For the Swedes, with their long record as champions of human rights, the key to the Egyptian deportation was a series of guarantees negotiated with Cairo not only that both the men "would not be subjected to inhuman treatment or punishment of any kind" but also that Swedish diplomats could verify their treatment by frequent visits to them in prison and by attending their trials. Time and again, in the months that followed, Persson and his officials and ministers stressed the frequent visits that Swedish diplomats made to see the two men in prison in Cairo. Yet with their reputations at stake, the Swedish ministers not only kept quiet on how the men were sent to Egypt. They lied about the two men's protests about torture.

On 30 January 2002, Jönsson was called in by Swedish immigration officials and was assured there had been "no complaints of physical violence."[34] In a letter to the United Nations Committee Against Torture (CAT) on 8 March 2002, the Swedish government spoke of how Ambassador Sven Linder had first been to see Ahmed Agiza on 23 January. They declared: "To the Swedish ambassador Ahmed Agiza conveyed no complaint about torture, or how he had been treated." Later, in another letter to the UN committee, dated 6 May 2003, the Swedish government asserted that Agiza's now-public complaints of having been tortured were not credible and "the government has had no information which casts doubts over this conclusion."

But this information was false. The government had released to its own parliament and to the United Nations an edited copy of Ambassador Linder's report from Cairo after his first meeting with the two prisoners. It stated:

Agiza and al-Zery had just been transferred to the Torah prison after having been interrogated for thirty days at the security service's facilities in another part of Cairo. Their treatment in the Torah prison was "excellent". ... (REDACTED SECTION)... It is not possible for me to assess the veracity of these claims. However, I am able to note that the two men did not, not even on my direct questions, in any way claim that they had been subjected to any kind of systematic, physical torture and that they consider themselves to be well treated in the Torah prison.[35]

The emphasis about Torah prison was misleading. The men's interrogation, as the lawyer al-Zayat had warned me, had taken place before they arrived. But at that first meeting, Agiza had made a series of allegations. This was what the 're-dacted section' actually said:

They had a number of complaints ... excessive brutality on the part of the Swedish police ... forced to remain in uncomfortable positions in the airplane during the transport to Egypt; forced to be blindfolded during the interrogation period; detention in too small cells 1.5 x 1.5 meters during the same period; lack of sleep due to surveillance in the cells; a delay of ten days before Agiza, following a medical examination, had access again to his medication for gastric ulcer; blows from guards while transported to and from interrogation; threats from interroga-tor that there could be consequences for Agiza's family if he did not tell everything about his time in Iran etc.

These were not, perhaps, allegations of actual torture. The men's detailed de-scriptions of their torture came later. But to state, as the Swedes had done, that Agiza "conveyed no complaint about torture, *or how he had been treated*" (my emphasis) was clearly false. The Swedes had assured the UN that Egypt's prom-ises of fair treatment had been met and it had "not received any information which could cast doubt on this conclusion."[36] Again, it was a lie. In another re-port it also stated that "Agiza said on 23 January that he had no complaints as to his treatment in prison."[37] Again, it was a lie. Later, the UN Committee ruled that Sweden had "committed a breach of its obligations" by not "disclosing to the Committee relevant information" nor voicing its concerns.[38]

The problem with assurances of good treatment by countries like Egypt was that they were almost impossible to enforce. Torture in Egypt was sophisticated. It was designed not to leave marks. Agiza and al-Zery's claims of torture could ultimately never be proved. While Swedish diplomats might diligently meet the prisoners in jail, those interviews were conducted in the presence of Egyptian intelligence officers. And, even if they weren't, the prisoners would know they would face reprisals if any kind of reports of torture in the jails emerged. The same problem would occur time and again when other countries tried to enforce promises by Arab states to treat their prisoners well.

Both Ambassador Linder and Agiza's mother saw Agiza in prison for the first time on 23 January 2002. Both had different impressions. The ambassador thought Agiza looked well. His mother said he looked badly beaten and imme-diately complained of torture. On 11 February, a correspondent from Swedish radio was allowed access to Agiza in jail, again with Egyptian intelligence officers present. He reported Agiza had a limp. When he asked directly if he was being tortured, Agiza refused to answer the question.

It took till the spring of 2003 for Agiza to have the confidence to speak to the Swedish diplomats of the torture he said he had endured, including electric shock treatment. They would not believe his story. In truth, there were few ways of verifying it. No independent doctor was allowed access to the prisoner, and the marks of electric shocks were easy to conceal. On 10 April 2004, Agiza was finally put on trial in Egypt's 13th Superior Military Court. Violating its written promises, Swedish diplomats were excluded from the first two hearings.[39] When Agiza's lawyer requested an adjournment so he could read 2,000 pages of charging material and prepare a defence, he was given just three days. Then the court rejected requests to call independent witnesses or to order a medical examination. On 27 April, Agiza was sentenced to twenty-five years, later reduced to fifteen years, on a charge of holding a leading position within the "Vanguards of Conquest", a wing of Islamic Jihad. Al-Zery meanwhile was quietly released after no charges were brought against him. But he was held effectively under house arrest and banned from talking about his time in jail or the pain of being sent back to prison. Jönsson, his lawyer, however, was adamant he obtained evidence that proved the depravity of al-Zery's treatment. His problem was that by protesting too loudly, he could get al-Zery into further trouble.

As the UN Committee was to conclude, there was no way of verifying the men's claims of torture, but Egypt had breached one clear promise in the case of Agiza — that of a fair trial. It was a concern I heard acknowledged from a Swedish diplomat I met in Cairo. "The key thing for us is the lack of fair trial. That's what we're watching out for," he said.[40] Until this point, what both Egypt and Sweden had done was to exclude any mention of the role of the United States in this whole case. No one apart from a handful of Swedish officials and secret agents were aware of the team of rendition agents, or the role of the Gulfstream jet.

Just a month after Agiza's trial, the secret of the Swedish case was finally revealed. A team of three Swedish TV journalists broadcast on 17 May 2004 the results of a five-month investigation and called their documentary "The Broken Promise". Its conclusions were clear-cut. They could reveal "it was a foreign intelligence agency that abducted the two men out of Sweden." Masked US agents had been allowed to operate on Swedish territory. They commented that "a few months after the attack on World Trade Centre, Sweden accepted to become a pawn in the United States's worldwide manhunt."[41]

Unaware of the Swedish case, and by pure coincidence, on the same day as the TV broadcast, writing in the *New Statesman*, I had published my first account of rendition and the CIA's secret fleet of planes, describing how the agency made use of a "fleet of luxury planes," including Gulfstreams, which, together with military transports, had moved prisoners around the world since September 11.

"Some of the prisoners have gone to Guantánamo, the US interrogation centre at its naval base in Cuba," I wrote. "Hundreds more have been transferred from one Middle Eastern or Asian country to another — countries where the prisoners can be more easily interrogated."[42]

What the Swedish journalists had done was to obtain the actual flight plan and the US registration number — N379P — of the Gulfstream plane. It was this information that was the starting point that helped me to track down thousands of flights by the CIA around the globe. Soon after the documentary, its claims were confirmed officially. Two documents were released. One memo from SAPO, dated 7 February 2002 (the same day that President Bush announced publicly that Al Qaeda and Taliban prisoners were not protected by the Geneva Conventions), revealed that "the American side" had offered to help in the deportation "by lending a plane for the transport." Lawyers at the Swedish justice department also wrote another memo that said "the transport from Sweden to Egypt was carried out with the help of American authorities."[43]

But was this plane just a special charter? And was the CIA really involved? Was it the FBI or the Pentagon? It took a further inquiry by Sweden's parliamentary ombudsman, Mats Melin, to prove the point. Arne Andersson, the head of the SAPO deportation operation, finally confirmed to him how they were glad to accept a CIA offer. He said: "In the end we accepted an offer from our American friends, so to say, their counterpart service [to us], the CIA, in getting access to a plane that had direct over-flight permits over all of Europe and could do the deportation in a very quick way." The Swedish case was now officially exposed as part of a CIA secret programme known as rendition.

Just two months after 9/11, and several weeks before the Swedish rendition, President George Bush was standing next to President Chirac of France when he declared that Allied nations needed to do more than express sympathy but "must perform". With a barely-concealed threat, Bush announced on 6 November that over time coalition partners would be "held accountable for inactivity". Helping the US could mean "different things for different nations. Some nations don't want to contribute troops and we understand that. Other nations can contribute intelligence-sharing. ... But all nations, if they want to fight terror, must do something." He added:

"You're either with us or against us in the fight against terror."

The United States would thus demand, not ask for, support in the war on terror. Across the globe, nations were already responding to 9/11 not only by pledging support but by helping practically: committing troops and assets for the invasion of Afghanistan, opening vaults of intelligence on Islamic militant groups, and by coordinating arrest operations of hundreds of militant suspects. Many of these offers of help were announced publicly. But of course there was also much that was secret, including plans for a worldwide traffic in prisoners.

Since 9/11 it had been fashionable to be "thinking out of the box" a
oping new methods of warfare against this new threat of terrorism. B
unconventional approaches were saluted publicly, what was not ann ...ced
was how, in dealing with its new prisoners, the US government proposed to
abandon the rule of law on a large scale. In the sort of double-think language
George Orwell in his novel *1984* had called "newspeak", the new measures
would not be described as "illegal" but instead US officials called the system
"extra-legal." In common language that meant outside any law, or in more
pejorative words "outlaw".

The objective of the extra-legal system was to take prisoners beyond the protection of any lawyer, US courtroom, or even military tribunal. Terrorists would
be dealt with, by preference, in a country that would handle them with the harsh-
ness politicians believed they deserved. CIA officers were more pragmatic. For
them, in the face of weaknesses in both US law and policy, transferring prisoners
beyond US jurisdiction was both more practical and more efficient. This system
came to be known as *extraordinary rendition* and one of the key vehicles of these
transfers was the plane from North Carolina.

The word "rendition" in our context meant the transfer of a prisoner by US
government agents without any kind of formal extradition proceedings or legal
hearing. As described in Chapter 6, such operations had been legal under US law
since the 1880s. But the "snatch," as it was often called, had nearly always been
geared to bringing the prisoner home to face justice in a US courtroom. As the
US confronted Al Qaeda, this principle was weakened and the "extraordinary
rendition" programme came to be adopted. This term "extraordinary rendition"
was never an official one and, when used, has been defined in many ways. When
I use the term, I refer to what became the CIA's principal tactic — the transfer of
a prisoner by US agents to any place but an American court of law.

Since 9/11, such extraordinary renditions occurred across the world. Prisoners were captured and transported by America not only from the war-zones of
Afghanistan and Iraq, but from countries including Bosnia, Croatia, Macedonia,
Albania, the Sudan, Somalia, Kenya, Zambia, the Gambia, Pakistan, Indonesia
and Malaysia. From these countries, prisoners were taken to a slightly smaller
list of destinations, including Egypt, Syria, Morocco, Jordan, Afghanistan, Uzbekistan and Thailand. (A list of known renditions, including examples of de-
partures from and transfers to all these countries is printed in the Appendix of
this book.)

Estimating the exact scale of the programme was always going to be hard and
imprecise because the details of these transfers were kept classified by the CIA.
George Tenet, when director of the CIA, testified to seventy renditions in the
(unspecified) years leading up to 9/11, of which some twenty were brought to
trial in the United States.[44] Since 9/11, no figures were officially given, although
CIA officials told journalists of a total of 100 to 150 transfers.[45]

My own research would suggest the total of renditions ran into many, many hundreds. From my own case files, I collected a list, published in the appendix, of eighty-nine renditions since 9/11, involving eighty-seven different individuals. But this list was a gross underestimate since only a small fraction of captured prisoners had been released to tell their story or were able to pass their accounts out of jail through their family or lawyers. After 9/11, Pakistan claimed to have captured a total of more than 600 Al Qaeda and Taliban suspects, of which the majority, said its officials, were rendered into US custody. Iran also said it captured over 1,000; most of these were handed into US control (although not generally directly). Egypt described the transfer of sixty to seventy into its jails alone. Sudan had acknowledged transferring fourteen into US custody, and its officials spoke of sending dozens more directly to Egypt. The key destinations of Jordan, Syria, Morocco, and Uzbekistan never provided any official figures on the prisoners they received, even though I had detailed information that they each received large numbers. [46]

Renditions were not only carried out by the CIA but also, in greater numbers, by the US military. Of the more than 6,000 prisoners captured in the Afghan conflict in 2001,[47] many were rendered to their home country — in official terms "repatriated" — for example to Uzbekistan.[48] According to the International Committee of the Red Cross (ICRC), international law required a hearing or independent review before anyone could be repatriated to a country where they might fear abuse.[49] No such hearings, according to US officials I interviewed, were ever carried out. The transfers of more than 700 prisoners to Guantánamo Bay, Cuba, were renditions too, since none were recognised officially as prisoners of war; all were international transfers without legal process or treaty. Studies of the case files of those at Guantánamo also showed that the majority, contrary to popular belief, had been rendered into US custody after being captured from outside the Afghanistan combat zone. Within four years of the opening of the Guantánamo prison, over three hundred had been rendered back to their home country, where they were either released or imprisoned again. In all, by my estimate, the military had carried out more than one thousand renditions.

There was one problem with all these transfers. The US had signed a series of treaties both against torture and also regulating its treatment of prisoners captured in a time of war. After 9/11, when many prisoners came to be captured as part of the declared War on Terror, and many were initially detained by the military in war zones such as Afghanistan, one of the big obstacles was the Geneva Conventions. These conventions demanded that prisoners be treated humanely and be given access to the Red Cross. They also, more importantly, placed strong restrictions on interrogations. In theory, prisoners could be compelled to answer little more than "name, rank and serial number." The convention on prisoners of war states bluntly that:

No physical or mental torture, nor any other form of coercion, may be inflicted on prisoners of war to secure from them information of any kind whatever. Prisoners of war who refuse to answer may not be threatened, insulted, or exposed to any unpleasant or disadvantageous treatment of any kind.[50]

Under the laws of war, the US *did* have extensive rights to hold prisoners without charge, for the duration of an international armed conflict. But the neutral ICRC would argue that such rights broadly ceased in the Afghan conflict with the establishment of a new government in the summer of 2002.[51] Moreover, the Red Cross said prisoners captured outside the Afghan or Iraq war zones — who, according to other sources, formed the vast majority of rendered terrorist suspects — were not subject to the laws of war but rather to the normal rights of criminal suspects, for example the right to challenge a detention in a civilian court of law.

The problem then was that, in the logic of the global War on Terror, many prisoners were captured for the very purpose of questioning. So the solution chosen by President Bush was to treat all captured terrorist suspects, wherever seized, as detainees held by the US under wartime powers, with no rights as civilians. But, regarding the global conflict with Al Qaeda in this way as a war, he would abandon the Geneva Conventions or at least those parts of the Conventions not considered appropriate by "military necessity."[52] Prisoners would be transferred and questioned at will, even if he directed that, in the military's hands treatment should continue to be humane.[53] With the terrorist threat proven by 9/11, the gathering of intelligence was paramount.

Another big problem for renditions was Article 3 of the United Nations Convention Against Torture that prohibited any state from transferring a prisoner to another country where there was a substantial risk that he or she would be tortured. This Convention was ratified into US Law by the Congress, with the only proviso that what constituted torture would be defined by US domestic law. Almost by definition, renditions involved the transfer to countries where the rule of law was weak and and therefore much more likely to tolerate torture. Countries with a strong legal system would rarely allow the transfer of prisoners without a proper extradition procedure. And in practice, rendition was also directed largely at Middle Eastern Islamic militants who were to be returned to mainly Arab countries. All of these had track records of using torture. It was almost endemic.

Just as Sweden had done in the case of Agiza and al-Zery, the US found a fig leaf to provide legal protection for renditions. Countries like Egypt were asked to provide a promise that they would not torture an individual prisoner. In this way, the US would argue, there were no grounds for imagining a "substantial risk" of torture. The downside was that when it came from a country like Egypt it would be hard-going to persuade anyone to believe that assurance. Most CIA insiders never bothered. As we shall see, they told the White House all along that anyone sent to Egypt would, almost certainly, be treated very brutally. Egypt was a country plagued by terrorism, having suffered more than fifty attacks in the years before 9/11.[54] It had dealt with the problem with ruthless repression.

In light of Egypt's record, few in Europe, or most Western countries, had been ready to send prisoners to face trial in Cairo. That is why the Swedish case was such an exception. For years, British prime ministers had tried to persuade their civil servants to approve extraditions to Egypt. Yet, time and again, the diplomats warned in none-too-welcome language that a passage to Cairo was a passage to the torture chamber. One former British diplomat recalled seeing an Egyptian dossier of evidence compiled against Yasser al-Sirri, the dissident in London mentioned above. "When I saw the file, it was like you could almost see the fingernails attached of the people they had questioned," he said.

The United States, and the CIA in particular, had never felt quite so constrained as the Europeans. On the quiet, secret renditions to dark dungeons had always been a part of covert life. According to Robert Baer, who had twenty-one years working the Middle East for the CIA till he left in the mid 1990s, renditions were always about more than sending terrorists to be locked up in countries like Egypt. It was also about making them talk, and different countries had different values. As he has remarked memorably: "If you send a prisoner to Jordan you get a better interrogation. If you send a prisoner, for instance, to Egypt you will probably never see him again, the same way with Syria."[55]

Countries like Syria might have been publicly classified as enemies of the United States, even as candidate members of Bush's "Axis of Evil", but they remained allies in the secret war against Islamic militancy. "The simple rule in the Middle East", said Baer, "is 'my enemy's enemy is my friend', and that's the way it works. All of these countries are suffering in one way or another from Islamic fundamentalism, militant Islam."

For years, the Syrians had offered to work with the US against Islamic militancy. "So at least until 11 September, these offers were turned down. We generally avoided the Egyptians and the Syrians because they were so brutal." One way or another, said Baer, the CIA had been carrying out renditions for years. What changed since 9/11 was the scale of the operations. It became large scale and systematic. According to Baer, hundreds of prisoners had been captured and sent by the United States to Middle Eastern prisons — many more than had been sent to Guantánamo. "September 11 justified scrapping the Geneva Convention," he said. It was the end of "our rule of law as we knew it in the West."[56]

Ever since the Camp David accords of 1978, no country in the Middle East bar Israel has been such a crucial ally for America as Egypt. [57] Their relationship has been cemented, above all, by money. Egypt receives more than $2bn a year from the US taxpayer, over 50% of which comes in the form of Foreign Military Financing (FMF),[58] which provides grants that enable Egypt to buy military goods, services and training from the United States. The two main recipients of FMF have been Israel and Egypt.[59] Since 1986, Egypt had typically received around $1.3bn annually from the FMF programme alone.

In the world of renditions, Egypt has been "Torture Central". Starting in the mid-1990s, as we shall see, more than one hundred prisoners were dispatched to Egyptian jails from countries around the world.[60] Often, as in the case of the two from Sweden, the renditions were portrayed as bilateral matters. The involvement of the United States had been concealed. But, time and again, the CIA had been the hidden hand. Since 9/11, my own records showed that CIA jets most directly involved in renditions had visited Cairo at least twenty times.[61] And on many occasions they have arrived with prisoners on board. Jack Cloonan, an FBI veteran and former senior agent in the FBI's Al Qaeda task force, has some experience of the Egyptian inclination to torture. Once the FBI had a witness, a pilot who had worked with Osama bin Laden and had agreed to testify against him. The FBI, in return, were offering him some protection. When this witness asked to go to Egypt to visit his family, the FBI pleaded with Cairo to leave him untouched. Yet even though he was a friend of the US and a witness against terrorism, said Cloonan, the Egyptian secret police insisted on arresting and beating him. "I was told they chained him to a toilet bowl," he said.[62]

Before he left the FBI in late 2002, Cloonan was one of those who advocated presciently that treating Al Qaeda suspects humanely according to the law was essential to bringing them to trial and to extracting good intelligence. He was angered when a key Al Qaeda logistics man, Ibn al-Sheikh al-Libi, was captured, questioned by FBI agents at Bagram airbase in Afghanistan, but removed from their custody by the CIA. Al-Libi was to be rendered for interrogation in Egypt, where his forced confessions reportedly became the source of false intelligence about links between Iraq and Al Qaeda. When he protested about al-Libi's rendition, the FBI director, Robert Mueller brushed him off: "It was like: 'why are you bothering me with this?'" From his experience, Cloonan said he knew terrorist suspects would remember experiences of mistreatment for generations. "What we don't seem to figure out is that when they are abused, they are duty bound to get revenge," he said.

Another prisoner sent to Egypt was an Australian called Mamdouh Habib. His case was an example that showed how rendition was used, not just to remove a terrorist out of harm's way, but to extract useful intelligence under torture. The information he provided in an Egyptian torture cell came to be used against him at a tribunal in Guantánamo. A former coffee shop manager from Sydney, Habib was on a bus in Pakistan, not far from the Afghan border, when he was arrested by local police. He had previously been living in Afghanistan, involved, it seems clear, with militant groups. He fled to Pakistan when the US invasion began. Although an Australian citizen, Habib was soon handed over to American agents. It is a familiar scene. Habib says he was taken to an airstrip and there American men in masks, t-shirts and boots stripped him, took pictures of him, shackled him, put a bag over his head and put him on a plane.[63] Then they flew him on to Cairo. It was here, explained his American lawyer, Professor Joe Margulies of the MacArthur Justice Centre of the University of Chicago, that Habib was continuously tortured for six months.

"The torture was unspeakable," said Margulies. "Mr Habib described routine beatings. He was taken into a room, handcuffed, and the room was gradually filled with water until the water was just beneath his chin. Can you imagine the terror of knowing you can't escape?"[64]

Under this interrogation, Habib confessed to his involvement with Al Qaeda. "'Whatever they wanted me to sign, I signed to survive," he said later.[65] Habib was then transferred back to American custody. He was first sent first back to Afghanistan, where he got to meet Australian officials and and, his government said later, "made some serious complaints about maltreatment during his time in Egypt."[66] He then was then sent on to Guantánamo. The confessions he signed in Egypt were now used against him in military tribunals. "Those combatant status review tribunals relied on the evidence secured in Egypt as a basis to detain Mr Habib," said Margulies.

After Margulies and others lodged public protests over his torture in January 2005, Habib was finally freed from Guantánamo and flown home to Australia. The government there said he would not be charged with any crime, although intelligence officials there would continue to accuse him of involvement with Al Qaeda. He still did not feel free. In an interview for Australian television he explained: "They doesn't [sic]want to leave me alone. So I feel free when these people leave me alone." He continued: "I've been released by United States and the United States say they dropped their case, they have nothing to do with me. I believe Australia shouldn't harass me anymore."[67]

Strikingly, Pakistan later confirmed that Habib had been sent to Egypt on US orders and for US purposes. "The US wanted him for their own investigations. We are not concerned where they take him," said Makhdoom Syed Faisal Saleh Hayat, the country's then Interior Minister. Egypt had not asked Pakistan for Habib's extradition, he said.[68]

Egypt then came in for much criticism. Its record both on human rights and on repressing democracy was lambasted annually by both the Congress and by the State Department. But in secret, men like Omar Suleiman, the country's most powerful spy and secret policeman, did our work, the sort of work that Western countries had no appetite to do themselves. Was such torture necessary? Was the threat really that great? Could the US and European legal systems not be tightened so as to deal with these prisoners ourselves, thereby saving the CIA from involvement in this business? These were questions I tried to answer again and again. While I had not yet arrived at a definitive answer, I was presented with an inescapable conclusion, namely that torture was being carried out in our name.

2

THE FOG OF WAR: THE "CONFESSIONS" OF A BRITISH "DIRTY BOMBER"

Flightlog

Registration: **N379P**;
Type: **Gulfstream V**;
Operator: Premier Executive Transport, Massachusetts;
Date: **Sunday 21 July 2002**

Flight plan:
Islamabad, Pakistan (dep. 11.35 p.m.)
Rabat-Sale, Morocco (arr. 3.43 a.m.)

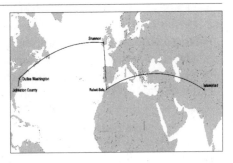

ISLAMABAD AIRPORT, PAKISTAN
21 July 2002

On the north-west Indian and Pakistani plains, stretched beneath the foothills of the Himalaya, the towering monsoon clouds were gathering at last. With them was coming a spell of welcome rain to a parched, brown landscape. As evening drew near, the silver-white frame of the Gulfstream began approaching into Pakistani airspace from the West, dodging the tall stacks of thunderclouds. Since the early hours of the morning, a 23-year-old Ethiopian man, a former London college student, had been waiting in a small room at Islamabad airport's military side. Binyam Mohamed, a tall and thin and rather gaunt figure with sad-looking eyes, was sitting on the floor. His hands were locked inside the steel rings of police handcuffs.

It was now just over a month since John Ashcroft, the US Attorney General, had announced the discovery of an Al Qaeda plot to explode a radioactive "dirty

bomb" on American soil. Its chief perpetrator, he declared, was a former junior
street gangster from Chicago called José Padilla, who was arrested on 8 May
when he landed back in the United States.[1] Later, much later, Binyam was publicly accused of being Padilla's chief accomplice. Both were said to have fought
in Afghanistan and then escaped together afterwards to Pakistan. In the upside-
down logic of the law after 9/11, Padilla as a US citizen would ultimately face no
charges over the plot that Ashcroft alleged and would be brought to a civilian
court to face much lesser accusations. Binyam, by contrast, was due to face the
charges in full at a military trial in Guantánamo Bay. But, captured back in April,
Binyam as yet had been asked nothing of these allegations. Today he knows only
that he is suspected of being with Al Qaeda.

In Washington, Ashcroft's announcement had been regarded as something
of a panicked affair, a weak move. He had interrupted a trip to Moscow to appear by live satellite link at a press conference to warn of the nuclear conspiracy.
Since Padilla had been arrested several weeks earlier, it was difficult to explain
the urgency of the announcement, except that Ashcroft and the FBI were coming under increased pressure. Just four days earlier, a whistle-blowing FBI agent
named Coleen Rowley had told Congress about how the FBI had ignored warn-
ings that Al Qaeda was training pilots to launch suicide attacks.[2]

All in all, things were not going too well in the global War on Terror. Since the
escape of bin Laden and more than 200 other key followers from the Tora Bora
mountains,[3] there had been some successes. The most important was the capture in Pakistan, at the end of March, of an alleged Al Qaeda leader named Abu
Zubaydah.[4] Yet Pakistan was still playing host to far more important terrorist
leaders — like Osama bin Laden himself and his deputy Dr Ayman al-Zawahiri.
The ringleaders of the 9/11 operation were still on the loose too: Khalid Sheikh
Mohammed and Ramzi Binalshibh. While the battle against Al Qaeda was therefore far from over, the attention of the administration was increasingly focused
on Iraq. That July weekend the head of MI6 returned from Washington to report
a shift of mood. "Military action was now seen as inevitable," he said.[5] To the
Defence Department, Ashcroft's announcement seemed not only an exaggera-
tion but a distraction. "I don't think there was actually a plot beyond some fairly
loose talk", said Deputy Defense Secretary Paul Wolfowitz, a day after Ashcroft's
declarations.[6]

The main trouble with Ashcroft's announcement of a "dirty bomb plot" was
that, while it raised fears about the terrorist threat, it seemed unconvincing.
Backed by no kind of evidence, it was a scare story. How then could interrogators obtain evidence to justify the alleged plot?

Since his arrest as he boarded a flight to Europe from Karachi airport in Pakistan on 10 April, Binyam, who still had not been named publicly, had been held
at a series of local prisons. While José Padilla's picture appeared on the cover of
every American national newspaper,[7] Binyam's alleged role in this plot remained

a secret. He had been questioned by both Pakistani and British intelligence, and by the FBI. But, he would later recall, he had at this stage confessed to nothing much more incriminating than his real name. It was time, his interrogators may have thought, to consider harsher methods.

On 19 July, two days before his flight, Binyam was brought to Islamabad from his jail in Karachi. His journey north had been on an ordinary domestic Pakistan International Airlines flight. He remembered he was in row 35 or 36. On the day of his departure he was taken by bus and pick-up truck to the airport, and was sitting patiently in handcuffs with another Pakistani captive. They were in a waiting room belonging to Pakistan's Special Branch police.

Just after 10 p.m. local time, the doors of the cells opened. A group of what Binyam took to be American soldiers walked in, wearing the black masks of the CIA's Rendition Group. "They stripped me naked, took photos, put fingers up my anus, and dressed me in a tracksuit. I was then shackled, with earphones, and blindfolded."[8] Soon, Binyam was being bundled onto a plane. With his vision obscured, he was unsure of the size or type. But he did decide it was military or something official: he could hear none of the normal noises of a civilian flight. He was sure too that there were two other prisoners on board. And so began Binyam's voyage into the netherworld of America's secret prisons. His journey was to take, he remembered, between eight and ten hours, long enough, as he sat blindfolded and tied up, to think again and again about how it had all come to this.[9]

Binyam Mohamed

Binyam Mohamed was born in Ethiopia in 1978, the son of an official at the Ethiopian state airline named Ahmed Mohamed.[10] In 1992, when he was fourteen, his family fled the country after the fall of the Communist regime. Binyam himself faced conscription into the Ethiopian army. They came first to the Washington, DC area, where Binyam already had three siblings. At home, he was remembered as meek and polite. His sister in Washington remembers him reciting dialogue from the film *Police Academy*, to his big brother's annoyance.[11] Binyam did not settle well in the US, his family recalled, so father and son moved to London, where Binyam was to remain for the next seven years.[12] Enrolling at what was then called Paddington Green College in West London,[13] he and his father settled in North

Kensington, with its eclectic mix of wealthy and fashionable white residents, as well as poorer immigrants from the Caribbean and Muslim countries.[14]

When his father decided to return to Ethiopia, Binyam applied for permission to stay in Britain and he moved in to a small flat off Golborne Road. He began studying for an engineering diploma. Making friends on the often rough streets of North Kensington, Binyam began picking up new habits — good and bad. Binyam loved music and enjoyed football, supporting Crystal Palace. As a player, he was thought good enough for a semi-professional career. He had been a gifted athlete, the fastest runner in his school track team.[15] Tyrone Forbes, his trainer, remembered: "He was a quiet kid, he seemed deep thinking, although that might have been because his language skills were not great."[16] Binyam also became something of a street kid and had friends who were dealing in cannabis. He picked up the habit of smoking it too. But then he also discovered Islam. He began to pray at the local al-Manaar mosque in North Kensington and became a volunteer at its cultural centre. "He is remembered here as a very nice, quiet person, who never caused any trouble," said Abdulkarim Khalil, director of the Kensington cultural centre.[17] Islam was the religion of his birth yet few in his family, he felt, had followed any of its practices or principles. He began to associate with "Al Tabligh", an international missionary group who aimed to bring wayward Muslims back to religion.[18] A friend would later recall walking down Golborne Road with Binyam as he repeatedly stepped aside politely for other pedestrians. "We have to try and emulate the conduct of the Prophet," Binyam had explained.[19]

In May or June 2001, Binyam left his bed-sit and travelled to Afghanistan, via Pakistan. According to Binyam, his reasons for going were partly religious and partly because he was determined to quit his drugs habit. He needed a change of scene, to get away from London's street culture. He explained later he felt he should live in a Muslim country and he decided to go and see if the Taliban regime was "a good Islamic country or not." He also, as both he and his friends acknowledged, had been incensed at television images of the Russians bombing what he regarded as innocent Muslim civilians in Chechnya. He thought of going to join the rebels there fighting the Russians.[20] As former intelligence officials acknowledge, many of the camps in Afghanistan labelled by the US as Al Qaeda were primarily set up to train insurgents for such conflicts, not to launch terrorist attacks against the West.[21]

To his family and friends, Binyam had always appeared a gentle person, not prone to any violence. Clearly his rediscovery of the Islamic faith had changed his character. He wanted to fight for its cause. Thoughts of fighting the Russians in Chechnya was one thing; many would consider it a just war. But plotting the deaths of civilians was another. Was he really someone who could be a terrorist?

CAMP ECHO, GUANTÁNAMO BAY, CUBA
Monday, 2 May 2005

Clive Stafford Smith, a British lawyer practising in the United States, was seated in a plastic chair as his new client, Binyam Mohamed, was brought into the cell. The prisoner was dressed in a beige polyester trouser suit, a signal from the US military that he was considered in their terms "compliant." Binyam's handcuffs were removed and a chain was attached from the shackles on his legs to a bolt in the concrete floor.

Binyam looked skinny, with a relatively trimmed beard, Stafford Smith would remember. All the hair was shaved from the top of his head, which was covered by a black skull cap consistent with his religious tradition. For thirty-seven months, till this moment, Binyam had been cut off from the world, a ghost prisoner who could not tell his own story. But now, after the US Supreme Court had granted the Guantánamo prisoners the right to see a laywer, he could at last start to tell his side of it, and to explain the story of his renditions across the world.[22] Binyam was a young man with a sense of humour, who could rarely resist a joke. "Binyam's remarkable feature is his bright eyes which glint continually unless he is depressed," recalled Stafford Smith. "He is an open book as the glimmer in his eyes is immediately switched off when he is not talking about a subject that he enjoys. But when he is on form, his retina tells the whole story, periodically complemented by a smile that illuminates him when a joke passes behind his eyes."

Binyam's family, based largely in the Washington, DC area, had been trying for nearly four years to discover his fate. They last heard from him in the spring of 2001 when they heard he was going abroad to study. Then, in the month that Binyam was arrested, they had a visit from two agents from the FBI who told them their brother was "in the custody of the Pakistani government." They showed Benhur, his brother, a picture of José Padilla and asked if he knew that man. But it meant nothing. After that the FBI refused to supply any information, and Benhur worried over his brother. He made a fruitless trip to London to find out if Binyam had returned, but he could find no trace at all.[23]

Beneath his good humour, Binyam had a terrifying tale to relate. It was dictated to Stafford Smith over the course of three days in Guantánamo. After his notes were declassified they were written up by Stafford Smith and became a diary of his torture, the most comprehensive compiled by any prisoner thus far. Binyam described the most horrific ordeals, from the psychological to the physical. In Morocco, he said, he had been cut over his body with razor blades, including on his genitals. After all that, he said, he had confessed to what the government had wanted him to say — that he was a dedicated terrorist who was plotting in Afghanistan and Pakistan with José Padilla and Al Qaeda's most senior leaders. Three months after meeting Stafford Smith, the results of those confessions became public. In an order signed by President Bush on 29 July 2005, Binyam and three others[24] were declared triable before a military commission at Guantánamo, accused of conspiracy to commit crimes including "attacking civilians; attacking civilian objects; murder by an unprivileged belligerent; destruction of property by an unprivileged belligerent; and terrorism."

There were two conflicting accounts of Binyam and his travels. One was the official account provided by the US government. The other was given by Binyam himself to Stafford Smith. The trouble in working out the truth was knowing whom to believe. The government declared he was an "unlawful combatant," and that such terrorists were trained to lie. Yet the government's own story was intrinsically weak, based on a series of confessions extracted in secret interrogation cells in the Middle East. Here then was the fog of war.

According to the government, Binyam was a trained electrical engineer who had arrived in Afghanistan in May 2001 after a recent conversion to Islam. He had been given training in light weapons at the Al Farouk camp. In the summer of 2001, Osama bin Laden himself visited the camps and announced "something big is going to happen in the future" and to "get ready" or words to that effect, said the government account. In August, Binyam was sent on to Kabul for a "city warfare course" where he was to receive ten days of pistol training, ten days on the AK47 assault rifle and ten days on "room to room"combat. Due to lack of ammunition, he was trained only on the AK47. From there, he had been sent north to the frontlines at Bagram, the old Soviet air base north of Kabul, where he received training in "firing mortars, map reading, targeting and firing." He returned to the city, and was then given a quick course on explosives and "home made" bomb-making. Also there, said the charge sheet, was Richard Reid, who was later convicted of trying to detonate a shoe-bomb on a transatlantic flight.[25]

Still in Afghanistan after 9/11, the charges tell that Binyam moved on from Kabul, to Kandahar in the South, to Zormat on the Pakistan border and then to a place called "Birmel". By now, he had been told that Al Qaeda had a mission for him, and he was introduced here to Abu Zubaydah, a leading member of Al Qaeda's Shura, or ruling council. His mission, as the indictment described, was to go to Pakistan to learn to build bombs to be used against US forces. Binyam, the indictment continued, now accompanied Abu Zubaydah onwards from Khost in Afghanistan across the Pakistan border, and then made his way to Lahore close to the Indian border. Along the way they had stopped at guesthouses and at a madrassa, or religious training school. And it was here that Binyam is said to have met up with José Padilla and other trainees also now accused of conspiracy. In Lahore, Padilla and Binyam were alleged to have studied computer guides on how to build an improvised "dirty bomb" — a conventional explosive device mixed up with radioactive materials. In theory it was designed by would-be terrorists to spread radioactive fall-out over a large area. The pair met Abu Zubaydah, who now asked Binyam to go on an overseas mission rather than return to Afghanistan. "Binyam Muhammed [sic] agreed to carry out an operation in the United States," said the charges.[26]

By now the prison at Guantánamo Bay was opened up and when Abu Zubaydah discussed other potential terrorist attacks — such as blowing up gas tankers and spraying people with cyanide in nightclubs — he mentioned that the reason for such attacks was to help "free the prisoners in Cuba." From Lahore and then Faisalabad, the northern city where Zubaydah was finally caught on 28 March, Binyam and Padilla were said to have travelled south and made contact with Khalid Sheikh Mohammed, the architect of 9/11, and Saif al-Adel, described by the Americans as the head of Al Qaeda's security committee. They were told their mission would now be "targeting high-rise apartment buildings that utilized natural gas for its heat and also targeting gas stations." This new plan involved renting an apartment, opening all the gas taps to let the gas leak and then setting it alight to detonate a gas explosion, collapsing all the floors above. "Binyam Muhammad and José Padilla agreed to conduct such an operation," read the charge sheet. In early April 2002, Binyam was said to have been given around $6,000 and José Padilla $10,000 to get to the United States. On 4 April, both went to Karachi Airport and tried to leave the country. Both were detained. Binyam was supposed to have a forged passport and Padilla had a visa violation. Mysteriously, both were apparently released the next day and Khalid Sheikh Mohammed was allegedly able to give Binyam a new passport to use. Then, on 10 April, Binyam tried to leave again, and this time he was again arrested for using a forged passport.

The story so far was the official version of events, as compiled by the CIA and the US military, and as later presented as an official indictment against him. It was supported by a series of confessions, not least by Binyam himself. But he claimed this statement was extracted under torture — after he was broken in a Morocco prison. Speaking to Stafford Smith, he said it was possible that he might have come across Padilla and others during his escape from Afghanistan, or in the months he hid in Pakistan. But he never knew Padilla personally or recognised his photograph. Yes, he had received military training but no, he was not any kind of terrorist. He had never been involved in any plot nor met or seen any of the big leaders of Al Qaeda.[27] Arriving in Afghanistan so soon before 9/11, he barely spoke Arabic. "What you had was a confession based on the imagination of his interrogators," said Stafford Smith. "They wanted to connect him with almost every possible person supposed to be of importance in Al Qaeda."

Some aspects of the government's account do make sense. It is certainly true that both Khalid Sheikh Mohammed and Ramzi Binalshibh were hiding in Karachi at the time when they were supposed to have met Padilla and Binyam. The proof comes from Yosri Fouda, a highly-respected Egyptian journalist and chief investigative reporter for the Arab TV station, Al Jazeera. It was in April 2002 that Fouda responded to an invitation and travelled to Karachi to carry out a secret interview with the two fugitives, their only ever meeting with a journalist since the 9/11 attacks.

At just the time when Khalid Sheikh Mohammed first contacted Fouda in London to invite him to record an interview, Padilla and Binyam were said by the government to have met with Khalid Sheikh Mohammed and Binalshibh for a "last supper" before their departure on their mission to the United States. Fouda finally travelled to Pakistan on 18 April and recorded the interview in a fourth-floor Karachi apartment the following day, 19 April. "People call us terrorists and they are right," boasted Khalid Sheikh Mohammed.[28]

Some other parts of the official accusations looked, at first sight, dubious. If the government was to be believed, after arriving in Afghanistan barely three months before 9/11, and with almost no knowledge of Arabic, Binyam was to be whisked at breakneck speed into a kind of terrorist fast-track. Most Al Qaeda attacks have borne the hallmarks of careful planning, some lasting several years. And yet here were Padilla and Binyam, in the space of several weeks, shifting their plans from exploding a nuclear radioactive device, to using cyanide in nightclubs, to blowing up the gas supply in apartment complexes. Fouda's encounters with Khalid Sheikh Mohammed also imply there was not a sense of haste or rush to the Al Qaeda planner's behaviour. Another oddity was the government's account of Padilla and Binyam's travel plans. Padilla was described as leaving Karachi in April 2002, on a flight to Zurich to "continue his journey to Chicago". And yet Padilla flew to Cairo, to visit his family, not to Chicago. He only reached there a month later.[29]

Binyam's diary of torture began from the moment of his arrest in Pakistan, at Karachi Airport on 10 April 2002. His ticket was for Zurich, from where he said he intended to fly home to London, where he had the legal right of residence. But he was soon accused of being a terrorist, and of wanting to fly to America. In Karachi, Binyam remembered being taken to a series of Pakistani interrogation centres.[30] He had tried to leave the country on a forged passport, he admitted, after losing his own passport during his travels. At first he tried to maintain his false identity but when the FBI turned up on 20 April and started asking serious questions, he knew the game was up.

Binyam remembered four of them. There was "Chuck", there was "Terry", there was a black man who could speak Swahili, and then there was a woman called "Jenny". Already the FBI had it in their heads that he wanted to fly to America. Binyam said the threat of rendition and torture came on the first day. Chuck told him: "If you don't talk to me, you're going to Jordan. We can't do what we want here; the Pakistanis can't do exactly what we want them to. The Arabs will deal with you." The threat was quite enough. Binyam revealed his real name and address and that, yes, he had been in Afghanistan. Chuck then came back and said the British had confirmed his identity. At one point they threatened to send him into British hands. "The SAS know how to deal with people like you," said Terry.

After the FBI questions came Pakistani ones. Binyam described how one officer loaded a pistol in front of him. "He pressed it against my chest. He just stood there. I knew I was going to die. He stood like that for five minutes. I looked into his eyes, and I saw my own fear reflected there. I had time to think about it. Maybe he would pull the trigger and I would not die, but be paralysed. There was enough time to think the possibilities through." Then two officers from British intelligence came to visit Binyam in jail. One was called John. He was white, about thirty with a goatee beard. Another, also white, was a stocky man aged about forty-five. Again, said Binyam, the threat of a rendition was made plain.

"They gave me a cup of tea with a lot of sugar in it. I initially only took one. 'No, you need a lot more. Where you're going you need a lot of sugar.' I didn't know exactly what he meant by this, but I figured he meant some poor country in Arabia." One of them told him then that he was going to get tortured by Arabs.

The British promised Binyam, who was still an Ethiopian national, that they would talk to the Americans about finding him a lawyer and about what would happen to him. But he heard no more from them. The visit did at least mark the start of improved treatment by the Pakistanis. (More than three years later, the Foreign Secretary, Jack Straw, confirmed that the meeting had taken place, but denied British officials were involved in either his capture or transfer from Pakistan).[31] After the British visit, Binyam refused to talk more unless he was given access to a lawyer, and he held out for the next few weeks as he was questioned by a succession of Pakistani officials.

As he was held, the hunt for the leaders of Al Qaeda was intensifying — as was Al Qaeda's own campaign in Pakistan. And as Binyam's interrogation progressed, Al Jazeera's Fouda was interviewing Khalid Sheikh Mohammed at his flat in Karachi about the 9/11 plot. If Binyam, as alleged, had truly met Khalid Sheikh Mohammed, there was little sign that the 9/11 ringleader was in any way perturbed either by Binyam's arrest, or by that of Abu Zubaydah three weeks earlier. "He made all kinds of mistakes, really; he was not terribly security conscious. He even insisted on walking me downstairs to say goodbye. He certainly was in no kind of panic," remembered Fouda.[32]

Meanwhile, in a secret CIA jail somewhere, Abu Zubaydah, who had been arrested at the end of March, had begun talking.[33] And it was he, by some accounts,[34] who seems to have first implicated Binyam and Padilla in a plot. At first Padilla's arrest on 8 May was kept secret while he too was questioned by the FBI. But on 9 June, the president handed him over to the Department of Defense and declared him an "enemy combatant," without the traditional rights of a criminal suspect to be charged or released.[35] On Monday 10 June, Ashcroft made his announcement from Moscow. "We have captured a known terrorist who was exploring a plan to build and explode a radiological dispersion device, or 'dirty bomb,' in the United States," he declared.[36] Ashcroft said the dirty bomb could "cause mass death and injury", and he named José Padilla as a terrorist with a US passport. The Attorney General made no mention of any accomplice but over the following days the papers had reports quoting Pakistani intelligence that there was an unnamed British suspect in custody. "Dirty Rat Pal Nabbed!" said the *New York Post*, citing the Pakistanis.

But for all the talk of a dangerous plot, Ashcroft revealed little convincing detail to show if the attempt was serious, or indeed if it ever had a chance of succeeding. One thing at least was clear: Abu Zubaydah had begun to talk, and the results of his interrogation were sparking new investigations. The first of at least six interrogations was noted in the 9/11 Commission Report as occurring on 10 July. It was not known if he had started talking earlier. Nor was it known how his confessions and accusations were extracted. Was Zubaydah also tortured? In the Palestine Branch in Damascus, some of his former companions, who were arrested with him and then sent on to Syria, described being shown photographs of a battered and bruised man who they were told was how Abu Zubaydah now looked. The implication was clear: 'Talk! Or you will look like this!"[37]

It was at 3.40 a.m., Morocco time, 22 July, that the CIA Gulfstream landed at Rabat airport.[38] Binyam was not alone; two other prisoners, he remembered, were also on board. The plane was, by then, a frequent visitor to Morocco. In total the flight logs were to indicate at least twenty-eight visits to the Kingdom by CIA jets since 9/11.

Binyam had flown into Morocco that weekend just as the attention of Washington had been diverted to a bizarre dispute on the country's north coast. A group of Moroccans had raised the flag on a tiny, uninhabited collection of rocks claimed by Spain that was known to most as Parsley Island. The Spanish had then retaliated by sending commandos in by helicopter. Tensions had mounted and now it was Colin Powell who was being asked to pull the parties apart. He spent the weekend on the phone, and a peaceful solution was reached. *The Sunday Times* noted that Morocco had some influence over Washington because King Mohamed VI was now seen as a key ally in the War on Terror.[39] The King's chance to return the United States' favour came as the CIA Gulfstream got clearance to land and stealthily unloaded its passengers.

On arrival at the Moroccan airport, Binyam remembered being placed in the back of a van and then driven for about thirty to forty-five minutes. He heard Arabic being spoken. He was taken to a prison outside Rabat that was made up a cluster of houses — each with about six rooms and a basement. Three were for prisoners, one for interrogation, one for the guards and one stood empty. The houses were surrounded by a metal fence and high trees, up to thirty feet tall. At first, he was placed in a large room with a white-washed wall and a large but shuttered window. Three weeks later he was moved to an end room by a toilet. This had wooden panelling. It was the torture room.

Binyam was describing all this many months later when he had reached Guantánamo and was finally able to see his lawyer, Clive Stafford Smith. All this came after he had been held in Morocco for eighteen months, kept for five months in a CIA jail in Kabul and another four months at Bagram Air Base, and then finally moved to Guantánamo Bay.

Soon after his arrival in Morocco, Binyam remembered asking one of the guards: "What kind of torture do they do in this place?" The guard responded: "They'll come in wearing masks and beat you up. They'll beat you with sticks. They'll rape you first, then they'll take a glass bottle, they break the top off and make you sit on it."

He hoped it was all threats, but after what his interrogators had told him in Pakistan he was not convinced. For all his time in Morocco, Binyam could never be sure if the jail was entirely Moroccan-controlled or was really an American facility. His jailers were in two teams: one mainly Moroccan and one that included foreigners. The local guards spoke both French and Arabic. The shift of "foreign" guards could speak English and what they usually spoke was not a Moroccan dialect but classical Arabic, of the sort spoken in the Gulf.

Binyam said he had a "torture team" that consisted of eight men and women. They included:

— "*Mohamed*", a Moroccan who was about six feet tall, well built, with blue eyes, brown hair, white skin, perhaps twenty-eight to thirty years old

— "*Sarah*", a thirty to thirty-five-year-old white woman, with blue eyes and blonde hair. She claimed to be from Canada and to be an intermediary between him and the Americans. But Binyam believed she was simply an American acting out a ruse. On 2 August, she told him: 'If you don't talk to me, the Americans are getting ready to carry out the torture. They're going to electrocute you, beat you and rape you." She had seemed blasé about this, as if this were something normal.

— "*Marwan*", about 6'2", weighing about thirteen stone, with brown skin, brown eyes, and clean shaven. Binyam described him as the lead tormentor who was in charge of much of the abuse. "He slapped me a few times during the interrogations, smoked Marlboro lights, and had a Motorola Wing telephone."

— "*Scarface*", who was about 5'10", with brown skin, brown eyes, and a deep voice. He was always masked and he did much of the questioning and the beating.

— "*The Boss*", who was about six feet tall, of white complexion with brown eyes, and "hair that was black but flecking to grey", a trimmed beard, well built. It was said of him that he had been to Guantánamo to interrogate the Moroccans there.

For more than eighteen months in Morocco, Binyam said he was subjected to one torture after another. In his diary of the events he dictated to Stafford Smith, he described his experiences in detail.[40]

From the beginning, the interrogators had asked searching questions. They asked him about Britain and London. They asked about the al-Manaar mosque in North Kensington. They even showed him pictures of people who attended prayers there.

On 30 July the diary recorded:

They also showed me photographs and files that they said came from Britain, from MI5. They called it the British file. It was then I realised that the British were sending questions to the Moroccans. I was at first quite surprised that the Brits were siding with the Americans.

But on 6 August, the torture began. In the morning Sarah and an interrogator named Mohamed had come in. At first it appeared he was about to be transferred out. They appeared all sympathetic and brought breakfast. They talked about politics and wars of the past.[41]

That night three men came in with black masks, some kind of ski masks that only showed their eyes. One stood on each of my shoulders, and the third punched me in the stomach. The first punch, I didn't expect it. I didn't know where it would be. I'd have tensed my muscles but I didn't have time. It turned everything in me upside down. I felt like I was going to vomit.

Within ten minutes I was almost gone. It seemed to go on for hours. I had prayed the sunset prayer, but I don't know what time it went on to. I was meant to stand, but I was in so much pain I'd fall to my knees. They'd pull me back up and hit me again. They'd kick me in my thighs as I got up. I vomited within the first few punches. I really didn't speak at all though. I didn't have the energy or will to say anything. I just wanted for it to end. I could see the hands that were hitting me. They looked like the hands of someone who had worked as a mechanic or chopped with an axe. They were heavy hands. There was dark black hair on the back of the hands and the fingers. I don't remember any rings. The wrists were thick, with shirtsleeves buttoned down all the way.

After that night, he continued, there had been no further "first class treatment". He was denied the use of the bathroom or even food.

A circle of torture began… They'd ask me a question. I'd say one thing. They'd say it was a lie. I'd say another. They'd say it was a lie. I could not work out what they wanted to hear.

They'd say there's this guy who says you're the big man in Al Qaeda. I'd say it's a lie. They'd torture me. I'd say, okay it's true. They'd say, okay, tell us more. I'd say, I don't know more. Then they'd torture me again.

Sometimes they left Binyam for days, even weeks, but they would always come back. He was informed during interrogations that senior figures in Al Qaeda had begun speaking about him. "They told me the US had a story they wanted from me, and it was their job to get it. They talked about José Padilla, and they said I was going to testify against him and big people." Among those named were Khalid Sheikh Mohammed, Abu Zubaydah and Ibn al-Sheikh al-Libi. Binyam claimed that when in Afghanistan and Pakistan his Arabic was so poor that he could not even have had a conversation with such figures. "The truth is I've never met any of them and how would I?… They told me that I must plead guilty. I'd have to say I was an Al Qaeda operations man, an ideas man. I kept insisting that

I had only been in Afghanistan a short while". "We don't care," was all they'd say.

Then came the worst of all tortures. It happened late in August 2002 when Binyam had made the mistake of insulting "Marwan", saying the Moroccans were not intelligent. Marwan had sworn at him. He returned later with three thugs.

"Strip him", shouted Marwan. They cut off my clothes with some kind of doctor's scalpel. I was naked. I tried to put on a brave face. But maybe I was going to be raped. Maybe they'd electrocute me, maybe castrate me. They took the scalpel to my right chest. It was only a small cut, maybe an inch. At first I just screamed ... I was just shocked, I wasn't expecting ... Then they cut my left chest. This time I didn't want to scream because I knew it was coming.

Marwan got agitated at this. "Just go ahead with the plan," he said.

One of them took my penis in his hand and began to make cuts. He did it once, and they stood still for maybe a minute, watching my reaction. I was in agony, crying, trying desperately to suppress myself, but I was screaming. I remember Marwan seemed to smoke half a cigarette, throw it down, and start another. They must have done this twenty to thirty times, in maybe two hours. There was blood all over."

They cut all over my private parts. One of them said it would be better just to cut it off, as I would only breed terrorists. I asked for a doctor. "The doctor's off," I was told. But in the end there would be two doctors who did see me and I did get treated. [42]

Binyam recalled the first doctor came in holding a briefcase but offered only to say some prayers. The second gave him an Alka-Seltzer for the pain, but when he examined his genitals gave him some proper cream and medicine.

Once the "razor treatment" had begun, it was repeated monthly. It was carefully controlled so the wounds would not be too deep and would not leave permanent marks. In the end, Binyam told his guards: "I will sign anything; confess to anything."

In the months that followed Binyam's first torture with the razor, he said that other techniques followed. During September and October 2002, he was taken by car to another place where they constantly played excruciatingly loud music, including hip hop and rock music such as Meatloaf and Aerosmith. Later they also may have experimented with drugs, said Binyam, putting something that felt like dope in his food. When he began a hunger strike to avoid the doping, they injected him with a substance with an intravenous drip. He said they also put him into rooms that smelled of urine, tried to tempt him with pornography or with the sight of naked or half-naked women they brought to the cells.

In all, this mental torture was worse than the physical pain. "I think I came to several emotional breakdowns in this time, but who was there to turn to?" In all the eighteen months Binyam was in Morocco, he said the most he saw of the outside world was by peering through the cracks in the shutters of an occasional cell. "I never saw the sun, not even once. I never saw any human being except the guards and my tormentors."

So here in these extracts was the account of among the worst kinds of torture imaginable. And yet Binyam was also accused of plotting to commit a terrible terrorist atrocity in America and of associating with some of the worst of the worst among Al Qaeda. So should the account of an accused terrorist like that be trusted or believed in any way?

In any normal circumstance, it might be possible to evaluate Binyam's descriptions by subjecting him to an independent medical check, or conducting a thorough interview of the guards who incarcerated and interrogated him. However until he reached Guantánamo, Binyam had no opportunity to raise any complaint with a lawyer or to speak to any outsider. And even when he reached Guantánamo and could finally speak to a lawyer, the US government would refuse to release any details of how he was arrested or where he was imprisoned. All were highly classified.

Some details of Binyam's account of rendition could be checked. His recollection of the dates of his journey from Pakistan to Morocco (21 July 2002), as described, matched the exact journey of the CIA Gulfstream V jet used for renditions; likewise his memory of his journey from Morocco to Afghanistan (21 January 2004), matched the log of a flight from Rabat to Kabul of a Boeing 737 business jet that was also used for renditions.[43] Because my flight-logs had not been made public by that date, Binyam had no means to concoct those dates from his prison cell in Guantánamo.

Likewise, Binyam's description of his interrogation centre in Morocco — a small group of houses, half-sunken, surrounded by tall trees and a chain-link fence and within forty-five minutes drive of Rabat airport — appeared to match an interrogation prison called Temara that was previously identified in reports by human rights organisations like Amnesty International.[44] The centre was just off the main highway to Casablanca, close to Rabat zoo, and some inmates reported even hearing sounds of the animals.[45] It was officially under the control of the Moroccan internal security service (Direction de la Surveillance du Territoire or DST) then headed by Hamidou Laanigri. Other former detainees have detailed not only the most extreme tortures but the presence both of outside interrogators and other prisoners rendered there by the United States. For example, a naturalised Italian named Abu al-Kassem Britel described his transfer to Temara from Islamabad on 24 May 2002 "by a small American plane," which I since discovered was the same Gulfstream that brought Binyam.[46] He was detained incommunicado for nine months.[47]

After Amnesty International investigated the centre in 2003, their report told of beating with metal rulers, electrocution, simulated drowning, and threats of raping suspects' wives or relatives.[48] "Interrogation" sessions in the centre can last as long as sixteen hours, during which suspects are often kept shackled and blindfolded while they are beaten.[49] Two detainees held at Temara have described to the International Federation of Human Rights how they were raped with bottles in the DST's custody, just as the guards had threatened to do to Binyam.[50]

Clive Stafford Smith said he never physically examined Binyam in Guantánamo. "I simply wasn't prepared to force him to drop his trousers in order to prove his claims," he said. But he said he did see physical scarring elsewhere on him.

Was Binyam innocent or guilty of plotting terrorism? It was impossible to tell. It was certain that he did go to Afghanistan and did end up in a training camp, albeit for a short period. But all further allegations such as his involvement in Padilla's "dirty bomb" plot, were all based on confessions originally obtained in foreign hands and most likely obtained by illegal means, including torture. By engaging in this out-sourcing of interrogation, the US government destroyed the credibility not only of Binyam Mohamed's statements to his interrogators, but of its own case against him in general. Here lay the central difficulty of using such methods in the War on Terror. If Binyam were really a terrorist, the case was a showpiece in entirely the wrong way to bring him to trial and secure his imprisonment. Instead, the government's charges simply left a gap between when he was captured and when he would record a confession back in the hands of US military interrogators — all protected by the demands or excuses of national secrecy. Ultimately he would be brought before a military commission to face the conspiracy charges, a process under suspension by order of the Supreme Court as this book went to press. José Padilla, meanwhile, had been transferred to a civilian court and was no longer accused of the dirty bomb plot, but of a separate, much lesser conspiracy with militants in the US.

While evidence obtained after years of prior torture seemed acceptable to the government for use in a military commission, its lawyers knew such evidence would be disallowed in a civilian court. And so the prime accused, Padilla, faced lesser charges in a public courtroom, while Binyam was accused of the most horrendous of plots. His imprisonment in Morocco was just the beginning of his ordeal.

3

MAHER ARAR

Flightlog

Registration: **N829MG**;
Type: **Gulfstream III**;
Operator: Presidential Aviation
Inc., Florida.
Date: **8 October 2002**

Flight plan:
Teterboro, NJ (dep. 5.40 a.m.)
Dulles

Dulles (dep. 7.46 a.m.)
Bangor, Maine

Bangor, Maine (dep 9.36 a.m.)
Rome (arr. 10.22 p.m.)

Rome (dep. 10.59 a.m.)
Amman, Jordan (arr. 1.55 p.m.)

Road traffic:
Amman to **Damascus**, Syria.

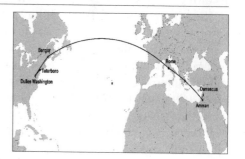

Over the Atlantic, at 30,000 feet

On board a Gulfstream jet, Maher Arar looked out through the portholes of
the private plane at the clouds beneath. Stretching out on the wide, uphol-
stered leather seat, he glanced across at the large video screen on which was
displayed the path of the plane from its departure point near New York, onward for a change of crew in Washington, DC and then to its final re-fuelling
point at Bangor, Maine, before heading across the ocean. As a telecommu-

Maher Arar and wife, Monia,
in Ottawa

nications engineer in Ottawa, Canada, Maher was used to air travel — but not to such luxury.[1] His fellow passengers — US federal agents — were preparing to switch on another in-flight film, an action movie. Maher could think only of the fate that awaited him when he reached the country to where the United States was now sending him — Syria. He recalled: "I knew that Syria was a country that tortured its prisoners. I was silent and submissive; just asking myself over and over again: 'How did I end up in this situation? What is going to happen to me now?' " He thought too of his young wife Monia and their two young children, all still on holiday in Tunisia.[2]

Maher had been arrested after arriving at New York's JFK Airport at 2 p.m. on 26 September to change planes; he'd been returning home from a long holiday in Tunisia. He found out that he'd been accused of membership of Al Qaeda and of knowing two other Canadians with Syrian families who were said to be terrorists.[3] Maher was baffled; he hardly knew the pair. They both seemed ordinary Muslims, like him: they did what their religion required. They fasted at Ramadan and went to the mosque for prayers on Friday. But they were hardly extremists, or so he thought.

It later became clear the reason for his arrest was information passed to the US by Canada.[4] Canada had its own secret investigation underway into a terrorist suspect in Ottawa. It seemed that Mr Arar had once used this man's name as an emergency contact when he signed for a lease on a flat. Though he was a Syrian national by birth, Maher was also a citizen of Canada and had lived in Canada for seventeen years. So he was surprised to be answering questions like this in New York that could so easily have been dealt with back home — in Ottawa. Despite his Canadian nationality, after interrogation in New York he was told he would be deported to Syria, not his adopted country. It petrified him.

Maher was finally released after nearly a year of torture and captivity in one of the world's worst jails. His story was emblematic of how an innocent man could be caught up and crushed by the manipulation of intelligence. It can happen to any citizen of either the West or the Orient. No legal charges were ever brought against him by either Canada or Syria, or by any country.[5] His story showed how normal relationships between individuals could be twisted to imply connections with terrorism. It also showed the human price of a system of justice created after 9/11 that appeared to ignore a basic principle of American law: innocent until proven guilty. Maher was simply lynched. On his arms and legs there were no physical marks left after his release: no welts, broken skin, or misshapen bones. He occasionally had real pain in his hips. But the harm he suffered was mostly in his mind; he was tormented by anger about his situation. It used to wake him up in a sweat. "I just feel angry," he told me when I met him in his Ottawa apartment, with his young children yelling behind. "I don't know who to be angry with. It's not directed at a single person yet I know what happened to me was wrong, and I know many people were complicit." In Canada, his case caused a political outcry, and in 2005 a public inquiry into his case was instigated in order to assess the actions of Canadian officials. A report was due to be published in the autumn of 2006.

Maher was the sort of man that America has always made welcome. He was intelligent, self-made and his priorities were focused on raising and protecting his family, and earning a good living. Born in Syria on 15 September 1970, Maher moved to Canada aged seventeen with his parents and became a Canadian citizen in 1991. His passion in life was for computers and technology. He studied engineering and eventually got a bachelor's degree in computer science at McGill University in Montreal, followed by a master's at the University of Quebec. At one stage, Maher was soccer-obsessed, playing striker in a semi-professional team. But it was technology and the idea of setting up in business that became his long-term goal. He recalled: "I suppose my idea of a good read was some business or electronics magazine." Was he a bit of a computer freak then? I asked him. "Yes, I didn't have too many hobbies or some big circle of friends," he replied. "My ambition was to make money and to raise a family."[6] It was at McGill that he met his future wife, Monia Mazigh, a young student from Tunisia. He would recall their engagement as "semi-arranged". He was not the sort of person to go out with girlfriends, so the pair were formally introduced through friends, and they fell in love and married in 1994. Three years later, they had a girl, Baraa.[7] Their son Houd was born in February 2002, seven months before Maher's arrest.

In December 1997, Maher had moved his family from Montreal to Ottawa and begun working in the high-tech wireless software field. He took a job with a firm called MathWorks that was based in Natick, Massachusetts. His work there involved travel all across the United States but he never had problems with the authorities. Then in 2002, Maher decided to stay in Ottawa and concentrate on starting up his own business, although he continued working for MathWorks as a consultant. That summer, Maher completed an article for a technical magazine, *Wireless Systems Design*. It was full of complicated jargon, meaningless to all but experts like him. It ended with the conclusion that: "Simulation results using 16QAM modulation prove that in the presence of light-to-moderate channel distortions, the new algorithm—known as baptized AMA—converges faster than CMA. Under severe channel conditions …etc". You get the picture. It was technology not radical *jihad* that filled Maher's head. That article was finally published in April 2003, six months into Maher's captivity in Damascus.[8]

In an emotional press conference when he was finally released from Syria, a sad and bearded Maher declared: "So this is who I am. I am a father and a husband. I am a telecommunications engineer and entrepreneur. I have never had trouble with the police and have always been a good citizen. So I still cannot believe what has happened to me, and how my life and career have been destroyed."[9]

Both Maher and his wife were Muslims. But both said they never supported any kind of militant politics. They supported the rights of Palestinians, like almost any Arab, but they never supported violence. Like many Muslims, after 9/11 Maher realised that things might get difficult. He knew he might be stopped from time to time and asked about his background. He also believed he had nothing to fear from such questions. Yet, unknown to him, his position was in growing danger. Canada's small Syrian community was coming under increased suspicion.[10] An inquiry had been launched by the "Mounties", properly called the Royal Canadian Mounted Police (RCMP). The inquiry's codename was "Project AO Canada"[11].

Ever since December 1999, when Palestinian Ahmed Ressam had crossed over from Canada intent on a Millennium-night bomb attack on Los Angeles' international airport,[12] the US government had been rightly worried about terrorists crossing from its northern border. As they contemplated potential suspects, they joined forces with both Canadian police and with the Canadian Security Intelligence Service (CSIS). As in many countries, attention turned to those Muslims who had returned from fighting *jihad* in Afghanistan. Time and again it was such Afghan returnees who had proved the hub of Al Qaeda cells. Who in Canada, the authorities asked, had been trained in terrorism at one of Osama bin Laden's camps? By the summer of 2001, attention was focusing in Canada on two particular suspects, both of them from the Syrian-Canadian community.

The first was Ahmed al-Maati, who, though born in Kuwait, was the son of a Syrian mother and Egyptian father, a retired accountant. In 1991, aged twenty-seven, Ahmed followed his elder brother Amr, who had left for Afghanistan three years earlier to join the US-backed war against the Soviet occupation. The brothers both joined Gulbuddin Hekmatyar's mujahideen faction, among the more extreme of those that fought among themselves after communist rule was toppled in 1993.[13] When the Taliban came to power in 1996, Hekmatyar's forces were driven out of the country. Ahmed fled to Iran from where he crossed to Pakistan. In August 1998 he returned to Canada. His brother Amr, however, remained in Pakistan, and remained involved with *jihadi* groups. Meanwhile, Ahmed and his father Badr were now viewed with high suspicion back in Canada. In the weeks before September 11, it seemed to some security officials that the suspicions against the family were justified. On 16 August 2001, Ahmed was stopped at the Buffalo border crossing into North America by US officials. In a bundle stashed inside his glove compartment, the customs men found a map of Ottawa that named several government buildings and a nuclear facility. Yet despite the discovery, he was allowed to continue.

Ahmed became a suspect after 9/11 for another reason too. In 1999, he had taken flying lessons at a school near Toronto. Ahmed said he found the lessons frightening and expensive and he gave up after a total of only five hours in the air. But all this strengthened suspicions.[14] A month after September 11, the FBI released a "watch list" of potential members of Al Qaeda. Leaked to a Finnish website, it listed the names of Ahmed al-Maati, his father Badr and brother Amr.[15]

By this time, another Canadian with a Syrian connection was under suspicion. His name was Abdullah Almalki, an Ottawa-based businessman, and father of four, involved in the export of electronic and communication equipment to countries including Pakistan. Back in the summer of 1998, Abdullah had been questioned by Canadian security agents, apparently interested in his firm's exports to Pakistan.[16] But, under questioning, Abdullah let slip something that had interested the agents more: while a student volunteer in Pakistan in 1994, working for the Muslim charity Human Concern International, Abdullah had not only crossed several times into Afghanistan but had worked under another Syrian-Canadian named Ahmad Said Khadr. It was Khadr who apparently raised a red flag. By the end of the 1990s, Khadr was seriously regarded as a member of Al Qaeda.[17] The fact that Abdullah and Khadr had never got on, and that Abdullah had quit Human Concern because of disagreements, did not lift the suspicions against him. In the two years before September 11, it seemed that American and Canadian suspicions were growing month by month. Abdullah was questioned four times about his business trips around the world, and about one of his friends who had a commercial pilot's licence.[18] So just like Ahmed al-Maati, Abdullah became a top surveillance target after 9/11. He began to notice that he was being followed everywhere by unmarked cars and a strange camera was installed across the street. His mail appeared to have been opened. The AO Canada inquiry was formally set up by the Royal Canadian Mounted Police in October 2001.[19]

Then, on 12 October, it was Maher who got caught in the tangled web. Maher, who was a friend of Abdullah's brother, met with Abdullah at 1.00 p.m. for a lunch of *shawarma* at the Mango Café in Bank Street, Ottawa.[20] A police surveillance team was watching and described later how they walked off together in the rain.[21] Maher remembered the weather as more like drizzle, if wet at all. He and Abdullah went off to buy a printer cartridge at a computer shop where Abdullah knew someone.

Nearly a year later, as Maher sat handcuffed in a cell in Brooklyn, New York, dressed in orange overalls, he was reminded of that same lunch visit. "Arar also admitted to the FBI meeting Abdullah Almalki at the restaurant where he and Almalki went outside and talked in the rain in October 2001, recorded the FBI."[22] By then, both Al-Maati and Abdullah had been arrested and taken to Syria's Palestine Branch interrogation centre. Maher would soon be on his way to join them. Maher had known nothing of either of their arrests. "When the FBI asked me of al-Maati's whereabouts, I said he was in Toronto. That's where I had last seen him years before. He was working in a garage where I went to fix a car. The last I'd heard of Abdullah was from his brother who told me he had gone to Malaysia."[23]

Maher's first taste of trouble came soon after his lunch with Abdullah. He was stopped on his way home from a business trip to the US by Canadian customs. He was allowed to continue but his laptop and Palm Pilot were seized. But still then, he didn't regard himself as under any real threat. He took it as the kind of thing that happened to Muslims after 9/11. In July 2002, Maher set off with Monia, Baraa and three-month old Houd for a long holiday at Monia's parents' house in Tunisia. In late September, his former employers, MathWorks, sent him an email offering him some consultancy work. And, using up some Air Miles, he booked a round-trip flight home to Ottawa, via Zurich and New York. His American Airlines flight arrived at JFK at 2 p.m. on 26 September. He knew he would have a few hours to wait there. Although only in transit, to travel onwards to Canada, Maher needed to go through passport control. He was stopped and taken aside. Soon he was in the hands of the FBI. He was shocked: "I worked in the States before, I travelled so many times. Part of my job is to provide support to the sales people and there was not a single time where I had problems in the US. It was a big surprise to me. I would never have expected such a thing to happen."[24]

In the official US version, Maher's was always a simple case of deportation. He had arrived in the US uninvited (although being a Canadian citizen he needed no visa), and was on a terrorist watch list (after being placed there by the Canadians).[25] As a dual national, he was simply deported to his country of birth, to Syria. After his arrest at JFK, Maher was first questioned by two FBI agents and a New York police officer for several hours. They asked if he was a member of Al Qaeda, and endless details of those he knew in Canada, including Abdullah Almalki. The questions continued the following morning. Finally, after a cold McDonald's meal, his only food, he was taken at 8 p.m. to the Metropolitan Detention Centre in Brooklyn, where he was strip-searched and put into an orange jumpsuit. It was the place where hundreds of immigrants had been taken in secret after September 11 and held as a precautionary measure. It was a grim place; the US Department of Justice's inspector general would later describe conditions there as "excessively restrictive and unduly harsh." The report described twenty-four-hour lighting, heavy restraints placed on detainees whenever they moved outside their cells and routine verbal and physical aggression from guards. The investigation also confirmed rumours that guards forced detainees to kiss a T-shirt bearing the slogan "These Colors Don't Run" beneath an American flag.[26]

On the morning of 8 October, Maher was woken at 3 a.m. Sitting on a chair in a Brooklyn cell, he was read a notice of a decision to deport him. Approved at the US Department of Justice by then Deputy Attorney General, Larry Thompson, it was signed by the regional director of the Immigration and Naturalization Service, J. Scott Blackman. Both classified and unclassified evidence, said Blackman, showed that Maher was a member of Al Qaeda. Among the evidence they cited was the fact that Maher had put Almalki's name as a contact when he signed a lease for an apartment in Ottawa. Crucially Blackman said the Commissioner of the Immigration and Naturalization Service (INS) in Washington, DC, James W. Ziglar, had certified the removal of Maher to be consistent with America's obligations under Article 3 of the United Nations Convention Against Torture.[27]

As mentioned, it was this Article 3 that banned the expulsion of a prisoner to a country where he was likely to be tortured. But the evidence from Syria was clear cut. The State Department's official report on Syria, published in March 2002, detailed "credible evidence" that security forces used torture, despite some improvements in 2001, and detailed their harsh methods, including electric-shock treatment.[28] So without a genuine guarantee of good and fair treatment, an expulsion of someone like Maher would be most likely illegal. In the days following his arrest, he repeatedly stressed that he was likely to be tortured. Among other reasons, a relation of his had been accused of membership of the Muslim Brotherhood: the Islamic militant group that remained the mortal enemy of the Syrian Ba'athist regime. In Syrian law, membership of the Brotherhood was a crime punishable by death.

"You know I told the Americans that Syria tortures people for all reasons and would have plenty of reasons to torture me. I told them my mother's cousin was in prison for nine years. He was accused of being a member of the Brotherhood. I told them I left the country without doing the military service. I told them I was a Sunni Muslim you know. But they didn't care."[29]

In May 2005, an expert in US immigration law from Cornell Law School, Stephen Yale-Loehr,[30] submitted to the Canadian public inquiry his analysis of the legality of Maher's treatment by US immigration officials. "The US immigration statute gives great authority and discretion to US officials in deciding who to remove from the United States and how. Such authority, however, is not unfettered. Article 3 of the Convention Against Torture prohibits US officials from sending a person to another country where there are substantial grounds for believing that he would be in danger of being subjected to torture. In my view, ample evidence existed that Syrian officials would torture Mr Arar if he was sent there. Moreover, Mr Arar told US officials he feared being tortured if sent to Syria. For these reasons, it appears that US government officials violated Article 3 of the Convention Against Torture by rendering Mr Arar to Syria."[31]

TETERBORO AIRPORT, NEW JERSEY
Tuesday, 8 October, 5 a.m.

At New York's business airport, across the Hudson River, little was moving so early in the morning. Gulfstreams, Learjets and Beechcraft were parked all around, their engines wrapped with canvas to protect them from the October frost. The night, though, had been mild, down to only 50F, and there was barely a shiver of wind. The windsock drooped vertical.[32]

At the centre of a convoy of police cars, a van approached with a cage in its rear containing Maher. He was taken into a building and then ushered up to the ramp of a fourteen-seat Gulfstream III.

This, according to flight records, was not one of the CIA's or any other official agency's own planes. It was a chartered jet from a private consortium called Presidential Aviation of Florida. The journey that lay ahead for this plane would normally have earned the company nearly $120,000 according to Presidential's website. Much later, the company's director of operations, Nigel England, was approached for a comment on the night's operations. "It's a very select group of people that we fly," he said, "from entertainers to foreign heads of state, a whole gamut of customers that we fly and wouldn't discuss one over the other."[33] By now — October 2002 — the CIA's programme of prisoner transfers was at maximum capacity. To boost its own fleet of planes, the Agency was beginning to hire such charter jets.[34] But Maher's deportation was also special because it took place from US soil. So, in charge until Maher reached the Middle East was the INS, under the US Attorney General, then John Ashcroft. The jet was hired by the Department of Justice.

The Presidential jet took off from Teterboro at 5.40 a.m. EST and set off on a course for Dulles international airport, Washington, DC. Here the crew changed, and at 7.46 a.m. the plane set off again: this time for Bangor, in Maine. Maher could follow the journey on the video screen.

Gulfstream IIIs have a range of only 5,000 miles,[35] so its course across the Atlantic was along the "spruce route" — refuelling up in Maine before taking off at 9.36 a.m. to turn east and fly non-stop across to Rome. Here the plane stopped for about half an hour. Then onwards again, this time for Amman, Jordan.

On board the plane was a federal agent who called himself Mr Khoury, and who explained that his family too was originally from Syria. Unlike Maher, Khoury was dressed smartly. Maher was now wearing brown overalls and was shackled with steel handcuffs and chains. During the flight, Khoury lent him a turquoise polo shirt, made in Canada. Maher would be wearing that shirt and nothing else for the next three months. He would be wearing it as his arms, his palms and the soles of his feet were beaten with electric cables.

I thought when they put me on this private jet with its leather seats, I started thinking about myself — who am I that they should do that? Am I that important for them? What kind of information could I offer to them? So I started thinking, what's going on here?

Later Maher sat down for a meal with Khoury, who seemed to struggle with his emotions.

The last two hours before we landed in Amman, they removed the shackles and chains and they allowed me to move freely on the plane. They gave me a very nice dinner, and I sat down with them, with the head of the team, Mr Khoury. That was a surprise, a big surprise to me. And he told me, I told him my story and he said why don't you talk to the Jordanians they might be able to do something for you. And he was very sympathetic, he didn't tell me directly, but I could tell in his eyes. I knew if I continued talking to him for another fifteen minutes he would just cry. You could tell.

Maher was going through his own turmoil.

So when they fed me this nice dinner, and there's a tradition, by the way, in the Muslim world called Eid, where they slaughter an animal, and before they slaughter the animal they feed him, and that's exactly what I thought when I was in the plane. I was always thinking how I could avoid torture, because at that point I realised that the only reason why they were sending me there is to be tortured for them to get information. I was 100% sure about that.[36]

At around 2 a.m. local time on 9 October, Maher's Gulfstream touched down in Jordan.[37] He was blindfolded and handcuffed and put into a van. They travelled for thirty minutes. If he tried to move or speak, the guards beat him. They led him into a building, where he was asked some basic questions and then taken to a cell. In the afternoon, he was put into another van, driven for three-quarters of an hour, beaten, he said, while his guards changed, and driven for another hour to the Syrian border. Three hours later, the van approached the outskirts of Damascus.[38]

At the presidential palace later that morning, Basher al-Assad was finalising a major announcement to be released in Beirut. Among the top items of his agenda was a shake-up of the intelligence agencies that sustained his regime. Ghazi Kanaan, the infamous chief of security in Lebanon, was being recalled to Damascus and given a new job — head of the political security agency that dealt with all dissidents.[39] It was now nearly two years since the cosmopolitan thirty-four-year-old had been ushered into office to replace his dead father, Hafez al-Assad. In his early years, Bashar had never expected to succeed his father. But the death of his brother, Basil, in a car crash in 1994 led him to begin preparations. He abandoned his work as an eye specialist in London and returned home with his wife Asma. Nowadays, Bashar was doing things his own way.

In the West, there were great hopes that Bashar's arrival could signal an end to decades of diplomatic isolation of Syria. His inscrutable father had proved a troublesome adversary. Still officially at war with Israel,[40] he had never accepted the loss of the Golan Heights, and so Syria both funded and provided bases to

Palestinian militant groups and their armed campaigns, as well as anti-Israeli factions in Lebanon such as Hezb'allah (the party of God), the same group held responsible for the capture of western hostages in the 1980s and the murder of a CIA Beirut station chief.[41] While economically weak, Syria had been funded until the late 1980s by the Soviet Union, and was widely suspected of having a chemical and biological weapons programme.[42] There were accusations too that Syria was involved in the Libyan plot that downed Pan Am flight 103 over Lockerbie.[43] In so many ways, Syria was a pariah state.

Always, though there were channels of cooperation and reasons for the US to enlist Syrian help. The Syrian takeover of Lebanon in 1989, for example, was widely accepted as bringing a welcome end to the Lebanese civil war.

By the time of Assad's death, some of the worst excesses of his rule were over. Amnesty International reported that, instead of thousands of political prisoners, there were now merely hundreds.[44] Bashar, when he came to power, declared a Damascus Spring with new freedoms for dissidents and intellectuals. But the traditions of repressive rule stayed strong. The Syrian Ba'athist party, as well its repressive organs like the secret police, were not ready to surrender anything. Soon enough then, the arrests and the crackdowns started all over again. The reaction was in full-swing in the first half of 2001.

Then 9/11 happened, and Bashar's repressions of freedom ceased to be a priority for the West. The War on Terror was everything. If Syria failed to cooperate, it would be President Bush's enemy. Already it was a candidate member for what Bush declared to be the "Axis of Evil." But if Syria co-operated in this new war then it would now be an ally — and would expect to reap all kinds of benefits.

Like President Pervez Musharraf of Pakistan, President Bashar made the decision to side with America. In his case, the decision was easier. Although Syria might hate Israel and shelter Palestinian groups like Hamas that the US labelled as terrorists, it had a common enemy in Al Qaeda and in militant Islam. The greatest sworn enemy of Bashar's regime was the Ikhwan, the Muslim Brotherhood. When they organised an insurrection in 1982, Bashar's father responded by levelling the entire city of Hama — with an estimated death-toll of 10-20,000 people.[45] So Bush's war on militant Islam provided the Syrian Ba'athists with a golden opportunity. They would open up their files on Islamic militants and share them with the West, offer to imprison and interrogate any suitable suspects, and, under this guise, help defeat some of their regime's most implacable opponents.

In the months that followed 9/11 real information was passed on by Damascus. This information, announced government officials, had "saved American lives."[46] But the full extent of the new cooperation was not made public. After all, Syria was still Syria. And a friendship with the Damascus dictatorship might well seem to be deeply hypocritical. In public, Syria remained prickly and hostile. On the morning of 9 October 2002, Tariq Aziz, Iraq's Deputy Prime Minister, praised Syria for resisting the planned invasion of his country. "All Arab leaders have abandoned us, but the Syrian regime led by Bashar al-Assad helps Iraq," Aziz said.[47] Much of the contact with Syria was therefore to remain furtive. For Western spies, Damascus always remained a dangerous place. Many key meetings, according to one former CIA officer, were held in Beirut, where Syria's secret police still held sway.[48] (According to one unverified account by dissident sources, the key link between the US and Damascus, including the rendition programme, was a general named Mustafa al-Tajer, who died suddenly in the autumn of 2004 of unexplained causes.)[49] It took the testimony of Maher and his fellow prisoners to finally reveal the true extent of secret cooperation.

It was just after 6 p.m. on 9 October when a car drove into a courtyard in western Damascus, and its engine was turned off. It was the Palestine Branch, chief interrogation centre for Syrian military intelligence. Maher was ushered inside the building. When his blindfold was removed he found himself in a small room with three other men, one of whom was a colonel. In the corner of the room stood a metal chair frame with no seat or back. The interrogators glanced at the chair frame and warned that it would be used to torture him. He would learn this was known inside as the "German chair". At this stage, in this first four-hour interrogation, these was only threats. Early the next morning, he was led downstairs to a basement. He was ushered inside cell no.2 — the same coffin-like cell he would occupy for ten months and ten days. As mentioned above, it was three

foot wide, six foot long and seven foot high. The walls were concrete, and the floor was tiled. There were two blankets, two plastic bowls and two bottles. There was to be no daylight coming into his cell nor any light source, just a dim glow through a hole in the reinforced concrete of his ceiling. Rats and cats used to wander above.[50]

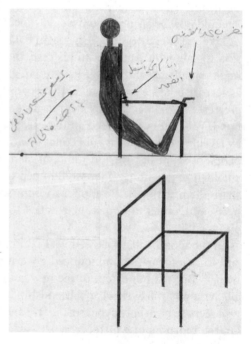

Maher couldn't keep track of the days but knew that about once a week he would be brought out to wash himself. By this time, when Maher arrived in Damascus, the Syrians were already filling their jail cells with prisoners like him who had been captured in the new War on Terror. The cells of the Pal-

The German Chair

estine Branch contained one prisoner after another that was accused of involvement with militant Islam and had been transferred to Syria by the United States or its close allies. Prisoners were being sent to Syria not simply to put them "out of harm's way", as President Bush would describe such renditions, but to be interrogated.[51] And it was a two-way traffic. America sent the prisoners. Syria supplied the confessions. The Palestine branch was a prison constructed with torture in mind. Everything about it was designed to break the soul. It was nearly enough to drive Maher insane. What did it mean to go through such anguish? For Maher, it was the mental pressure that became most severe:

You know the first two weeks, the beatings, especially the first week, the beating was intensive. And when I was put back in the cell, even though it was one of the worst places on earth, I just said to myself they can keep me here for six months but I won't want to talk to them anymore. That's the kind of feeling.

As time passed, Maher felt increasingly desperate:

I was ready to accept any sentence, even though I was innocent. I told them just take me to a place where I can live like a human being. And I was ignored.[52]

One by one, the three suspected Syrian-Canadians were put through the torture mill. One by one, each confessed to their terrorist "crimes." This process was not conducted by Damascus alone. Everything pointed to the direct involvement of foreign agencies, not only in their arrests, but in the management of their interrogation.

Foreign intelligence agencies, like Canada's CSIS, would justify their actions by implying they remained mere consumers of torture evidence. The Canadian government declared that CSIS would not reject evidence obtained by torture out of hand, if it could "corroborate that information from other sources"[53] Yet, this story is a circular tale of both information flow and interrogation. The West first supplied suspicions. When the Syrians supplied information to confirm those suspicions, the Americans and Canadians wanted to know more. And the Syrians obliged with torture. It was a circle driven by genuine fears of a terrorist threat but it was a process that made it more, not less, difficult to work out what was true.

The first into the Palestine Branch was Ahmed al-Maati. He arrived in Damascus on 12 November 2001 to marry his sweetheart, Rola. But she and her family waited at the airport in vain. Held in cell no.5, and subject to beating with electric cables and burning with cigarettes, al-Maati confessed not only to knowing Almalki and Maher but also to seeing them in Afghanistan.[54] And he confessed to participating in a plot to blow up the Canadian parliament in Ottawa.

Al-Maati's interrogations were based on information supplied by Canada and the US. As mentioned above, he had been caught back in August that year at the Buffalo border crossing in possession of a map of Ottawa with key government buildings marked. He had already been questioned about it back in Canada. On

12 October 2001, the same day Abdullah met Maher at the Mango Café, the *Los Angeles Times* splashed news, quoting anonymous US agents, that revealed how a 36-year-old man, al-Maati, had been found with documents that identified Canadian government buildings, including sensitive research laboratories. It all sounded highly suspicious — except for the fact those "documents" were nothing more than a tourist map of Ottawa — and an outdated one at that — that was issued to drivers like al-Maati for doing deliveries in the city.[55]

Whether groundless or not, al-Maati's "confessions" caused excitement in Canada. In January, a RCMP liaison officer came to Damascus to interview Gen. Hassan Khalil, then head of Syrian military intelligence, about the interrogations. The same month a search was carried out at the al-Maati family home in Toronto. On 25 January Ahmed al-Maati was rendered by plane to Cairo for his questioning to continue. On 17 July that year, the RCMP cabled Egypt to ask for access to al-Maati "in order to further a major investigation in Canada."[56]

In Damascus, meanwhile, it was time for the next torture victim to arrive for the treatment. Abdullah Almalki had heard nothing of al-Maati's arrest. Flying to visit his ailing grandmother and some business contacts, Abdullah arrived in Damascus on 3 May 2002. He too went straight to the Palestine Branch and he would stay there — in cell no.3 — till August the following year. Again the questions asked by interrogators in Syria appeared to be written not in Damascus but across the Atlantic. Time and again he was asked about his friends in Canada. And among those he admitted to knowing was Maher. Four months later, Maher was arrested in New York. The news flashed across the Atlantic. And as the INS considered his fate, the Syrians at the Palestine Branch worked hard to supply their confession. Abdullah was being threatened with the most gruesome treatment unless he confirmed that Maher had been in Pakistan or Afghanistan. Salloum, his chief interrogator, told Abdullah that Maher "would be there soon" and that if he lied to him he "would be put in a barrel of excrement…. The food and drink he was allowed [would be reduced] and then [he would be put] in the chair till he was paralysed" (according to Abdullah's account). Before Salloum left, said Abdullah, he told the interrogator to torture him till he needed to be hospitalised.[57]

So finally, it was Maher's turn to be placed on the rack. In a way, Maher was lucky, lucky above all in love. Because, 5,500 miles away, his wife Monia had come home to Canada and was raising his case in public. Though naturally shy, and abiding by the Muslim traditions of female modesty, Monia was no submissive or silent wife. In the months that followed, she would mobilise a nation on Maher's behalf.

His interrogations took place upstairs: every day for the first twelve days. He recalled the first time, the first morning after his arrival and his initial questioning:

The interrogator said, 'Do you know what this is?' I said, 'Yes, it's a cable,' and he told me, 'Open your right hand.' I opened my right hand and he hit me like crazy. It was so painful, and of course I started crying and then he told me to open my left hand, and I opened it and he missed, then hit my wrist. And then he asked me questions. If he does not think you are telling the truth, then he hits again. An hour or two later he puts me in this room sometimes where I could hear people being tortured. [58]

For Maher, the physical torture was relatively short-lived. Pressure by his wife had galvanised Canadian authorities to seek access. On 23 October, after an official Canadian protest to the US about Maher's deportation to Syria, the Canadian consul in Damascus was able to meet Maher in jail. Before the meeting Maher was taken to another building and ordered to say nothing of his torture or the conditions of his cell. But, at least, the physical beating largely stopped from then on. For him, the torture was now mostly psychological. Stuck in the darkened cell, it was an existence which he could barely have imagined. For the next ten months, apart from the consul, Maher's only human contacts were those guards and torturers — and so they too became not only his enemies but his friends. His ultimate humiliation came when one of his torturers, a colonel, pretended to know his brother.

I started telling them about the names of my brothers in order. I told them the name of one of my brothers, and the Colonel, he said to me, 'he's my friend'. And I started crying again and I said I was so happy to have met someone who knew my brother, who could help me. I was in such a helpless state and I just wanted someone to save me, someone to do something for me, but of course it was all a lie. I even told him I was going to kiss him, and I would never do that in a normal situation, right, and he told me, "no don't" because the other guy was with him. That's when I realised it was all not true.

"You offered to kiss him?" I asked Maher.

Yes. I wanted to hug him because he was the friend of my brother, that's what he told me, it's mind games. And if he was not satisfied with the answer he would beat me and give me an answer, I would resist for a while then, I would say when I was not able to take it any more, I would say yes.[59]

As they had with al-Maati and Almalki, Canada continued to press for the results of the Syrian torturers' work. Maher's native government was playing a double game. Following Monia's protests, in public the Canadians were protesting over Maher's treatment. In private, they wanted the results of his questioning. Franco Pillarella, Ottawa's envoy in Damascus, met with a Syrian official on 22 October and asked for an update.[60] He was told Maher's questioning was continuing but the official promised to pass on what information could be gleaned. Again on 3 November, Pillarella asked for a "resume of information obtained from Maher so far."[61] He passed the results back to Canada.

In Canada, the director general of the foreign ministry's security and intelligence branch, Dan Livermore, on 30 October 2002, wrote a secret memo stating the RCMP was, according to a redacted version, "seeking either to directly interview [blank] or to send their Syrian counterparts a request that [blank] be asked questions provided by the RCMP." Michel Cabana, head of the RCMP investigation into Al Qaeda, told one of Livermore's deputies that month: "We would be prepared to share with Syrian authorities if they felt it could be of assistance to their investigation, this in light of their sharing info with us in the past."[62]

Maher remained in the same coffin-like cell till 19 August 2003. He was then transferred to Sednaya prison, a general prison north of Damascus, also under the control of military intelligence. Here, at last, he could speak with other prisoners and he finally met with Abdullah, who reached there on 6 September. And he heard news of other prisoners like the German-Syrian prisoner Zammar, a suspect in the 9/11 plot, who had languished in the Palestine Branch since December 2001.

Meanwhile, the campaign for his release intensified. On 5 October 2003, after a week of being held back again in an interrogation cell at the Palestine Branch, Maher was finally flown home and was met by Monia at the airport. His struggles were not over though. Anonymous stories continued that accused him of terrorist links. And he was filled with a rage of frustration. It was the beginning of a long struggle to win justice.

In Egypt, al-Maati was still going through torture. He was transferred from one prison to another in Cairo. His freedom came on 11 January 2004, after his Egyptian lawyer obtained a court order for his release. Almalki, meanwhile, remained in Sednaya prison. He was finally released on bail in March 2004, acquitted of all links to Al Qaeda in a court hearing on 25 July. He then arrived home in Canada on 2 August to a quiet welcome from his family. Undergoing treatment for post-traumatic stress disorder back in Canada, he eventually decided to go public and agreed to a full investigation of his case. "I need to clear my name. I need to know the truth. Every citizen of this country and who cares needs to know the truth," he said.[63]

In Canada, a determined campaign by Maher and Monia led to a public inquiry being launched into the circumstances of his arrest. As this book went to press, the results of that inquiry were still awaited.

A chain of circumstances had convicted Maher and snared an innocent man. He had shared a meal and walked in the drizzle with another man, Abdullah Almalki, who once worked in Afghanistan and who exported electronic goods to Pakistan. He also vaguely knew another man, Ahmed al-Maati, who had fought in the American-backed jihad against the Soviet invasion and whose brother remained in Afghanistan, fighting in the civil war. All this justified a year of torture and confinement in some of the world's worst jails. This traumatic experience had done some good: Maher had caught a glimpse into a secret world and his testimony provided positive proof of a secret channel now established between the United States and one of the Middle East's most dictatorial regimes. As the three Canadians left Syria, they left many prisoners behind in the jails of Damascus, many rendered to the country by American hands. Some were innocent and others guilty of crimes. All received the same treatment.

4

MISTAKEN IDENTITY
A GERMAN CITIZEN'S JOURNEY TO
AN AFGHAN HELL

Flightlog

Registration: N313P;
Type: **Boeing 737 Business Jet (BBJ)**;
Operator: Premier Executive
Transport, Massachusetts;
Date: **23 January 2004**

Flight plan:
Palma, Majorca (dep 6.40 p.m.)
Skopje, Macedonia (arr 8.56 p.m.)

Skopje (2.30 a.m.)
Saddam International Airport, Iraq (arr. 9.53 a.m.)

Saddam International Airport (dep. 11.15 a.m.)
Kabul, Afghanistan (3.44 p.m.)

In the morning in the Balearic Islands, off the Mediterranean coast of Spain, the wind generally blows from the warmer sea onto the dry land; by mid-afternoon and into the evening, the winds are reversed. The breeze now blows out from the warmer island onto to the colder sea.

On the evening of 22 January 2004, a Boeing 737 Business Jet approached from the south. It then turned right into the wind onto a north-east bearing of 60 degrees. Descending from 4,000 feet, it passed the city lights of Palma and its marina on the left and set an approach straight-in for the airport's left-hand runway, 06L. At 10.20 p.m. the plane's wheels touched down, and it taxied across

N313P / © Toni Marimon

to a small business aviation terminal. Ready to meet the plane was the ground crew and handling agents of Mallorcair, a company that for the last fifteen years has provided fuel, catering, and general facilities for the VIP passengers who thronged to the island by business jet, particularly during the short but hot summers. Many customers kept their multi-million pound yachts moored in the city's seafront marina.

According to the Spanish police, in a report compiled a year later, the name of the pilot on the plane's flight plan was Capt. James Fairing, aged 49. He came with a flight crew of three, and with seven passengers, all American citizens. Though his name was registered as a pilot with the Federal Aviation Administration, Captain Fairing's home address was given as a postbox in north Virginia. Fairing was a CIA ghost pilot, and his passengers were members of the CIA's top secret Rendition Group, based in Langley, Virginia. They had no idea that within months their mission into Palma would help unleash a political scandal in Europe that would shed light on the secret world of the CIA's prisons.

One thousand miles away, after a twenty-two day ordeal of being kidnapped, beaten up and having no contact with his family, a German citizen named Khaled al-Masri had finally won hope. Locked up in a hotel room in Macedonia in Eastern Europe, he would recall thinking that his captors from the country's secret police had at last realised that they had captured the wrong man. So when they told him that a plane was coming to take him home, it had made sense. The mistake of his abduction could finally be corrected, he thought.[1]

As they disembarked back in Palma, Fairing's crew was asked, like anyone else, to show their passports to Spanish immigration. Among them, five carried passports with numbers that began with '90', an indicator they were official US diplomats.[2] "I remember the immigration officers sometimes thought it strange that they were carrying diplomatic passports. It's not ordinary for crew members," recalled Francisco José, a manager at Mallorcair. "But they essentially shrugged their shoulders. They were obviously important people," he said.[3]

The arrival of such a Boeing Business Jet (BBJ) raised some eyebrows but was not completely unusual. If you compared executive planes to executive cars, the BBJ was a sort of stretch-limousine. The BBJ was rather too large to land at small airports and, even for multi-millionaires, considered something of an extravagance. "The BBJs are often used by music groups, travelling rock bands like the Rolling Stones. The idea is they can transport everyone together," said José. "They are also used by Arabs sometimes so they can travel with their large families and all their wives!"[4]

With more than 3,000 planes handled each year, José and his partner Miguel Mudoy were not certain his staff could recall every detail of this plane's arrival, nor the other six visits of the CIA planes handled by his company. But, if their memories served them correctly, on this occasion the pilots wore blue airline-style uniforms, and were accompanied on-board by a mechanic, a normal thing on a 737. Before leaving the plane, the pilots changed out of their uniform into casual clothes, just like the passengers. The company's minibus loaded their luggage on board. And, after completion of formalities, they were whisked away to their chosen hotel, just fifteen minutes away down the motorway. "These people were very friendly, normal Americans. There was nothing out of the ordinary that any of us saw," José said.

It had been a gruelling day of long-haul flights for Capt. Fairing and his crew. Earlier that morning, they set off in darkness on a three-stage 8,000-mile journey that began with a flight from Rabat, Morocco, to the Afghan capital of Kabul, continued from there to Algiers, Algeria, and then finished with a half-hour hop across to Palma airport. Among the passengers that day was Binyam Mohamed, who after eighteen months in Morocco, was being taken on to a new jail cell in Afghanistan. From later police inquiries, it would emerge there were two women aboard the BBJ when it arrived in Palma: Patricia, who was 59 years old, and Jane, whose age is unknown. On his flight, Mohamed remembered one woman, possibly Jane, as one of the few people who ever seemed to care about his plight.

"There was a white female with glasses", he recalled later at Guantánamo. She had been taking pictures and had been shocked by the sight of the injuries caused by his razor blade torture, he said. "She was one of the few Americans who ever showed me any sympathy. She was about 5'6", short, blue eyes. When she saw the injuries I had, she gasped. She said, 'Oh, my God, look at that!' Then all her mates looked at what she was pointing at and I could see the shock and horror in her eyes."[5]

That evening, the CIA crew tried to forget the traumas of the day. They settled into the five-star Marriott Son Antem golfing resort, with its well-stocked bar and thick-carpeted corridors arranged around a series of courtyards and fountains. When they awoke the following morning, 23 January, most had the opportunity to relax. One passenger, John, found time to book into the hotel's holistic health spa with its "Therapeutic Thermal Water". Maybe he had read the brochure which offered the chance to "journey to deep inner peace."[6] At this off-season time of year, there were few other guests. Just a party of mostly German lawyers from the legal firm Freshfields, and from Markem, a German engineering company. The room rate was cheap for such a luxury place, only 135 euros per night. In the hotel bar, one member of staff later recalled they used to often get pilots and aircrew. "We always ask who they work for and they always refused to say," she told me.[7]

Between 3.49 p.m. and 5.26 p.m. the CIA crew checked out of their hotel, settling their bills individually on their credit cards. The last to check out was John D., nicely relaxed after his massage.

The plane took off at 5.40 p.m. — bound for Skopje, the capital of Macedonia in Eastern Europe. There, in another smart hotel, was a German citizen who was being prepared for a trip in Captain Fairing's plane. The thirty-nine year-old had spent the last three weeks in the room — with the curtains firmly drawn and surrounded, night and day, by armed guards.

SKOPJE, MACEDONIA
The Skopski Merak Hotel, 23 January, late afternoon

Khaled el-Masri was looking rather pasty and weak. Normally, his dark eyebrows were set in a cheery, if rather chubby, round face. But, after refusing food for ten days, he was looking haggard. He had not shaved properly in the last three weeks and his thick hair was getting wild.

For all that, Khaled's spirits were now running high. After what seemed an endless captivity, he had been told an aeroplane was on its way to Skopje to take him home to Germany. A team of seven or eight Macedonians had entered his room and asked him to stand by the wall and record a video statement. They wanted him to declare before he could return home that he had not been harmed. Then they led him downstairs and put him into a jeep waiting outside the hotel. He was handcuffed and blindfolded. About half an hour later (just as Capt. Fairing's BBJ and its seven passengers were touching down on the runway after their two hour flight from Majorca), Khaled arrived at the airport terminal. He could hear the sound of airplanes.

The Macedonians told Khaled he would now be receiving a medical checkup, and still blindfolded, he was led into a room. "And then they beat me from all sides, from everywhere, with hands and feet." Then using knives or something else sharp they began to cut up his clothes. "They tried to take off my pants. I tried to stop them so they beat me again."[8] Khaled heard the clicks of photographs being taken. Then they lifted his blindfold. What he saw may now sound familiar.

"There were seven or eight people." He said that "all the people were in black clothes and black masks."[9] The men then put him in a dark blue suit with cut-off arms. "They put earplugs in my ears and a sack over my head."[10] Tieing his arms behind his back, and putting chains on his legs, he was led onto the plane which had just landed — but it was not taking him home to the wooded slopes

Khaled el-Masri

of southern Germany. It took off in the early hours of the morning from Skopje, turned east and set a course for Kabul, with a stop-off in Baghdad. Khaled thought he was on a cargo plane. "I couldn't make out any seats and there was metal, I think. They threw me on the floor."[11] At this point they injected him. "They put me on the floor and injected me with something. I blacked out. At some point, I smelled the kind of alcohol they have in a hospital. I received another injection."[12]

The way Khaled's story had begun was bizarre. A car salesman by profession, he had been struggling to find work in his home city of Ulm, south Germany, and his marriage was in trouble; he was constantly arguing with his wife. In an effort to gain some breathing space he had decided to go on a few days holiday, he said later. He found a cheap package trip to the Balkan state of Macedonia and bought a round trip on a bus.[13] And this was how he disappeared for five months into the black hole that was the dark side of the War on Terror.

His story seemed so strange that, at first, he hesitated to recount it. "One person told me not to tell this story because it's so unreal, no one would listen," he recalled.[14]

It was 3.30 p.m. on New Year's Eve 2003, when the coach full of tourists had pulled up at the main border crossing into Macedonia from Serbia. Khaled was singled out. His passport was confiscated and the bus left without him.[15] He was taken to a windowless room by three local men with holstered pistols. They accused him of being a terrorist. His first response — and it was the request he repeated more than any other — had been to ask to call either the German Embassy or his wife Aycha, he recalled. (One of the worst things about his ordeal was that he had left his wife in the middle of a row, and it plagued on his mind.) But his request, he said, was ignored.

Instead "they asked a lot of questions — if I have relations with Al Qaeda, Al Haramain (an Islamic charity), the Islamic Brotherhood," he remembered later. "I kept saying no, but they did not believe me."[16] By then it was 10 p.m., and the Macedonians said it was time to go to a hotel. Dressed in civilian clothes but armed with handguns, the men took him outside where a convoy of cars was waiting. He was driven about thirty minutes to a large hotel. As he stepped in, it all seemed normal. There was a reception to the right and sofas and coffee tables in the foyer. Khaled was taken up four or five floors in an elevator and ushered into a room. It seemed quite a luxurious place. There was an en-suite bathroom, a television and an air-conditioning unit, and a computer with Internet access. It was located just 200 metres from the US Embassy and opposite the city zoo.[17]

As Khaled sat down in the hotel room, the questions continued.

It was New Year's Eve and they started to drink champagne in my room. They offered me a glass; but it was not out of being friendly, they were trying to see if I drank alcohol. ...They asked me where I came from, what I wanted to do in Skopje, the same questions again as earlier, whether I have connections to aid organisations, whether I am a strict Muslim, whether I drink alcohol. How many times I pray during the day and questions like that.[18]

Then they started asking about the mosque where he prayed and all the details of his life.

Though born in Kuwait of Lebanese parents, Khaled had come to Germany in 1985. In the following eighteen years, he had settled, become fluent in German and taken on citizenship. The couple's four sons aged 7, 5, 4 and 2 were all born in the country. But his and Aycha's social life was still centred around their mosque.[19]

Khaled continued to ask his captors whether he could phone his local consul, or his wife. But his pleas were met with blank stares.

On the third day I deliberately got off the bed, after I had to stay on the bed all the time, even when I had to go to the bathroom, I had to leave the door open and they kept looking in. So, I got off the bed, put on my shoes and then we started arguing heavily with each other. I yelled at them in German and they said something in Macedonian. I did not understand them and then they pulled their weapons and they stood around me, one at the window, the other at the door and another next to the bed. They were really threatening me. I realised that the situation was really serious.[20]

Guarded round the clock by a team of three Macedonian security agents, the questions from his captors were both vague and open-ended: effectively, they were point-blank demands that he confess to being a terrorist. Was Khaled a member of Al Qaeda? Who did he know? Had he met Mohammed Atta, the 9/11 pilot from Hamburg? Or Ramzi Binalshibh, one of the 9/11 ringleaders? But they never asked him about any particular incident or episode.

In fact, it seemed as if they had no idea who he actually was. There were things they could have asked him about. He knew people who sympathised with the goals of the Taliban government in Afghanistan. Like most men of his age from Lebanon, he had fought as a teenager in his country's civil war — in his case for a group influenced by the Muslim Brotherhood.[21] He also travelled frequently, to the United Arab Emirates, Morocco, Jordan and Eastern Europe. But that was not what they asked him about. Instead they seemed to be fishing for information, he thought.

At various points, the questioners did appear to have something in their head.

Somebody who appeared to be the boss visited after about a week. He was maybe 55 years old. ...... He said that I am not Khaled el-Masri and this is not my passport. I was supposedly in Jalalabad [a town in eastern Afghanistan which before 9/11 had several Islamic militant training camps] and I was seen there. And then he showed me a photo of an Arab-looking guy and he said he had seen me there and he knows me.[22]

Supposedly this man was waiting in the corridor outside. But when Khaled told them to bring him in, no one came.

Back at home in Germany, Khaled's wife, Aycha, had no idea where her husband was. She was terrified, alone with her children, spoke little German and now her husband had left for a low-cost trip to Macedonia after one of the worst fights they had ever had. She and Khaled and their sons lived off social benefits in a one-room flat.[23] Khaled had not had any work as a car dealer for over ten months. She found life in Germany difficult, and had made few German friends outside of the mosque despite living in Ulm for over seven years. She could not understand how cruel Khaled could be simply not to call or send a postcard or a message through one of his "brothers" as he called his fellow believers.[24]

Khaled was a strict Muslim, and for Aycha, the idea of going to one of his friends directly, that is, a woman approaching a man without her husband knowing it, was unthinkable. So she went to her friend, the wife of her husband's best friend, Reda Seyam to ask for advice. What should she do? The two women decided together that she should go and live with her parents back in Lebanon until she heard from her husband. Aycha sold the family car to a fellow Muslim who attended the same mosque to pay for her flight with the children back to Beirut.[25]

After thirteen days in the hotel room, not permitted to get up from his bed except to go the bathroom, al-Masri began a hunger strike in protest. He ate nothing more during his last ten days in Skopje. It was at this point that they told him that he was going home, back to Germany. But in reality, the BBJ chartered by the CIA was on its way to take him elsewhere.

During the three weeks or so that Khaled was in Macedonia, the 737's pace had been frenetic. Leaving Dulles on 6 January, it went to Frankfurt and then to Jordan. Here it picked up a Yemeni prisoner[26] and flew him to Kabul. It then returned to the Czech Republic and back on to Washington, then to Shannon, Ireland, and Larnaca, Cyprus. Here the CIA held a brief meeting. (The CIA's Gulfstream V arrived at the same time.) Afterwards the Boeing 737 flew on to Morocco. That was where the plane picked up Binyam Mohamed and flew him to Afghanistan.

On the same day as Binyam's second rendition, Capt. Fairing and his crew returned to Palma via Algiers. Nothing has yet emerged of why this journey took place. But one clue may be a file released from Bagram Airbase, referring to three "repatriations" from Afghanistan on that date.[27] "Repatriation" is a military euphemism for a rendition back to a detainee's home country. As already noted, Capt. Fairing's flight continued on to Palma, and then on to Skopje to pick up Khaled.

ON BOARD THE CIA BUSINESS JET
24 January, 3 p.m.

In his cockpit, Capt. Fairing began his descent for landing into Kabul. His passenger in the back, Khaled el-Masri, was feeling heavily drugged. He remembered little of this journey, one that he had hoped would have returned him home but instead took him many thousands of miles further east. Back in Majorca, the plane had been packed with a supply of airline meals, including breakfast and dried fruit,[28] but Khaled would have no memory of what fare was being offered. The plane travelled first to Baghdad and then onwards to Afghanistan. Occasionally he had awoken and then, drugged again, he had drifted off back to sleep. He said his headphones had slipped and he did occasionally hear some noises. But his mind had been in a haze. One thing he now knew for certain, he was not going home.

When the plane landed in Kabul, Khaled was placed in a room where through looking at newspapers he began to realise that he was in Afghanistan. Then he was put into the boot of a car and driven for about 10 minutes. "I awoke in a small, dirty cell," he said. "It was like a basement room with a tiny window. There was Arabic and Farsi writing on the wall from other prisoners. It was then that I knew for sure that I was in Afghanistan."[29] The cell he was in had a small window at the top of the wall. The light of a setting sun came through. He realised he had been travelling for more than twenty hours.

Both Khaled and Binyam Mohamed were now in the hands of Americans, although their guards were often Arabs or Afghans. They were now in a network of jails controlled directly by the CIA itself.

Previous chapters have dealt largely with the out-sourcing of interrogation: the transfer of suspects into the hands of foreign interrogators. But, apart from the very public Guantánamo Bay and jails run entirely by foreign governments, like Egypt's Torah prison, America's prison network also included a series of jails run by the CIA itself. Unlike Guantánamo, they provided no access to the Red Cross or even attempted to provide even lip service to the Geneva Conventions. In theory, this was because these jails catered for the real "worst of the worst of the worst", such as Khalid Sheikh Mohammed. Rather than putting those responsible for 9/11 into a Nuremburg-style trial, they were interrogated relentlessly, and held in top secret prison centres around the world. Apart from the very secret jails — the "black sites" where those like Khalid Sheikh Mohammed were held — there was another category of jails, also controlled by the CIA but operated by local staff. These held a lower category of prisoners, those like Khaled and Binyam. Khaled's prison came to be known as the Salt Pit and the prison where Binyam was being held was named the Dark Prison, also known to inmates as the Music Prison. Both had Afghan guards.

On 28 June 2004, the US Supreme Court ruled that the US prison at Guantánamo was subject to Amarican laws.[30] So did those prisons in Afghanistan where Khaled and Binyam were sent in 2004 match up to US standards, for example the prohibition against the use of torture?

The jail where Khaled was held, the Salt Pit, was an abandoned brick factory north of Kabul.[31] It consisted of nine separate cells, as well as interrogation and guard rooms. Khaled found no bed, just an old dirty blanket and some tattered clothes to use as a pillow. He was not alone in the jail. The inmates included a Pakistani, three Saudis and two Tanzanians. The place was run by Afghan guards, and any complaints about the conditions were directed to them. The interrogations themselves were carried out by Americans. Some spoke Arabic and others used Palestinian or Lebanese interpreters. The "prison director" was also an American.

In Khaled's cell the only water he had was a stagnant yellow colour and stood in a filthy plastic bottle; but stricken with thirst he tried some. "I really tried to drink some of that water but it really stank, I could smell it from far away. I held my breath and took a sip. But the aftertaste stayed for more than an hour. That was really disgusting."[32]

On the night of his arrival Khaled was first taken out of his cell to an examination room by some masked men. They undressed him and took some pictures, as well as a blood sample. The doctor, who wore a mask and a pair of jeans, spoke in English, with a Palestinian interpreting into Arabic. Khaled complained about the water. The doctor said that was a problem for the Afghans. Later, Khaled was taken from his cell again to an interrogation room. Again everyone was masked. The chief interrogator spoke in Arabic with a Lebanese accent

In the following four days there were a total of four interrogations. The questions were no different from those in Macedonia. They asked about the Multicultural Centre, Khaled's mosque in Ulm, whether he knew Mohamed Atta, but never about any specific crime or terrorist act. After a while, it seemed the interrogator merely gave up. "He said I wasn't being cooperative and they would simply forget about me in the cell. He didn't have any time to play around with me any longer. For maybe three weeks or so no one ever came to my cell. I was in there all the time."[33]

The conditions in his cell, said Khaled, were grim. Three times a day he was allowed to use the toilet but otherwise he was left completely alone. Food came from the Afghans — boiled skinless chicken in water. Sometimes there was some mouldy yellow lettuce. "The food always caused me and the other prisoners to have diarrhea; we were not sure if it was injected with something or if it was just bad."[34]

In theory, he was not allowed to communicate with other prisoners. But when the guards stepped away, whispered conversations were possible between the cells. The inmates also left notes for each other in the toilets. In this fashion,

Khaled learned there were nine of them in this section of a prison, each in a separate cell.

Although he had been beaten in Macedonia, in the prison it was milder. The worst physically was how they moved the prisoners about in chains. "They would push us around, with our arms high up, and then rush down the stairway. I almost broke my shoulder because I simply wasn't fast enough."[35] In all, Khaled said he was roughed up in interrogations, was beaten in Macedonia, photographed nude, and both injected with drugs and given suppositories against his will; later, when on hunger strike, he was forcibly fed. Yet, he made no claim at all that he was physically tortured.

In answer to the claims of torture by many former prisoners, Defense Secretary Donald Rumsfeld and many in the US government often insisted that such claims have been invented, citing evidence from a jihad training manual that circulated widely on the internet and had been found in the homes of many militants.[36] But Khaled was an example of a prisoner who often understated his experience, never trying to suggest, for example, that he was ever beaten in Afghanistan. In fact, in his first interview, the day after his return home with his friend Reda Seyam, he emphasised that he had undergone a horrendous experience, but that the others were treated far worse than he was and he assumed that was because he was a German citizen.

Khaled's ordeal was mostly mental. Any complaints of his were met with shrugs. But his troubles were "not like the others." There were people he came across who had come from much worse places in the prison network where the treatment was more severe. These prisoners gave descriptions of a "music prison" where they were held for months in complete darkness. Said Khaled:

There was very loud and annoying music and this darkness. And they were either tied to the ground. So they could not sit or stand up. ...Or some had their hands chained to the ceiling, their body hanging down. All naked, no food, no water, for five days. One, when they got him down had swollen legs, he was treated with injections. Another, from Tanzania, had a broken hand, because he had been beaten up. He was also forced to crawl into some kind of a very small suitcase. In there he must have thrown up all the time, his stomach was empty after that.[37]

"I had heard so much from the others about the Dark Prison that I came to feel personally the horrors there."[38] It was to the same Dark Prison that one of Capt. Fairing's other passengers had been taken in the same CIA Boeing 737: Binyam Mohamed. As noted, he arrived in Kabul just two days before Khaled. In his account of his treatment in American captivity, dictated in Guantánamo, Mohamed also called the detention centre the Dark Prison.

The primary weapon at this jail, said Binyam, was rock music played incessantly at high volume. It was a psychological tactic used by the US military to dislodge General Manuel Noriega from the Vatican Embassy in Panama in December 1989. The most repeated track played at the Dark Prison was 'White America' by Eminem. Binyam reported that: "The noises were so horrible and loud that I used to stick anything — toilet paper if I had some, or parts of the one blanket I got — in my ears just to minimise the sound. Others tried to do this but I know at least one who got perforated ear drums from all the noise." It was at this point that Binyam had folded and agreed to sign anything. He was soon transferred to Bagram military base and then moved on to Guantánamo.

Left alone in his cell, Khaled felt desperate. It may not have been physical torture, but he felt psychologically tortured. And the only way he knew to protest was to go on a hunger strike. After organising other inmates around him, prisoners on Khaled's wing started refusing both food and water. After a while, they started drinking water, stale and smelly as it was. Many prisoners, already weakened by months of poor treatment, could not hold out for long. But Khaled kept on going and going, holding out for thirty-seven days. Finally, his American interrogators intervened to keep him alive.

They came and told me that possibly in three weeks I could be released. I should stop [my] hunger strike. I said no and that I wanted some kind of a guarantee. They brought me back to my cell. Maybe twenty minutes later four masked men, all in black, walked in. They handcuffed me and put on the chains and then carried me again to the interrogation room. They tied me to a chair. One other man bent my head towards my back with his arm. Then the doctor came with some kind of a tube with a funnel on the one end. He stuck the tube through my nose down my stomach and forced some nutritious liquid through it. That really was hard and painful. And he told me, they could do it that way every time: you cannot force us to follow your wishes. So we negotiated. They promised me to from now on give me better food, especially for me. And better water and books and so on.[39]

Khaled had made his point. His CIA captors knew that a death in custody could be highly damaging. The case, according to a later New York Times report, had also now been raised at the highest levels. George Tenet, the CIA director was informed. So was Condoleezza Rice, the then National Security Advisor.[40] Khaled would have to be released. But here was the rub: how could they release Khaled and prevent him from exposing the CIA's secret prisons? Should the German government be officially informed?

In the final days of his imprisonment in Afghanistan, Khaled was not only questioned about information from Germany, he was introduced to a new interrogator who implied he was from the German government. It happened at the beginning of May, when Khaled was recovering from over a month spent on hunger strike. In the interrogation room was the American director of the prison, another American, and a German with a northern accent. He called himself "Sam" — slim, maybe 1.80 m high, blond, a little longer hair, maybe 40 or 45 years old — and he said "they would talk about everything now, openly."

"I asked him: 'Are you from the German authorities?' He said: 'I do not want to answer that question.' When I asked him if the German authorities knew that I was there, he answered: 'I can't answer this question.'"[41]

Khaled asked how they could speak openly when Sam refused to answer even the most basic of questions. But Sam said Khaled was not to talk, only to answer his questions. "He began asking all the same questions as the Americans, about Dr Yusuf, the leader of the mosque, and about the persons at the Multicultural House in Ulm."[42]

All this could have been a ruse. Some British Guantánamo detainees, for example, described being questioned by an MI6 agent in Afghanistan. And yet I later met the American interrogator, who admitted he was the agent. He had pretended to be British in order to persuade those men to talk. Khaled was convinced that Sam really was German.[43] But the German government was to deny this. The German foreign intelligence service, the BND, informed the German government in a special report they had details of two German-speaking Americans who had worked for US intelligence in Germany. One might have been the man in question.[44] The possible identity of "Sam" was named in one account as "Thomas V" who had worked in the American consulate in Hamburg in 2000.[45]

Sam, whoever he was, told Khaled that he was finally to be released but that America would try to keep his capture secret. "Sam told me that the Americans didn't want to admit to anyone that I had been here and because of that the journey back to Germany would be a bit more complicated. So no one could find out where I was coming from and where I had been. That simply would take a while but I shouldn't worry. That I was going to get free 100 per cent."[46] Khaled's food ration changed. Through the diarrohea, lack of food and water, and the stress of not knowing why he was in prison, he had suffered radical weight loss. But after Sam's promise, it started to change. He was given milk and meat. They were clearly trying to fatten him up, he thought.

Finally, on 28 May, Sam's promise came true. Khaled was taken on a ten minute drive to the airport and placed on another executive plane. Accompanying him was Sam.[47] But rather than being flown home to Germany, Sam took him to Tirana, the Albanian capital. His captivity was still not over. He was driven six or seven hours into the countryside down a series of bumpy pot-holed roads. Eventually the car stopped and his captors took off the rope binding his hands and they removed his blindfold. He was told to walk down the path he saw in front of him and not turn round once. All the way along he felt a tingle of fear in his back. "I was very much afraid. I thought maybe they just let me walk a couple steps to then shoot me. So that frightened me. But I thought why should they do it that way. There are cheaper ways to get rid of someone."[48]

At the end of the path he found three uniformed men. They appeared to be expecting him and had a plastic bag with a packed lunch waiting for him. They asked for his passport and then said he was in the country illegally and they would drive him to Tirana. They revealed he had been driven down to the border triangle of Albania, Macedonia and Serbia. Departing at around 10 p.m.

they drove him straight back to Tirana airport After buying his own 320 euro ticket at the airport, he was placed on an Albanian Airways plane to Germany. It was an ordinary civilian flight.

BORDER CONTROL, FRANKFURT AIRPORT
29 May 2004, 8.40 a.m.

Arriving home after 149 days of captivity, Khaled approached the German border guard, who, examining his passport, said "This photo is not you." He now looked several years older than his picture. "No," said Khaled, "the photo is recent. It was taken just eight months ago." Producing other identity cards, he convinced the guard but he realised now how much he had changed. [49] While in captivity he had lost more than four stone in weight.

It was late when Khaled finally got back home to Ulm. He had with him the suitcase he had packed for his short holiday six months earlier; it was almost untouched. It was eerie. His clothes were still folded as he had folded them, his toiletries were all there. Even the money he had packed and his keys were still there.[50] His first port of call was his apartment on Bahnhofstrasse 18, where he had last seen his wife and children. He first found the mail box stuffed with advertisements and mail. There were threatening letters from bill collectors and demands from the unemployment office for his appearance. When he entered the apartment he was shocked: the entire apartment seemed ransacked, the sofa ripped apart. There was no sign of his wife or of his four boys.[51]

Not knowing what to do, he immediately ran over to the home of his friend Reda Seyam. It was 11 p.m. when he rang the bell. Seyam could not believe what he saw. Khaled had lost 60 pounds, had a long beard and longer hair. But it was his sad, tired and worn out eyes which most shocked him. Seyam told him to come in, and that he immediately should eat and then get some rest. And when he awoke, the next day, Khaled began to tell him his story, and Reda Seyam took out his video camera and said: "You have to tell me this on camera."[52] This private account, which I obtained for this book, was intimate. But, in its detail, it did not in any way contradict the public account Khaled later gave of his ordeal.

After a few days of sleep and recovery, Khaled el-Masri set out to try to rebuild his life. Khaled heard from Seyam that his wife, Aycha, was living with their four boys at her parents' home in Lebanon. He called her and immediately arranged for the family to return to their home in Germany. A week later there was a tearful reunion at Frankfurt airport. Eventually, with the help of a lawyer, Khaled filed an official complaint about his treatment with the German police. In June, both the German Office of the Chancellor as well as the Foreign Ministry received complaints describing his kidnapping.[53] After hours of questioning, a federal prosecutor in Munich came to believe that what Khaled was saying was true. He found corroboration of his trip to Macedonia (for example witness statements from other bus passengers) and used a sample of his hair to determine that his account of being on hunger strike was likely true.[54] Flight data of the BBJ's movements, as described, matched precisely his description of his rendition from Skopje to Afghanistan. Munich prosecutor Martin Hofmann said: "I have no indication that Masri is not telling the truth."[55]

As his story emerged, the biggest puzzle for Khaled and for everyone around him was — why was he ever arrested? What was behind his rendition?

The most convenient and well-publicised explanation for Khaled el-Masri's kidnapping to Afghanistan was that the CIA had made an innocent mistake. It was convenient because it implied that, while Khaled had regrettably suffered in error, there was nothing essentially wrong in principle with what occurred in his cases: the kidnap, covert transport and secret imprisonment of someone without charge or any legal process. In any war, innocents would always be hurt. Even if it was proven that Khaled was completely innocent then it would not matter; because, as realists would argue, accidents will happen.

When Khaled first described his treatment publicly, at the beginning of 2005 and when his account was corroborated, among other things by the flight logs, the US government could no longer pretend that such renditions did not occur. The key thing was to argue that no torture was intended, and if torture did occur, it was all a dreadful mistake. After all, Bush had previously stated the US was "leading this fight" against torture by example.[56]

Rocked on its heels, the CIA began to defend itself. In Khaled's case, it was, yes, a terrible error, a mistaken identity. In April 2005, the *New York Times*, quoting CIA sources, reported that "Macedonian and American authorities believed he [el-Masri] was a member of Al Qaeda who had trained at one of Osama bin Laden's camps in Afghanistan. But within several months they concluded he was the victim of *mistaken identity*, the officials said. His name was similar to an Al Qaeda suspect on an international watch list of possible terrorist operatives, they said. The American officials acknowledged "the detention had been a serious mistake and that he had been held too long after American officials realised their error." [57]

Later, the blame was pinned more firmly on junior officials in the CIA's Counter-Terrorist Centre. One former CIA official told the *Washington Post*: "Masri was held for five months largely because the head of the CIA's Counter-Terrorist Centre's Al Qaeda unit 'believed he was someone else. ... She didn't really know. She just had a hunch.'"[58]

Later the same year, when Condoleezza Rice, now Secretary of State, faced a storm of anger in Europe over the CIA's abductions and secret flights, she hinted at this simple error. "If mistakes have been made, they are always corrected rapidly" she said in public. In private, while meeting the new German Chancellor,

Angela Merkel, she repeated the mantra, but was said to have added a specific apology for Khaled, although she denied it later.

By this time, the end of 2005, the Khaled el-Masri case seemed to me increasingly intriguing and I set out to try to grasp what had really happened. To what extent, I asked first, could Khaled's capture have been this simple error?

The most obvious reason why an innocent mistake *could* have been made in Khaled's case was that he shared a name with a man alleged to have assisted the 9/11 conspirators in Germany. According to the United States' 9/11 Commission Report, a Khaled al-Masri (let's call him the "Hamburg Khaled") was a link between the trainee pilots in Hamburg led by Mohamed Atta and the Al Qaeda leadership in Afghanistan. At the time of Khaled's arrest, this Hamburg Khaled was still listed as a wanted man. So it was plausible that when Khaled crossed the border into Macedonia his name was flagged up as a suspect terrorist. This could at least explain his initial arrest.[59]

Yet if the Macedonians may have believed they had captured Hamburg Khaled on the border, it was implausible to imagine the same mistake was made by US intelligence for very long, and not for the five months he was held in Afghanistan. Khaled had lived openly in Ulm for many years and had a history that was easy to verify with the German government. He had attended a mosque that was under heavy surveillance. If there were any suspicion at all of his involvement in 9/11, the German authorities would not have hesitated to arrest him. But he had faced no police questions, not even over a parking fine.

Just say though — in an assumption at odds with years of cooperation — the CIA distrusted the Germans and believed it unwise to arrest him in Germany. Would they not, at least once, have asked Khaled himself if he really was Hamburg Khaled? Would they not have tried to check his identity and ask if he really was on the train in Germany when Hamburg Khaled met Atta? Yet Khaled himself remembers no such questions. He was indeed asked in CIA captivity if he was a member of Al Qaeda. He was asked too if he knew Mohammed Atta and Ramzi Binalshibh. They were the sort of questions asked of all terrorist suspects from Germany. But there was nothing specific. There was no clue of what he was actually accused of.

How then did Khaled explain the events? He found the idea of a mix-up unconvincing. "They told me that they had confused names and they had cleared it up, but I can't imagine that. You can clear up switching names in a few minutes."[60]

Perhaps the CIA had some other specific intelligence. Perhaps they believed him guilty of some other crime or that he played another role in Al Qaeda. Yet why was he never asked about such reports? The CIA had used extreme and expensive means to take him to Afghanistan by executive jet. And yet, when in their hands, when they got him to their prison, it was if the CIA men were trying to justify their actions in hindsight. Rather than defend *their* kidnap, Khaled was asked to invent *his* crime and to justify what had occurred. Like a scene from

Franz Kafka's *The Trial*, when Josef K is asked to confess to an unknown crime, Khaled remembered an exchange when he was asked to justify his detention: The interrogator, he said, started "to scream out at me and asked if I knew at all why I was there. And I said, that was actually my question. ...I said I wanted to know why I was there. And he said you are here in a country without laws and no one knows where you are. Do you know what that means?"[61]

So the nature of the questions asked of Khaled, I thought, pointed not to the idea that he was being held on some mistaken charge (except perhaps in his initial arrest at the border), but rather that he was being held as part of a strategy to gather information. Rather than being asked about any specific offence, still less his *intentions* to commit a crime, Khaled was asked mainly about his *associations*. Who did he know? Who did he meet and on what date? As Khaled said: "Nothing speaks for the mix up theory. I think it had to do with my contacts. They wanted to know what the Multicultural Centre, Dr Yusuf and Reda Seyam, were up to. They thought, 'something is happening there, we will find out what if we put this guy in this difficult situation, then he will tell us'."[62] This focus on associations was important because it is a clue to the Khaled case — and a clue to a strategy that emerged after 9/11, one that former CIA officers insisted would never previously have been sanctioned. If Khaled's contacts and friends could be considered evidence of guilt and justification enough for his lengthy detention, then his case would suddenly make sense. In the post-9/11 world, and when it came to his associates, Khaled rang nearly every possible alarm bell:

• First, Khaled was a member of a radical mosque, the Multicultural Centre, with a track record of recruiting young Muslims to fight for Islam. Two worshippers from the mosque fought in Chechnya against the Russians and died in 2002 and 2003.[63]

• Second, Khaled knew the Mosque's leader, Dr Yehia Yusuf. Known for his anti-western sermons, Yusuf was described by the Bavarian interior minister as a "preacher of hate". The minister was determined to expel him from Germany. Dr Yusuf's son, Omar, also had militant viewpoints and also was a friend of Khaled. He was eventually expelled from Germany in June 2002.

• Third, and most importantly, one of Khaled's best friends, Reda Seyam, was an open supporter of global Islamic jihad. He had fought in Bosnia and then had toured the Far East making militant propaganda videos. When the Bali bomb exploded in October 2002, Seyam was arrested in Indonesia as a suspected conspirator and, though released, was deported back to Germany. His opinions did not shift. In 2005, he had a son and named him Jihad.

This, then, was how Khaled might have appeared to be a potential terrorist. It was the Ulm connection that had done for Khaled and particular his connection to Dr Yusuf. "I think there is a link. Because, again and again, I was asked about him," he said.[64]

All roads then seemed to lead to Ulm.

THE SWABIAN ALPS, SOUTHERN GERMANY
19 March 2006

Driving from the city of Stuttgart across the snow-covered hills, I was headed to the medieval city of Ulm to try to reach my own conclusion about why Khaled really was kidnapped, and to what extent Germany itself was involved in the affair.

A little way to the West, part of the same range of hills, lies the Black Forest, the source of the mighty Danube River that flows down through Ulm and then across through central and eastern Europe to reach the Black Sea — a route that was broadly followed by Khaled's coach when he had travelled to Macedonia through Vienna and Belgrade. Within Germany, the river is also the boundary between two German states: The north of Ulm, where Khaled lived, is in the state of Baden-Württemberg. But as I crossed an old bridge across the river, I entered "New Ulm", and found a sign that welcomed me to the "Free State of Bavaria." It was on this Bavarian side of the city that I found the Multicultural Centre, the controversial mosque that Khaled and Seyam had attended. I found it on an industrial estate, next to a centre for asylum-seekers. It had been closed down a few months earlier, by order of the Bavarian government; a legalised brothel had been licenced next door, with heart-shaped red flashing lights.

"What you must understand is that everyone wanted to follow this mosque," a security official explained to me. "It was like an Oriental bazaar, an intelligence market, with everyone competing to recruit sources," he said. The disaster of 9/11 — led by an Al Qaeda cell in Hamburg — had put everyone in Germany on alert to find other sources of Islamic extremism. The mosque at Ulm was one of the top places of suspicion. "Everyone wanted to get in on the act; suddenly everyone decided they would start to hunt for terrorists," he said. But the division of the city between two states, he explained, made understanding what happened really quite complex. Under German law, each state had its own domestic intelligence agencies (part of a system of checks and balances established after the Second World War to prevent the creation of a new Gestapo). So with the mosque in Ulm, the agencies from the two states — local police, state police, and intelligence services — all had competed to penetrate the mosque. "In all I can count at least eight German agencies involved," he said, "and that is before we count foreign intelligence."

The officer, who I was interviewing back in Stuttgart, one of a series of security officials that I managed to track down with a colleague, laughed as he recalled what sounded like a circus. "I'm pretty sure we had Egyptian intelligence, Saudi intelligence, and Moroccan intelligence; and that's of course excluding the Americans and Israelis who had a close interest." No wonder, in the months before he disappeared, that Khaled and his friends had hints there was something strange going on. "There were strange new faces in the mosque and people taking pictures. Khaled and Seyam both had the feeling there were cars following them as well," their lawyer, Manfred Gjindic, told me.

But with all this attention, what intelligence had emerged? Had Khaled ever been considered a suspect? It turned out, the security officials told us, they had known *plenty* about Khaled — long before he was kidnapped. They too believed he might have been captured because of his associations; but basing any assumption of guilt on these, they argued, had been exceedingly foolish. "Khaled had been in the background of the mosque for some time," one told me, "but he really was not important. Of all the people that you might suspect of being a threat to security, he was really at the back of the list, a really minor player in the scene." Even those characters at the mosque regarded with the greatest suspicion — those like his friend Reda Seyam, and Dr Yusuf — were generally considered a long way from being actual terrorists. Seyam might have praised or even advocated jihad, but there was no evidence of any involvement in anything more than propaganda. In Indonesia, the US had ample opportunity to arrest him but they chose not to. As for Dr Yusuf, he certainly had extremist views, but he was also someone in close dialogue with the German authorities. He had in fact, I confirmed, been for years an agent of the local state security office, for which he received only expenses. Who at the mosque, I asked one officer, was not working as an informer? He just chuckled.

The consensus among those who knew most about the Ulm mosque was clear then — the pursuit of Khaled el-Masri by the CIA was a red herring; a fact explained either by misinformation or a motive other than concrete suspicion.

But what of German involvement — had the CIA used information supplied by the Germans?

While he was being held in Afghanistan, Khaled became convinced that the information he was being asked about had to have been provided from his home country. Almost all of the questions he faced were about people he knew in Ulm and Neu Ulm or about the Multicultural Centre. The interrogators even knew fine details about what kind of food could be purchased in the mosque's shop. How could they have known to ask such detailed questions if they did not have some cooperation with the German authorities?

A pointed question about who he knew in Norway indicated to Khaled el-Masri that the interrogators — the Americans — clearly had access to information about his bank account. Norway "is the only place where I had received large sums of money. I have a very good customer in Norway and he had transferred once 50,000 euros to my account in order to buy cars for him. When they asked me about Norway I just played dumb. But I thought, 'Aha, they know about my bank account'. Maybe the CIA has its own access to my bank account, but it seems to me that they may have gotten the information from the Germans."[65] Another question that the American interrogators asked Khaled in the Salt Pit prison in Kabul had also, he said, implied German cooperation. His friend Reda Seyam drove a Renault which was registered to Khaled's wife Aycha. Khaled says that virtually no one the two men associated with was informed about the arrangement. "You had to have access to official government records to know that."[66]

All these examples certainly demonstrated to me that the CIA had been following closely events and people at the mosque. Yet given what I'd heard about the scale of penetration of the mosque by multiple agencies, it would be hard to pin down who exactly had handed over the detailed files, always assuming the CIA had stuck to the rules which prohibited its case officers from running unilateral operations within German territory.

At a local level, the German agencies denied handing over information on Khaled. One intelligence officer said the CIA's station chief in Munich had frequently asked for updates on information collected about the Ulm mosque — but she had never asked for specific information on Khaled. At a higher level, however, German intelligence analysts, in a series of interviews in Berlin, pointed out that given the closeness of relations between the CIA and both domestic and foreign German services, the CIA would have been given detailed access, without even asking, to a great deal of reporting about what was happening in Ulm. Whatever Germany's public disagreements over American foreign policy were at the time (for example over the invasion of Iraq) German spies had worked hand-in-hand with American ones.[67] Even during the Iraq invasion, on-the-spot operatives from the country's foreign intelligence service (the BND) were providing detailed information to the United States. They assisted in identifying targets in Baghdad, and ruling out non-targets, such as sensitive civilian buildings.[68] So did the United States obtain their information on Khaled from one of the local German services, from an Arab intelligence service also active in Ulm, or through routine intelligence exchange at a national level? In each of those cases, the information would not have been hard to get.

More broadly, there was much about Germany's position in the Khaled el-Masri case that was less than convincing. On the morning of 31 May 2004, just after he was released in Albania, the then US ambassador, Daniel Coats, went to tell Khaled's story to Otto Schily, then the German Interior Minister[69] and the head of the Terrorism desk in the ministry's vast Law Enforcement unit.[70] According to the official account, the US admitted kidnapping the German citizen but said that he had appeared on a "Watchlist" and that they thought he had been carrying forged documents. Coats apologised for their mistake, but said that Khaled had been released after they determined that his passport was genuine and apologised for their mistake, receiving in turn a promise of silence from

Germany.[71] No notes were made of the meeting, the ministry later claimed, and when a federal prosecutor in Munich began investigating the case, and asked the government what it knew, the ministry did not tell the prosecutor about the US ambassador's visit. It was strange behaviour for a government that professed ignorance of the whole affair. As Khaled said in an interview for this book, if the CIA had doubts about the authenticity of his passport and his real identity, it stretches imagination to contemplate they would not have contacted German intelligence for help.[72]

For years, and particularly after 9/11, the CIA had been using Frankfurt as its main logistics base in Europe. It also served as the main staging post for rendition operations around the Middle East. Located just outside Stuttgart in Vaihingen was the European headquarters of the Defense Intelligence Agency (DIA) — one of the closest partners of German intelligence.[73] Had Germany been so foolish to allow such activity on its soil without knowing what was going on? "Of course not," answered one former CIA operative, who knew of the CIA's counter-terrorist operations in the first three years after 9/11. "With the Europeans, and the Germans in particular, it was always a case of don't ask, don't tell. They wouldn't know the specifics, but they knew the sort of things we were up to." At the time of writing, these issues remained under investigation by the German parliament.

For all the potential complicity of the Germans, however, it was ultimately the Americans who had kidnapped Khaled, who had let him be beaten by the Macedonians, who interrogated him in secret, who had force-fed him and then dropped him in the Albanian mountains. From the evidence I saw in Germany, it seemed ever clearer that, while Khaled had kept the company of those thought suspicious, there was never any serious evidence against him. He had been someone who, to use police jargon, "fitted the frame," who had the right profile. It seemed an incredible basis on which to put him through such an ordeal.

Ultimately, if Khaled *really* had been considered that important, his case could have been dealt with within days. The validity of his passport could have been verified with the Germans. Instead, after his initial interrogations, Khaled had largely been left to stew alone in his cell in Afghanistan. Much of this case was still a mystery. Yet the more I looked into it, the more it appeared like a cover-up rather than a mix-up.

It was in January 2006, a couple of months before this trip to Ulm, when I had finally taken a flight out to Majorca to find out about how Khaled's rendition operation had been staged. At a late night meeting in an air-conditioned office I was shown the documents of one of the most detailed police investigations into the CIA's aviation operations — an inquiry launched reluctantly by the local prosecutor after complaints from the island's human rights activists.

The investigation was conducted by a captain from the Guardia Civil, Antonio Tarifa. It was he who had identified the crew of the planes that transported both Khaled and Binyam Mohamed. After Khaled had begun speaking publicly, and my flight logs had confirmed details of his flight from Macedonia, a local journalist, Matías Vallés, had noticed that the same Boeing 737 was a frequent visitor to the city's airport and contacted me for more information. He also realised that the journey to pick up Khaled el-Masri had begun in Palma. Prompted by the articles by Valles and his colleagues, a group of campaigners and lawyers filed a complaint to the island's chief prosecutor, alleging that torture victims might have been transported through Majorca. As a result, the prosecutor in turn asked the Guardia Civil to investigate.

Capt. Tarifa examined twelve visits by the CIA planes to the airport. He began his investigations at Mallorcair and Assistair, the two local ground agents for handling the arrival of the planes. The operators of the CIA's Gulfstream V and Boeing 737 were revealed as a company registered in Tennessee, Stevens Express Leasing. Companies like Mallorcair do not keep a record of the names of passengers and crews of visiting jets. But they did have a record of the hotels to which the crew were taken to rest overnight. These records revealed the CIA crews' visits to the Marriott Son Antem. But their most popular destination was the Gran Melia Victoria, a five-star hotel in Palma city centre that overlooks the yacht marina.

"They were all just ordinary people. They came down and drank in the bar like anyone else," the Gran Melia's manager told me. Like ordinary guests, the CIA crew had also left their names and addresses, as well passport numbers and credit card numbers. It was the first time that crews of these CIA jets had been identified.

As the police investigation showed, after completing the renditions of both Binyam Mohammed and Khaled al Masri, Capt. Fairing and his crew returned to Majorca on 26 January 2004 for two nights of rest and recreation at the Melia Victoria. Snow and ice had sealed off Dulles airport to incoming flights.

As they prepared to return home, their jobs done, their Boeing 737 was loaded up with an unusual amount of ice — 30 kilos of ice cubes and dry ice. And dipping into Mallorcair's drinks cabinet, they selected for themselves three bottles of fine Spanish wine, two of Pesquera and an Alion, along with five crystal glasses. All were charged to the CIA plane's bill.

By 28 January, the weather in Dulles had cleared. At 10.09 a.m. Capt. Fairing opened the throttle on his 737 and took off for Washington, DC. The rendition group's work was over — for now.

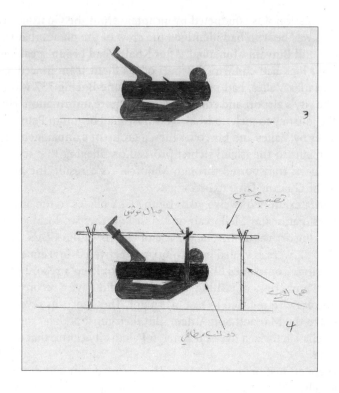

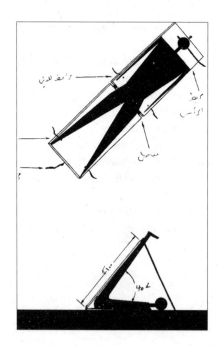

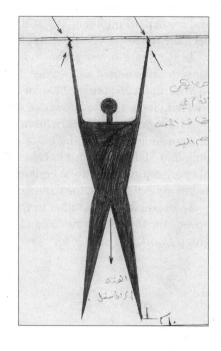

PART TWO
AIR AMERICA

5

COVERT ACTION
UNMASKING THE NEW AIR AMERICA

Flightlog

Registration: **N6161Q**;
Type: **Dehavilland Twin Otter**;
Operator: Aviation Specialties Inc,
Maryland;
Date: **4 November 2001**

Flight plan:
Glasgow
Frankfurt Rhein AFB

Frankfurt Rhein AFB
Dushanbe, Tajikistan

Dushanbe, Tajikistan
Sherkat, Afghanistan

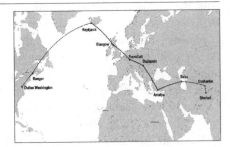

GULBOHAR, AFGHANISTAN
Sunday, 4 November 2001

Seven days before the fall of the northern city of Mazar-i-Sharif and nine days before the fall of Kabul, B52 bombers were pounding the Taliban frontlines facing the Northern Alliance in the Shimali plain north of the Afghan capital. For a month, engineers had been levelling a dirt airstrip on uncultivated flood land at Sherkat, close to the village of Gulbohar and its cotton factory, about fifty miles north of Kabul and at the point where the Panjshir Valley drops down out of the Hindu Kush. It was close to the headquarters of the Northern Alliance and controlled by militia loyal to Burhanuddin Rabbani, the self-proclaimed Afghan president. The British first used the same plain as an airstrip in 1919. That morning, a small white twin-prop aircraft appeared from the clouds. It circled, turned abruptly, and then dropped down onto the strip. Out stepped what appeared to be US agents, wearing chinos and baseball caps. Others also arrived in what appeared to be Soviet-made Mi-17 helicopters. "They looked like us, except without all the dirt on their clothes", recalled a witness.[1]

The plane was a Canadian-built Twin Otter aircraft and its passengers provided one of the first open glimpses of members of the CIA's Special Operations Group, its paramilitary arm. They were the same team whose members included Mike Spann, who would become the first US casualty in the War on Terror, killed at the prison in Mazar-i-Sharif on 28 November. The group deployed to Sherkat were part of a CIA team operating under the code-name "Jawbreaker".[2] At the time, no one harboured more than suspicions of who these men were. And the incident was soon forgotten. There was just one small reference in a British military magazine that identified the registration of the plane as N6161Q. It reported the plane was owned by a Washington DC-based company called Aviation Specialties Inc. According to the magazine, the plane had flown to Afghanistan from the US via Glasgow Airport in Scotland, the US Rhein-Main air force base in Frankfurt, Germany, and Dushanbe in Tajikistan.[3]

Nearly four years later I would take this work onwards — tracing how this same plane, a Twin Otter, belonged to Johnston County in North Carolina — home to the CIA's aviation fleet and to the Gulfstream jet used in rendition flights. I would trace the same plane to a remote military airstrip in Virginia called Camp Peary.[4] This was a restricted base known to the CIA as "the Farm"; it used to have the codename "Isolation" and was the agency's main training base. I realised that this plane's appearance in Afghanistan was not just the first sight of the CIA in that country, but was the first glimpse in public of one of America's most secret assets — the Agency's private aircraft fleet. It was the discovery of these planes that helped unlock America's torture scandal.

All this was to come later. For now, the mystery had yet to be uncovered — and this visit to the Panjshir was just a clue left awaiting detection. Because, time and again, when America turned to clandestine action, it was the public discovery of secret airplanes that exposed those operations. As this chapter describes, my aim as a journalist was not to expose a well-justified covert action such as the delivery of the Jawbreaker team into Afghanistan but to expose a questionable one — the Agency's new practice of out-sourcing torture. As a freelance journalist, my resources were meager. I was investigating an agency with a budget of many billions.[5] But, as a technique of investigation, there was no better place to start looking than at its airplanes.

Ever since the CIA turned to clandestine warfare, it had needed a discreet aviation wing. Planes could land and pick up agents behind enemy lines. They could survey difficult targets, drop supplies, and could also transport prisoners away. But planes are also quite difficult to hide.

When the United States fought Communists in South-East Asia, the CIA made use of Air America, a group of private companies that it secretly owned. It was a thin secret though — mainly because of the sheer scale of operations. In the early '70s, Air America was reputed to have become the biggest commercial airline in the world.[6] Its motto was "Anything, Anywhere, Anytime — Professionally." Air America's operations were centred on Laos. According to an authorised account of the war by Professor William Leary of the University of Georgia, published on the CIA's website: "The largest paramilitary operations ever undertaken by the CIA took place in the small Southeast Asian Kingdom of Laos. For more than thirteen years, the Agency directed native forces that fought major North Vietnamese units to a standstill."

In remote Laos, this airline was used for the secret supply of an anti-Communist rebel army based on Meo tribesmen. Yet the flow of airplanes and helicopters to the Meo bases exposed this operation. Leary gave a sense of the scale of the project: "Air America, an airline secretly owned by the CIA, was a vital component in the Agency's operations in Laos," he wrote.

By the summer of 1970, the airline had some two dozen twin-engine transports, another two dozen short-takeoff-and-landing (STOL) aircraft, and some 30 helicopters dedicated to operations in Laos. There were more than 300 pilots, co-pilots, flight mechanics, and air-freight specialists flying out of Laos and Thailand. During 1970, Air America airdropped or landed 46 million pounds of foodstuffs — mainly rice — in Laos. Helicopter flight time reached more than 4,000 hours a month in the same year. Air America crews transported tens of thousands of troops and refugees, flew emergency medevac missions and rescued downed airmen throughout Laos, inserted and extracted road-watch teams, flew nighttime airdrop missions over the Ho Chi Minh Trail, monitored sensors along infiltration routes, conducted a highly successful photo-reconnaissance programme, and engaged in numerous clandestine missions using night-vision glasses and state-of-the-art electronic equipment. Without Air America's presence, the CIA's effort in Laos could not have been sustained.[7]

But the Meo, it emerged, were not only fighting the Communists. They were also, from their bases at the centre of the Golden Triangle, helping to corner the world supply of opium. The more well-known Air America became, the less useful it became for the CIA and the more the CIA's reputation was tarnished by the rough connections of its allies.[8] In the mid-1970s, when the United States withdrew from Vietnam, Air America was shut down. By then, many of the CIA's activities were under investigation — most notoriously by a Senate committee headed by Senator Frank Church.[9] Testifying to that committee in 1975, the CIA's (unidentified) chief of cover and commercial staff, said that if an operational requirement like the South East Asia conflict should again arise "…I would assume that the Agency would consider setting up a large-scale air proprietary with one proviso — that we have a chance of keeping it secret that it is CIA."[10]

In the years that followed, the CIA had only mixed success in keeping its air operations under wraps. For all the protests and investigations of the 1960s and 1970s, the desire by successive presidents of the United States for an effective covert action capability had hardly gone away. Both the debacle of the failed military attempt to rescue hostages in revolutionary Iran and the Soviet invasion of Afghanistan underlined this need. So, very quietly, the Agency got back into the aircraft business.

Sometimes the plane of choice was a charter, not Agency-owned. Brian Martin, an adventurous British pilot, showed me his log books that described covert missions into East Berlin in a jet chartered by the CIA to buy Soviet weapons from under the KGB's nose.[11] Ostensibly buying AK47s and ammunition to supply Soviet allies in Africa like Angola, once out of Communist airspace the plane's flight plan was altered and it diverted to Washington, DC's National Airport (now Reagan Airport), just by the Potomac river. The weapons, he said, were unloaded there into military trucks and soon diverted to the CIA's own purposes — like the mujahideen in Afghanistan or the Contra rebels in Nicaragua.

The CIA also created its own new airlines, some run by former pilots of the old Air America. In 1989, one such airline, Tepper Aviation of Florida, was caught using a Hercules plane to fly weapons to Unita rebels in Angola in violation of United Nations sanctions. This news was first reported in February that year by a British journalist, Alan George, whose article recorded that Bud Peddy, the head of Tepper, "categorically denies that the Hercules has been in Zaire or Angola."[12] But on 27 November that year, the same plane crashed at the Unita-held Jamba airfield. Among those killed were two West Germans, a Briton, and several Americans…including the same Bud Peddy.[13]

Other planes were used to support the CIA's backing for the "Contra" rebels against the socialist Sandinista government in Nicaragua. Among the CIA operations was one to place mines inside Nicaraguan harbours.[14] Again, it was the crash of a CIA-chartered plane that helped expose a scandal — the secret diversion of aid intended for the Contras to purchase arms for Iran in exchange for the release of American hostages in Lebanon. This so-called Iran-Contra affair began unravelling on 5 October 1986, with the shooting down by the Sandinistas of a C123 cargo plane. Among the crew was an American, Eugene Hasenfus, who told reporters he worked for the CIA. With the cover of the aid network now blown, the trail to Iran-Contra led from there.[15]

LONDON
July 2003

I wish I could say that when I began my journey I had a clear idea of the path ahead, of how I and others could possibly get any proof at all of the CIA's rendition programme. For the last two years I had been at the helm of the *Sunday Times*'s Insight team, its investigation unit. But now I was turning freelance. I was determined to spend more time on my own projects, and in particular to try to run down reports of a story that I had never had time to tackle properly. This was the one I had heard from sources that Guantánamo was just the tip of the iceberg. Apparently there was a whole network of prison camps across the world. As I left, I spoke to Bob Tyrer, one of the paper's senior editors and alternately my harshest critic and best ally, and told him of my objective. He wished me good luck. "You don't exactly pick the easy ones," he said. "How the hell are you going to find this out?" As I left the building, I thought to myself: "I wish I knew."

I had been covering the War on Terror as a journalist pretty much since George Bush declared it. In the days after 9/11, I arrived in New York on one of the first flights across the Atlantic. Ground Zero was still smouldering. My concentration was on the counter-terrorist fight back — the struggle to hunt down the perpetrators of 9/11 and the ringleaders of Al Qaeda. What intrigued me most was what I knew least about — the undercover war. I knew it had successes and failures. And, from the hints I received in the months that followed, I began to learn it might involve methods about which America could be acutely embarrassed. I knew that exposing the facts of those methods was a worthwhile journalistic endeavour. But how should I probe beneath the surface?

Many journalists, of course, claimed frequently to know and write the truth about the CIA's secrets and some got quite close.[16] Some have written a plethora of "inside accounts". There were detailed narratives like Bob Woodward's *Bush at War* that described covert operations in great detail. But accounts like these often provided only the illusion of access. The very references in these accounts to "secret" and "classified" documents often betrayed the fact they had been fed certain choice tidbits of information that, whether officially or not, were cleared for release. How could I tell this story as a Washington outsider, how could I find out about such secret operations without being manipulated or being used for a hidden agenda?

In reporting on the secret world of intelligence, the most important thing was to unearth some hard facts. Rumours and conspiracy theories are easy to find. So are stories based on anonymous sources. And however wild the latest report may be, it rarely forces a secret service like the CIA to respond to the charges. It simply adds to the agency's mystique. The key thing for a covert operation is to maintain "deniability": the ability of the government to deny all knowledge of the involvement of the United States. When a covert operation is ordered, there is a fair chance that its existence would eventually become public knowledge. But the key thing is to be able to distance the US and particularly the President from whatever has occurred. Extraordinary rendition, with its unsavoury whiff of cruel torture, was exactly such a covert policy. It was acceptable for it to be public knowledge that a terrorist was sent from Albania to

Egypt, and even that he was tortured. It was acceptable for anonymous sources to allege the US had arranged the whole thing. But it was definitively unacceptable for the CIA to have a *proven* role and for the President to be implicated. This then was the challenge: to find a firm link between the rendition operations and the US government. Only then could the agency and its masters begin to be held accountable.

To discover the truth of rendition what I needed was the testimony of a real credible witness or some undeniable piece of physical evidence. As in all good detective stories, the clues were all out there. At this stage, I just hadn't spotted them.

One of those clues was a story published in *The News International*, a paper in Karachi, Pakistan, on 26 October 2001. The reporter, Masood Anwar, wrote a story headlined "Mystery man handed over to US troops in Karachi".[17] It said a "suspected foreigner", possibly a Yemeni student at the city's university named Jamil Qasim Saeed Mohammad, was picked up by a "Falcon aircraft owned by the US Air Force" which was parked "in a remote, dark and isolated area at the old terminal." Anwar's source told him the entire operation was so secretive that the people involved, including the US troops, were wearing masks. One US operative was also making a video film of the entire operation. The plane had arrived from Amman, Jordan, at 1 a.m. and it took off to return to Jordan less than two hours later.[18]

Anwar's story was describing a classic rendition operation. Qasim, an Al Qaeda suspect, was not being deported to his country of origin, nor to a country where he was being wanted for some particular crime. He was being rendered to Jordan for interrogation. Yet the most important thing in Anwar's scoop was in the second paragraph. The aircraft, he wrote, was "having registration numbers N-379 P". Here was the classic investigative fingerprint. He had found a clue that could allow someone to track the CIA's most secret operations for at least the next three years. But, although published on the internet, there were few who spotted his story. If I had known about the registration number I could have learned everything, from almost the beginning of when it started.

Five months later, in March 2002, a more prominent article was written with more clues, this time on the front page of the *Washington Post* and with a dateline from Jakarta, Indonesia.[19] Like the article in Pakistan's *The News*, the *Post* quoted only anonymous sources, but it spoke of a much wider system of rendition by the United States of terrorist suspects. Among those was an alleged Al Qaeda operative named Muhammad Saad Iqbal Madni who had been transferred from Jakarta on 11 January and sent to Cairo. The CIA had told Indonesian intelligence that Madni was an associate of the shoe-bomber Richard Reid. And then a formal request came from Egypt to transfer Madni — a Pakistani citizen — to Cairo on unspecified charges. Under pressure to do more to fight terrorism, Indonesia had reacted fast. On 9 January, Iqbal was arrested. The article reported that two days later, without a court hearing or lawyer, "he was hustled aboard an unmarked, US-registered Gulfstream V" and flown to Egypt.

In many ways this newspaper article had it all. The reporters, Rajiv Chandrasekaran and Peter Finn, provided one of the first potted histories of rendition, describing a series of transfers. They also pointed up its dilemmas.

The suspects had been taken to countries, including Egypt and Jordan, whose intelligence services have close ties to the CIA and where they can be subjected to interrogation tactics — including torture and threats to families — that are illegal in the United States, the sources said. In some cases, US intelligence agents remain closely involved in the interrogation, the sources added.

Yet, the article was, in a way, mistimed. Less than half a year since 9/11, America's mood was still raw and angry and there was little thought to what the consequences of a policy of rendition might be. The article, with its anonymous sources, also contained little proof. I heard later that the *Washington Post*'s reporters had, like Anwar, also learned the registration of the Gulfstream that took Iqbal from Indonesia — the same Gulfstream V with the registration N379P. For the moment, after this stunning reporting, the *Washington Post* dropped the ball and it never seemed to inquire further into this mysterious jet plane.[20] Others would soon pick up that story.

STOCKHOLM, SWEDEN
17 February 2004

The phone rang at the home of a reporter from the country's Channel 4 Television. He lifted the receiver.

Caller: — "Hello, my name is Mikael Lundstrom. I work with the Security police. I call because you have been in contact with US authorities, concerning a certain person."

Reporter: — "OK"

Caller: — "My question is then, do you work for a government authority?

Reporter: — Why do you ask?"

Caller: — "If I put it like this, we have been contacted by our US cooperation partners in this matter."[21]

Fifteen minutes earlier, the reporter had been on the telephone to a number in Virginia. He was talking to a woman called Mary Ellen McGuiness. She had the mistaken impression he was a Swedish official who was trying to charter the Gulfstream jet, registration N379P. "That was our aircraft. You came to the right office," said McGuiness. The jet was owned by a private company but it was not available, it seemed, for private hire. Was it necessary to go through the US government? asked the reporter. "We only lease through the US government, we are on a long term lease with them. Let me see if I find someone to call you back," she said. That was just before Lundstrom, from Sweden's internal security police, SAPO, had come on the phone.[22]

The reporter from TV4 was trying to get on the trail of the ghost plane, the Gulfstream V. Now, at last, he had confirmation of who really controlled it. It was none other than the United States government.

The story of the Swedish investigation began some three months earlier. Three journalists from TV4 — Fredrik Laurin, Joachim Dyfvermark and Sven Bergman — all worked together in an investigation team. Around the Christmas of 2003 they were looking for a new subject to investigate and turned their attention to the story of the two Egyptians, Ahmed Agiza and Mohammed al-Zery, who had been expelled from Sweden in December 2001 and sent to Cairo, as described in Chapter 1. Both men's lawyers were now complaining their clients had been tortured. Assurances of good treatment given to Sweden by Cairo were now the subject of fierce controversy. But was there more to the story? "I'll be honest, initially I wasn't so keen on it. It seemed like just another human rights story with not much new to find out," recalled Dyfvermark.[23] For now, no hint had appeared anywhere that the American government was involved in the transfer. As they planned their inquiries it was looking like another domestic piece of reporting, with possibly a foreign trip involved to Cairo. Maybe they might get some evidence about how those men had really been treated. Eventually, however, they got word from their sources that a private plane was involved that night. An official at the country's aviation authority provided its registration number, N379P. The 'N' at the start of the number meant it was American. But what was this plane? Who did it belong to? Was it simply a charter plane that was hired by the Swedish government?

An internet search revealed the article by Masood Anwar and the fact it had been used in a prisoner transfer before. Suspicions grew. A check with the website of the Federal Aviation Administration and with their officials showed the plane's owner was Premier Executive Transport Services, a company based at Washington Street, Dedham, Massachusetts. The address turned out to be the office of a lawyer, Dean Plakias, but who did he represent?

The TV4 team decided to launch an undercover investigation. They had to be careful. Under Swedish law it was an offence to impersonate a government officer. "We just said we were a different agency in Sweden that wanted to hire the same plane for a different mission," said Dyfvermark. "We didn't spell out that our 'agency' was a TV company." A reporter placed a call to Plakias who gave them a number for McGuiness in Virginia, saying she was the plane's operator. Now, with the call back from Swedish security police, confirming that McGuiness represented the "US authorities," the circle was complete — the plane was on official business.

The Swedish journalists went on to probe what happened with Agiza and al-Zery's case. They discovered how the US agents arrived in masks, how they stripped and bound the two Egyptians in a waiting room at the Stockholm airport, and they heard evidence of how the men were tortured back in Cairo. The first part of their programme — entitled "The Broken Promise" — was broadcast on 17 May 2004. That week, my first piece on rendition had been filed from a hotel in Basra, Iraq and was published in the *New Statesman* on exactly the same day as the broadcast. I had written of a whole network of terrorist prisoners. Some of them had gone to Guantánamo, Cuba but "hundreds more have been transferred from one Middle Eastern or Asian country to another — countries where the prisoners can be more easily interrogated." I wrote of how the CIA made use of a "fleet of luxury planes," including Gulfstreams, which, together with military transports, had moved prisoners around the world since September 11.[24] But Laurin and the team had gone one better and established the plane's registration

LONDON
July 2004

Back from Iraq at home in London, I was fired up by news of the Swedish discovery. I called up Laurin in Stockholm: if we could only track his plane across the world, perhaps we could trace the whole pattern of renditions. Proving US involvement in the transfer of prisoners would destroy Washington's "deniability" about renditions. But I knew time was running short. After the Swedish report, the CIA would be covering its tracks. Data would be erased or altered. Cover identities might be changed. Aviation officials and allies would be told to keep quiet. There was no time at all to be lost. What I desperately needed was a source, my own "Deep Throat," who might have access to the movements of the planes. But, in the meantime, I discovered there were many means to track an aeroplane. It was clear the security of the CIA's covert jets was compromised in one way after another.

The most obvious source of data was from plane enthusiasts. Across Europe, there were spotters who spent every bit of spare time sitting in the cold at the fence outside airports and noting every movement of every plane. And they would also take pictures of each new plane and publish them on the Internet. In some countries this might be called spying. But across the continent it was widely tolerated as a legitimate hobby, even outside military bases. The result was a series of sightings and snatched pictures of the CIA Gulfstream V.

Some Internet websites published by plane-spotters seemed to be remarkably well informed. They gave details of the plane's airport of origin and where it was flying to next. How could they obtain such information? Did they have inside sources at the airports? I had a suspicion they might be a little more devious. Then, as I picked up an aviation magazine, I noted the advertisements for scanning devices that intercepted something called "ACARS" standing for aircraft communication addressing and reporting system, a digital signal given out by a modern plane as it travels through the air. The information sent through this means would include the height of the airplane, its exact positions, messages to the airport and to the plane's owners, and, routinely, its flight plan. And all of this could be intercepted, perhaps illegally, by an amateur enthusiast with a handheld scanner and laptop computer.[25] The movements of any civilian airplane were thereby liable to be intercepted and tracked. In this way, I suspected, highly confidential data was ending up on the Internet. And it was all useful to me.

Another open door to aviation security came from the United States. Because of the Freedom of Information Act, the Federal Aviation Administration (FAA) was providing a live feed of electronic data to aviation databases that operated websites with titles like Flight Explorer. These websites provided a live picture of the exact location and intentions of almost every civilian aircraft in the United States. Based on the electronic flight plans and position reports filed automatically by an aircraft, these databases could even give you advance notification of the arrival at a particular airport of the plane you were seeking to track. And this data was accessible from anywhere. Osama bin Laden in his Afghan cave (if equipped with an Internet connection) could have watched the four flights of September 11 as they veered off their normal course and began heading towards the World Trade Centre. For my purposes, many of these websites also had a facility to search an archive of all previous flights, in one case back to November 2001. So it was possible to get a history of a particular plane's movements. There was one security feature. The owner of the plane could ask, for the sake of privacy, for its movements to be "blocked". Under a voluntary code, none of the aviation websites would then publish its data. Curiously, in the case of CIA planes, the Agency appeared remarkably slow in using this feature. Time and again, they seemed to ignore the most obvious ways of keeping their operations secure.

These three loopholes — the information from plane spotters, the flight plans published on the Internet, and the American flight-tracking software — all were to provide a breach of security that helped track the CIA's Gulfstream V, my original "Ghost Plane", and later many other CIA planes. Yet the data collected had its limits. The data from plane spotters was patchy and confined in the main to arrivals at European airports. And the data from the FAA, provided by those American websites, only showed flight plans of journeys that ended or began within US airspace. To solve the mystery, I needed to go much further and to track flights of the CIA planes around the Middle East and within Europe. Only then could I see evidence of the actual rendition flights.

Then I found my Deep Throat. There was a man who I'd known all along in the aviation industry. I wish I could tell you more about him but, for reasons that will become obvious, he preferred to remain in the shadows. He said the answer to my search would be at the offices of air traffic control centres. "They know everything. They track these planes everywhere," he said. "Could you get this data?" I asked. "Well, of course," he said. "Which plane do you want to track?" This man was to be a key to unlocking proof of the whole CIA rendition programme.

In early September, he came on the phone. "I've got your data," he said. "What's your fax number?" I gave him an unlisted number. And then from the whirring machine came a list of code-words:

9/1/02 KIAD — HECA

30/7/03 OAKB — UTTT

3/12/03 GMME — MUGM

And so it continued. I quickly searched on the Internet for what these codes meant. They were codes for airports designated by the International Civilian Aviation Organisation (ICAO). I began decoding the list. This source, I realised, had a key to the goldmine. And this information I was looking at was gold dust. One by one, the key destinations became clear:

KIAD — Washington, DC — the main base

MUGM — Guantánamo, Cuba

HECA — Cairo, the destination for many renditions

UTTT — Tashkent, Uzbekistan, one of President Bush's most controversial allies and the US's main base to the north of the Afghan war zone.

OAKB — Kabul, Afghanistan, where prisoners were sent both to and from

GMME — Rabat-Sale, Morocco, another destination for renditions

It was almost an atlas of the War on Terror, and this plane was clearly a key asset in that war. But could I prove the plane's involvement in renditions, and hence US complicity in those transfers? The journeys themselves seemed to match what we had heard of renditions.

Kabul — Cairo

Kabul — Jordan

Pakistan — Cairo

Kabul — Tashkent

So far, of course, it was difficult to match those flights to particular cases; most renditions had occurred in great secret. Apart from Maher Arar in Canada, almost no terror suspect who had been rendered had emerged from captivity to give their story and to provide exact dates for their transfer. I could, however, see a flight out to Cairo on 9 January 2002; that appeared to match the case of Muhammad Iqbal — the suspect who, as we've heard, was flown from Jakarta to

Cairo on 11 January "in a Gulfstream jet". The flight logs showed that, after its trip to Asia, the plane returned from Cairo to Washington on 15 January.[26]

There was one flight that stood out as odd. On 8 December, the plane flew from Washington, DC to Banjul, the capital of the Gambia in West Africa. This was important because it was here that three British residents, including a British citizen, had been arrested as Al Qaeda suspects when they arrived on Gambian soil a month earlier. Two had been flown on to Afghanistan and then Guantána-mo. The time of their departure from the Gambia matched the arrival of the Gulfstream on my flight logs. I later confirmed the flight carried onwards to Kabul via Baghdad.[27]

SWEDEN, STOCKHOLM ARCHIPELAGO
13 September 2004

I was on an island near Stockholm surrounded by lapping water. We'd arrived by a chugging motor boat from the car park nearby. The boat was tied up by Fredric Laurin's young children, dressed in orange life-jackets and perfectly competent in handling the boat. In a couple of months they would be skating to reach the car park. The school bus, provided by the government, was a little hovercraft. In a tall wooden house they built themselves, we sat down to a din-ner of smoked fish and blini. Present were the entire Swedish team, as well as Kjell Jönsson, the lawyer for Mohammed al-Zery.

I'd agreed to share my flight data with Laurin and the team and to pool our resources. By now, he'd found a witness to go on camera and describe the night at Stockholm airport when the Gulfstream V had visited. It was the policeman Paul Forell, who, as described in Chapter 1, had seen the men in masks that emerged. We sat down and watched the latest broadcast of their investiga-tions.

The next morning, Laurin took me to meet the team again at their office in central Stockholm and we shared some of the data we had collected. Detailed documents obtained by him from the FAA showed more of the corporate his-tory of the Gulfstream jet, which had now switched its registration number from N379P to N8068V. The jet had been purchased in November 1999. Most of its maintenance appeared to be handled not by Premier Executive, its official owners, but by a company in North Carolina called Aero Contractors. This company was based at Johnston County airport, a small regional base largely used by amateur pilots. Flight data from the plane showed that, after finish-ing its missions, the jet appeared to return regularly to this airport. Was Aero Contractors the real owner of the plane?

Back in London, I phoned Aero Contractors to ask them directly. I knew now from Laurin there was also another company involved called Stevens Express Leasing of Tennessee. Both appeared to operate the Gulfstream jet and its sister plane, a Boeing 737, also owned by Premier Executive. But which of the companies was carrying out the rendition flights? Answering the telephone at Aero Contractors was the friendly voice of its general manager, Jack M. He was friendly but dismissive and said his company was just "one of several companies that lease those airplanes as needed." Yes, he did missions for the US government but there were many private companies who serviced such contracts. Most of his work was straightforward contracts with the military, he said, adding: "There is no branch of government that we don't contract with.... We just fly them and crew them when we have them on lease." And no, none of their work had involved the transport of prisoners, he claimed. "We just have the misfortune of using planes that other people use for other things," he said, elliptically.[28]

It was time to publish what I knew. Under the headline "US accused of 'torture flights'" I revealed the existence of the flight logs and their link to a series of rendition cases. The article ran in the *Sunday Times* — on page 24 — but it made headlines around the world.[29] Soon, other publications were in touch, trying to get hold of copies of the flight logs I obtained. For now, though, I didn't want to publish the full details. Was it right to reveal to anyone — including potential terrorists — the exact movements of the CIA's jets? I wanted to investigate more before deciding. Moreover, if I published the exact details, would prisoners concoct accounts of their transfer in these jets? It was far better for now to obtain their accounts first and then compare them to the data that I had. For now I also made no mention of Aero Contractors; I still was not sure of its role. Was it a government contractor, or really an agency of the government? Curiously, within days of my article, the two planes were sold by Premier Executive to two different companies.[30] Were they trying to escape attention? There was another interesting development: among the calls was one from a prosecutor in Italy, Armando Spataro, who was investigating a potential CIA kidnapping in Milan. It was an investigation that was to lead to criminal charges against twenty-two alleged operatives.

Meanwhile, I was curious to find out more about the *other* jet owned — until my article was published — by Premier Executive. This was the Boeing 737 Business Jet that came into service in January 2002, three months after 9/11.[31] Was it too involved in any rendition cases? Was it also hired by the CIA? In January 2005, the fax machine started whirring again. Again my source had come up trumps, with more than 150 flights of this jet.[32]

Once again it was astonishing to see how little effort the CIA had made to protect its cover. Internet flight track services (such as fboweb.com) could still freely track the movements of this jet round the United States. And then on 5 February, I had an *advance alert* that the plane was coming to Britain and was about to take off from Washington, DC at 11.40pm GMT. By now I was working with the CBS *Sixty Minutes* programme to help make an item on renditions.[33] So I got on the phone to Graham Messick, the report's producer, in New York. "You won't believe this," I told him, "there's a plane heading right here." Messick scrambled into action and dispatched a cameraman to await the plane's arrival at Glasgow. He could have been a terrorist and scrambled a SAM 7 missile. But at any rate, we had obtained the first TV footage of a CIA plane in action.

The most exciting thing in the new flight logs of the Boeing 737 were details of a January 2004 flight from Macedonia to Afghanistan. A few weeks earlier, as mentioned above, the German citizen Khaled el-Masri had described his kidnapping from Skopje and transfer to a CIA-controlled Afghan jail.[34] Here, for the first time, was some proof of his account. Anxious to get some wider coverage, I had passed the flight logs on to *Newsweek* investigative reporters Mark Hosenball and John Barry. Both were one-time reporters for the *Sunday Times*. Their piece "Aboard Air CIA," which contained many new details, was published on 28 February.[35] Journalists from ZDF television in Germany also independently confirmed details of this flight.

By now it seemed crystal clear that all these planes were being used almost exclusively by the CIA. But even so the evidence was circumstantial. I had no direct documentary proof that these were CIA planes. And was this just a couple of planes or, as my sources were telling me, a whole fleet? As I worked away, the stakes were getting higher and higher. By now, as I describe in the next chapter, I had found sources within the CIA who, for the first time, were confirming details of the rendition programme on the record. The deniability was fading fast and the Agency was now on the back foot: passing the buck by telling reporters that all its operations were clearly ordered and authorised from the White House. Yet the President was announcing that *no prisoners* were being sent to countries that practised torture.[36] Yes, they all acknowledged, there had been some mistakes. But reports that the CIA was systematically out-sourcing torture were wildly exaggerated. It was clear I needed to find a lot more evidence.

CAMBERWELL, SOUTH LONDON
March 2005

Glued to my chair in my attic office, and fuelled by coffee and cigarettes, I was surrounded by pieces of paper and numbers. I'd now spent more than 100 hours staring at the computer screen and my eyes were getting sore. Confronted with the need to obtain more evidence, I had been vacuuming up huge amounts of data. I was looking now not just at the flight logs of two executive jets, but the global movements of hundreds of jets. More than 12,000 flight plans were now stored in my computer. I was trying to narrow things down — find the pattern that lurked beneath all this data and the identity of the CIA's planes that might be involved in rendition. When I started my investigation, I had almost no information but now I was almost swamped. I turned to a software programme called Analyst's Notebook, a tool used normally by the police or intelligence organisations to solve complex financial crimes or even murders. Its job was to find connections within exactly such a mass of data.

The first task I set the computer was to wrestle with the question of Maher Arar's deportation from JFK to Canada. I'd last seen Maher in a café in Ottawa on a snowy day in January when I had told him about the flight logs I had obtained on the CIA's main rendition jet, the Gulfstream V. Maher was feeling slightly down. He was naturally disappointed that I had no evidence of his flight into captivity. Finding details of his journey would corroborate his account of his bizarre deportation by luxury jet to Jordan, from where he was driven across the border to a prison cell in Damascus. So I turned to my computer to see if I could find the exact plane that took him from New York on 8 October 2002. Maher had alleged he was taken from an airport near New York that he believed, from a glance at the motorway signposts, was probably in New Jersey. He said he was then taken to Dulles, Washington DC and then onwards to Amman via refuelling stops in Portland, Maine and Rome. He said he could follow the flight's progress because there was a screen in the jet that showed the aircraft's position, the same as on most commercial flights. Using the link analysis software, I obtained the logs of all US flights with a destination to both main Rome airports, Leonardo Da Vinci and the smaller military-civilian Ciampino airport. I also looked at all flights into and out of Portland, Maine. And I looked at flights to Dulles from Teterboro, the New York business aviation airport, twelve miles from midtown Manhattan in New Jersey from where Maher's Gulfstream had most likely taken off.

These were all the flights listed from Teterboro (TEB) to Dulles (IAD):

N199BA	CL60	TEB	IAD	10/8/2002 5:45:40 am EST
N829MG	GLF3	TEB	IAD	10/8/2002 4:40:19 am EST
OPT611	BE20	TEB	IAD	10/7/2002 6:21:30 pm EST
BLR8023	CRJ2	TEB	IAD	10/7/2002 5:02:20 pm EST
	GLF5	TEB	IAD	10/7/2002 4:17:09 pm EST

Just two planes, N199BA and a Gulfstream III, N829MG had left Teterboro in those early hours. And only one of those could be seen as arriving later in Rome, Italy. These were the American-registered flights into Rome Ciampino (LIRA):

AEU821P	XXXX	EGKK	LIRA	10/8/2002 4:10:24 PM GMT
GOE903	XXXX	EGSS	LIRA	10/8/2002 2:47:58 PM
N829MG	GLF3	BGR	LIRA	10/8/2002 1:36:08 PM
RYR3004	XXXX	EGSS	LIRA	10/8/2002 10:12:30 AM
RYR3002	XXXX	EGSS	LIRA	10/8/2002 7:06:31 AM
GOE905	XXXX	EGSS	LIRA	10/8/2002 6:59:55 AM
RYR3006	XXXX	EGSS	LIRA	10/7/2002 4:47:49 PM

There was no match with any plane into Rome from Portland, Maine, but this plane, N829MG, had come in from Bangor, Maine. It seemed Arar had made a simple mistake. Sure, enough, when I looked at all the flights into Bangor (BGR) that morning, here was its journey from Washington Dulles (IAD). The last connection was established:

PDT3224	DH8B	PHL	BGR	10/8/2002 7:20:34 PM EST
N899DM	H25B	TEB	BGR	10/8/2002 6:47:46 AM EST
N829MG	GLF3	IAD	BGR	10/8/2002 6:46:43 AM EST
WIG8406	C208	PWM	BGR	10/8/2002 6:44:29 AM EST
TEL1660	C208	MHT	BGR	10/8/2002 6:40:33 AM EST

In other words, no other plane recorded in the public database had travelled on more than one of the three legs: Teterboro to Dulles, Dulles to Portland or Bangor, and finally Portland/Bangor into Rome. Furthermore the departure times of the flights also provided strong evidence that this plane was indeed Maher's plane, as they matched the times provided by Maher Arar himself.[37]

The mystery of Maher Arar's flight to captivity was solved. I found a picture of the plane, a Gulfstream III, on the website of its operator, Presidential Aviation. It showed an interior of brush brown leather seats, just as Maher had described. After I sent him the photograph of the plane and described its flight path, Maher was elated. He told me: "I think that's it. I think you've found the plane that took me." He added: "Finding this plane is going really to help me. It does remind me of this trip, which is painful, but it should make people understand that this is for real and everything happened the way I said. I hope people will now stop for a moment and think about the morality of this."[38]

So far I had looked at particular renditions and at two particular suspect planes. But I wanted now to cast the net much wider. Using the information I had so far, could I go back to first principles and attempt to identify the CIA's entire fleet of planes? Again, I turned to my detective software — and to a police technique used to narrow a wide field of criminal suspects. Imagine the CIA plane was like an individual, I thought. If I had a crime, I would create what the police would call a "profile" or "frame", a bit like a description on a "wanted" poster. It's what they would call the duck principle — "if it walks like a duck and quacks like a duck … then it is a duck." You can't look in a phone book under "bank robber": so you start searching for bank robbers by looking at people who do the type of things that bank robbers do, like buying face-masks or handguns. The crime to investigate in my case was rendition and torture and the suspect in the investigation was a CIA plane. How would that CIA plane quack? I drew up the following profile:

— It would have permission to land at US military bases across the world.[39]

— It would visit key destinations in the war on terror, like Guantánamo, Kabul, and Baghdad.

— It would visit "allied" countries where the CIA sent prisoners — like Egypt, Morocco, Jordan, Uzbekistan and Syria.

— It would visit the CIA's own bases, like Camp Peary, the CIA's training base in Virginia.

— It would visit Special Forces military bases and come to Washington, DC.

— It might meet with other planes that were known CIA planes, or were owned or operated by the same people.

Of course, making the computer understand this profile was easier said than done — and hours and hours passed by. But eventually, from the thousands of flights and hundreds of planes in my database, the software drew up a short list of "suspects" that matched at least four or five of these characteristics. Some planes — like the original Gulfstream V and Boeing 737 — matched every one of my factors. But there was another group of twenty or so "suspect" planes that matched almost every one.

Leaping from this list of suspects, for example, was, amazingly a plane that appeared to be in regular use by the Boston Red Sox baseball team. It carried the team's logo on its tail. I noticed the plane, registration N85VM, was in Cairo, Egypt, on exactly the night, 18 February 2003, when a rendition had allegedly taken place. Bingo! This was the kidnapping of the cleric Abu Omar from Milan — the same story that Armando Spataro, the Milan prosecutor, had phoned me about the previous October.[40] Later, Phillip H. Morse, the owner of the plane and minority owner of the Red Sox, confirmed that his plane was indeed regularly hired out to the CIA. "It's chartered a lot," Morse told the

Boston Globe from his winter home in Florida. "It just so happens one of our customers is the CIA. ... I was glad to have the business, actually. I hope it was all for a real good purpose."[41]

By its transparent ownership, the Boston Red Sox jet had all the characteristics of a genuinely private-owned jet — simply chartered on occasion by the government. But there were others with much more opaque ownership that might be wholly government-owned jets, operating under civilian guise. From my list of suspects, some company names stood out, among them: Rapid Air Transport, Stevens Express, Devon Holding and Leasing, Aviation Specialties and the Path Corporation.

By now, I was working with the *New York Times* and their investigation team. Their formidable reporter Margot Williams had just joined the paper from the *Washington Post*, where, in an article on 27 December 2005, she and her then colleague Julie Tate had used corporate records to establish that the directors of Premier Executive were most probably using fake names.

Each of the officers of Premier Executive is linked in public records to one of five post office box numbers in Arlington, Oakton, Chevy Chase and the District. A total of 325 names are registered to the five post office boxes, the article reported. An extensive database search of a sample of 44 of those names turned up none of the information that usually emerges in such a search: no previous addresses, no past or current telephone numbers, no business or corporate records. In addition, although most names were attached to dates of birth in the 1940s, '50s or '60s, all were given Social Security numbers between 1998 and 2003.[42]

Looking at our new "suspect" companies, Margot discovered a similar pattern of corporate officers who were using names like "Philip Quincannon" and "Erin Marie Cobb" that were probably fake and had social security numbers registered as recently as the 1990s — implying a freshly-created identity. Examining the corporate records of the aviation empire, we were stunned to see just how badly they were put together. The CIA had left behind a paper trail for us to follow. Each different company was connected to another. So, Premier Executive, which owned our original ghost plane Gulfstream V, shared Quincannon as a company officer with Crowell Aviation and Stevens Express. Devon Holdings had the same registered agent as Stevens. Cobb was an officer for both Devon and Stevens. The result was a web of connections that showed all the companies were part of the same group. It was all one fleet and it owned a total of twenty-six planes in all. The fleet included C130 Hercules cargo planes, and small, propeller-driven short take-off and landing planes like the Twin Otter N6161Q that, as we've heard, had been seen in Afghanistan. They were useful for landing at covert strips. The flagships of the fleet were clearly the Gulfstream V and the Boeing 737 business jet. The 737 was too large to land at Johnston County itself so was housed at nearby Kinston jetport, about an hour's drive away. In sum, we had identified the new Air America.

As I showed the results to one former CIA officer, he just laughed. The whole point, he said, of using these civilian companies was a "cut out". — a trail that would lead an investigator to a brass plate by a lawyer's office entrance, but no further. Yet here the "cut out" was not cutting out at all but leading us on: helping connect the web of companies together. Meanwhile, Scott Shane, a *New York Times* reporter based in Washington, had tracked down some former pilots from Aero Contractors. It turned out they were hired after responding to adverts for CIA pilots and had been interviewed down in Langley, Virginia. "We are the bus drivers in the War on Terror. I didn't use to check who was in the back," one former Aero Contractors pilot recalled.[43] It was final proof that Aero Contractors and its allied companies were not just working for the CIA. They were the CIA.

Here then was the story that emerged: back in the late 1970s, after the disbandment of the old Air America, a former chief pilot of the deceased CIA proprietary airline, Jim Rhyne, had been asked to found a new proprietary for the CIA. The hub of the new operation was a company they called Aero Contractors based at Johnston County. Professor Leary remembered Rhyne as "one of the great untold stories of heroic work for the US government." [44] Former colleagues recalled how Rhyne had an artificial limb after losing a leg from anti-aircraft fire in Laos as he kicked out supplies from an open cargo door. When President Carter prepared to order his ill-fated Iran hostage rescue attempt in 1980, it was Rhyne who was sent off in advance to test out the secret landing strip. He was killed one cloudless evening on 2 April 2001, while trying out a friend's Skybolt aerobatic biplane, at Johnston County airport. Rhyne had just recently fitted a new artificial leg. The accident report showed Rhyne had logged 25,000 hours as a pilot or nearly three whole years of his life in the air.

One former pilot said Rhyne had chosen the rural airfield because it was close by to Fort Bragg and many Special Force veterans. There was also no control tower that could be used to spy on the company's operations.

Aero Contractors Limited pilots had flown King Hussein, the former ruler of Jordan, on shopping trips around the United States. They flew both declared and undeclared missions for the drugs war in Colombia, helped supply the Contra rebels in Nicaragua, and had taken weapons and food to Jonas Savimbi's UNITA guerrillas in Angola. On some of these missions, a pilot told me, they would "fly the crease". That meant, to avoid being compromised if their plane was captured, instead of following a marked route they would simply follow a fold in their charts. They often flew with night-vision goggles, and when spotted by enemy planes would have to "get down among the reeds" — diving down to low altitudes. Some of their planes had glass bottoms through which surveillance photographs could be taken. During the Afghan war, Aero pilots helped supply mujahideen rebels with the shoulder-launched Stinger missiles they used against

Soviet helicopters and planes. "We flew out to Afghanistan to take in the missiles. Then, when the war was over, we flew out again to try and buy the missiles back up again," said one pilot.

As other former pilots told me, covert operations made for the best kind of exciting flying — coming down without electronic landing aids under cover of darkness, on the smallest of air strips, and being prepared to take on-coming fire. The launch of the rendition programme in the mid 1990s saw the airline's growth. Since 1990, Aero had acquired a Gulfstream III jet and it became a workhorse for, among other things, the transfer of prisoners. Adopting the cover of a VIP jet, the air crew now donned a fake uniform — a pair of blue trousers and a blue jacket. There were no neck ties, however — Rhyne hated formality. While abroad, the air crew would claim to represent an aviation company called "Stevens Express". It was the cover operator, designed to have no links back to Johnston County. Nor did the pilots ever use the term "rendition". We just called them "snatches". You would just notice someone not too happy was in the back but we didn't ask too many questions. The deal was that if the "client" came forward to talk to us, fine, but otherwise we would shut the cockpit door and stayed out of it."

Was Aero a company that worked for the CIA or was it actually a branch of the CIA? "Put it this way," replied a pilot, "I joined after replying to a CIA job advertisement, after having my background checked out by the CIA, going on the 'box' [the polygraph] at a hotel near the CIA headquarters at Langley, and then by going to the CIA headquarters to pick up my alias." As he signed for Aero, the pilot said he did however sign a form that declared "I was not working for the CIA and would never claim to be a CIA operative." The CIA kept all copies of the forms. But it was all a fiction. "We all knew who we were working for. How else could I walk into a state driving license office and they would usher you upstairs and say here you are Mr X and here is your new license; or get a credit card in this new name; or get a brand new pilot's license in a fake name."[45]

After 9/11 Aero's operations expanded rapidly as it became the lynchpin of rendition operations. Aero's staff grew from forty-eight to seventy-nine during 2001-4, according to *Dun and Bradstreet*,[46] and federal records showed that ten new planes were purchased in the same period. The Gulfstream III had already been sold off and the company had bought a top-of-the range Gulfstream V, followed, in 2002, by the Boeing 737 business jet. "All change is good," said one pilot, "we got to fly something new."[47] This rapid expansion did not go without hitches — in the electronic age, it was more difficult for a covert airline to cover its tracks. In 2003, one of the CIA's new planes, a Hercules C130 operated by Tepper Aviation, the same airline that had supplied UNITA forces in Angola, was intercepted over Austrian airspace by fighter jets after filing a suspicious "civilian" flight plan from the Frankfurt US air base to Azerbaijan. The US Embassy assured the Austrian authorities the plane had no connection with the US government even though corporate records now showed us it was owned by the CIA.[48]

I had discovered too that the "cover" for the CIA's front companies was paper thin, and was able to obtain thousands more flight logs showing the detail of the CIA's flights around the world. The flight logs had not been obtained from any super-secret or classified sources. They were widely available in the airline industry, and the CIA had made little effort to cover its tracks. "Whatever you can find out as journalists, be assured there are other more hostile governments who have found it out already," one former CIA officer told me.[49] The data exposed secret operations by the CIA across the world — even the mysterious presence of planes used by the CIA in Venezuela at the same time as activists there were alleging the CIA was plotting a coup.[50] Most importantly it showed up some of the secret side of the War on Terror. Concealed behind the movement of innocent-looking civilian jets, the flight data showed the agency was working with some of the most repressive countries of the world. But were disclosures justified? Was it right to reveal such secrets?

When we first revealed the existence of this new Air America, many argued that we were shamefully revealing national secrets, thereby putting the lives of undercover agents in danger. "Let's Dare Call it Treason," said Phil Brennan, a former staffer on the House Republican Policy Committee, headlining an article critical of us on NewsMax.com.[51] Another critic, Frederick Turner, a professor at the University of Texas at Dallas, said that our article had significantly increased the risk to the life of a friend of his who was being dispatched abroad on a mission for US intelligence. Writing for *Tech Central Station*, he said: "They should know that, if a certain civilian plane comes down over an unnamed Middle Eastern country, and all the US personnel aboard are killed, there is one compatriot who will regard them as murderers."[52] Another blog asked simply: "Shane, Grey and Williams: Are They Human?"[53]

The reaction was understandable, if overblown. Contacted by the *New York Times* beforehand, the CIA had raised no objection to the publication of our article.[54] As one former CIA operative told me afterwards: "This wasn't really some grand secret, hardly a great journalistic coup; you can't really hide a fleet of airplanes." But, for us, it had only been by uncovering the tentacles of the CIA's air operations that I had been able to prove the involvement of the US government in these otherwise secret operations — and prove that rendition had become a key part of the War on Terror. In essence the CIA's air-fleet had provided the link connecting all the different nodes of this new global prison network. As we saw in the cases of Maher Arar and Khaled el-Masri, all described above, it was the confirmed presence of one of the CIA jet planes from North Carolina and other bases that proved what otherwise might have seemed the untrustworthy allegations of an alleged terrorist. The same was true of claims by Binyam Mohamed of his rendition and torture in Morocco and Afghanistan. In his statement at Guantánamo, Binyam had given some precise details that matched the flight data I had collected. This confirmed, as he claimed, that he was flown from Pakistan to Morocco by the CIA on 21 July 2002, and that precisely eighteen months later, 21 January 2004, he was flown on again to a CIA prison in Afghanistan.[55]

In the next year, more and more cases emerged and I matched more than fifteen different flight logs to the accounts of rendition flights given by prisoners. With the flight data and personal testimony, the systematic rendition of prisoners by the US to destinations around the world was increasingly case proven. What remained was to prove the real purpose of these transfers. Who ordered the programme and why? And how could this potentially damaging outsourcing of intelligence-gathering really serve any useful purpose? These were the questions I turned my attention to next.

6

COVERT ACTION
THE SECRET WAR AGAINST AL QAEDA

Flightlog

Registration: **Classified**;
Type: **Predator un-manned spyplane**;
Operator: **United States government** (Central Intelligence Agency).
Date: **7 September 2000**

Flight plan:
████████, Uzbekistan
Kandahar, Afghanistan
████████, Uzbekistan

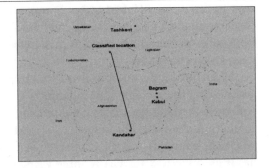

WASHINGTON
7 September 2000

It was 2 a.m. when Michael Sheehan took a call in the kitchen of his home near Georgetown, Washington, DC. On the line was Richard C. Clarke, the chief of counter-terrorism at the White House. He was sounding excited for a change. But this was special. He was calling from the CIA at Langley and had been there since midnight. "Want to come out and take a look?" he said. Sheehan got dressed and climbed into his car.[1]

A former Green Beret colonel, Sheehan had been working on combating terrorists for years, from the time he led a uniformed counter-terrorist squad in El Salvador; and later in the White House.[2] After retiring from the Army, he had

now risen to be the State Department's counter-terrorism coordinator, responsible for persuading or sometimes bludgeoning other countries into taking the
issue seriously. It could be a frustrating role. He knew that diplomacy could go
only so far to deal with Al Qaeda. He also hated the sort of bureaucratic turf-war
that seemed to epitomise Washington. What he hankered for was not a bureaucratic offensive but for someone to take risks and some real action — political
action against regimes whose policies were failing to disrupt Al Qaeda, or military action if necessary — to take out Osama bin Laden and his camps in Afghanistan. But the latter meant galvanising the leadership of the Department of
Defense. And, though a former soldier, that wasn't his job.[3]

Within an hour, Clarke and Sheehan joined Cofer Black, the CIA counter-
terrorism chief, in the Global Response Centre at the CIA's headquarters in the
woods of Langley. These three knew each other well — they were part of an inner
circle that had spent hours pondering how to deal with Al Qaeda. While now
dark in the eastern United States, it was broad daylight in Afghanistan. They
clustered round a television screen and watched a picture that had been beamed
from half-way round the world. A man in flowing white robes was striding into
view: Osama bin Laden.

The picture of the six-foot-five-inch bin Laden towering above his acolytes
and moving from building to building was being shot from 15,000 feet by an
American Predator spy-plane. It was circling above Tarnak Farm near Kandahar,
southern Afghanistan, the hideout to where the CIA had successfully tracked the
Al Qaeda leader.[4] It was the culmination of a secret war against Al Qaeda that
has been underway for nearly three years. But ultimately it was unsuccessful.
Clinton refused to order Special Forces to go in and arrest bin Laden; the risks
seemed too high and intelligence too uncertain. And soon the one Predator in
operation crashed on take-off on an ice-bound airport in Uzbekistan. The CIA
and Department of Defense argued over funding another three million dollars
for a replacement drone,[5] then the weather turned bad. Until 11 September, the
surveillance operation was suspended. The delays and excuses had maddened
Sheehan. "Don't tell me the damn thing doesn't work. You just don't want to do
it," he remembered shouting.[6]

For those who had tracked Osama bin Laden and what later came to be called
Al Qaeda, the failure of the Predator programme was just the latest chapter of
a frustrating story of emerging danger coupled with political failure to take the
risky decisions to confront that emerging threat.

The Jeremiahs

Like modern day Jeremiahs crying in the wilderness, a small band of highly-
placed insiders had by the mid-1990s come to regard bin Laden as one of the

biggest global threats to the United States. This group included Clarke, Shee-han, and a maverick FBI special agent named John O'Neill,[7] who was later killed in the World Trade Centre on 9/11. In the mid-1990s, along with CIA colleagues, all had at one time been part of a White House committee, Clarke's Counter-terrorism Security Group (CSG) that struggled to create a workable strategy to defeat Al Qaeda. These men, who regularly warned of a potential threat of mass casualties in the United States, often felt themselves a belea-guered minority. While senior leaders, like President Clinton and his National Security Advisers, Anthony Lake and then Sandy Berger, provided lip service to the importance of defeating Al Qaeda, to this group they seemed unwilling to take many of the risky political decisions that would have countered threats like bin Laden effectively.

It is by looking through the prism of men like these — reviewing the tribula-tions of officials who tried and failed to reshape US anti-terrorism strategy in the run-up to 9/11 — that the policy of rendition can be understood, if not accepted. After a series of interviews with many senior officials involved, it is clear that rendition was never their weapon of first choice to defeat Osama bin Laden. It emerged as a compromise solution because the CIA's ultimate political masters were unwilling to take the bolder decisions required to declare an effective war on Al Qaeda. It was their frustrations that drove them to create a programme that was, they considered, one of the least bad ways of disrupting both Al Qaeda and the wider network of Islamic militants.

For Richard Clarke, who headed the CSG for President Clinton's National Security Council (working from the same suite of offices used by Colonel Oliver North in the late 1980s), the threat of Islamic militancy had already become a top priority by late 1994 — four years before bin Laden made his public declaration of *jihad* against the United States.

Clarke was convinced by then that the network which later was called Al Qae-da presented a new kind of trans-national threat that had to be dealt with by new methods. The old law enforcement approach — launching a federal investigation only with "probable cause" — needed to be reinforced by direct action against the terrorists who have shown themselves capable of striking across the world, but yet co-ordinate their operations and train themselves within lawless, inac-cessible states.[8] An array of special operations was eventually developed to target bin Laden in his Afghan hideouts. The CIA deployed the Jawbreaker teams into northern Afghanistan to establish listening posts in opposition Northern Alli-ance territory. A desert airfield was also surveyed close to the ruling Taliban's headquarters in Kandahar, southern Afghanistan.[9]

But, despite the formidable technology available, capturing bin Laden and destroying the terrorist camps would ultimately require the deployment of US ground forces. After the Somalia debacle, in which US troops in 1993 became embroiled in deadly fighting after being deployed initially to help famine relief in a lawless state, there was little or no political will, either from the Clinton White House or its Republican opponents, to risk US lives.[10] Jack Devine, who retired in 1998 after serving as CIA station chief in London, had been a director of clandestine operations in the early 1990s. He said his former department became wary of taking risks when considering covert action, which he now considered a "dying art". "With hindsight," he told me, "even in the early 1990s, when bin Laden was in Sudan and was beginning to emerge as an identified threat to America and the West, the use of covert action might have been effective in neutralising his activities."[11]

Michael Sheehan, at the State Department, as well as supporting Clarke's call for direct US-led covert actions, had also argued for much firmer diplomatic pressure. He believed the administration was far too weak with both Pakistan and Saudi Arabia, both of whom, he felt, were propping up Afghanistan's Taliban regime and allowing many Al Qaeda operatives to move around unchecked. Yet, even in this, his demands for action were rebuffed.

So, confronted with the large threat they perceived and with few weapons in their armoury, Clarke and the CIA devised a way of attacking Al Qaeda that would at least cause some disruption to the network, even if it left their main bases untouched. Instead of direct action, a policy of indirect action was created: a policy we now know as "extraordinary rendition". Sandy Berger, Clinton's National Security Adviser, signed off on the idea. He called it a "new art form."[12] But to those involved at the CIA, it was an art they had known of for some time, albeit in different form.

MEDITERRANEAN SEA, OFF LARNACA, CYPRUS
13 September 1987, aboard the yacht Skunk Kilo

They heard the speedboat before they saw it. Below deck on the 81-foot executive yacht were members of an armed FBI hostage response team. They had been waiting too long for their suspect. Visibility was poor and their radio connections with the CIA's case officers, monitoring events from a hotel onshore, were constantly breaking up. The sound of the motor grew louder and louder as the vessel approached. Below, the FBI agents clenched like a spring. The boat carrying Fawaz Yuniz, a wanted terrorist, moored alongside and he clambered onto deck. Then the FBI pounced and the trap swung shut. CIA officers would recall how Fawaz suffered fractured wrists from the force with which he was cuffed.[13]

This was the successful Operation Goldenrod, one of the first publicised examples of a rendition organised by the CIA to capture an Islamic terrorist. Yuniz had been lured to Larnaca from his home in Beirut to face criminal charges for his role in a hijacking two years earlier. Four days later, after a transfer to the aircraft carrier *USS Saratoga*, Yuniz was on a plane for Washington, where he later received a thirty-year sentence.[14]

So, the concept of rendition was not something invented after the events of 9/11 or in the struggle against bin Laden. Howard Safir, former head of the US Marshal's Service, said federal agents started using the terms "rendition" or "extraordinary renditions" back in the 1970s.[15] Some marshals used to refer jokingly to renditions as "informal renditions" or even "Mexican extraditions."[16] Still, the idea was always to bring a fugitive back to the US to face justice; it was never intended to ship them off to some foreign dungeon. Safir said they once even planned to render, in effect kidnap, the billionaire trader Marc Rich, who in 1983 had fled the US for Switzerland to escape charges of evading some $48 million in tax. Discussing the case with Larry King on CNN after Rich was pardoned by Clinton in January 2001, Safir said the operation was aborted when the Swiss warned the US agents they would be arrested if they tried anything.

"Did you ever come close, Howard, to, as they say, nabbing him," asked King, "for want of better term, kidnapping him?"

"Well, we call them extraordinary renditions," replied Safir to laughter.

"That is a great term", said King.[17]

It was under President Reagan in the 1980s, with operations like Goldenrod, that renditions became an acknowledged weapon against terrorists.[18] The architect of the Mediterranean snatch was Duane Clarridge, who had founded the CIA's Counter-Terrorist Centre (CTC) in 1986. It had a specific mission of using covert action. In June 1988, the Justice Department issued a legal opinion that, according to William Webster, then CIA director, speaking a year later, was aimed at permitting the CIA or FBI to seize terrorists in lawless countries like Lebanon. It finally placed "rendition" into the official lexicon as a term for the act of capturing and bringing back to the US a criminal suspect.[19]

Even in those Cold War days, the rules for renditions seemed very tight. The CIA's involvement in such operations was justified by Executive Order 12333 issued on 4 December 1981 which authorised the CIA to "render any other assistance and cooperation to law enforcement authorities not precluded by applicable law."[20] But while the CIA might lure a suspect into a trap, they could not actually arrest him. The Justice Department, which commands the FBI, insisted on a clean capture. Said Clarridge: "This meant that Yuniz had to be apprehended by the FBI in international waters or airspace, remain in constant custody of the feds, and remain clear of the turf of any sovereign nation — for the entire duration of his four-thousand-mile journey to the United States."[21]

I bumped into Clarridge, then a sprightly 72-year-old, at a breakfast table in Baghdad in 2004. Though long-retired, he had lost none of his enthusiasm for covert action. He was scheming a new private plan to capture a wanted terrorist who was living freely in a Middle Eastern capital (I had better not say where: he might still just do it!). Yet, as he told me, some of his big successes were not actually through covert means. Clarridge's CTC effectively destroyed the Abu Nidal terror network not through clandestine action but via public diplomacy: the publication and global distribution of intelligence about Nidal's network that galvanised countries worldwide to arrest, expel or otherwise disrupt the terrorist leader's operatives and financial assets.[22] As a case study in effective anti-terrorism, Clarridge thereby showed that covert action was not the only weapon in the agency's armoury.

The law on the sort of renditions like Clarridge's snatch of Fawaz Yuniz, was well established. One of those who tracked it down was Barbara Olshansky, a lawyer at the Centre for Constitutional Rights in New York, who also cited a detailed joint study on the case law by the New York City Bar Association and NYU law school.[23]

As she explained, the US courts themselves had never been too concerned about the exact details of foreign arrest operations. The 1990 capture of General Manuel Noriega, for example, had been a high profile example of what she called old-style rendition. Noriega, then president of Panama, was indicted in 1988 by the Drug Enforcement Agency as a cocaine smuggler but was not extradited to the US through normal channels. Instead, US Marines in 1989 invaded the country and captured the Panamanian leader and brought him home to be successfully convicted in Miami.

The law that allowed such snatches, she said, was both old and clear cut. It dated back to the 1880s when federal courts held they had no interest in the *means* by which a suspect was arrested and brought back into US jurisdiction. This gave federal agents carte-blanche to employ special methods to capture wanted criminals or terrorists —in short, to bypass local laws and the normal process of extradition.

The Supreme Court's *Ker v. Illinois* of 6 December 1886, discussed the case of a Frederick Ker who was convicted in Cook County, Illinois, of larceny after being "kidnapped and brought to this country against his will." Bypassing an extradition procedure, Ker had been seized in Lima, Peru, by a federal agent and put aboard a US ship, the *Essex*, before being transferred by various ships by way of Sydney, Australia, and San Francisco, California, and then back to Cook County. The Supreme Court judged his manner of arriving before the court was of no importance to a US court.[24]

In 1952, the Court had again re-affirmed what had then become known as the "Ker doctrine" when it said the federal Kidnapping Act was of no help to a murderer Shirley Collins who wanted his conviction in Michigan quashed because, while living in Chicago in the state of Illinois, officers from Michigan came and "forcibly seized, handcuffed, blackjacked and took him to Michigan." There was "nothing in the Constitution that requires a court to permit a guilty person rightfully convicted to escape justice because he was brought to trial against his will."[25] Again in 1992, the court had approved the prosecution of a Mexican, Dr

Alvarez-Machain, who was brought to the US by abduction rather than the extradition treaty between the US and Mexico. He was accused of complicity in the slow torture and then murder in 1985 of a US Drugs Enforcement Agency agent. The court argued that, as a matter of law, it was blind to his kidnap (though he was later acquitted by a lower court on the facts of the actual charges).

Though effectively sanctioning kidnap, all these cases had involved the return of suspects into US jurisdiction, to face a normal trial. "Previously," said Olshansky, "the US would always use any measure to get an individual back to be tried in front of a court here. The end notion would be that they would be tried in a court of law." But when the CIA started covertly targetting Al Qaeda in the mid-1990s, the approach was different. This was now what the NYU study defined as "extraordinary rendition" — the transfer of the suspect not back to the US but to a third country, usually the suspect's native home, for incarceration and imprisonment there. Said Olshansky: "Now, this entire idea of rendition was turned on its head. We now had extraordinary rendition, which meant the US was capturing people and sending them to countries for interrogation under torture: rendering people for the purpose of extracting information. There was no planned justice at the end."[26]

Those involved at the CIA would dispute Olshansky's definition of the purpose of these new renditions. They would insist that, at least at the outset, the purpose was not to torture, even if it was a certain outcome. But all agreed it was a new approach. So what prompted the change?

In the mid-1990s, when what became the rendition programme was formulated, it was a hybrid strategy. The focus would remain on rendering suspects back to US courts, in the traditional way, but it also had a new component — the idea of sending a suspected terrorist to a third country to be imprisoned. The policy was set out in President Clinton's Presidential Decision Directive, PDD-39 of 21 June 1995. It stated that: "When terrorists wanted for violation of US law are at large overseas, their return for prosecution shall be a matter of the highest priority and shall be a continuing central issue in bilateral relations with any state that harbors or assists them."[27]

This could be accomplished by rendition: "*Return of suspects by force may be effected without the cooperation of the host government*, consistent with the procedures outlined in NSD-77, which shall remain in effect." NSD-77 was a previous directive issued in 1982 by President George H.W. Bush that remained classified. There was now an additional component, which also stayed classified. It was summarised later in a staff report of the 9/11 commission: "If extradition procedures were unavailable or put aside, the United States could seek the local country's assistance in a rendition, secretly putting the fugitive in a plane back to America *or some third country* for trial."[28] Here then was the beginning of "extraordinary rendition" as we have come to know it.

The timing of Clinton's 21 June orders was no accident. Two months before, a bomber had struck in Oklahoma City and killed 168 people. Despite early fears, there was no connection with Islamic militants. But the incident had served as a wake-up call. A wider strategy was drawn up to combat these threats —in particular from Sunni Arab extremists, of which Osama bin Laden at this time was just one major name. Still in Sudan (he moved to Afghanistan in May 1996), bin Laden was already the subject of a special CIA tracking unit. But he was then seen as just one component of a much wider threat, part of a network of Sunni radicals that were a legacy of the war in Afghanistan war against the Soviets. Many of these militants had been part of the Saudi-backed force of foreign fighters that had fought alongside the US-backed Afghan mujahideen. Some had remained in Afghanistan, others had travelled to the Balkans to join the Bosnia war, and others had returned to Egypt, which was now an epicentre of terrorist violence, much of which was targetting foreign tourists. Some had even reached the United States and had been responsible for the 26 February 1993 attack on the World Trade Centre.[29] Rendition as a tool was directed at this wider threat, not simply against bin Laden. In 1995, bin Laden was widely regarded as an important terrorist financier, but not yet as a leader of this whole network.

The problem for the CIA in confronting this group was that while the threat appeared to be large, much of the information collected was based on intelligence material, much of it from foreign governments or from classified intercept systems, that would be difficult to use as evidence in a normal criminal trial. So the possibilities for a traditional rendition back to a US court were strictly limited. None in the Clinton administration would have contemplated changing the law to allow the detention of these militants based only on this kind of intelligence material.

In many ways what was now contemplated was a failure of imagination. Past experience, for example Clarridge's successful campaign by the CIA versus Abu Nidal in the late 1980s, had shown that effective public diplomacy, including the publication of intelligence, could be at least as effective as covert action in persuading governments worldwide to confront a terrorist threat. And yet, while launching their new covert actions, US officials still made scant public references to either Osama bin Laden or to Al Qaeda (the latter did not receive a single reference in public print before the August 1998 African Embassy bombings). Those like Dick Clarke, who believed in the threat, had failed to convince their own government.

At the time of the growth of the militant network which came to be labelled "Al Qaeda", the CIA's clandestine branch was also at a historic low point. Rundown after the Cold War through incessant budget cuts, desperately short of Arab linguists and specialists, and ordered by Clinton to perform a "wash" of unpalatable sources who might be tainted with involvement in criminal acts, the Agency was not well placed to gather much direct (and therefore publishable) intelligence on Al Qaeda nor to carry out its own large-scale interrogations of terror suspects.

Introduced by John Deutch, CIA director from May 1995 to December 1996, the new rules prevented the CIA from hiring people with a dubious background without senior-level permission. It was hard to conceive of anyone inside a terrorist group that could possibly meet this test. The result was what CIA operatives refer to as the infamous "scrub" of 1995. From top to bottom, the CIA reviewed its list of informers and part-time agents, eliminating swathes of human intelligence sources. "We basically scrubbed assets, fired anybody who had ever said an unkind word to anybody," then-Congressman Porter Goss told me in 2001. "No smart career officer was going to send in a little cable to headquarters saying 'I've got this really great guy, now he killed his wife and he murdered his children, but he knows what the [X group] are doing.' That just isn't going to happen."[30] For Jim Woolsey, Deutch's predecessor, the collapse of basic spying inside Islamic groups at that time because of such funding cuts set the scene for 9/11. "Human intelligence is a long-term operation. It's like growing orchids, it takes a long time," he told me.[31] Increasingly, others said, the agency was relying on intelligence on terrorism from "liaison services": essentially the secret police of the same Middle East governments whose repressive policies had helped to spawn that terrorism. According to insiders, one fifth of the agency's operational spending was cut in real terms during the 1990s, with covert intelligence stations removed from many Third World countries, including some in east Africa, where Al Qaeda was active.[32] According to Senator Richard Shelby, former Chairman of the Senate Intelligence Committee, these cuts were substantial. "I can tell you, after 1990, there were huge cuts in the intelligence budget, because a lot of people thought, 'Gosh, we've won the cold war, we don't have any problems in the world'. Such naive thinking." The agency's lowest point came in 1995 when only twenty-five trainees became officers.[33]

It was at this point of weakness that the rendition policy was developed. In essence, the US government chose to outsource its handling of terrorists because neither Clinton nor his Republican opponents was prepared to establish a proper legal framework for the US to capture, interrogate and imprison terrorists itself; nor to take the more direct military or diplomatic action required to eliminate the leadership of Al Qaeda in Afghanistan; nor to confront countries like Saudi Arabia or Pakistan whose policies helped to encourage the growth of terrorism; nor to strengthen adequately the CIA's own key capabilities.

As Roger Cressey, Richard Clarke's deputy at the National Security Council, told me:

In the pre-9/11 world, rendition was viewed as one of the most aggressive and effective options available to the US policy maker — at a time when no consensus existed on making terrorism a priority at the expense of other issues on the foreign policy agenda. Rendition has a limited utility but, at that time, it was one of the few options available to be proactive.

One of the key men who confronted those dilemmas was Michael Scheuer, then head of the CIA's bin Laden unit, which came to be called the "Alec" station, named after his young son. Like Clarke, Scheuer had often found his battle against bin Laden to be a lonely one. "One of the things that I think is probably not very well appreciated is that even within the Agency, people thought we were nuts" he told me.[34] It was Scheuer who essentially founded the new rendition programme, even if at the agency they never used the label "extraordinary" for them.[35] Scheuer later retired from the agency at the end of 2004 and I interviewed him shortly afterwards at his home in Falls Church, Virginia. He summed up to me how rendition was not some policy of first choice, but a response to the limited options made available by the policy-makers.

He explained:

The practice of capturing people and taking them to third countries arose because the Executive Branch assigned to us the task of dismantling and disrupting and detaining terrorist cells and terrorist individuals. And basically, when CIA came back and said to the policymaker, "where do you want to take them," the answer was — "that's your job". And so we developed this system of assisting countries who want individuals who have either been charged with or convicted of crimes to capture them overseas and bring them back to the particular country where they are wanted by the legal system.[36]

But, said Scheuer, it should never been a policy pursued in isolation. The programme began with transfers to Egypt.

UNITED STATES EMBASSY, GARDEN CITY, CAIRO
Summer 1995

It was the kind of regular meeting that filled the Ambassador's diary; but for this one he had to leave his well-appointed office, a room that by its architecture was judged "open to penetration". Edward Walker Jr walked down to the Embassy's secure area, a place regularly swept for bugs and with thick walls to prevent electronic interception. Waiting for him was the CIA's chief of station in Cairo who had an unusual scheme to outline.[37]

Since his arrival a year earlier, Egypt had been rocked by terrorism. And in the previous five years, there had been 43 terrorist attacks, killing 38 people and injuring 147. In the worst of these, 11 Israeli tourists had been killed, and 19 wounded, when their bus was attacked near Cairo in February 1990. The majority of attacks were carried out by the Islamist militant group, Gama'a al-Islamiyya, and aimed at foreign tourists. Spanish, Austrian, British, and Japanese visitors were targetted in almost monthly attacks throughout 1993-4.[38] In this violent climate, Walker had been ordered to assist the Egyptians in every way.

Much of the work was done by the FBI but their main effort was to gather evidence that could be used in a US court and that, recalled Walker, was "not an efficient way of fighting terrorism".

For many months, the CIA had been working hard on additional covert help to the Egyptians. CIA stations across Europe and Scheuer's OBL unit at Langley were working together. They were tracing the support network that supplied money and recruits to the Egyptian militants and were organising their propaganda. The CIA intercepted telephone calls and opened mail, said Walker, and suspects were identified both in Egypt itself but also in mosques centred in several European capitals — including Milan, Oslo and London. "We had a fairly-effective effort to help them uncover these problems," he said.

Now, the CIA chief was outlining to Walker a novel approach, sanctioned in Washington; the US would actively seek out and render Egypt's most wanted prisoners back to Cairo. Apart from more traditional assistance, the US was now developing "this question of rendition with the Egyptians where we would bring people who were suspects for further interrogation in Egypt and we did so."

Walker recalled he approved completely of what was planned. "I thought it was a good thing. Because I could see very well how limited we were in our ability to deal with these guys through normal police channels. I was convinced that in virtually all of these cases they were bad guys, and they were set on causing harm. And you know, it's not a perfect world."[39]

Back at Langley, Michael Scheuer and others had devised the rendition programme because it suited both countries' interests. "What was clever was that some of the senior people in Al Qaeda were Egyptian," Scheuer said. "It served American purposes to get these people arrested, and Egyptian purposes to get these people back, where they could be interrogated."[40] According to Scheuer, the programme began with a secret agreement in 1995 with the government of Egypt. The US offered its resources, including a small fleet of planes, to track down and capture terrorists and bring them back to Cairo.

Scheuer made clear that this new policy was signed off at all levels, ultimately by the White House. Clinton had just signed the directive, described above, instructing CIA to carry out renditions if they would assist US national security.[41] And each operation was approved by lawyers. Said Scheuer: "There is a large legal department within the Central Intelligence Agency, and there is a section of the Department of Justice that is involved in legal interpretations for intelligence work, and there is a team of lawyers at the National Security Council and on all of these things those lawyers are involved in one way or another and have signed off on the procedure. The idea that somehow this is a rogue idea that someone has dreamed up is just absurd."[42]

Within the CIA, the authority for each operation, said Scheuer, had to come from the director of central intelligence, then George Tenet, or his assistant director. "So basically the number one and two men in the intelligence community are the ones who sign off," he said.[43] It was a tight circle of people who knew about the programme, however; Sheehan, at the State Department, was not informed, even if he later supported its importance.

Back in Cairo, the negotiations with the Egyptians were handled by Walker's chief of station. "[The negotiation] was done by the Agency," he said. "I was involved only in that I was Ambassador. I had to approve of this kind of activity. But this was also approved in Washington." President Clinton, he said, had to sign a "finding", the official term for an executive order to the CIA. "It was new to me. It seemed to be new to the sort of Agency people who arranged it. It was a sort of outgrowth of efforts that they had been making to capture people on the ground."

Like Scheuer, Walker stressed that all operations were approved at a high level, including, in general terms, by congressional oversight committees. And there were certain requirements: "We had to have an assurance from the Egyptian security authorities that people would be re-tried, and they'd have a fair trial, and they wouldn't be tortured.[44]

To negotiate those "assurances" the CIA dealt principally in Egypt through Omar Suleiman, chief of Egyptian general intelligence (EGIS) since 1993. It was he who arranged their meetings with the Egyptian interior ministry, said Walker. Suleiman, who understood English well, was an urbane and sophisticated man. Others told me that for years Suleiman was America's chief interlocutor with the Egyptian regime — the main channel to President Mubarak himself, even on matters far removed from intelligence and security. "He was a very bright guy, very realistic," said Walker. "And he was often at odds with the way the interior ministry was dealing with things. He understood the consequences of some of the negative things that the Egyptians engaged in, of torture and so on. But he was not squeamish, by the way." Formally, the programme was required to establish that each of the rendition targets was wanted in Egypt on a criminal charge. So this required the cooperation of the Ministry of Interior and its then minister, Hassan El-Alfi.[45]

Though Walker oversaw the CIA's secret operations in Egypt, he was also responsible for the embassy's reporting on human rights. The State Department was consistently describing Egypt's severe torture methods and "it wasn't a question of mincing words. ... I think the human rights reports were correct." But, as Ambassador, he could not inform his diplomats working on human rights what the CIA was up to. There was a kind of Chinese wall to keep the CIA's secrets. "The walls were huge," said Walker "and they only come together at the ambassador level... [The diplomats working on human rights] might have been a little upset if they knew what was going on." Not everything was inconsistent, though. The CIA was funding one programme to train Egyptian special operations forces in counter-terrorism arrests. The trouble was "too many people that died while fleeing." It was more of a hit squad than arrest squad. So in 1998, the funding was terminated. "It got to be a little too obvious, and the Agency got very nervous about this."[46]

While Walker and the CIA station chief in Cairo arranged the reception committees, back in Langley the Osama bin Laden unit — headed by Scheuer — was getting reading to extend "invitations" to several Egyptian militants. The first of these new rendition operations, initially an ad-hoc one that was put rapidly together, took place on 13 September 1995, when the CIA took custody in Croatia of one of Egypt's most wanted terrorists, Talaat Fouad Qassem. He was implicated in the assassination of Egyptian president Anwar Sadat and already sentenced to death in his absence. After being interrogated aboard a US warship in the Adriatic, Qassem was flown back to Egypt and later executed.[47]

The CIA men and women who used to carry out such snatch operations were not ordinary case officers. As the secret war against OBL got underway in the 1990s, George Tenet had revived the Agency's Special Operations Group — Special Activities Division, essentially the direct action department of the CIA. It was a fusion of military, ex-military, and undercover operators with their own dedicated aviation assets and special equipment, prepared to deploy anywhere round the world.[48]

To organise the renditions they needed transport, and the CIA turned to its aviation front company, Aero Contractors. As mentioned earlier, in the 1990s the company had bought an executive jet, a Gulfstream III, and this became the workhorse for the movement of prisoners. Aero worked hand in hand with Special Forces. Their headquarters, Johnston County, was deliberately located near to Pope Air Force base, where the CIA pilots could pick up paramilitary operatives that were based at Fort Bragg. The proximity to such an important military base was convenient for other reasons too. "That supported out principal cover," one former pilot told me, "which was we were doing government contracts for the military, for the folks at Fort Bragg."

Gradually, the rendition programme picked up pace. The explosion at Khobar Towers in Saudi Arabia on 25 June 1996, killing nineteen US servicemen and a Saudi citizen, added new impetus, even if it took the CIA time to pin down responsibility for the attack. In 1997, the Counter-Terrorist Centre established a "Rendition Branch", also known as the Rendition Group. It was an operational unit with a specific brief to track down wanted fugitives. Case officers were given "man to man" responsibilities to track down the key people like Khaled Sheikh Mohammed. In 1998, there were further changes. In February, Osama bin Laden issued his famous *fatwa* from Afghanistan that effectively declared war on the United States. Clinton followed with a Presidential Decision Directive PDD-62, signed 22 May, that established Dick Clarke as new national co-ordinator of counter-terrorism and included further detailed instructions, still classified, on "Apprehension, Extradition, Rendition and Prosecution".[49] After the Embassy bombs of August 1998, the President's instructions were now increasingly fo-

cused on bin Laden himself and his close circle. A series of Memoranda of Notifications (MON), executive orders to the CIA, signed August 1998, July 1999,
and December 1999 gave escalating covert orders to the CIA to deal with bin
Laden. The last of these, according to the 9/11 Commission, confirmed the CIA's
authority "to use foreign proxies to detain bin Laden lieutenants, without having
to transfer them to US custody."[50]

The biggest pre-9/11 rendition operation by the CIA took place in Albania in
the summer of 1998, just before the explosion of the Embassy bombs in Tanzania and Kenya. As disclosed by Albanian intelligence officers, the CIA brought a
team to Tirana that helped track down a cell of Egyptian nationals that was allegedly plotting to blow up the US Embassy. Albania's then-President, Sali Berisha,
later recalled the relationship between the CIA team and his intelligence service
had been one of "total cooperation. They worked in Albania as if they were in
New York or Washington."[51] From June to August 1998, a total of four suspects
were arrested by Albanian authorities, interrogated by CIA agents in a disused
airbase and flown back to Cairo on an executive jet. One suspect was shot by
Albanian police and two others evaded capture. A fifth member of the "Tirana
cell", as it became known, was arrested in Sofia, Bulgaria, and flown back to
Egypt where he received a ten-year jail sentence.[52]

Mission accomplished? The cell was wound up and put out of action. But the
trial of these men — known in Cairo as the "Albanian returnees" — became a
cause célèbre that galvanised Islamic feeling. And the men were brutally treated.
Two were executed over charges for which they had never attended a trial.

After being handed over to the Egyptian government, this is what happened
to them:

Ahmed Saleh was suspended from the ceiling and given electric shocks; he was
later hanged for a conviction resulting from a trial held in his absence.

Mohamed Hassan Tita was hung from his wrists and given electric shocks to his
feet and back.

Shawki Attiya was given electric shocks to his genitals, suspended by his limbs
and made to stand for hours in filthy water up to his knees.

Ahmed al-Naggar was kept in a room for thirty-five days with water up to his
knees; had electric shocks to his nipples and penis; he was later hanged without trial for the offence; his sentence of death had been pronounced before
his arrival.

Essam Abdel-Tawwab also described more torture for which the prosecutors
found "recovered wounds"[53]

There was another consequence: the CIA had rattled OBL's cage. On 4 August,
Ayman al-Zawahiri, the Al Qaeda leader's deputy, reacted to the Albania arrests.
Published in the Arabic press, he issued a statement in the name of Islamic Jihad
in Egypt and referred to the "handing over of three of our brothers from some

Eastern European countries [to Egypt]". The three were accused, he said, of declaring jihad against "America, Israel, and their clients."

Ominously he declared:

We are interested in telling the Americans, in brief, that their message has been received, and a reply is currently being written. We hope they read it [the reply] well, as, God willing, we will write it in the language they understand.[54]

Three days later, on 7 August 1998, came Al Qaeda's response. Bombers struck the US embassies in Nairobi and Dar-es-Salaam. 257 people were killed and more than 5,000 were injured.

A kind of duel now developed between the CIA and al-Zawahiri. In 1999, both of his brothers were captured; both of them were rendered back to be interrogated in Egypt: in the spring, Mohamed al-Zawahiri was captured in the United Arab Emirates. A military commander of the Islamic Jihad, he disappeared for many months after his arrival. Dissident sources said he was interrogated within Omar Suleiman's General Intelligence holding centres. He later appeared in Torah prison. His brother Husayn had no known involvement with terrorism. He was picked up in Malaysia in November or December 1999, and released in 2000 after six months of interrogation by Egyptian authorities. Years later he remained effectively under house arrest, banned from any contact with anyone but his family.

In all, Tenet later testified, there had been a total of seventy renditions in the years before 9/11,[55] including "two dozen" between July 1998 and 2000.[56] But throughout these renditions under Clinton's presidency, there was a hybrid strategy, with covert transfers combined with overt ones. A series of prisoners were either extradited or rendered back to face normal criminal charges in US courts and these cases were publicly announced. Between 1993 and 1999, there were nine renditions and four extraditions to the US. They included:

— *Mahmud Abouhalima*, extradited from Egypt in 1993 for his role in the 1993 World Trade Centre bombing. In 1994, he was found guilty and sentenced to 240 years in prison.
— *Eyad Mahmoud Ismail Najim*, extradited from Jordan in 1995 for his role in the 1993 World Trade Centre bombing. He also received a 240-year sentence with no chance of parole.
— *Ramzi Yousef*, rendered from Pakistan on 7 February 1995, and sentenced to life imprisonment for his role in the 1993 World Trade Centre Bombing, as well as a plot to simultaneously detonate bombs on eleven international flights.
— *Mohamed Rashed Daoud Al-'Owhali*, rendered from Kenya in 1998 for his role in the bombing of the US embassy in Nairobi in 1998. In October 2001, he and four others were sentenced to life without parole.[57]

After 9/11 this policy of traditional rendition back to US justice was almost completely abandoned. Secret renditions to foreign jails became the norm. With the exception of a Yemeni cleric, Sheik Mohammed Ali Hassan al-Moayad, and his assistant, who were extradited from Germany to face charges for financing terror groups, not a single major terrorist was returned to the US to face trial in the first five years following 9/11.[58]

In the final days of Clinton came the attack on the USS *Cole*, a US destroyer docking in Yemen. A speedboat approached the destroyer, but under rules of engagement the sailors could not fire and the boat exploded with the loss of seventeen lives. The explosion, having caused a forty-foot square hole in the hull near the engine room, came close to sinking the ship. Once the flooding was contained, the ship listed 4 degrees.[59] Although the initial intelligence was hazy, to all concerned there was no doubt this was an Al Qaeda affair. It seemed to trigger not a resolve for action, but rather another bureaucratic row — something that seemed almost an instinct in the Clinton White House.

Bush takes over

When President George W. Bush took over in January 2001, it looked at first as if the covert war against Al Qaeda might be run down not expanded. The new administration's obsessions were Iraq, China and Iran and most of the key players in counter-terrorism — men like O'Neill at the FBI, Mike Sheehan at the State Department, and Dick Clarke at the NSC — were marginalised, or resigned. By the summer of 2001, the Predator programme was still effectively in mothballs and, despite preliminary moves to authorise a new covert action programme in Afghanistan, including capturing Al Qaeda leaders, there was no serious consideration yet of a snatch operation against Osama bin Laden.[60]

APPROACHING JOHN F. KENNEDY AIRPORT, NEW YORK
17 September 2001

It was a glorious sunny day, with clear blue skies, as my British Airways plane circled, ready for its final approach to land in New York. After waiting for days around London airport for flights to resume across the Atlantic, I was finally arriving to cover the aftermath of the September 11 attacks.[61] Through the window, I could see Manhattan's famous skyline, denuded now of its Twin Towers.

At the moment when Mohammed Atta and his hijackers struck the North Tower at 8.45 a.m. Eastern Standard Time, I had been sitting on a wooden bench in the peaceful surroundings of Jesus College, Cambridge. My mobile phone was switched off as I chatted to John Moscow, then a Manhattan prosecutor. We were attending a conference on organised crime. When I finished the interview, I switched on the mobile phone and I realised something was up. Four messages had been left in the space of ten minutes: the voicemails from my office at the *Sunday Times* described how one plane and then another had struck the towers. I knew immediately I had to get straight back to London. But first I ran back to find Moscow in his room, to relay the news. There are no televisions in college rooms. He took the information in silence, hardly reacting. Moscow had good friends who worked at the World Trade Centre. Then as I walked back across the college quad, he suddenly appeared out the door and chased after me. "You are joking, right?", he said, as he grabbed me. "No, it seems unbelievable, but it's true," I replied.

A week later, I travelled into New York and, like many others, went straight to Ground Zero to witness the devastation. There was still a strange smell of wet dust in the air. And the mood of people was still confused. A stranger on the subway turned to me suddenly (an unusual event in itself) and said: "I never thought it would happen like this. A colleague at work, who is a Sikh, wants to spend the night at my house. He's afraid of being lynched: everyone thinks he is a Muslim." Yet, for the most part, the mood in New York was one of solidarity, not of anger or reprisals. Everywhere across the city and across the US billboards began to go up: "United We Stand". As I stayed in New York and then Washington for the following weeks, I felt the mood swiftly harden. Many felt the angry need for reprisal. President Bush, people said or implied, should invade and bomb Afghanistan not next week, but today. At a political level, this mood that sanctioned a "by any means necessary" approach breathed new life into methods of action that had not been employed since some of the darker days of the Cold War. Direct actions by US operatives that President Clinton might have previously refused were now given the green light. With all the talk of "new paradigms", of a new form of war, many began suggesting publicly that torture too should now be considered. And leading the charge were many who, hitherto, might be considered to be liberal.

Writing in *Newsweek* in November 2001, Jonathan Alter, who was considered something of a progressive, wrote: "In this autumn of anger even a liberal can find his thoughts turning to . . . torture." He added that he was not necessarily advocating the use of "cattle prods or rubber hoses" on detainees. Only, "something to jump-start the stalled investigation of the greatest crime in American history."[62]

Alter's comments were almost a manifesto for what, as we've seen already, was to transpire after 9/11. He continued:

Couldn't we at least subject them to psychological torture like tapes of dying rabbits or high-decibel rap? [The military has done that in Panama and elsewhere.] How about truth serum, administered with a mandatory IV? Some people still argue that we needn't rethink any of our old assumptions about law enforcement, but they're hopelessly "Sept. 10"—living in a country that no longer exists. ... We can't legalize physical torture; it's contrary to American values. But even as we continue to speak out against human-rights abuses around the world, we need to keep an open mind about certain measures to fight terrorism, like court-sanctioned psychological interrogation. And *we'll have to think about transferring some suspects to our less squeamish allies,* even if that's hypocritical. Nobody said this was going to be pretty. (my emphasis)

Alter said shortly afterwards that he was surprised that his article had not caused a public outcry. What he found most surprising, especially given all the sensitivities about torture, was that many people "who might be described as being on the left [were] whispering 'I agree with you'."[63]

The theme was continued by the pen of many commentators. In a cover story in the *Atlantic Monthly* in October 2003, ironically during what transpired to be the worst period of abuse at the Abu Ghraib prison in Iraq, the author of *Black Hawk Down*, Mark Bowden, declared the Bush Administration had "exactly the right posture" in its statements and actions on torture. His piece argued for "coercive" interrogations — exactly what was proscribed as illegal for prisoners of war under the Geneva conventions.

"Candor and consistency are not always public virtues," he wrote.

Torture is a crime against humanity, but coercion is an issue that is rightly handled with a wink, or even a touch of hypocrisy; it should be banned but also quietly practised. Those who protest coercive methods will exaggerate their horrors, which is good: it generates a useful climate of fear. It is wise of the President to reiterate US support for international agreements banning torture, and it is wise for American interrogators to employ whatever coercive methods work. It is also smart not to discuss the matter with anyone.

He concluded:

If interrogators step over the line from coercion to outright torture, they should be held personally responsible. But no interrogator is ever going to be prosecuted for keeping Khalid Sheikh Mohammed awake, cold, alone, and uncomfortable. Nor should he be.[64]

Shortly after Alter's *Newsweek* article, leading lawyer and legal scholar, Alan Dershowitz, suggested in an article in the *Los Angeles Times* that torture was not unconstitutional and, as a result, ought to be allowed under special judge-issued "torture warrants". He did point out that the results of such warrants could not then be used in a criminal court since this would be a violation of the Fifth Amendment, a defendant's right against self-incrimination.[65] A few years later, Dershowitz explained that it should be used as "a last resort in a ticking-bomb case", and if used, "it ought to be done openly, with accountability, with approval by the president of the United States or by a Supreme Court justice."[66]

Another trait of the torture debate was the "relativity" of certain methods. It seems that everyone agreed that the torture used under Saddam Hussein was horrific (fingernail pulling, electric shocks, rape and the like), but what these commentators were thinking of was somehow a lesser form of torture, and therefore more acceptable.

Two factors then set the backdrop for a revival of renditions. Torture, if in a limited form, was suddenly no longer considered taboo. A wider sense of psychological shock also played a part. After what was being called the largest terrorist crime in history, and as intelligence chiefs struggled to assess whether further large scale attacks were planned, pressure increased for employing "any means necessary".

I was affected too with this enthusiasm too — shocked by events, I also wondered if I had become too squeamish. I had not yet contemplated what that kind of attitude would mean.

New operational requirements

President Bush put a new rendition programme into operation within days of 9/11. A "memorandum of notifications" was signed on 17 September that authorised the CIA to conduct renditions without any advance approval from either the White House or the Department of Justice or Department of State. [67] The New York Times would later report these transfers could take place even if no criminal charges were contemplated: "Before September 11, the CIA had been authorised by presidential directives to carry out renditions, but under rules much more restrictive than those now in place. As part of its broad new latitude, current and former government officials say, the CIA has been authorized to transfer prisoners to other countries solely for the purpose of detention and interrogation." [68]

The shock of 9/11 had prompted some to demand a re-think of options. The idea was to "think out of the box" and to define a new imaginative response to the new threats. In the days and months that followed, the promise was unrealised. Bush decided to leave the leadership of the CIA under George Tenet intact. So instead of re-conceiving their approach, the rendition programme was dusted off and revitalised. The policy of rendition and out-sourcing, what had been Clinton's "least worst" compromise, was not wound down but was vastly expanded. As Reuel Marc Gerecht, the former CIA covert operative, stated, before 9/11 renditions were a "low-profile counter-terrorist tool" but afterwards they became a "standard operating procedure, critical to the way the CIA wages its battle against Islamic extremism." [69]

The expansion of rendition was not just the result of some new enthusiasm for torture, although these new moral attitudes played a role. As in the Clinton era, it was largely a policy selected once again as a short cut dictated by limited options and political fix. While policy makers promised a new "no holds barred" re-think of counter-terrorism policy, Washington's instinct was to dole out more of the same. Again it was a political fix, a compromise justified not only by the CIA's catastrophic shortage of its own well-trained and Arab-speaking interrogators, but by the rush to launch a global war that declared almost any Islamic militant group as an enemy and which left both the military and the Agency swamped with prisoners and potential targets, as well as a lack of imagination to devise something better.

With the new global war on terrorism now effectively labelling tens of thousands of Islamic militants as "enemies", Afghanistan invaded and with Osama bin Laden's escape from the battle of Tora Bora, the main problem at the close of 2001 was that both the CIA and the US military were now inundated with prisoners and potential prisoners. And yet, confronted with its failures to predict 9/11, the CIA particularly was under unremitting pressure to deliver new intelligence fast.

While under Clinton, risky military options were ruled out, under Bush they were sometimes tried and botched: Osama bin Laden got away at the battle of Tora Bora after a failure to deploy US military forces to block the passes.[70] And, haunted by its past mistakes, the CIA rushed to expand one programme they could at least perform effectively and that might just yield a new supply of information. Yet, as before 9/11, most insiders were well aware that rendition was hardly a war-winning tactic.

At the CIA, there were certainly now fewer qualms about handling interrogations directly. Secret detention facilities were built for "high value detainees". But, after being rundown for years, former insiders claim the CIA's clandestine department was simply unable to handle the numbers of people involved. It had just a handful of the mainly Arab-speaking interrogators who could bond with detainees effectively enough to extract intelligence.[71]

And so, in the hurried march to war, rendition was vastly expanded. As I've described in Part 1 of this book, hundreds of prisoners were now transferred across the world to face interrogation and imprisonment in foreign hands. One former senior officer in the Directorate of Operations told me: "Before 9/11, these renditions were much simpler. They looked at people who were wanted in those countries and brought them back there. But that's quite a different scale to what happened after 9/11."

For CIA case officers, the programme had one important point. Every decision was signed off at the highest level, ultimately by President Bush himself. As one former CIA official, who was directly involved in renditions, told me: "Everything we did, down to the tiniest detail, every rendition and every technique of interrogation used against prisoners in our hands, was scrutinised and approved by headquarters. And nothing was done without approval from the White House — from [National Security Adviser] Condoleezza Rice herself, and with a signature from John Ashcroft [the Attorney General]". Under the expanded programme, according to those former and serving CIA sources I interviewed, operational approval for individual renditions could be given on the authority of the head of the CIA's Counter-Terrorist Centre (CTC), but only within a clear set of guidelines and rules approved by the attorney general and the President's National Security Council. Any changes to rendition procedures would be briefed by the head of the CTC or his deputy to the National Security Council Staff. Congressional oversight committees would also be informed. In addition, each individual operation required legal approval. A detailed legal brief needed to be prepared, and this went for approval not only to the CIA's general counsel and to the CIA director (or his deputy) but also to the NSC's lawyers. So, one way or another, the White House was always informed. At least four other former and serving CIA officers I interviewed, all of whom had access to details of the rendition programme, told the same story: it was a policy dictated from on high. "Our backs were relentlessly covered," one said. [72]

In their haste to acquire intelligence on Al Qaeda's plans and find places for its prisoners, the CIA established closer than ever relationships with Middle Eastern dictatorships like Syria and Egypt. At least in the early days, the politics of the moment gave little opportunity for reflection on whether, without proper safeguards to ensure humane and *effective* interrogations, and to encourage an end to wider repressive policies, these renditions might be counter-productive.

Bureaucratic rivalries also played their part. The CIA was anxious to keep the top Al Qaeda prisoners within its programmes. Military interrogators describe receiving batches of prisoners in Afghanistan with key members of a group missing — having been taken away by the CIA to its own facilities. As one Army interrogator told me, it was like getting "… a box with puzzle pieces in it and one of the crucial pieces seems to be gone".[73] But though the CIA wanted to keep control, many of these prisoners were not retained by the Agency but simply passed on to countries like Egypt. And so, to the surprise of law enforcement officials, key suspects like Ibn-al-Sheikh al-Libi, who was captured after fleeing Afghanistan, and who might have provided crucial evidence in terrorist prosecutions, were placed in the hands of foreign intelligence services where any statements obtained would be useless in any US court of law.

In hindsight, many former CIA insiders, considering the ten-year history of renditions, think they might have done better — "It was never meant to be anything more than a complement to economic, political, military programmes," said Scheuer. But though not the best overall solution, few of those involved seem deeply affected by unease.

But mistakes would happen, as they always did, and innocents might be captured. "It is impossible not to have a mistake in the business of espionage and intelligence. There was never anything flip or blasé about the way this was approached. It was a deadly serious business, and if we were wrong, we were wrong. But the evidence pointed us toward what we did."

Asked about the danger these men might be tortured, Scheuer appeared to have few qualms about the matter. "The bottom line is getting anyone off the street who you're confident has been involved or is planning to be involved in operations that could kill Americans is a worthwhile activity."

Even if he might be tortured?, I asked.

It wouldn't be us torturing them, he replied. And I also think that there is a lot of Hollywood involved in our portrayal of torture in Egypt and in Saudi Arabia. It's rather hypocritical to worry about what the Egyptians do to people who are terrorists and not condemn the Israelis for what they do to people they deem terrorists. Human rights is a very flexible concept. It kind of depends on how hypocritical you want to be on a particular day.[74]

PART THREE

BACKLASH

7

THE ICE MAN

NEW YORK
28 April 2004

Journalists at CBS headquarters were preparing a sensational and damning ex-
clusive. They had sat on the story for several weeks. They, together with Seymour
Hersh, the journalist who exposed the My Lai massacre in Vietnam, were to reveal that night some shocking news — pictures of abuse at Abu Ghraib in Baghdad, a jail once used by Saddam Hussein as a centre for torture and execution.

One of those pictures showed Specialist Sabrina Harman, 26, the daughter
of a homicide detective from Arlington, Virginia. She was standing before the
bruised torso of a man. He was slumped in a shower, dead, covered in ice and
wrapped in tape. She had a fixed grin and gave the thumbs up. The morning after
the picture was taken, the dead man had an intravenous drip inserted into his
arm so that, as he was carried out, other prisoners would not realise he was dead.
Thus was his corpse taken from the prison and transferred later to a US military
mortuary at Camp Sather, at Baghdad Airport.[1]

In the days that followed the story of Abu Ghraib abuse would dominate the
front pages of newspapers across the world; the photographs became an iconic
image of the dark side of America's wars in Iraq and against terror.[2]

On 5 May, George Bush addressed the Iraqi people, in an interview with a
correspondent of Alhurra Television, the US-funded Arabic satellite channel.
"First, people in Iraq must understand," he said, "that I view those practices as
abhorrent. They must also understand that what took place in that prison does
not represent the America that I know." Referring to "the actions of these few
people," Bush promised a full investigation. In a democracy, mistakes would be
made. "But in a democracy, as well, those mistakes will be investigated and people will be brought to justice. ...We're a society that is willing to investigate, fully
investigate in this case, what took place in that prison."[3]

The dead prisoner was an Iraqi called Manadel al-Jamadi. He was, it emerged, suspected of involvement of a bomb attack that destroyed the Red Cross head-quarters in Baghdad on 27 October. Unlike the other prisoners, shown naked in the Abu Ghraib gallery, al-Jamadi had been in the custody of the CIA and had been captured in a night raid by US Special Forces, the Navy SEALs. Military pathologists determined his death was "homicide". Despite Bush's promises of a full investigation, for at least two and a half years the CIA made no official com-ment on his death and no prosecution was brought against the Agency inter-rogators involved.

Al-Jamadi had died under CIA interrogation on 4 November 2003, at the height of the abuses at Abu Ghraib. It was at this time, between October and December 2003, that members of the 372 Military Police Company were said by the subsequent official inquiry of Major General Antonio M. Taguba to have committed "sadistic, blatant, and wanton" criminal and intentional acts that in-cluded:

— Punching, slapping, and kicking detainees; jumping on their feet;
— Videotaping and photographing naked male and female detainees;
— Forcibly arranging detainees in various sexually explicit positions for photo-
  graphing;
— Forcing detainees to remove their clothing and keeping them naked for sev-
  eral days at a time;
— Forcing naked male detainees to wear women's underwear;
— Forcing groups of male detainees to masturbate themselves while being pho-
  tographed and videotaped;
— Arranging naked male detainees in a pile and then jumping on them;
— Positioning a naked detainee on a box, with a sandbag on his head, and at-
  taching wires to his fingers, toes, and penis to simulate electric torture;
— Placing a dog chain or strap around a naked detainee's neck and having a
  female soldier pose for a picture;
— A male MP guard having sex with a female detainee;
— Using military working dogs (without muzzles) to intimidate and frighten
  detainees, and in at least one case biting and severely injuring a detainee;

Other credible allegations, he said, included:

— Breaking chemical lights and pouring the phosphoric liquid on detainees;
— Threatening detainees with a charged 9mm pistol;
— Sodomising a detainee with a chemical light and perhaps a broomstick.[4]

Few were to realise that within Tier 1, under control of the 372nd, was a section Alpha devoted to CIA prisoners.[5]

In a damage limitation exercise, the Defense Secretary, Donald Rumsfeld, would emphasise again and again that it was only a small group that had car-ried out these acts. "You know," he said, "what was going on *in the midnight shift* in Abu Ghraib Prison halfway across the world is something that clearly someone in Washington, DC, can't manage or deal with" (my emphasis).[6] By 2006, Rumsfeld was still talking of "what was done by *that midnight watch* group of people at Abu Ghraib, and was so terrible in terms of its effect in the world" (my emphasis).[7]

Rumsfeld and others maintained strongly that what happened at Abu Ghraib was abuse, not torture. It was not part of the interrogation process. It also went against military training doctrines. He stressed that "all of our rules, all of our procedures, all of our training is against abuse of people that are detained."[8] The abuses were also something at complete odds to what the President wanted. "The president from the beginning had a policy of humane treatment and torture was not allowed," said Rumsfeld. "We had a policy that reflected the president's policy. It went right down." Subsequent Pentagon inquiries found that some of the abuses did occur as part of interrogation. There were orders, for example, to use military working dogs to intimidate the prisoners. The military police-men accused of abuse, Gen. Taguba found, were also "actively requested" by both Military Intelligence interrogators and those from the Other Government Agencies (OGA), a military euphemism for the CIA, "to set physical and mental conditions for favorable interrogation of witnesses."[9] A further inquiry in 2004 by Major General George Fay concluded:

CIA detention and interrogation practices led to a loss of accountability, abuse, reduced in-teragency cooperation, and an unhealthy mystique that further poisoned the atmosphere at Abu Ghraib.[10]

Neither the CIA nor Military Intelligence gave any formal orders to the military policemen to carry out abuse. The inquiries all found that the worst excesses at Abu Ghraib, such as sexual abuse of prisoners, had not been ordered by anyone in the military chain of command.

What did emerge, however, was a series of orders and legal opinions from political leaders in Washington that exposed how the definitions of prisoner abuse and of torture itself had been re-defined in the quest to defeat terrorism. Of themselves, these memos did *not* provide instructions to carry out what was seen at Abu Ghraib. Yet those in Washington did establish a new legal frame-work in which the traditional rules for dealing with prisoners did not apply. This new framework applied in Abu Ghraib, but also defined the conduct of Ameri-can men and women in prisons and interrogation centres across the world. It defined the government's attitude to conduct in America's own jails but also to conduct in many of the foreign jails involved in the CIA's rendition programme. Both soldiers and CIA officers had to navigate in this new environment, often without being equipped with an effective compass to guide them. Abu Ghraib, then, changed the terms of the debate. The extent of the depravity exposed on Tier 1 posed a series of searching questions about what had been going on, often covertly, in America's name. And, as this process of questioning gathered pace, the consequences for the CIA were just as great as those for the Pentagon and its military. The working logic of the war on terror had begun to be laid bare.

The story of America's invasion of Iraq and the details of the scandal at Abu Ghraib are not central to this book's account of America's secret rendition programme and its network of secret prisons. And yet the scandal's revelation in April and May 2004 was significant because it defined a moment in time, a high water mark of abuse. It was the beginning of a backlash in which so much was revealed and so much had to change.

In Iraq, the Abu Ghraib affair could not have emerged at a worse moment. Since early April fighting of unparalleled atrocity and lethality had erupted. The US Army was fighting a war on two fronts: against an insurgency in the Sunni triangle, backed by foreign militants, and against the Shia militias of the Mehdi Army in Baghdad and the holy city of Najaf. A spate of kidnappings had been launched. And now Abu Ghraib would focus the anger of many Iraqis against American forces.

I was in Iraq at that time, reporting from the southern city of Basra, to witness the effect caused by these pictures of abuse. I had heard tales of abuse by former Iraqi prisoners before. In February, one alleged victim from Baghdad had drawn detailed diagrams for me of the type of torture he had endured at a US military holding centre at Baghdad airport. At the time, few would believe these allegations. The man I interviewed was a Sunni from a district of Baghdad known to be hostile to the American presence. How could I be sure his allegations were not invented? How could I level such serious charges without any more detailed proof? (The irony of victimisation is that the more people are victimised and made to suffer, the less one is inclined to believe their accounts of such treatment.)[11] So, with so much else going on, I never wrote up his story. Yet now, we were seeing photographs, acknowledged as genuine, that were appearing on television. We had concrete proof that these stories were true. In southrn Iraq, many hardened Shia had little sympathy with the victims of torture. "They're all from Fallujah and terrorists; what kind of treatment do they expect?" one told me. But, all the same, these very people realised that these revelations would harden attitudes in Sunni areas and potentially prolong the insurgency and potential civil war.

For myself, I also realised it was time to publish the first part of my research that showed the wider network of abuse tolerated as part of the rendition programme and authorised at a high level. By satellite telephone from Basra, I filed a long piece for the *New Statesman* that described in detail what the magazine headlined as "America's Gulag." As mentioned earlier, it described the existence of a secret airline run by the CIA to transport prisoners. The same day my article was published, the Swedish documentary that revealed the identity of one of the fleet's planes, the Gulfstream V, was broadcast.

If all these scandals and such articles and broadcasts affected the CIA rendition programme, it is hard to gauge. But, whether by coincidence or by reaction, in the weeks following Abu Ghraib, there were some changes. On 29 May, the German car salesman, Khaled el-Masri, whose story was described in Chapter 4, was finally released from the CIA jail in Afghanistan. At the same time, the former London resident Binyam Mohamed, as described in Chapter 2, was transferred from another CIA prison in Afghanistan to the military base at Bagram airport. He was finally a ghost prisoner no more. At last he had access to the Red Cross and, after his two years in captivity, they could inform his family of where he was. In September, a total of fourteen prisoners, all apparently former CIA ghost prisoners and including Binyam, were transferred from Bagram to Guantánamo.[12] It seemed the CIA was clearing out its stable.

In its specifics, and though hardly publicised at the time, there was much too much that could be learned from the Abu Ghraib scandal about the CIA's wider programme of prisoner detentions. By the end of 2003, with an insurgency now raging, Iraq had become a major outpost of the War on Terror. The CIA was forced to mobilise more and more of its resources into the country, diverting them from other quarters. Acquiring intelligence became vital, particularly from prisoners. And so the CIA became increasingly involved in the interrogation of both Iraqi prisoners and of foreign militants who were captured in Iraq. By the middle of 2004, the US had handled more than 43,000 prisoners in Iraq.[13] The CIA brought to Iraq not only its interrogation teams trained for the War on Terror, but also its new methods and rule books developed since 9/11. The exposure of what happened at Abu Ghraib helped reveal those methods.

More than anything, Abu Ghraib threw attention and criticism on to the military. But, just as the activities of the military policemen raised wider questions, so the death of al-Jamadi and his photograph provided an uncomfortable glimpse into the wider world of CIA interrogations, and into the Agency's detention of prisoners without trial or formal legal procedure. While the US military may have been criticised most strongly, its prisoners at least were formally logged and registered and given access to the Red Cross. The CIA's prisoners were held in secret and without access to any outsiders. Al-Jamadi was an example of a ghost prisoner. And his case provided the first public glimpse since 9/11 of an alleged homicide in CIA hands.

The month when al-Jamadi died, November 2003, was the height of the panic over the relatively new Iraq insurgency. Six months after the "liberation" of the country, the rebels were gaining in strength, and many Americans, who believed their presence had been welcomed, were shocked at its ferocity. The UN headquarters had been blown up on 19 August and on 27 October the Red Cross headquarters was reduced to rubble. Most distressing of all was that Saddam Hussein was still at large and there was little concrete intelligence about where he might be hiding.

Three agencies were competing to interview prisoners. First there was the CIA-directed Iraqi Survey Group, which handled most of the high-value prisoners and, although set up to help hunt for WMD, it had been ordered also to help with the hunt for Saddam. Then there was a special operations covert fusion group — Task Force 121, that included the CIA; it was set up in Afghanistan to hunt for Osama bin Laden but had been brought over to Iraq to be the key agency directing the hunt for Saddam.[14] Finally there were the military's own intelligence assets, concentrated both at Abu Ghraib but also deployed on the ground.[15]

In the race to find Saddam, the pressure drove each of the agencies to pull out the stops to find useful intelligence. The military policemen said they were told by both Military Intelligence and the CIA to prepare the prisoners for interrogation.[16]

At this time, the CIA's fleet of planes became frequent visitors to the former Saddam International Airport in Baghdad. "We used to see these Gulfstreams and executive jets on the tarmac," former Brig.-Gen. Janis Karpinski told me. "We assumed they were hired by TV journalists. Only later did we find out they were OGA."[17] Two days after the Red Cross bombing, and five days before the raid on al-Jamadi's house, a CIA Gulfstream flew into Baghdad from Kabul. CIA planes arrived too at the time of other crucial investigations and interrogations. Within a day of Saddam Hussein's arrest on 13 December, both the Gulfstream V and the Boeing 737 had arrived in Baghdad.[18]

It was about 2 a.m. on 4 November when a convoy of Humvees and blacked-out Chevy Suburbans approached a three-story apartment block where al-Jamadi lived. SEAL Dan Cerrillo was first in and rushed the door, striking Jamadi with it and then hitting him on the face with two fists.[19] The pair struggled ferociously, and his stove fell on him. Then al-Jamadi was grabbed and thrown into the back of a Humvee.

The SEALs took al-Jamadi back to their Navy camp near Baghdad Airport, known as Camp Jenny Pozzi. The commander of the SEAL platoon, Lt. Andrew Ledford, was later put on trial at a court martial in San Diego accused of allowing al-Jamadi to be severely beaten. He was cleared by the jury of improper conduct.[20] But in testimony, eye-witnesses said al-Jamadi was punched, kicked and struck by the SEALs at the camp, among other places in a tiny space known as the Romper Room. Al-Jamadi was stripped, and water poured all over him.[21] Among those there were the SEALs and CIA officers including an interrogator and polygraph expert named Mark Swanner[22] and "Clint C", a private contract translator for the agency.

One CIA interrogator, recalled a SEAL, had pushed "his arm up against the detainee's chest, pressing on him with all his weight." A CIA guard also testified he heard an Agency interrogator threaten to "barbecue" al-Jamadi if he didn't

begin to talk. He apparently moaned "I'm dying, I'm dying" to which the interrogator responded: "You'll be wishing you were dying."[23]

As he was taken away to a waiting Humvee, the court heard, al-Jamadi was
"body-slammed" into the vehicle by SEALs, who confessed he presented no
threat. On arrival at Abu Ghraib, al-Jamadi was still walking freely. Jason Kenner, an MP on duty, said al-Jamadi had been stripped of his underwear and
was naked but for a purple t-shirt and purple jacket. He had a green plastic
sandbag over his head. But he was walking and spoke normally.[24] Al-Jamadi
was put in a holding cell at first. His remaining clothes were taken off and he
appeared to have no injuries, said Kenner. Then, the MPs were told to put
the prisoner into an orange jumpsuit and take him to Tier One — Alpha, the
wing of Abu Ghraib used by the OGA. The "Alpha" section, which typically
held about twenty prisoners, was part of the overall Tier 1 that was policed by
the 372 Military Police Company, the unit held responsible for the worst Abu
Ghraib abuses. Jamadi did not resist the transfer. At Tier 1 Alpha, his interrogation took place in a shower room.

Several MPs now noticed that al-Jamadi was having trouble breathing. An
autopsy later found he had six broken ribs. Swanner told the military policeman
not to let al-Jamadi sit down but instead to raise his wrists behind his back and
attached the metal handcuffs to the wall behind him. He could stand up but if
his knees buckled then he would be left hanging from the wall. One account
described this as a form of torture known as "Palestinian hanging".[25] With his
ribs now broken, it must have been excruciatingly painful if he lent down. Once
attached, al-Jamadi was left alone with Swanner and the translator "Clint". A little later, they were summoned again by Swanner and found al-Jamadi hanging
slumped from the wall, with his knees bent. Every time the soldiers attempted to
raise him, he flopped down again. Walter Diaz, a military policeman present recalled: "All his weight was on his hands and wrists — looked like he was going to
mess up his sockets."[26] Swanner allegedly told Diaz that the prisoner was faking
it, "playing dead"; another MP, Sgt. Jeffrey Frost, said Swanner had said he was
"playing possum". Frost was unconvinced and lifted al-Jamadi's hood and found
his face bruised and lifeless. The men lowered al-Jamadi to the floor and "blood
came gushing out of his nose and mouth, as if a faucet had been turned on," said
Frost. [27] Within forty-five minutes of arriving in the shower block, al-Jamadi was
now clearly dead. It was just before 7 a.m.

In detailed investigations into al-Jamadi's death, the New Yorker's Jane Mayer,
Seth Hettena of the Associated Press, and John McChesney of National Public
Radio, quoted witnesses who recounted how CIA officials took away the prisoners' bloodied hood, thus destroying the evidence. After being kept overnight on
ice, al-Jamadi's body was removed from the prison.

An autopsy was not conducted for another five days. Military pathologists
called his death a homicide caused by "blunt force trauma to the torso compli-

cated by compromised respiration". But much later, al-Jamadi's autopsy results were looked at again by two medical examiners, Dr Michael Baden and Dr Cyril Wecht, on behalf of one of the accused SEALs. Both rejected the conclusion that blunt force injuries to his head played any part in his death. Instead both said he died because of "compromised respiration" caused by the combination of broken ribs and the painful position in which he was held. Dr Baden, then the chief forensic pathologist for the New York State Police, told Mayer, that "you don't die from broken ribs. But if he had been hung up in this way *and* had broken ribs, that's different." In his judgment, "asphyxia is what he died from — as in a crucifixion." Dr Wecht, former president of the American Academy of Forensic Sciences, drew the same conclusion, telling her that "the position of the body was in would have been the cause of death."[28]

At the time of writing, neither Swanner nor any other CIA official had faced any criminal charges in connection with al-Jamadi's death.[29] An investigation by the CIA Inspector General's office had been passed to the Department of Justice where the file awaited any action. Proving the cause of death or the extent of injuries inflicted by the CIA officers in particular would be hard. But a summary of the basic facts give a fairly brutal picture of rough justice: al-Jamadi was arrested without any charge, was subjected to no initial medical examination (as required by international law), nor was his arrest registered officially. He was then physically beaten as part of the interrogation procedure. After his death, his body was dispatched out of the prison in disguise. Al-Jamadi was a fully-fledged ghost prisoner: dealt with — and finally disposed of — outside the rule of law.

In June 2004, a month after the Abu Ghraib scandal and al-Jamadi's picture were first broadcast and published, the world was still struggling to comprehend what had occurred. In Washington, political and military leaders denied that any such abuse had been ordered.[30]

But then the so-called "torture memos", legal opinions endorsed by the Department of Justice,, were made public, in a series of disclosures beginning in that month. These showed how the official rules for dealing with prisoners had been re-defined. And they showed why the Geneva Conventions had been abandoned so that prisoners could be intensely questioned.[31]

Back in early 2002, in the early stages of the War on Terror and when the camp at Guantánamo was just opening up, the White House chief of counsel, Alberto Gonzales was considering all the legal issues. What he understood clearly was the central importance in this War on Terror of the capture and interrogation of prisoners. The United States was facing a new enemy whose intentions and plans were unclear. Defeating that enemy — the terrorists — required first and foremost good intelligence. And the most ready source of that intelligence was from captured prisoners. So it was essential to have a rule book that could allow good and effective intelligence. Yet there was a problem. The Geneva Convention on prisoners of war placed clear limits on their interrogation.[32] Essentially there was a ban on almost all types of aggressive questioning or any kinds of incentives provided to those who talked. It states: "No physical or mental torture, nor any other form of coercion, may be inflicted on prisoners of war to secure from them information of any kind whatever." Similar protection existed for captured civilians from "physical or moral coercion. ... in particular to obtain information from them."

The solution then was clear to Gonzales: abandon those Geneva Conventions. In a memo to President Bush on 25 January 2002, Gonzales had spelled this out:

"The nature of [a "war" against terrorism] places a high premium on. ... factors such as the ability to quickly obtain information from captured terrorists and their sponsors .... and the need to try terrorists for war crimes. ... *[t]his new paradigm renders obsolete Geneva's strict limitations on questioning of enemy prisoners...*" (my emphasis)[33]

On 7 February 2002, the President wrote to Vice President Cheney, Rumsfeld, Secretary of State Powell and others, confirming that he accepted the legal conclusion of the Department of Justice and determined that the Geneva Convention did not apply to "either Taliban or Al Qaeda prisoners." Based on this, he declared that Taliban detainees were "unlawful combatants" and "because Geneva does not apply to our conflict with Al Qaeda, Al Qaeda detainees also do not qualify as prisoners of war."[34]

If the US could escape from the Geneva straightjacket then the President could set his own standards of what would constitute torture and would therefore be illegal. Although the US remained bound to oppose torture itself, the definition of torture could be relaxed. A definition of what constituted acceptable conduct, in response to a request for advice from the CIA, was later sketched out by the Department of Justice, in a memo on 1 August 2002 by assistant attorney general Jay S. Bybee. Torture as defined in US law, he said, "covers only extreme acts." He added:

Where the pain is physical, it must be of an intensity akin to that which accompanies serious physical injury such as death or organ failure. Severe mental pain requires suffering not just at the moment of infliction but it also requires lasting psychological harm, such as seen in mental disorders like post-traumatic stress disorder. ... Because the acts inflicting torture are extreme, there is a significant range of acts that though they might constitute cruel, inhuman, or degrading treatment or punishment fail to rise to the level of torture. [my emphasis].[35]

Bybee's memo was important, because it provided an excuse to authorise all kinds of stressful questioning procedures. When this memo was made public in June 2004, it caused an outcry and was withdrawn, the Department of Justice said. But a new, more moderate memo still contained some of the same thinking. While the requirement stated in Bybee's memo that physical torture needed to amount to an *"intensity akin to that which accompanies serious physical injury such as death or organ failure"* was withdrawn, the policy confirmed the US believed that mental torture was only legally "torture" if it was severe enough to cause long-term harm. A footnote confirmed that the revised policy would have made no difference to the Attorney General's verdict on what interrogation techniques were considered legal.[36]

More broadly, Bybee's thinking was just one part of the series of re-examinations of the basic principles by which America should treat its enemies. With Geneva swept aside, the agencies that handled prisoners, the military and the CIA, were navigating in clear blue water — choosing a course with no obvious landmarks to steer by.

In the military, the new post-Geneva policies began to be applied a fortnight before the President formally ruled on 7 February that America's new enemies were excluded from Geneva protections. On 19 January 2002, Donald Rumsfeld ordered the US chiefs of staff to inform commanders in Afghanistan that Taliban and Al Qaeda captives should only be treated humanely "to the extent necessary and appropriate with military necessity."[37] The President had set the tone for how this policy would be applied when, in a press conference on 28 January, he referred to the Guantánamo prisoners as "enemy combatants" and praised the valiant efforts made by troops "to make sure that these killers — these are killers — were held in such a way that they were safe." Although the decision to drop Geneva was widely discussed, few realised that the real aim of this move was to open the field for harsher questioning. A press notice issued by the Pentagon listed the types of Geneva rights that would be denied to Guantánamo inmates, among them the ability to purchase food, soap, and tobacco, have a monthly advance of pay, or "receive scientific equipment, musical instruments, or sports outfits". No mention of the right not to be subject to "physical or moral coercion" to talk.[38]

The definition of acceptable interrogation had long been set out for the Army in its Field Manual (FM 34-52), which included a list of seventeen approved techniques.[39] But in December 2002 Rumsfeld authorised a set of enhanced techniques specifically for use in Guantánamo, some of which required his personal approval when used.[40] These were partially rescinded the following January, but by then these practices, including sleep deprivation and forced standing, had already been passed on to Afghanistan where Special Forces teams were engaged in hunting remnant Taliban and Al Qaeda forces.[41] Deployed alongside them were members of the 205 Military Intelligence Brigade and its 215 Battalion (Alpha Company), the same unit that later ended up at Abu Ghraib and was accused by General Taguba of asking the military policemen to set the conditions for interrogation. It was interrogators from the 215's Alpha Company that were later found responsible for the deaths of two prisoners at Bagram, Afghanistan — Mullah Habibullah on 4 December, and a taxi-driver named Dilawar on 10 December 2002. According to military prosecutors the former died after having been repeatedly assaulted and was kept awake for days "by shackling him in a standing position with hands suspended above shoulder level for a prolonged period of time."[42] A military lawyer at Bagram, in a secret report written on 24 January 2003, confirmed that interrogators in Afghanistan were using the same Rumsfeld-approved techniques that were seen at Guantánamo.[43]

The commander of Alpha Company at Bagram was a decorated officer, Capt. Carolyn A. Wood. After a brief return to Fort Bragg, she was then drafted with her company on to Iraq. According to the report by Vice Admiral Albert Church following his investigation ordered by Rumsfeld into military interrogation methods, it was she who drafted interrogation policy for Abu Ghraib in August 2003 that was "based in part on interrogation techniques being used at the time by units in Afghanistan."[44]

If the military had its new rules after 9/11, what had emerged now of the rules for the CIA? In a normal conflict, the rules of the Geneva Convention would apply as much to the CIA (or KGB or any secret agency) as to any part of the military. A prisoner of war should be treated according to the rules of war, regardless of what agency might carry out the interrogation. But if, in the new War on Terror, the Geneva Conventions did not apply to the Pentagon, as the President had ruled, then they certainly did not apply to the CIA. Like the military, the CIA would have to rely on its own new "blue water" definitions of what might be acceptable limits of legal interrogation. One point missed from public debate was the decision to exclude the CIA from the president's directive to the military to follow Geneva's provisions where possible. As one February 2002 official memo noted:

"CIA lawyers believe that, to the extent that (the Geneva convention on prisoners of war) protections do not apply as a matter of law but those protections applied as a matter of policy, it is desirable to circumscribe that policy so as to limits its application to the CIA. The other lawyers involved do not disagree with or object to the CIA's view."[45]

The detail of what exact methods the CIA was now entitled to use was for long to remain classified. Two memos, one written in August 2002 and another in March 2003, were said to define the detail of "enhanced"interrogation techniques permitted for CIA use, including some quite shocking.[46] Among those techniques was said to be "water-boarding", the simulated drowning of a prisoner.[47] At the San Diego trial of the SEAL commander, Lt. Ledford, two CIA representatives appeared in court to ensure that none of these secrets were revealed. When defence lawyers asked a witness "what position was al-Jamadi in when he died" the CIA objected that this information was classified, as they did when asked about the role of water in al-Jamadi's interrogation. The hearing was frequently conducted behind closed doors, with reporters and the public told to leave.[48] Effectively, Ledford was on trial for what his men did prior to the CIA interrogation, with what actually happened at the interrogation kept secret. Not surprisingly, the jury found Ledford not guilty.

Most observers and witnesses did generally report that the CIA's interrogations in Iraq and Guantánamo were often far more professional and subtle than those of military interrogators.[49] They were far less prone to the kind of random violent abuses and frustrated lashing-out by some poorly trained army interrogators. Whatever the CIA did was more deliberate. It emerged that the CIA came not only to resort to torture by proxy (through the rendition programme) but, in some specific cases, made a calculated use of what many would regard as severe torture itself. Legal authority for using new "intensive methods" of interrogation was requested and granted after the CIA struggle to get useful information from several key "high-value" prisoners held at undisclosed locations. It was after the capture of Abu Zubaydah in Pakistan in March 2002, and when he had become unhelpful despite an initial period of co-operation, that the CIA was said to have requested and won clearance to use techniques like "water-boarding".[50] Water-boarding was also allegedly authorised for the interrogation of Khalid Sheikh Mohammed, who was captured in 2003.[51] One de-classified military memorandum showed how the use of water treatment, described as "use of a wet towel and dripping water to induce the misperception of suffocation", was, though refused for use in Guantánamo, considered to be permissible legally "if not done with the specific intent to cause prolonged mental harm, and absent medical evidence that it would."[52]

All these revelations about the "new paradigm" that defined America's treatment of its enemies came to light in the months after Abu Ghraib. Faced with worldwide horror about what happened at the Iraqi prison, it was as if the events shocked many involved in the War on Terror into realising that unconstrained warfare — even against an evil foe like Al Qaeda — would be counter-productive. The images of Abu Ghraib came to express what was wrong in the War on Terror and were the catalyst that prompted a backlash against all the tactics that had been employed since 9/11. In this new atmosphere of public self-criticism, those internal critics of the conduct of the war felt able at last to come forward and speak publicly. They could now argue convincingly that public comment was needed to prevent further outrages.[53]

As the backlash continued, a series of rulings by the Supreme Court on 28 June 2004 that gave detainees at Guantánamo the right to file lawsuits for *habeas corpus* provided a crucial opportunity for these stories of abuse to emerge.[54] The Court said the President could declare both a US citizen and a foreign citizen to be an "enemy combatant" but that such detentions could be challenged in US federal courts. The ruling did not make it plain if such rights were to be extended beyond the US and Guantánamo to other US-controlled prisons, for example in Afghanistan. Sandra Day O'Connor, one of the judges, declared that "a state of war is not a blank cheque for the president." After this ruling, detainees at Guantánamo such as the former British resident Binyam Mohamed and the Australian national Mamdouh Habib, began to have access to their own independent lawyers and were at last able to recount their stories of rendition and torture.[55] After Abu Ghraib, the accounts of detainees like these who protested of their torture were at last taken seriously.

The discovery of prisoners like Binyam in military custody at Guantánamo who had previously been interrogated in Egyptian or Moroccan hands then provided confirmation that the foreign torture cells of Cairo or Damascus and the US jails at Guantánamo and Bagram were part of one interconnected gulag in which prisoners were swapped both between countries but also between the CIA and the US military. It became clear too that evidence obtained in these foreign jails were being used against prisoners at Guantánamo: in other words the rendition process was not just to send prisoners back home to be jailed but had an intrinsic purpose of interrogation. For example, under torture in Cairo, Habib had confessed to be a member of Al Qaeda in Afghanistan; now he faced the same accusation at Guantánamo.[56]

If 9/11 produced an "autumn of anger" that justified a relaxation of standards and resort to torture, as investigations got underway into the abuses at Abu Ghraib, at Bagram and at Guantánamo, a "spring of doubt" set in. Military and intelligence officials were beginning to wonder if the mission had been betrayed. Would they be left taking the rap for misconceived methods and tactics that could eventually lose the War on Terror?

8

THE SPECIAL RELATIONSHIP
OUR MAN IN TASHKENT

THE BRITISH EMBASSY, TASHKENT, UZBEKISTAN
22 July 2004

Down the corridor from the Ambassador's office was a large metal door, opened with a combination. Behind it was a small room, hardly bigger than a cupboard.

It was 3 p.m., the time for the afternoon telegrams. Her Majesty's Ambassador, Craig Murray, walked into the grandly-named Registry and checked an urgent telegram, addressed to the Foreign Secretary, Jack Straw MP. Unusually, this telegram, sent through an encrypted computer system, was marked not only for London but for copies to go to British missions around the world. The Ambassador wanted to make sure his views became known. The subject of his message was the CIA and torture. It began:

"CONFIDENTIAL

FM TASHKENT

TO IMMEDIATE FCO

TELNO 63

OF 220939Z JULY 04

INFO IMMEDIATE DFID, ISLAMIC POSTS, MOD, OSCE POSTS UKDEL
EBRD LONDON, UKMIS GENEVA, UKMIS NEW YORK

SUBJECT: RECEIPT OF INTELLIGENCE OBTAINED UNDER TORTURE

SUMMARY

1. We receive intelligence obtained under torture from the Uzbek intelligence services, via the US. We should stop. It is bad information

anyway. Tortured dupes are forced to sign up to confessions showing what the Uzbek government wants the US and UK to believe, that they and we are fighting the same war against terror."

Murray was writing about intelligence supplied by Britain's Secret Intelligence Service (SIS), also known as MI6. It contained reports, passed by the CIA, of interrogations conducted under torture. His own deputy, he said, had visited staff at the US Embassy in Tashkent who "readily acknowledged torture was deployed in obtaining intelligence." Not only, he said, was Britain and America condoning the torture but they were also being cheated. The "confessions" were being manipulated to tell the story that Uzbekistan wanted their allies to hear: that local Islamic dissidents were in league with the forces of Osama bin Laden.

On the usefulness of the material obtained, this is irrelevant. Article 2 of the Convention [Against Torture], to which we are a party, could not be plainer: No exceptional circumstances whatsoever, whether a state of war or a threat of war, internal political instability or any other public emergency, may be invoked as a justification of torture. Nonetheless, I repeat that this material is useless — we are selling our souls for dross. It is in fact positively harmful. It is designed to give the message the Uzbeks want the West to hear.

Murray's telegram reminded the Foreign Secretary of how he had spoken publicly against the use of torture. And yet this intelligence collusion stood in direct contradiction to his public stance. There was a postscript too. The British and the Americans were not just *receivers* of the intelligence. They had *instigated* some of this torture too. Prisoners captured in Afghanistan, he said, had been sent back to Uzbek jails. They had been rendered.

Plainly it was a breach of Article 3 of the Convention (Against Torture) for the coalition to deport detainees back here from Baghram, but it has been done. That seems plainly complicit.

It was the last telegram the British Ambassador would ever send. One week later, Murray flew to London on his annual leave and to have some medical treatment. Month after month his return was delayed. Then on 13 October the telegram was leaked to the media. Speaking in public, he defended its contents. Within four days, he was withdrawn from his post.

For more than two years after he arrived, Our Man in Tashkent had been clashing with his own government. Impulsive and perhaps arrogant, Murray was a man who took risks. He took risks in his job and took risks in his private life. But, though perhaps self-destructive, he had at least accomplished one thing. He had focussed attention on the most corrupt of regimes and one of the most questionable destinations of the CIA's rendition programme — a country ruled by an ex-Communist, President Islam Karimov, that, eight hundred years after Genghis Khan, still boiled some of its prisoners alive. Murray helped expose how intelligence gleaned from such tortures was routinely circulated and consumed by the West.

Craig Murray was never your typical British diplomat. Educated at a grammar school and Dundee University, rather than the more traditional Eton and Oxford, he shunned the old-school network. An eccentric, he wore smart three-piece suits combined with Wallace and Gromit ties. He drank heavily, enjoyed late-night bars, and had a succession of extra-marital affairs, including with a fellow Ambassador's daughter. I once asked Murray what the best thing about being a diplomat was? "Oh, the sex," he replied, half-seriously.[1]

But what had troubled Murray's superiors more than his *personal* conduct was the lack of inhibition in his professional life. Murray showed no concern for the polite conventions of diplomacy: he was a passionate individual prepared to abandon form and euphemisms and prepared to speak forcefully and publicly about what he believed. From almost the day he touched down in the capital of Uzbekistan, Murray had been battling from the inside to expose what he saw as a scandal — the West's support for a ruthless regime.

Many said Murray's campaigning zeal made him unfit to be a senior diplomat. Yet, fit or unfit for the post for which he had been selected, Murray would throw a spotlight on a thorny dilemma like no-one else: how, in fighting for a goal of spreading global freedom across the world, the West had ended up extending support for some of the world's least free regimes. In Britain, Murray's accusations had an additional explosive mix. Prime Minister Tony Blair had vowed to be America's closest ally, to maintain what London still called the "Special Relationship". At the heart of that relationship lay the exchange of intelligence. Every key piece of information in the war against terrorism should, by secret treaty, be exchanged across the Atlantic.[2] Murray, by speaking of the CIA's secret intelligence reports, had broken a cardinal rule. Nothing should *ever* be revealed about each other's information. In doing so he had assaulted that relationship, but he had also opened up its contents to public scrutiny. The CIA's traffic, he said, contained information obtained from torture. Some were the fruits of the agency's rendition programme. Was Britain, in taking part in this exchange, now complicit in some ways with the CIA's own torture programme?

I first met Murray that summer, in the month before he was fired. He was staying in a luxury apartment overlooking the Thames. Belonging to a friend, it was beautifully furnished, but Murray had managed to make a complete mess. There were papers scattered everywhere, empty coffee cups in the sink and an atmosphere of confusion as Murray chased around the flat looking for things he had lost. I liked him immediately. In many ways he seemed quite a typical "whistleblower", a risk-taking maverick prepared to lose everything in his quest to do things his way.

By then I had heard about Murray's July telegram but had not seen it. There was a buzz among diplomats that it concerned "extraordinary rendition" — the very topic I was researching. Murray then surprised me. "It was actually your piece that helped inspire me to write that," he said. "I read your article in the

New Statesman and by then I realised it was happening in Uzbekistan too." He was referring to the article I had published in May that had reported on America's network of prisons and of planes. Since that piece, I had started to track the movements of the fleet of CIA planes. And I was curious as to why Uzbekistan should be so important. After two years of frequent visits to Tashkent, the CIA planes' visits seemed to have stopped overnight in September 2003.[3] Had there been a rupture in relations?

The importance of Uzbekistan to the CIA was obvious from its geography, as obvious it was to the great generals of Alexander the Great, who reached its frontiers, to Genghis Khan, who marched through and sacked its cities, to Tamburlane, who made the southern city of Samarkand his capital, and to the Russians and British who jostled for influence in the nineteenth-century's espionage war. When Murray first met President Karimov, he reminded the Ambassador of this Great Game. "The greatest misfortune in the history of the Uzbek people, is what happened in what you call the Great Game," he told Murray.[4] Located on the ancient Silk Route between the great civilizations of East and West, Uzbekistan stood within striking range of China. It controlled the route south from Moscow towards Iran, Afghanistan and India, and it stood at the north-eastern frontier of Islamic influence. After the fall of the Soviet empire in 1991, the CIA moved quickly to win new influence and, touring the region, offered to establish a formal relationship with President Karimov. This move angered the Russians. The then prime minister, Primakov, telephoned the CIA to register his protest. "We know what you're doing there," he said, "trying to establishing relationships with the Near Abroad; It's not acceptable. The Near Abroad is ours." But the CIA persisted.

In the 1990s, the CIA had a more specific interest in common with the Uzbeks. The decline and then end of Communism in Uzbekistan saw the revival of religion and with that the emergence of new Islamic political forces. Brutally repressed by Karimov, these forces splintered into different factions, including some that urged a violent revolt or *jihad*. Most of these Islamic groups were purely national in character, seeking merely to challenge Karimov's rule. But across central Asia, tensions were boiling, heightened by the brutal actions by Russian troops in Chechnya. Some of these groups were prepared to support the wide international *jihad*, both against the Russians and against all secular forces, including the United States. The victory of the Taliban in Afghanistan in September 1996 had provided a home for those escaping Karimov's repression and, for the Uzbeks and the CIA, it also now provided a common enemy. In practical terms, Tashkent became the only practical base for operations against the Taliban, and against Osama bin Laden, who lurked within their borders. The only outpost of revolt against the Taliban within Afghanistan, the Northern Alliance, was located in the northern Afghan mountains of the Hindu Kush. Nearby Pakistan was actively supportive of the Taliban, Iran was a "no go area" for the CIA, and Tajikistan, though lying closer and also hostile to the Taliban, was too unstable a place for an effective agency base (as well as hosting a garrison of Russian troops). Karimov approved a plan, devised by the CIA's CTC, to stage a snatch operation for Osama bin Laden out of an airstrip in his country.[5] Then in September 2000, it was from Uzbekistan, as mentioned in Chapter 6, that the CIA launched its secret unmanned Predator spy plane flights against bin Laden. The agency paramilitary Jawbreaker teams also deployed from Tashkent to provide direct covert assistance to the Northern Alliance and install a covert listening post to intercept communications.[6] After 9/11, the Jawbreaker programme was revived. The CIA's Counter-Terrorist Centre deployed the first teams of US operatives on the ground. They flew by CIA Hercules from Frankfurt, assembled their gear in Tashkent, and then moved south by road, and then in an old Russian Mi-17 helicopter or light plane.[7]

After 9/11, the public face of cooperation with Uzbekistan became the giant ex-Soviet base in the south, near the towns of Kharshi and Khabanabad and known to all as K2. Lying 90 miles north of the border, it was once a supply route for the Russians into Afghanistan. It was now a supply route for the American military. Named Camp Stronghold Freedom, the base earned Karimov $15 million a year from the Pentagon in leasing fees till 2003, and a total of $280 million in US aid between 2002, 2003 and 2004.[8] American, British, Canadian, and Australian Special Forces all mounted their operations south from this huge base in the desert. With victory assured in Afghanistan, the Uzbek base became less important. America's giant transport planes could fly direct to Kabul and south to Kandahar. But, having established the base, the US was not going to give it up easily. As a crucial strategic foothold in a hostile region, what was now being called a "lily-pad", the K2 base was considered a model for future operations — one of a chain of outposts that could be used as part of Defense Secretary Donald Rumsfeld's concept of a modern form of rapid-deployment flexible warfare. This then was the public side. The maintenance of the base became a crucial US goal. But there were other operations, managed by the CIA, that were considered important too. This was the darker side of this new relationship.

MUNICIPAL COURT, TASHKENT
20 August 2002

The British Ambassador stood, within a crowded throng, sweating in a three-piece suit. Before him, inside a crudely-made cage, painted white, was a thin twenty-three-year-old man, the youngest of six defendants on trial. The judge, who sat with no jury, could barely disguise his anger or his prejudice. "I don't suppose anyone could hear you through your long Muslim beard" he said, laughing at his own joke.[9] Isanker Khudoberganov was not laughing.[10] Like the others he knew he faced the death penalty by firing squad. Khudoberganov said he was seriously tortured, and three members of his family said they had even witnessed some of it. The judge, a smug figure named Nizamiddin Rustamov, was not impressed. "You are just telling us about torture, and not about your crimes," he told Isanker. Another time, when he complained of torture marks, Rustamov stopped him to remind him he had been at the Ministry of Internal Affairs which was, in the judge's words, "not a holiday resort."[11] For Murray, the trial of Khudoberganov was an introduction to reality, what he later would call his "awakening".

Murray had arrived in Tashkent just a few days before, travelling first class with his wife Fiona and his children, Jamie and Emily, on an Uzbek Air 747 jet. It landed at 2 a.m. and he was greeted at the airport by his key staff: Karen Moran, his deputy head of mission, and Chris Hirst, his information officer and Karen's partner. It was a small posting, small for its significance, with just four fully-accredited UK diplomatic staff, as well as about a dozen local and British non-diplomatic staff. Outside the terminal was waiting his official flag car. It was not a Rolls Royce or Jaguar, like at bigger, more prestigious embassies, but instead a rather humble Land Rover. Still, as they drove away, he was proud of the Union flag fluttering on the bonnet and its number plate 16 CMD — "16" was code for a British diplomat and "CMD" meant *chef de mission diplomatique.* Twenty minutes away was his new embassy, an old two-storey building surrounded by a fence, a small garden and concrete anti-blast barriers. Long ago, it had been the home to Alexander Kerensky, the leader of the first post-Tsarist government in 1917. Now its grandeur was subdued by the demands of its many functions. The staff of the mission was due for expansion and a new separate residence for Murray was under construction. When completed at Christmas it would be lavish, boasting an eight-seater Jacuzzi, a sauna, and en suite bathrooms for each of its five bedrooms. The garden included a fabulous water feature installed at Murray's request. For now though, the Ambassador and his wife were lodged in what was effectively a flat over the shop. A door from the residence led straight into his office.[12]

Murray's appointment to Tashkent had been announced in April in the diplomatic column of *The Times.*[13] At forty-three, he was to be one of Britain's youngest ambassadors, although not the youngest. The next few months required an intensive course in Russian and his preparation ended with three weeks of briefings. These had concentrated, said Murray, on three crucial areas — the department's management system, on Uzbekistan's role in the War on Terror, and the Central Asian country's vital economic potential (its cotton industry and, above all, its oil and gas). There was little discussion, he claimed, about the regime's human rights record, and yet he was able to garner some basic facts. Karimov, as all knew, was essentially an old-style Communist. After years in the party, he had seized power in 1989, while the country was still under Soviet control. When the Moscow regime collapsed, he held onto control. He had re-named his party the People's Democratic Party but left the system and one-party rule almost entirely intact. His last election saw him win with an impressive 91.9 per cent.[14] All major sectors of the economy remained in state hands. Karimov was also proudly repressive. Back in 1999, he said: "I am prepared to rip off the heads of 200 people, to sacrifice their lives, in order to save peace and to have calm in the republic."[15] He boasted of executing about one hundred people a year. More than 6,000 political opponents were locked in his jails. Threatened by the revival of Islam, he ordered a huge crackdown on religion. The definition of "crime" came to include having a "Muslim" beard, or holding a prayer meeting at home.[16] Tortures were said to include the ripping out of nails, the pulling of teeth, electrocution, suffocation and rape.

It was in that Tashkent courtroom that Murray saw the reality of state-sponsored torture. In a letter to his mother and sister, written a month after the trial in which his confessions were recorded, Khudoberganov wrote of how he endured weeks of torture in the hope of a fair trial. "They tied my hands from behind, hit me with truncheons and chairs and kicked me on the kidneys. They hit my head against the wall until it was bleeding." Starved of food and with his family threatened, he had only then confessed to being a terrorist.[17] Murray had seen how these kinds of accusations were treated — with complete disregard.

More tangible evidence emerged a few days later. Murray was shown an envelope of photographs of the body of a dissident named Muzafar Avazov, aged thirty-five, that was covered in burns, with a wound on the back of his head and with fingernails missing. Avazov had been detained in the prison of Jaslyk, where he was serving a sentence for membership of Hizb-ut-Tahrir al-Islami, the Islamic Freedom Party. This banned organisation, popular across Central Asia, had disavowed violence as a means to achieve power and establish an Islamic state. But the Karimov regime had repressed its members brutally and pressed Western governments to declare it a terrorist group.[18] Avazov's 63-year-old mother Fatima had brought the photographs herself to the British Embassy. (She was later thanked by the regime with a six-year jail sentence for attempting to "overthrow the constitutional order".)[19] Murray sent the photographs back to London for analysis. A report from the University of Glasgow pathology department, headed by Dr Peter Vanezis, declared his death had followed severe torture. "The pattern of the scalding shows a well demarcated line on the lower chest/abdomen, which could well indicate the forceful application of hot water whilst the person is within some kind of bath or similar vessel."[20]

Murray was now enraged by what he knew. And yet he found little interest in raising these subjects, particularly among his fellow Ambassadors. The problem, as we've discussed, was Uzbekistan's strategic importance. Was it wise to start rocking the boat? In an angry telegram dispatched on 16 September, the Ambassador laid down his conclusions. It was just over a month since he had arrived. The telegram began:

Confidential

FM Tashkent

TO FCO, Cabinet Office, DFID, MODUK, OSCE Posts, Security Council Posts

16 September 02

SUBJECT: US/Uzbekistan: Promoting Terrorism

SUMMARY

US plays down human rights situation in Uzbekistan. A dangerous policy: increasing repression combined with poverty will promote Islamic terrorism. Support to Karimov regime a bankrupt and cynical policy.

Murray wrote of the 7,000 to 10,000 political and religious prisoners in jail. The boiling alive of dissidents like Avazov, the committal of two leading dissidents, Elena Urlaeva and Larissa Vdovna, to a lunatic asylum, and the fact that all political opposition groups remained banned. "Terrible torture is commonplace" he said. Yet, just a week earlier, the State Department had declared that Uzbekistan was improving "in both human rights and democracy", freeing up a $140 million aid programme for the country. British policy was one of engagement with the Karimov regime, and yet to make sense "it must mean grappling with the problems, not mute collaboration." It was time, he felt, to up the ante.

FREEDOM HOUSE, TASHKENT
17 October 2002

John Herbst, the lean and gangly Ambassador of the United States, was first to step up to the podium. A 51-year-old career diplomat and fluent Russian speaker, he had been in Tashkent for three years. Before him was an audience of diplomats, campaigners, and Uzbek officials. The occasion was the launch of Freedom House, an US organisation dedicated to the spread of democracy. In Uzbekistan, as everyone knew, there was precious little evidence of this. Herbst, however, was there to emphasise the positive. Uzbekistan, he said, choosing his words carefully, had "made public commitments to democratic reforms and the protection of human rights". It had made "some progress towards meeting those commitments", was his guarded comment.[21] One observer, a local human rights activist, was to describe his speech as "pale, watery by comparison with the one that followed".[22]

When Her Majesty's Ambassador Murray stood up to speak, he began innocuously. Whisky and liberty, he said, went well together, and how difficult it was to find real whisky in Tashkent. He became blunt: "Uzbekistan is not a functioning democracy, nor does it appear to be moving in the direction of democracy." The audience looked shocked. He spoke of the cases of Avazoz and Alimov "apparently tortured to death by boiling water" but stressed that "all of us know" it had not been an isolated incident. "Brutality is inherent in a system where convictions habitually rely on signed confessions rather than on forensic or material evidence."[23] As Murray said "thank you" and stepped down, the backlash was already beginning.

Back in London, at the Foreign and Commonwealth Office's Eastern Department, the mandarins were not amused. Behind the formulation of a speech lay a bitter dispute. In one corner was "Our Man in Tashkent". In the other, back in Whitehall, were his supervisors. At its heart was the question of tact — in the art of diplomacy, should brutality be called brutality?

The FCO believed Murray was fast becoming a campaigner. "You're an ambassador: not an NGO," an official wrote to him, two days before the speech.[24] A day later, the same official wrote to one of his bosses in the FCO: "we are fast developing a problem with Craig Murray,"[25] a view the senior official endorsed. But Murray was having none of it: "My style is more direct, and in my view, more effective. I am sorry but I am never going to turn into Polonius."[26] Another FCO official told Murray to avoid "language which is too outspoken," what they called "the soapbox tone of the peroration." In particular, he was told in no uncertain terms that the word "brutality," should definitely be cut.[27] But Murray had other allies outside the Eastern Department, including in the Foreign Office's human rights department. And so, approved by fax from London, the word "brutality" had survived, and so had the outspoken tone.

The president of Uzbekistan was not used to such criticism. In London, the Uzbek ambassador, Dr Alisher Faizullaev, came to protest to a top official at the Foreign Office and was told that London was behind her Ambassador. In the telegram to Tashkent that followed, Murray was told "the Uzbeks are clearly riled to have been told some home truths."[28] But still many at the Foreign Office believed Murray's loud approach, if continued, would reduce British influence with the Uzbek regime. Murray disagreed, believing it was pointless to try to seek to influence an ex-Communist dictator like Karimov with quiet words — a strategy of "mute collaboration" as he called it. It was pressure that was needed, he thought. For now, though this dispute was a secret. Murray's speech became part of the official record and was republished in full in the Foreign Office's annual human rights report.

As an ambassador, Murray's contacts were not just with his direct superiors, the Eastern Department, but also with policy experts in all areas, as well as other government agencies including the intelligence services. Twice a day, going to the Embassy's tiny registry, Murray would pick up the latest telegrams. The most sensitive ones, containing secret intelligence, were known as CX traffic and were generally for the Ambassador's eyes only. It was among these that Murray would make his most important discovery.

Britain's Secret Intelligence Service, he had been briefed, had no declared station in Uzbekistan. In fact, as he reported later, they had no operative "within a thousand miles." Without an official liaison with Uzbek intelligence, it meant that most intelligence from the Uzbeks was coming from the Americans. CX traffic was routinely marked "from a friendly intelligence service." The information about Uzbekistan, he noticed, often contained information derived from the confessions of captured prisoners. Sometimes they referred to "detainee debriefing." Murray was clear in his mind about what had happened. "This was information obtained under torture. That's how they do interrogations here," he said. "It was clear the CIA was just picking it up and we were buying what they told us." Murray said he sent Moran, his deputy, to check the facts at the American Embassy. She reported back that the Americans acknowledged that torture was plainly involved.[29]

Murray now believed he had discovered a major issue. If Britain was receiving intelligence obtained under torture, albeit from the CIA, then British ministers were effectively colluding in that torture. To that effect, he wrote a telegram to London, marked "Top Secret", that warned ministers of this torture evidence circulating in intelligence reports and that the government could be in violation of Article 2 of the UN Convention Against Torture, which banned any "complicity" in such acts. As he also noted, much of the information was also unreliable. One CX report spoke of a training camp in the hills of Samarkand. Yet his own military attaché, he said, knew exactly the same area and that there were certainly no training camps. It was not till March the following year that he received a full reply to these allegations from London — a month when the Ambassador's life would turn a corner in many different ways.

RAWALPINDI, PAKISTAN
1 March 2003

The events of that month would begin in Pakistan, in a small apartment in an outer suburb. It was here, after years of searching, that the CIA would finally capture one of its biggest prizes. The architect of 9/11 and of many of Al Qaeda's biggest attacks was now in US custody. He was transferred quickly to a secret location. Just eighteen days before the US and Britain invaded Iraq, the CIA had begun questioning him. On 2 March , a plane set out from Washington, the CIA's Gulfstream V. Pausing to refuel in Prague, the Czech Republic, it flew on with a new flight plan: "Prague — Tashkent, Uzbekistan". Time and again, after a key arrest or key event, the same pattern had been repeated. *The plane's movements were a log of what the CIA considered important.* Arrested in Pakistan, the CIA's top prisoner had been flown on to a secret location. Was this Tashkent? Or was the plane merely stopping off, heading for another "black site" in an allied country further east, like Thailand? I never discovered the plane's final destination. But one thing was apparent — the capital of Uzbekistan had become a vital hub in the CIA's world operations. No other destination east of Jordan had received so many flights from the CIA fleet, nor from the particular planes like the Gulfstream that were used in renditions.

That year, a Danish journalist named Michael Andersen was following events in Uzbekistan. A distinguished radio reporter, he criss-crossed much of Central Asia and had followed closely the resurgence of Islam. The most militant elements of that revival, he knew well, were based in the countryside, such as in the desperately-poor Ferghana Valley, a region that is shared between Kyrgyzstan, Tajikistan and Uzbekistan itself. Under pressure from the Karimov government in Uzbekistan, many young Islamists had fled the country and ended up in Afghanistan. And after 9/11, when American forces entered, they began to be captured, both in Afghanistan itself and next-door Pakistan. "As I travelled around, I spoke to many of these men's families," he recalled. "And I began to realise what was happening. These militants were being sent home." Sometimes, the returnees would be interrogated and then freed and forced to appear on local television. "It was like something from Soviet Russia. They would stand up and make a confession — admit they had been with Al Qaeda, apologise for all their crimes and be publicly shamed." Others, it was clear, were simply transferred into prison. "Their families would get word they were back in the country and that they were in the hands of state security." Andersen knew who was behind these transfers. "Everyone knew it was Americans. Several family members told me that their sons had told them that Americans had been transferring them back. They were organising a repatriation into Uzbek jails, and of course that meant a transfer into torture. ... This was a country that boiled people alive."

In early March, Craig Murray was in Brussels, attending a conference on EU policy toward Central Asia when he received what he called a "rather terse summons" to a meeting in London. After his protest about torture and American policy, Murray was convinced he was about to be sacked. But the meeting, in fact, was to answer the question he had posed — was it right to receive intelligence obtained from torture? As was his habit, Murray arrived a little late. All the other key people were already in place, seated round a mahogany table. The tone of the meeting, said Murray, was brusque. He was told that the FCO "does not think it is wise to commit such matters to paper". But the matter had now been considered at the "the highest level", including with Jack Straw and with "C", the traditional reference to the head of MI6. The legal viewpoint was now presented to him. Nothing in the UN Torture Convention prevented *receiving* torture intelligence. The only ban was on using such intelligence in court. A letter would confirm this advice in writing, an official admission that the receipt of torture evidence was considered legally acceptable. The use of intelligence from torture "did not create any offence" under law, the letter's author wrote. [30] Another official present — there to represent the views of MI6 — described the material from the Uzbeks as "operationally useful". He would not elaborate. In just a few minutes, the meeting was over. Murray left with a sense of renewed outrage. "I just had the impression they did not really care," he recalled. "I was the one that dealt with the victims, the people who had been tortured but for them it was just not important."[31]

Murray had failed in his battle with Whitehall. Intelligence from the CIA — regardless of how it had been obtained — would simply not be turned away nor not passed around; and yet he had confirmed one important thing — the Foreign Office, under a Labour government that once had spoken proudly of creating an "ethical foreign policy", was fully aware that some of its intelligence was being obtained under conditions of torture. Could Murray himself turn away from the subject? Only seven months into the job, his reputation back in Tashkent was made. Like it or not, he was an Ambassador of Human Rights. Dissidents and campaigners turned up again and again at his door. How could he just walk away?

Later that March, Murray had a guest in town, his Foreign Officer manager, on a two-day visit. On the second day they drove to Samarkand and had two key meetings. The first was with the regional governor or *hokkim*, Shavkat Mirziyaev.[32] And the second was with Jamal Mirsaidov. He was a literature professor at the city's university but he was also a leading Tajik dissident. They arrived at Mirsaidov's house at about 4.30 p.m., and the professor greeted the pair with a spread of dried fruit and pastries. It was a pleasant exchange. The shock came the next day. In the early hours of the morning, a badly-bruised body was dumped on the doorstep of the professor's house. It was Mirsaidov's own grandson, Shukrat. "The lad was eighteen. His knees and elbows had been smashed by blows from a hammer, or perhaps a spade or rifle butt. One hand had been immersed in boiling liquid until the flesh was peeling away from the bone. He had been killed with a blow that caved in the back of his skull."[33] Murray, who was informed of the death later that day, after his boss had already left the country, interpreted the killing as a punishment. "The Russian Ambassador told me, from his excellent sources, that this was intended as a warning to both dissidents and me not to meet each other."[34] The shocking death of Mirsaidov's grandson, apparently as a direct result of his meeting, hardened Murray's determination to continue his struggle. And yet the escalation of the conflict was putting lives in danger. Could he really survive the mental pressure? Did he have the personal strength to confront or persuade both Karimov and his own Foreign Office? The sad truth was that Murray did not have such strength. Here then, was the root of what became his own tragedy.

Murray, as described, was no ordinary ambassador. It was his desire to be different that had put him into contact with the regime's opponents, and had taken him beyond his embassy's walls to discover the reality of its repression. But the same contrary nature infected his personal life too, and he had struggled for years to stay faithful to his family. That March, in the midst of his turmoil, Murray was in his favourite nightspot when he became particularly attracted to a young dancer. Her name was Nadira. After pursuing her for several days, he started an affair.

Back in his small embassy, Murray had other problems too — ones of considerable advantage to the Karimov regime. His Third Secretary, Chris Hirst, was being accused of a bizarre assault, attacking a neighbour with a baseball bat and his Rottweiler. To complicate matters, Hirst's partner, as mentioned, was Moran, Murray's deputy. In May, Hirst was withdrawn back to London, and he quietly resigned from the diplomatic service. But, back in Tashkent, the atmosphere had become poisonous. Some staff blamed Murray for the man's dismissal. When a Foreign Office official visited in June to discuss the matter, he picked up details not only of the diplomat's conduct but of a series of rumours about Murray himself. Murray by now was in mental turmoil. A doctor diagnosed acute anxiety.

THE OLD ADMIRALTY BUILDING, THE FOREIGN AND COMMONWEALTH OFFICE
London, 21 August 2003

In a bland office just off St James' Park, Craig Murray faced his accusers. He heard a list of extraordinary charges:

Allegation 1
That he had facilitated visas for girlfriends, paying money for air tickets, receiving sexual favours in his office in return.

Allegation 2
That he regularly turns up at the office drunk or hung-over and late before going home to "sleep it off", then returning to the office at 16.50 p.m. demanding people start work late with him.

Allegation 3
That he took a girlfriend as an interpreter on an up-country trip after which no note was produced.

...

Allegation 5
That at an away-day Murray encouraged drivers to take embassy vehicles down staircases.

...

Allegation 8
That he "knows" the SBU [local intelligence service] are watching him but doesn't worry because he is open about his behaviour. But he is scared his wife will "find out" and divorce him,
taking the children

Allegation 9
That certain locally-employed staff —"dolly-birds"— are employed in e.g. visa section at double normal rates "because he says so".

...

Allegation 12
That he frequently takes the flag car out (with driver) until 02.00-04.30 a.m.[35]

All of those charges were ultimately to be withdrawn, but Murray was now
caught in a pincer movement. The Foreign Office had decided the ambassador
must go. Murray had returned that morning, summoned from a holiday in
Canada. He discovered that while he was away an FCO official had travelled to
Tashkent and collected a total of eighteen allegations. Each, he reported, was
supported "by at least one member (often up to four) of the UK-based staff."
Though varying in seriousness, for an ambassador these matters were hardly
frivolous. The Foreign Office had a clear duty to investigate. But had Murray
been set up? To some it had all the air of a quiet hint from on high, just like
that of King Henry II, when he declared: "Will no one rid me of this turbu-
lent priest?" Internal documents, though revealing nothing of such an order,
do reveal a clear desire to find a basis for firing Murray. While he holidayed
in Canada, one official was warning: "I'm not sure we can lay a trap for him
before he returns to post."[36] Another appeared to recommend a manipulative
approach: "Very helpful in clarifying for me the kind of person we're dealing
with. I agree we should call him back; say we've been reflecting on his own
self-questioning. ... say he should leave quickly on operational grounds and go
to London."[37] The response from above was curt: "Fine. Please go ahead. It will
be messy."[38]

The confrontation, as it turned out, was both messy and Kafkaesque. It
started not with the serious disciplinary allegations but with a simple demand
that Murray resign from his post. The request for resignation, they said, was
on "operational grounds", not because of the disciplinary allegations. Murray,
though exhausted with jet lag, refused to quit. He saw it all as a devious ma-
noeuvre to force him out. And the charges themselves, he said, were ludicrous
and without foundation. The Foreign Office now issued some further "advice".
While the investigation occurred, Murray could discuss the allegations with
no one in Tashkent.[39] The Foreign Office feared he would put under pressure
local staff, over which he had great power. But Murray was outraged: "It was
all utterly unbelievable," he recalled. "I was faced with these incredible accusations made by anonymous individuals and was told I had almost no means of

defending myself and no-one that I could go to for advice. Can you imagine the mental strain?"[40]

TASHKENT
23 August

Back home at the residence, Murray pondered what to do. In post as Ambassador now for just over a year, he had challenged his superiors on every level, forcing them to approve his robust speech at Freedom House and pressing them over intelligence from torture. But his dissidence, till now, had been largely internal. Murray had bent the rules but not openly contravened them. Now, when his job and his reputation had been placed squarely on the line by those in London, Murray decided to cross that line and fight back.

The only way to win was to take the Foreign Office on and to gather support. Orders or no orders, he would return to the embassy and speak to his staff. Gathering key people in his office, Murray told them "the view had been reached in London that this post would operate more efficiently" if he were to leave.[41] By about 5 p.m. Tashkent time, Murray's staff had drafted, signed and faxed a letter to London that protested his innocence. Other British expatriates were informed too, and they too signed a letter that was faxed off to London.

On 28 August, the struggle escalated. In an email, Murray was told he had flouted the "advice" given to him and he was now told to "remain off the Embassy premises until further notice". The email continued however to emphasise that "you're not being suspended from duty: you remain HM Ambassador to Uzbekistan. ..." But it was essential "you do not speak further to your staff — UK-based or locally-employed — about this matter."[42]

Banished to the residence, Murray now lobbied his friends and they intervened. On 7 September, a British businessman in Tashkent wrote to *The Times* in protest: "The common belief here is that Mr Murray is being sacrificed to the Americans, since the US Embassy makes no effort to conceal its inveterate dislike of the way in which he repeatedly and unequivocally slams the Human Rights record of a region so heavily under US influence."[43] On 1 October, *The Times* reported that "The Foreign Office insisted that it supported Mr Murray's line on Human Rights in Uzbekistan". But it was the beginning of a storm of press allegations.

By now the stress was getting to Murray. At the beginning of September, an official, Tony Crombie, came to investigate the charges. A day later, Murray had collapsed with acute anxiety and he was medivacced to London and put on suicide watch. While he sat in hospital and then convalesced, the case of Craig Murray was now becoming a celebrated cause. "Ambassador accused after criticising US," the *Guardian* reported. Many hinted the "sick leave" was a ploy by the Foreign Office. And yet, Murray's health problems were far from fictitious. On 14 November, he returned to Tashkent, but in 48 hours he had collapsed ill again. It was an attack of pulmonary embolism, blood clots on his lungs that deprived him of oxygen. Rushed to the hospital, he was lucky to survive and was then flown back to London by air ambulance. In Tashkent meanwhile, Crombie had combed through the allegations but he was later to conclude they contained almost no substance. One internal document concluded that "in by far the majority of the allegations, there is no case to answer in conduct and discipline terms and that, where there is a case to answer, Mr Murray's behaviour does not seem to him [Crombie] to constitute gross misconduct."[44] Murray might have been a socialite. He might have visited bars after dark. But there was no evidence this had affected his work. The British press was also at work, swarming to Tashkent to investigate the claims. They too could not prove any impropriety. Most left concluding they were a simple smear.

In January, Murray left the hospital and returned to Tashkent. All charges had now been withdrawn, except for the offence of speaking to his staff about the initial charges. He received a reprimand, and was told to return to his post.

But Murray was now a deeply troubled man. Wearied by illness and months of confrontation, he no longer had the energy for his interventionist approach. It got worse in March when the *Mail on Sunday* carried an extravagant headline: "Torture row British ambassador dumps wife for 22 year old Uzbek hairdresser." The story was out about Murray's affair with Nadira and the fact his wife Fiona had returned home to Britain. Life for Murray, then, was unravelling.

Murray's stay in Tashkent was nearly over, but not quite. The story of investigations of torture took one final twist. The scandal of Abu Ghraib had now broken, and he read my account of the CIA's rendition system. He thought back now, he said later, of some people he met. They were pilots and ground crew from an American company who used to go drinking in the expatriate bar called the Lionheart.[45] Their missions, they said, were for the US government. And they had even flown prisoners from Bagram in Afghanistan to Tashkent. "They told me they were in the aviation business, doing contracts for the US government," he would say. "It was clear they were doing something special." One of them had even married a local Uzbek, and then suddenly just disappeared and left her behind. The only news of him was a brief phone call from Frankfurt. Murray by then had also met Michael Andersen, the Danish journalist, and he heard from him of the wider story, how men were appearing in Uzbekistan's jail after their capture by the US in Pakistan and Afghanistan. Now, he believed, his discoveries made sense. The CIA, it was clear to him, was not only taking evidence from torture; it was actively *procuring* that torture. Many of the prisoners had been delivered to the Uzbeks. They were handed over to face torture.

In July, Murray sat down to compile his conclusions and to write the telegram on rendition that would, ultimately, end his career.

Two months later, when I met Murray in his flat, he was still officially Her Majesty's Ambassador but, in truth, he knew the game was over. The issues he had fought for were now too important. "I'm not going to apologise. I'm not going to be silent." I wished him well and left London shortly afterwards for a trip to Baghdad. While I was away things moved fast. His July telegram was leaked to the *Financial Times* and he was formally withdrawn from his post by email. And then Murray went on BBC Radio 4, criticising the government. The same day, 15 October, he was suspended from duty.[46] Murray found a lawyer and threatened to sue the Foreign Office for unfair dismissal. He finally left the service with a £300,000 redundancy package and a Foreign Office explanation of "compassionate and medical circumstances".[47] He instantly vowed to continue his battle politically, taking on Jack Straw as an independent candidate in the British general election of 5 May 2005. He received just five per cent of the vote.

ANDIJAN, FERGHANA VALLEY
13 May 2005

Protestors had seized a government building and demanded the release from jail of a group of businessmen, members of an Islamic group that was considered by most as moderate. A crowd, most of the town, was milling around outside. Then without warning, at 5.20 p.m., the armoured cars arrived and starting firing. Estimates said between six hundred and one thousand people were killed.

Galima Bukharbaeva, an American-trained journalist, was a witness:

As they drove up to the square, they opened fire without warning, and everyone ran. I also ran... . The bullets flew at such a rate that it seemed hail was falling on all sides. ... I ran in fear amid the roar of weapons, and saw several men who were running next to me fall down... The shooting stopped for a while. The first row of APCs [Armoured Personnel Carriers] had done their work. But scarcely a minute had gone by when a second row of APCs appeared which also opened fire. ... Only when back in the hotel did I get my notebook with telephone numbers. I opened my backpack and saw that a bullet had passed through my notebook, along with the. ... journalist identity card.[48]

In the days that followed the world reacted with outrage. A State Department spokesman, Richard Boucher, at first urged caution, warning of the escape of prisoners "including possibly members of the Islamic Movement of Uzbekistan, an organisation we consider a terrorist organisation." But later the US too realised that what had occurred was a massacre, and joined condemnations of the Uzbek government by Jack Straw and European governments including Greece and France.[49] The State Department was unable to certify the country's record on improving human rights and a tranche of US aid was now blocked.[50] The

Russians and the Chinese chose a different approach, refusing to interfere in the country's "internal affairs". Two months after the massacre, President Karimov announced the closure of America's K2 base and strengthened his relations with the Russians and Chinese instead.[51]

In some ways, there had always been a simple choice: to work with Karimov and to accept or at least try to soften his abuses, or to condemn him and lose all cooperation. Craig Murray had chosen to force not only his government but the hand of the United States. As an Ambassador, chosen to represent his government, he had exceeded his role. As an individual, he had achieved a great deal — opening a window on another frontier of the rendition system, and showing how a dictator would share evidence obtained under torture with Western intelligence agencies for his own political purposes: to secure international support or acquiescence for his own ruthless clampdown on the dissidents who opposed him. He had exposed to the world a very uncomfortable alliance — between a superpower that proclaimed human rights and an unreformed Communist who boiled his prisoners alive. Steve Crawshaw, UK director of Human Rights Watch, remarked: "Craig Murray may not have been a good ambassador; that's not for me to judge. But the abuses he pointed to were real, horrific."[52] If this was the War on Terror, many would ask, was it really worth fighting?

9

THE ITALIAN JOB

Flightlog

Registration: **Spar 92**;
Type: **Learjet 35**;
Operator: US Air Force.
Date: **17 February 2003**

Flight plan:
Aviano AFB (dep. 6.20 p.m.)
Ramstein AFB (arr. 7.30 p.m.)

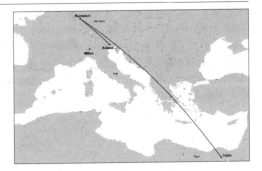

Registration: **N85VM**;
Type: **Gulfstream IV**;
Operator: Richmor Aviation

Flight plan:
Ramstein AFB (dep. 7.52 p.m.) —
Cairo (arr. 12.32 a.m.)

MILAN, ITALY
20 April 2004

In a small second-floor apartment, the hand of a 35-year-old woman in Islamic dress reached over and, with shaking fingers, dialled the 12 digits of a number in Alexandria, the ancient port on the Mediterranean coast of Egypt.[1] The woman, Nabila, was nervous because she could not quite believe the news she had just heard. The phone was answered and a man's voice appeared on the line, speaking in Arabic.

— "Nabila," he said.

— "Abu Omar," she replied.

— "May peace be with you."

— "How are you?"

— "I'm fine, thank God, where are you calling
　　from?"

— "I'm calling from home."

— "Are you still in that house?"

— "Yes."

Abu Omar

At first, the conversation was stilted. Nabila could
not really believe it was her husband on the line.
His name was Osama Nasr, known to his family
and friends in the Arab tradition as "Abu Omar",
meaning "the father of Omar", the name of his
then seven-year-old son.[2] An Egyptian citizen who
was granted asylum in Italy, he was under investigation by the Italian police for
potential involvement in plotting terrorist crimes in Europe. But he had disappeared thirteen months earlier and till today neither Nabila nor the Italian authorities had heard any news at all of him.

— "Are you well? How are you doing financially?" he asked.

— "I'm fine, I'm fine, thank God," she said.

— "Are there any other problems?"

— "I'm well, I'm well, everything is good!"

— "Are you serious?"

— "I swear! How are you? What are you doing?"

— "I'm fine, I'm fine"

— "You're fine?"

— "I'm fine, I'm fine!"

— "Really?"

It was clear now that Abu Omar had spent months in prison. He had last been
seen walking down the street in Milan on the way to midday prayers at the local
mosque where he sometimes preached. Somehow, he ended up in the hands of
the Egyptian secret police. But Osama was reticent to describe what had happened and he talked with a rich irony.

— "I'm fine, I'm fine!" he repeated.

— "Really?" she asked.

— "I swear! They brought me food every day."

— "Really?"

— "Sure, they brought me food from the fanciest restaurant!"

— "Thank God."

— "The matter is very simple, unfortunately a hitch cropped up... so... they
were meant to keep me one month... but they held me longer, anyhow I praise
the Lord."

— "Thank God!"

But he hinted that he had more to tell.

    — "Listen, I want us to talk…but don't call me from the home phone."

    — "Allright, if God wills it."

    — "Do you understand?"

    — "Yes, yes."

The previous afternoon, at 3 p.m., Abu Omar's brother, Magdi, who was home in Alexandria, had received a call from the local police station. "Come and pick your brother up straight away. Just don't ask what happened," they told him. Magdi and another brother, Isham, set off immediately. But when they arrived at the station, they were turned away. At 2.30 the next morning, the police called again: "If you don't come now, you'll never see him again."[3] The brothers raced round again and this time they found Abu Omar waiting. Hours later, the family were still in shock.

As their conversation continued, Nabila and her husband talked over some practical matters: Osama was concerned whether some of his friends had been jailed in Milan and whether the police, when they visited his house, took possession of his personal computer. "No", said Nabila. "Are you allright?" he asked. "I miss you Osama!," said Nabila. He said to take it easy. He was fine but he was banned now from leaving Alexandria. And he warned her not to come to Egypt to visit because, although they promised she would be safe, he was concerned that he would be barred from leaving again. And then, his guard slipped.

    — "Anyway, look, now we've spoken…keep calm, we'll talk later and I'll tell you everything."

    — "All right."

    — "Take it easy, there are no problems for me, there won't be a second kidnapping… there won't, there won't, you understand?"[4]

While they spoke, the lights on a box of electronics at a police station of the Carabinieri in via Lamarmora, central Milan were blinking.[5] The telephone conversation, like dozens of others across the city,[6] was being recorded onto a digital disk. As part of a wider investigation into Islamic militancy in Milan, Nabila's phone was being constantly monitored. The conversation of that evening would be replayed to investigators the following morning. It was to be their first concrete evidence that Osama did not just return peacefully to Egypt or elsewhere: he was kidnapped.

Was anyone else listening? America's National Security Agency? The Italian secret service? Egyptian intelligence? Either way, someone tipped off the Egyptians that Abu Omar was talking. This phone call and a few other calls home to friends provided Abu Omar with just a brief window of opportunity to tell his story before he was re-arrested and shut back up in jail. The phone call was also to set off a chain of inquiries that would prove to be one of the CIA's most embarrassing episodes since the attacks of 9/11.

THE PALACE OF JUSTICE, MILAN
21 April

In this tall grey-marble building, towering like a square fortress over surrounding streets, the sound of footsteps and animated conversations was echoing through the wide corridors that circled around the building's wide inner courtyard. At his desk on the fourth floor was Armando Spataro, the silver-haired deputy chief prosecutor of Milan and co-ordinator of all terrorism investigations. On the wall above was a collection of prints of the American painter Edward Hopper and a photo finish from the 1999 Chicago Marathon — a time of 3 hrs, 13 minutes, and 45 seconds. "Nothing I've done in the legal profession makes me as proud as my personal best in the marathon," the fifty-six-year-old said proudly. Also on his wall were many plaques and certificates. They recorded his co-operation with US prosecutors, with the FBI, with the US Drug Enforcement Agency, and with the Anti-Terrorism Branch at Scotland Yard.

That morning marked the beginning of a long legal journey for Spataro that would lead him to both confront the CIA, and, according to Italy's then justice minister, would come to threaten the country's entire relations with the US.[7] "The first person to tell me what had happened was a fellow prosecutor, Massimo Meroni. He was running an investigation, un-connected to the kidnapping, that had arranged for Abu Omar's home to be tapped," he recalled. Later, another prosecutor, Stefano Dambruoso, also phoned to mention the phone taps of Abu Omar calling from Egypt. It was Dambruoso who had run the kidnap investigation so far but he was clearing his desk ready to leave for a new job working for the United Nations in Vienna. He was about to hand over the entire case file to Spataro. "It was stunning news really, just to hear that Abu Omar was alive and had appeared again in Egypt. Of course, we immediately wanted to know much more. Just from his conversation with Nabila, it was clear he had been held in prison but we still had no details how he got there."[8]

A prosecutor for twenty-eight years, it was now over a year since Spataro had been working back in Milan.[9] Until the beginning of 2003, he had been working down in Rome and on 17 February that year, when Abu Omar was kidnapped, Spataro was still settling in to this new job. Under Italy's legal system, developed to combat the mafia and terrorist groups like the Red Brigades, a prosecutor like Spataro takes complete charge after a crime is reported — ordering inquiries by police and also conducting key interviews. Prosecutors make their investigations independently without any political control. "Under the law, if a crime is reported then we are obliged to open an investigation." If a case is solved then the prosecutor must draw up charges and then put them before a judge for approval. For now, though, he was only an observer on this case. "I do remember hearing about his mysterious disappearance. It quickly seemed like a kidnap," he recalled. "But back then I didn't even have an office in the building. I wasn't really involved."[10]

It was between 11.30 a.m. and midday on 17 February when Abu Omar had disappeared. He had set off from his home for the ten-minute walk down Via Guerzoni to join midday prayers at the Viale Jenner mosque, one of the two centres for radical Islam in Milan. Abu Omar told his wife Nabila he would go after the prayers to pay the rent and then come home.

Three days later, Nabila walked into a police station and reported him missing. The same day, an Italian lawyer, acting for the Islamic community, also asked at the Milan headquarters of DIGOS, one of the Italian police units dealing with terrorism cases, if they had arrested Abu Omar.[11] The police confirmed they had no such prisoner.

Police inquiries discovered a witness to the presumed kidnapping. An Egyptian woman, Merfat Rezk, was walking home with her two daughters after buying some bread. She remembered being forced to cross the road because a light-coloured van was blocking the pavement. In front of it, she said, was "a dark-bearded Arab man dressed in a traditional tunic". There was also another man, Western-looking and wearing sunglasses, "who was talking into a mobile phone resting between his head and shoulder," she said, and he appeared to be examining the Arab man's papers.[12]

During both interviews with police, on 26 February and 4 March, Rezk appeared terrified. She claimed she saw nothing of what happened next and soon after the interviews she fled the country to Egypt. But later her husband, Shawki Salem, confirmed she had indeed seen what happened next. The Arab man, who she didn't recognise, had "struggled and cried for help while being violently grabbed and forcibly made to enter a van," said Salem. The van drove off at high speed.

Salem said his wife had gone back to Egypt because of a mixture of "fear" and their poor economic circumstances in Italy.[13]

It was after these interviews that Dambruoso, who was then in charge of most terrorism cases, opened an official inquiry into a possible crime of kidnapping (a violation of Article 605 of the Italian criminal code, with a penalty of at least four years in prison). The DIGOS office, and the head of its Milan counter-terrorism section, a young inspector named Bruno Megale, were put in charge of the investigation. Conscious that Rezk had spoken of a man "who was talking into a mobile phone," Dambruoso ordered the collection of all information possible on mobile phone traffic in the area at the time. He also obtained authority from a judge for a permanent phone tap to be maintained at Abu Omar's family home and those of some other relatives.

Inquiries by Dambruoso and Megale were initally largely fruitless. A later police report noted that for over a year "no significant progress was made". It said the investigators had "almost disregarded the matter" after they were passed a secret intelligence report that suggested Abu Omar had gone back to the Balkans. The message, dated 3 March 2003, was passed by the chief of the CIA station in Rome, Jeffrey Castelli,[14] who operated under diplomatic cover, to Italy's central police intelligence unit, the DCPP.[15] Its full text read:

"MEMORANDUM FOR: DCPP

SUBJECT: INFORMATION ON USAMA MUSTAFA NASR
REFERENCE:
3 MARCH 2003

SECRET//RELEASE TO ITALY ONLY

WE HAVE INFORMATION SUGGESTING THAT USAMA MUSTAFA (NASR) AKA (AMU 'UMAR) AKA ABU OMAR AL-(ALBANI) MAY HAVE TRAVELLED TO AN UNIDENTIFIED COUNTRY IN THE BALKAN REGION. TO DATE WE HAVE BEEN UNABLE TO VERIFY THESE ACCOUNTS; HOWEVER, WE WILL KEEP YOU INFORMED SHOULD HIS LOCATION BE FURTHER IDENTIFIED.

SECRET//RELEASE TO ITALY ONLY"

As a police report was to state: "The statement made to the Italian authorities would later be proven to be utterly groundless."[16]

Just how groundless the CIA report was would become very clear to Spataro in the days soon after Nabila's phone call to Abu Omar on 20 April. With case files now on his desk, Spataro ordered all key witnesses to be interviewed again and all important phones of Islamist militants to be tapped. Most were already. A month earlier, on 11 March, a slew of bombs had exploded in Madrid, killing 191 people, and Italian police were on the look-out for any connection to their own Islamist radicals.[17] The Abu Omar case was still a side show.

One of those already under surveillance at the time in Milan was a 47-year-old Egyptian named Mohamed Reda Elbadry.[18] Although cleared later of any crime, he was then suspected, like Abu Omar, of being part of a cell of militants that had been in contact by satellite phone with militants based in Herat, Afghanistan who had moved after 9/11 to northern Iraq. (They included Abu Musab Al Zarqawi, the militant who later boasted of orchestrating many terror attacks against US troops and civilians after the invasion. He was killed in an air strike in May 2006.) Although Elbadry was himself not charged with any crime, as no evidence was found against him, others in the Milan cell were later convicted of recruiting young volunteers to go and wage *jihad*.[19] On 8 May, a telephone tap recorded Abu Omar on the phone from Egypt again, this time to Elbadry. At last it provided some hints about his treatment and a confirmation that he was indeed kidnapped, as originaly suspected. As Elbadry later explained, Abu Omar had made a deal with Egyptian authorities not to speak about his treatment or his torture. And so when he talked on the telephone, he spoke often in irony. Even Elbadry did not always seem to pick up the hints. Recounting his experiences, Abu Omar hinted of a hunger strike, describing it as a "fast":

— Thank God I'm well, he said. When I was put away [imprisoned], God gave me strength. I fasted for two months and didn't even skip one day. I was well, I had never dreamt such a good thing could happen in my life... It was the best year of my life...thank God ...and are you well?

Elbadry responded:

— Well, thanks. Everybody sends their greetings...As you know the situation here is quite awful, you know what it's like. ... We've never had it so bad... We were prisoners worse than you.

Abu Omar, though guarded, seemed none too impressed with Elbadry's view that conditions in Milan had been worse than for him. He hinted directly at his torture:

— They bothered me with their questions on many things... I was freed on health grounds, I was almost paralysed. Still today, I cannot walk more than 200 yards. I always stay seated. I was incontinent, suffered from kidney trouble, and high blood pressure... so they let me go on health grounds...

The conversation continued and then he blurted out: "They took me straight to a military base and there they put me on board a military plane...and then."

Elbadry interrupted him and Abu Omar revealed little more. He did not directly say the kidnapping was the fault of the Americans. But when Elbadry stated it, he agreed.

— We spoke about this in the mosque, in newspapers....I told them these same words, I said: this is not your style of kidnapping, this is the way Americans do things ...

— Yes.

— "...And you [the Italians] are allies of the Americans, while we accuse you.... because this man had refugee status, and was under your protection, and you failed to protect him, so your responsibility is great...".

— Yes.

On 9 May, Spataro was informed about Elbadry's phone tap conversations. His attention was now completely engaged. Could this whole story amount to a kidnap operation in Milan by the Americans, even by the CIA? "I always had a feeling that the CIA might be involved in this disappearance," he would recall, "but then in this business there is a huge difference between proof and suspicion." He added: "Some accusations, particularly in Italy, remain hanging there for years."

A month later, Spataro, who had waited while the phone tapping operation continued, got to hear Abu Omar's full story. Agreeing to come to the Justice Palace, Elbadry sat down in Spataro's office on 14 June with an interpreter. This interview was to prove extraordinary. Elbadry, a known Islamic militant, was himself a suspect in a series of criminal investigations into alleged terrorist conspiracies. And yet he decided to speak frankly not only about Abu Omar's kidnap but about the key personalities in the Italian Islamist movement. Most importantly, he revealed he had had several conversations with Abu Omar beyond the intercepted phone calls. And from these he could lay out a detailed account of what happened:

On the morning of 17 February, Abu Omar had left to pray at the Jenner mosque and had noticed, close to his front door, a white van with two people inside. He walked onwards and then as he approached the mosque saw the white van again. It had clearly driven round the block. It could not follow him directly due to the one way system. The two men then jumped out of the van and asked him in Italian for his papers and he showed them his passport which declared he enjoyed political asylum in Italy.

Elbadry continued:

At that point one of them sprayed something on his mouth and nose....and they pushed him into the van.... Abu Omar had just enough time to notice an Arab woman with two kids who had witnessed the scene.... Inside the vehicle the two men also applied a plaster to his mouth.... Abu Omar did not lose consciousness and was well aware. Speaking Italian, the two men told him to be quiet or they would kill him. The windows were also tinted from the inside so he hadn't seen what direction the vehicle had taken nor what route it followed. Thanks to his wrist-watch, though, he noted that the two men had driven him around for about five hours. ... He just told me that he had been gagged for the duration of the journey and the plaster had only been removed once they had reached their destination.

The destination proved to be the Italian-American air base of Aviano. The two kidnappers, who spoke Italian, then handed him over to people at the base. Abu Omar believed them to be Americans because he "clearly spotted US military aircraft...bearing the US flag," said Elbadry. At the air base, Abu Omar had his first questioning, he said.

The two left him with a number of people who spoke English and Italian and who anyhow had an interpreter for Arabic. Those who spoke English and Italian... who Abu Omar believed to be American ... beat him whilst repeatedly asking questions on three specific issues: on his relationship with Al Qaeda, on his involvement with the Iraqi war (asking if he was sending volunteers in that area to fight Americans), and on his dealings with Albanian radical Islamic circles. He told me he was beaten, tortured and interrogated. And at dawn he was loaded onto a US military aircraft.

From the air base, Abu Omar was flown onwards for a short flight to another airport near a big city. He guessed it was Rome. The airport seemed large and he appeared to be inside a restricted, perhaps military area. He was taken off the plane and into another military aircraft, also with US insignia and the plane "took off immediately". Eventually the plane reached Cairo. Abu Omar was blindfolded and driven to Lazoghly Square, the notorious headquarters of the Egyptian interior ministry and its secret police. There he was taken directly to meet the minister of interior himself, General Habib al-Adly. He was told bluntly that "if he agreed to work as an infiltrator for the Egyptian secret service, he would be home in forty-eight hours. Otherwise he would have to bear full responsibility for his refusal. ... Abu Omar refused." He was then taken onwards to another secret police building in Cairo where he was held until his release on 20 April the following year.

In the months that followed his capture, Abu Omar was subject to pitiless, physical torture, said Elbadry.

The first measure was to leave him in a room where incredibly loud and unbearable noise was made. He has experienced damage to his hearing. The second kind of torture was to place him in a sauna at tremendous temperature and straight after to put him in a cold storeroom. It caused terrible pain to his bones — as if they were cracking...The third was to hang him upside down and apply live wires to give electric shocks to the sensitive parts of his body including his genitals. He suffered damage to his motory and urinary systems and became incontinent.

Under torture, the Egyptians had accused him of being an Al Qaeda militant plotting against the Egyptian regime. They told him to consider himself, along with Elbadry, Abu Imad (the leader of the Jenner mosque in Milan) and Abu Saleh (the former leader of the mosque) as terrorists. If they did not surrender, all of them would be kidnapped. The torture had been "particularly ferocious" for the first seven months in jail. Then it had gradually diminished.

In the end they told him he could be released "under surveillance" if he promised to tell no-one about his abduction or his torture. According to Elbadry, Abu Omar asked for advice from other inmates at the jail and they told him no-one left the prison alive, so he should take his chances. "He was ordered not to disclose anything to anyone, neither in Italy, nor Egypt, and certainly not to the press." [20]

Elbadry's statement was explosive. His allegations would have to be proved. And yet months later a police report would record an "utterly amazing aspect" from a study of technical evidence. What Elbadry had described was proven true in almost every detail.

Here then was an account of a kidnapping to Egypt and of severe torture and interrogation. But who was responsible? It was so far a crime without a suspect.

MILAN, VIA FATEBENEFRATELLI, DIGOS HEADQUARTERS
Late June 2004

In his office in central Milan, Bruno Megale sat down with his team to plan the next part of his investigation into Abu Omar's disappearance. At thirty-seven, Megale was young to be leading such an important unit. But he had already distinguished himself with a series of key investigations, mainly into terrorist cells.

Megale's thirty detectives were in an up-beat mood. On 6 June the same team had arrested in Milan a man who was suspected of being one of the key architects of the Madrid bombings, a thirty-two-year-old named Rabei Osman Sayed

Ahmed.[21] He was caught after his phone and his house were bugged for weeks. The arrest of Rabei had been a joint inquiry with the Spanish police. Such co-operation was routine. Since just after 9/11, when they rounded up a series of militants, DIGOS was well-known to be working routinely with foreign agencies, including both the FBI and CIA. But, behind the scene, such liaison had been going on for years.

Rifa Ahmed Taha
or Abu Yasser

The police in Milan had even worked directly with Egyptian general intelligence (EGIS) on a job known as Operation Sphinx that began in 1993, three years after Megale had joined the police.[22] Another major Italian police operation with the CIA also had an Egyptian connection. In the late 1990s, DIGOS helped track down a notorious leader of the Gama'a al-Islamiyya known as Rifa Ahmed Taha or Abu Yasser, who refused to accept the group's ceasefire. He was one of the signatories of Osama bin Laden's declaration of war against the United States in February 1998. The Italians were able to tap the phone of a mosque leader in Milan, Abu Saleh, who was talking to Abu Yasser as he travelled between Iran, Sudan and then Syria. (Other calls were also monitored by the FBI in New York, via a phone tap on a US-based associate. These calls included the instructions for the raid that led to the Luxor massacre.) The operation ended with Abu Yasser's arrest in the spring of 2001 in Syria and his rendition, with a little help from the Americans, to Cairo.[23] Many thought he had then been executed, but one of the phone taps of Abu Omar's calls home now revealed some important news. Abu Omar told Elbadry:

— "I want to tell you something that you must relay immediately ... tell him Abu Yasser is well, and was in a neighboring cell to Abu Omar."

Now, Megale was being asked to carry out an enquiry that could potentially lead to exposing the very allies of the DIGOS in these investigations. On his desk now was a set of instructions from Armando Spataro, the prosecutor, on how the police should proceed. In his file too was a list of the statements and phone tap records the police and Spataro had collected so far. Abu Omar had dropped some clear hints about what had happened to him. Elbadry's statement was more definitive. But it was essentially all hear-say evidence. Elbadry himself was a direct witness to nothing, and anyway no court would place too much credence on what he said unless it was verified elsewhere. After all, he was a suspected Islamic militant himself. Nor was there any indication about the identity of the kidnappers, other than that they spoke Italian and English, wore western clothes, and had taken Abu Omar to an American base. Crucially, though, he kept coming back to that statement of Rezk, when she talked of seeing one of them "talking into a mobile phone."

To set the alleged kidnapping in context, Megale was asked by Spataro to answer three specific questions:

— Did this type of kidnapping fit into a pattern of similar abductions of alleged terrorists anywhere else in the world?
— Was Abu Omar wanted officially for any crime by Egypt or by any country?
— And were there any military bases, either belonging to America or Italian bases used by America, that fitted Abu Omar's description of being five hours from Milan? [24]

For Megale, the first question was not difficult to answer. Under the Italian judicial system, prosecutors like Spataro were prevented by a kind of Chinese wall from having any access to intelligence reports or intelligence agents. But police units like DIGOS were directed not only to work on investigations ordered by the prosecutor's office but also to work with intelligence agencies. Based on intelligence reports, Megale was well aware of an operation back in September 1995 that was remarkably similar to Abu Omar's abduction. This was the CIA snatch of Abu Talat Al Qassem in Croatia (described in Chapter 6). Italian police and intelligence had earlier been involved in tracking Abu Talal, who, though living in Denmark, had been a regular visiting imam at Milan's Jenner mosque. Abu Talal, who had already been condemned to death after a trial in his absence, subsequently disappeared and was believed executed by the Egyptians.[25] In retaliation for the kidnapping, an extremist from Milan drove a car bomb to Croatia which was detonated on 20 October 1995 outside the offices of a police station in the town of Rijeka (Fiume in Italian), killing one person and wounding 29.[26]

The second question was more difficult to answer. The Egyptians ignored all formal legal requests for co-operation in their inquiries. But Egypt was a member of Interpol and routinely issued international arrest warrants for militants wanted by its judicial system. Megale discovered there was no such arrest warrant issued. This was a crucial fact since, in the pre-9/11 programme, renditions had been specifically targetted against suspects who were formally wanted by the country of destination.[27] Without such an arrest warant, the abduction would then have been straying into illegality. Sending Abu Omar to Egypt would be a particularly egregious breach of the law, the police believed, because the Italian state had granted him political asylum — thus officially acknowledging he would face persecution in his home country.

Answering Spataro's last question, about the location of the base, was not going to be difficult. By July, Megale could formally report that of military bases used by American planes, only the Aviano AFB north of Venice lay around five hours drive from Milan, as described by Abu Omar.[28]

And there remained the thorny question of the identity of the kidnappers themselves. With the CIA now in the frame, here was the awkward part for Megale and his team. Since 9/11 and before, DIGOS had been at the forefront of efforts in Italy against terrorist networks. And, in this, Megale and his team had worked closely with both the FBI and with CIA officers stationed in Italy. One of those, who had arrived in September 2000, was the CIA station chief in Milan, Robert Seldon Lady, known to them as "Bob". Born in Tegucigalpa, Honduras, on 2 May 1954, Lady had started his career as a New York City police officer but had joined the Agency in the mid-1980s. A veteran of operations in Central America, he was well-liked by his Italian comrades. At the US consulate, Lady operated under diplomatic cover as a deputy consul but his true secret role was declared to Italian authorities. Megale and his team usually shared specific operational details with their more direct counterparts like the FBI, not the CIA. But Lady had made himself popular by helping with technical work. By one account, he supplied DIGOS with a particularly long-lasting bugging device that could be installed inside some of Milan's mosques.[29]

Megale also remembered that back in 2002 and early 2003, Lady had shown particular interest in the Viale Jenner mosque and Abu Omar specifically. Now piecing things together, Megale remembered that after Abu Omar's disappearance, Lady's contact with DIGOS had petered out, although he would still pop round occasionally. If Lady had been involved in Abu Omar's kidnap, in Megale's mind, it would be a betrayal. As one police source in Milan said: "For years he really was the face of the CIA in Milan. All the chiefs of the cops and Carabinieri knew him. He had official contacts also with our secret services both military and civilian. Before and more so after 9/11. He helped our investigators, especially with sophisticated technology. He was considered a kind of tech-genius."[30]

The CIA's interest in Abu Omar was not hard to explain. Although never considered among the most important militants in Milan, Omar was a former member of the Gama'a al-Islamiyya, previously one of Egypt's most feared militant groups. The Gama'a had in 1999 declared an official ceasefire with the Egyptian government. Yet it was unclear whether many of its former members abroad accepted the movement's cessation of violence.

Just ahead of the Iraq war, which began on 19 March 2003, Abu Omar, like Elbadry, was being specifically investigated for his alleged involvement in a cell that was said to be recruiting volunteers to join Al-Zarqawi in northern Iraq to prepare for the US invasion. Italian officials stressed though that he was never considered the ringleader of that cell.[31]

For now, though, the CIA and Bob Lady's involvement in Abu Omar's kidnapping was speculative. It was time to start examining the cell-phone traffic. This, of course, had been one of the earliest ideas for investigation after Abu Omar had disappeared. But things were delayed by a clerical error. Between April and October 2003, Megale had been waiting for full details of the cell phone traffic on the day of the kidnap. But when it arrived he discovered

Dambruoso had asked for traffic from the wrong date: his request had been for traffic on 17 March 2003 rather than 17 February 2003. There was nothing to do but make the request again. The data did not arrive until the spring of 2004.[32]

MILAN, PALACE OF JUSTICE
Early September 2004

Armando Spataro remembered the phone call when it all came together. Bruno Megale was on the line. "Armando, you won't believe what I've discovered. It's incredible," he said.[33] Over at DIGOS headquarters, Megale was staring at an intricate diagram. On it were marked little picture icons that each represented a mobile phone. Each was used on the day of Abu Omar's kidnap in Milan. And each, he now believed, could be traced back to the CIA.

Megale was using a police technique they had used to catch members of the Mafia, like the murderers of two leading judges, Giovanni Falcone and Paolo Borsellino in 1992.[34] When a cellphone is switched on, regardless of whether a call is made or received, it registers itself with a local base station. Working backwards, and by collecting data from mobile phone companies, the police could tell which mobile phones were switched on at a particular location on a particular date. This data is retained for up to four years by the Italian phone companies.

So what Megale did was to locate the base stations near the area of the kidnapping and then ask the telephone companies for a list of all telephones switched on between 11 a.m. and 1 p.m. on the day of the kidnap and all the calls they made. Megale then fed the data into a computer programme that analysed all the 10,718 calls made.[35] He had a programme similar to the one I had used to study the CIA plane flight logs. From these calls emerged a ring of eleven cellphones that were both at the scene and in contact with each other. There were another six in contact with these eleven that were located nearby. He noticed something peculiar about these cellphones. All had accounts that were created after November 2002 and before January 2003, and all had been closed down within three days of the kidnapping. Most were registered to fake-sounding names: six to a Romanian citizen named "Timofte Mihai" and another three to a "Riva Beniamino". Only one, a Vodafone, was registered to a real-sounding person. This phone belonged to an American citizen, Monica Adler.

The most telling information came when Megale's team began to track where this group of cellphones went after the time of the kidnapping. They discovered the cellphones had not just been activated near the scene of the kidnapping but could be traced along the motorway all the way to Aviano. Moreover some had called numbers that could be traced back to American officials at the Aviano airbase, including a Lt.-Col. Joseph Romano III, who controlled access to the base.[36] Here then was clear evidence that the users of this group of cellphones were involved not only in the snatching of Abu Omar but in his removal to an American airbase five hours away — just as Abu Omar had described on the phone from Egypt.

The next task for any high-tech policeman, after identifying the cellphones involved, would be to trace their real owners and to "house" the suspects: identify their real addresses. The kidnappers made this easy by frequently calling their own hotel or hotels used by members of the team. All these clues led to a series of top hotels in Milan. From analysing the cellphone records over a series of days and the call lists, Megale could tell which days the kidnappers checked in and which days they checked out. His team examined the records of hotels in the neighbourhood and matched those dates with guests who checked in and checked out those days. By these methods, they found, by mid-2005, a total of twenty-two names of possible kidnappers.[37] All had American passports and many had left a credit card number and even a frequent flyer number or hotel loyalty card so they could earn points for their stays in Milan.

There were still more clues. The itemised phone bills included calls not only to hotels but to car hire offices and travel agents. The same people who rented rooms at the hotels were also found to have hired cars in the same names, or purchased air tickets. In some cases, they left behind photocopies of their passports.

One intriguing detail was a number — a Milan Vodafone cell phone number 3480614737 — which two of the alleged kidnappers (George Purvis and Ray Harbaugh) had been calling since December 2002. On the day of the kidnap itself, Harbaugh called the number just after 12:56, and then again at 14:20, 14:28 and 16:25. Cellphone records also revealed the phone had travelled to Egypt shortly after the kidnapping. A call was made in Egypt on the telephone on 3 March and the records suggested the phone was "most likely" there since 22 February, according to the police report. A quick check with Vodafone revealed this was registered to none other than an employee of the US Consulate in Milan. Her name was Barbara P, described as an "administrative technician," and born in 1956 in Kansas City.[38]

Megale quickly obtained a copy of Barbara P's mobile phone account and he began to study the calls made from it.

As he looked down the list of numbers, he felt a chill as he noticed among the itemised list of phone calls a number for the DIGOS office itself. One of those involved with the kidnappers had been in regular touch with his own team. A police report stated bluntly: The number 3480614737 (registered under the name of Barbara P) has contacted several times the staff of Milan DIGOS."[39] But Megale was still confused. Barbara P, though registered as working at the US Embassy, was not a name that he or his team recognised.

Then he spotted another item on the itemised bill: a total of 156 calls to a landline in Milan. This traced to Robert Seldon Lady, the man known to Megale as "then attaché to the US Consulate and CIA superintendent", i.e. the CIA station chief for Milan. And there were calls to and from another mobile, 3357504143, a number billed to the consulate that Megale recognised as Bob Lady's mobile. Or as the police report noted drily "with this same cell phone, the man had business communications with the DIGOS staff." Did all this suggest that Barbara P was working for Lady and keeping in touch with her boss, or was Lady using her phone? Further clues pointed to the latter. Frequently, between October 2001 and February 2003, all calls to Lady's mobile phone were simply placed on automatic divert to Barbara P's number. Sporadically, the SIM cards for both numbers had been used within the same Motorola cell phone.

Bob Lady obviously had a strong connection to this phone number close to the kidnappers and registered to Barbara P. But how could it be proved that this number was in fact his own property? Again, Megale turned to the techniques of cell tracking. His team studied where Barbara P's phone had been used between 9 p.m. at night and 10 a.m. They found it had been connected 270 times to a cellular base station on the Via de Alessandri, about 100 yards from Lady's old address in the centre of Milan: Via Cimarossa 22. They also noticed it was connected 49 times to the rural base station at Moncalvo, within one mile of Lady's new retirement home in the hamlet of Penango, in Asti.

Crucially, the first time the phone was connected to this rural base station was on 10 September 2003. Bob Lady had registered a change of address on 9 September 2003.[40]

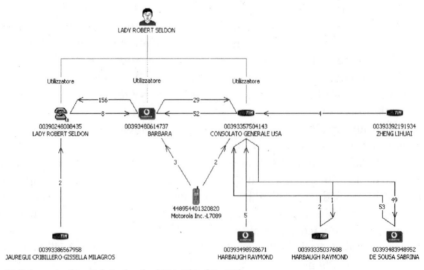

Cellphone trail to Bob Lady, the 'CIA Chief' in Milan

LONDON
October 2004

The answering machine at my home in south London was full of messages. My article had just appeared in the *Sunday Times*, "US accused of torture flights", that revealed the flight logs of the CIA's Gulfstream V and its movements around the world. Journalists, mainly from America, were calling for more details. There was also a message in accented English from a prosecutor in Milan, Armando Spataro. He was involved in an investigation into a potential rendition from Italy, he said, and could I call him?

Until then the ongoing investigation into Abu Omar's disappearance had remained entirely secret.[41] But the Italian press were aware of the case and had noticed my article. Could the movements of the CIA's "torture plane", as they called it, be connected to the Abu Omar case? Spataro asked the same question. I called and agreed to see him.

Two weeks later, at his office in the Justice Palace, Milan, Spataro explained the basics of the case, of how Abu Omar had disappeared completely till his phone calls home that April. He was tracking down movements of all jets that had flown to Italy back in February 2003, trying to find out any that might be linked to the case. As a journalist, I said, I could only confirm what I had published, not reveal sources. But I was happy to explain the facts that had appeared in print. The existence of a rendition programme, I said, had been publicly confirmed by the CIA's George Tenet and, as my *Sunday Times* article explained, my research had confirmed the use of executive jets for the transport. Sadly, I had no trace of the plane used for Abu Omar's kidnapping, although I would certainly try to find and publish the information. (At the time of the kidnapping, the Gulfstream V was sitting back in Johnston County, North Carolina.)[42]

Spataro then swore me to secrecy and, over a cup of coffee, said he already had "certain elements" that indicated the involvement of the CIA in the operation. He refused to elaborate. But he said what saddened the police in Milan was that, since long before 9/11 they had been working closely with the US authorities to combat terrorism in Europe, and Al Qaeda specifically. At the time of his disappearance, Abu Omar had been under investigation by those policemen and his kidnap had undermined a prosecution not only of Abu Omar himself, but of a cell of activists in Italy and around Europe.

Late that same night, on a bench outside Milan central railway station, I met up with a journalist from the *Corrierre della Serra*, Paolo Biondani, who had close police contacts. He showed me a transcript of a bugged conversation inside a Milan mosque. In it, Abu Omar had received an unidentified visitor who spoke of being part of a network of militants in Austria, Poland, and Great Britain.

— Visitor: We must find money because our objective is to form an Islamic Army which will be known as Force 9.

— Abu Omar: How are things going in Germany?

— Visitor: We can't complain, there are already ten of us and we are also concentrating our efforts on Belgium, Spain, the Netherlands, Egypt and Turkey. But the hub of the organisation remains London.

By now, as I flew home and prepared for another trip reporting in Iraq, the Italian press were getting wind of the CIA connections to the inquiry.[43] With the Milan police now checking hotel registers, car hire firms and travel agents around Milan, the CIA too had become aware that Spataro was serious in tracking them down. Bob Lady by now had retired from the CIA and he hoped to settle at his home in Penango. But, under advice, he was forced to flee to Geneva, Switzerland, at least till things cleared up. Just before Christmas, Susan Czaska, a friend from the Milan consulate wrote him an email.[44]

From: Susan Czaska—@msn.com
Sent: Friday, December 24, 2004 2:47 AM
To: lady—@hotmail.com
Subject: Merry Christmas
Dear Bob,
I am so glad to hear from you. Since I got your last note, I suddenly got an email through work which was entitled "Italy, don't go there." It was from Maura, giving a short rundown regarding the Milan Magistrate's intentions. I was a bit taken back by all this ... I was truly concerned that you were sitting in some Italian holding cell. I sent a note to Torya, telling her to get some more information (since everyone seems to be so tightlipped), and she said that she had gotten a note from Sabrina telling her that could [sic] not visit Italy and that you were in Geneva until all this blew over. I was extremely relieved to get your note—do be careful, and let me know if I [sic]help in any way.
My Best to you and your family for a Joyous and Safe Holiday and New Year. Do stay in touch and let us know if you need anything.
Hugs,
Sue[45]

All these emails were discovered much later when police were to raid Bob Lady's villa in Penango.

In January, I returned to Milan to record an interview with Spataro.[46] I asked him what it would mean if CIA agents were involved in the kidnap. "If it was true, it would be a serious breach of Italian rules. It would be absolutely illegal," he said. I also published an article in the *Sunday Times*, the first about the investigation in the English language press, that warned the net was closing in on the CIA. Imam Imad, the head of Viale Jenner, where Abu Omar was heading on the day he was kidnapped, said Abu Omar had spoken to him too from Egypt. "He can't be sure if it was the Italians or Americans who took him," Imad said. "He was blindfolded. But they were Western people. It was certainly not the Egyptians who captured him and took him to Cairo."[47]

By now, Spataro and Megale had almost completed their investigation, at least of the CIA agents' involvement. Studying the latter's hotel bills, they were staggered to find that they had spent a total of $144,984 on accommodation. Perhaps maintaining cover as rich businessmen, they had chosen nothing but the best in their accommodation. Two others allegedly involved in the CIA operation, Monica Adler and John Duffin, for instance, spent nearly $18,000 during their three weeks at the Milan Savoy hotel.[48]

The investigation had now uncovered a total of more than thirty-five names of Americans involved in the CIA operation.[49] The Italians knew, however, that most of the names were probably fake. Only Lady and another six of the twenty-two were registered as diplomats in Italy. The others were probably using cover identities. This impression was enhanced by a glance at the credit cards issued to the operatives. Many of the numbers were issued in a sequence, and five of them had closely-matched Visa numbers. Two more had similar Visa numbers and another two had similar Diner's Club numbers.

On 23 March 2005, Spataro finished his report and dispatched it to the judge. I alerted news organisations that a potentially sensational story was about to be published. Would the judge agree to press charges against members of the CIA? Would political pressure be brought to bear on her by the Italian government quietly to shelve the matter? Spataro, however, was by now determined to bring a prosecution. If the judge rejected his request for an arrest warrant then he would file an appeal — and the matter would become public anyway.

In the end, the judge, Dr Chiara Nobili, spent thirteen weeks pondering her decision.[50] In the meantime, relations between Italy and the United States had soured. An Italian secret service agent, Nicola Calipari, was killed by US soldiers at a checkpoint in Baghdad on 4 March when he went to recover a freed hostage, the fifty-six-year-old left-wing journalist Giuliana Sgrena. Some colleagues speculated whether she had delayed her report so as to avoid the impression her decision would be a political retaliation.

By now, as described earlier, I had begun trying to track down much of the CIA's airline fleet and noticed that a charter plane belonging to an owner of the Boston Red Sox was in Egypt at the time of the kidnap and appeared to be the plane used in the kidnap.[51] Meanwhile, from air traffic authorites, Spataro had independently discovered the same fact. His information showed a military Learjet, using the call sign Spar 92, had flown from the US airbase at Ramstein, Germany, into Aviano and made a return trip to Ramstein, departing at 6.20 p.m. and landing at approximately 7.20 p.m. Here the plane met up with a Gulfstream IV, the Red Sox plane, and it seemed that Abu Omar was rapidly transhipped onto the Gulfstream. This plane took off for Cairo at 7.52 p.m. (local time) and landed at 12.32 a.m. (local time). The plane returned to the US the following day, refuelling at Shannon Airport in Ireland.

The use of Germany as a transhipment point for Abu Omar was intriguing and potentially very damaging for the United States. Despite extensive bases across Germany, the US military operated in the country under German law and its constitution. The bases could be used for legal purposes but certainly not for a kidnapping operation, nor even for any form of detention of prisoners who were not US servicemen.[52] The German prosecutor at Zweibrucken, the civilian legal office that has jurisdiction for Ramstein, was later to open an investigation against unknown persons for the crime of kidnapping. Not surprisingly the US Air Force refused all cooperation.

PENANGO, ASTI
23 June 2005, sunrise

At dawn Bruno Megale and a team of seven detectives rang the bell of a renovated country villa, Bob Lady's retreat in the Piedmont hills. Lady was not at home but his wife, Martha, was there and she answered the door. "She was not terribly happy to see us," recalled one Italian detective.

Searching through the house, Megale's team zeroed in on Lady's personal computer. And on it they were to make a surprising discovery — records of an internet search by Lady to find the quickest route from where Abu Omar lived to the Aviano Air Base. On a separate floppy disk they also found three pictures taken by the CIA surveillance team. All showed Abu Omar walking down the road. And in the waste paper bin were a copy of some emails, including the Christmas good wishes from Susan Czaska that revealed the CIA had issued a message: "Don't Go to Italy." All in all it was a profitable raid. It seemed a surprising breach of tradecraft by Lady to have left this data at home.[53]

A day earlier, 22 June, Judge Nobili had issued the arrest warrants for thirteen CIA agents. She declared that Abu Omar's kidnap represented a "very serious violation to the national sovereignty that cannot absolutely be justified." Such a serious crime could mean a jail sentence of more

Abu Omar, CIA surveillance picture

than four years for the accused, if convicted. A former diplomat like Bob Lady, as he had retired in 2004, had no protection under the Vienna Convention, she asserted. And given the sophistication of the kidnap, there was a "concrete danger that those persons involved in our case could commit other crimes similar to the one of this procedure."[54]

As the news broke, there was consternation in the United States. I was in Milan covering the story for the BBC and the *New York Times* and my report for the latter made the front page (my first front page dateline with the *Times*). The BBC filmed me as I met contacts and retraced the steps of the CIA team. We organised a re-enactment of the kidnapping with actors. After obtaining a copy of the judge's arrest warrant and attached police report, we began investigating the names listed. Most appeared to be false. But checking online databases in the US, Margot Williams at the *New York Times* confirmed that two of the names mentioned, Ben A. Harty and Michalis J. Vasiliou, used a box at the same post office in Dunn Loring, Virginia, that was also used by Philip P. Quincannon, an officer of Premier Executive Transport Service, the former owner of the two main CIA rendition planes, the Gulfstream V and the Boeing 737. It was another indication of the CIA connection.[55]

With all the traces that the CIA team had left, there was intense speculation that the Italian secret service must also have been involved in the operation. Why else would the Americans have been so careless with their tracks? On 30 June, the *Washington Post* quoted former and serving CIA agents who claimed the entire operation had indeed been approved by Italy. The article quoted officials involved in the Milan operation asserting it was conceived by the Rome CIA station chief, organised by the CIA's Counter-Terrorist Centre and approved by the CIA leadership and at least one person in the National Security Council. One official involved said the Italians approved it "at the national level, among senior people." But the report cited conflicting accounts of whether it was Gen. Nicolo Pollari, head of the Italian military intelligence service, SISMI, or a lower-ranking official who was consulted.[56] Michael Scheuer, the former head of the CIA's Osama bin Laden unit, went further in an interview later for Al Jazeera. He claimed the operation had actually been asked for by the Italians.[57]

Armando Spataro was resolute however. The Italian secret service had no authority to order an illegal kidnap. Under the Italian constitution no one, including a state agency, has the power to deprive anyone of their liberty without the approval of a judge. If an official of the Italian secret service had given the green light, and evidence of this emerged, then he would merely ask for their names to be added to the indictment. The proper authority for investigating and dealing with terrorists was the police and judicial authorities. No spy agency had the right to break Italian domestic law.

In a secret letter to the Milan prosecutors, the office of the then Italian prime minister, Silvio Berlusconi, had already asserted the Italian secret services, which came under his control, had no knowledge of the Abu Omar affair. Berlusconi's ministers repeated this denial to his parliament. And he summoned the US Ambassador on 1 July as a protest, demanding the US show "full respect" for Italian sovereignty.[58] Many suspected all the denials were a sham. Spataro and Megale kept open minds, but were determined to keep their inquiry going — and to charge any Italians who might be involved.

As this book went to press, Spataro's allegations were yet to be tested in a court trial. But the investigation, which had employed the most advanced police methods, was impressive.

In the following weeks, more names were added to the indictment, bringing the total to twenty-two. But although international arrest warrants were now issued for all the alleged kidnappers, the then Italian justice minister, Roberto Castelli, from the right-wing Northern League, resisted issuing an extradition request to the US. "The interests of the state are on the line," he said, accusing Spataro of left-wing, anti-American bias.[59] (Spataro's friends remembered the prosecutor had spent years investigating the left-wing Red Brigades, who had even murdered a close friend of his.)

In the spring of 2006, former CIA officials in Washington, some with knowledge of the case, told me they were certain that Italy had been informed of the operation. Abu Omar was not such a valuable prize to have risked the United States relationship with such a close ally as Italy. But even if an Italian official had given the green light, there was consternation at the tradecraft employed by the CIA team that allowed their movements to have been so closely tracked. One former senior officer of the Directorate of Operations told me: "Even if the Italians were involved, this whole operation was botched. Using such a large team, involving the local station, staying in such luxury and making such a large scale use of cellphones and traceable credit cards was only asking for trouble."

For the CIA, the Italian investigation had blown several cover identities and working methods and prevented many operatives from travelling to Europe indefinitely. In Europe, the clearcut evidence of a CIA rendition operation within European territory, based on an official police report rather than mere journalistic inquiries, provided a clear impetus for politicians to begin hounding the CIA and to open up a series of judicial and parliamentary inquiries.

For Spataro, however, his operation showed above all how the use by the CIA of extra-legal methods like rendition was damaging overall to the fight against terrorism. The Abu Omar rendition had not only damaged relations with the Muslim community in Milan, it had disrupted a specific Italian police investigation into a terrorist cell in the city, and its exposure would undermine confidence in cooperation with the United States against terrorism.

LONDON
7 July 2005, 8.50 a.m.

Synchronised by the alarms on their mobile phones, three suicide bombers detonated their explosives on crowded rush-hour Underground trains. A fourth bomb exploded at 9.47 a.m. on a bus. The total death toll was fifty-six people. With traffic disrupted, I cycled to the scene of the no. 30 bus explosion in Tavistock Square. The carnage brought to mind what I had seen on the streets of Baghdad, with blood spattered across the marble frontage of the British Medical Association headquarters. A few days later, 21 July, terrorists attempted to blow up more Underground trains, including one heading for my local station. One of the suspects, Hussain Osman, fled abroad.

In Milan, Megale's team swung into action. Using the same techniques employed against the CIA, they tracked Osman's mobile phone to an apartment in Rome. He was arrested on 29 July (and, at the time of writing, had yet to face trial). The investigation against Robert Lady and his team had been a diversion. They were back in their normal business of catching the criminals, the ones, that is, that wanted to blow up trains.

10

THE TORTURE LIE
RENDITION AND THE LAW

WASHINGTON, DC, THE WHITE HOUSE MAP ROOM,
28 April 2005

President George W. Bush stepped up to the podium before the White House press corps and took a question about the rendition programme.

Question: "Mr President, under the law, how would you justify the practice of renditioning, where US agents brought terror suspects abroad, taking them to a third country for interrogation? And would you stand for it if foreign agents did that to an American here?"

The transcript recorded his chuckles. "That's a hypothetical," he said.

We operate within the law, and we send people to countries where they say they're not going to torture the people.

But let me say something. The United States government has an obligation to protect the American people. It's in our country's interest to find those who would do harm to us and get them out of harm's way. And we will do so within the law, and we'll do so in honoring our commitment not to torture people. And we expect the countries where we send somebody to, not to torture, as well.[1]

His remark, one of his first before the cameras after years of official silence on renditions, was well prepared. His very first comments were made in a *New York Times* interview four months earlier, and were somewhat different. Then he stated that "torture is never acceptable, nor do we hand over people to countries that do torture."[2]

The remarks at the press conference had the appearance of a lawyer's draft. The United States had obtained assurances, he implied, that countries like Egypt would not torture a suspect that was rendered into their custody. But both statements, as we shall see, contained a lie. For more than a decade, under both Presidents Clinton and Bush, the rendition programme had sent prisoners to foreign jails in the full knowledge that they would be tortured.

The difference between Bush's remarks in January and April masked a real weakness with the rendition system: the fear it could be in violation of both domestic and international law and of a clearly stated policy to abhor all forms of torture. The suggestion made by President Bush in January that a country like Egypt did not torture was clearly unsustainable. So, with the help of his advisers, Bush had inserted a new clause. And his use of the reference to places "where they say" they would not torture was a reference to one of his administration's crucial legal arguments in its efforts to defend renditions. Egypt, as recorded by the State Department, might indeed torture and torture frequently. But, for prisoners sent by America, they had promised not to follow their normal practice. So rendition might just be legal, his advisor insisted.

As the facts of the rendition programme have become public, the President's lawyers have been busy supplying such arguments. Their central arguments have been two-fold: first, that neither the CIA nor any US agency had sanctioned torture by any foreign government; and second that the US itself did not carry out any such torture. In the face of the facts, both claims required a rafter of specialised arguments. All of them were comparable to rather ropey old corks hammered inexpertly into leaking dams.

What, then, were the laws, both foreign and domestic, which gave the White House so many headaches, and which forced them to be so economical with the truth?[3]

In arguing its first claim — that the US never sanctioned the torture by others — the first hurdles to jump were the Geneva Conventions. As described in Chapter 7, these treaties, signed after the Second World War by the United States, required all prisoners of war and captives generally to be treated humanely, to be protected from all forms of coercive interrogation, and to have access to the Red Cross. The rendition of a prisoner to a country where they might face torture would amount to complicity in violating these very provisions. The issue of repatriation — as the US military labelled many renditions — had long been a sensitive one. After the Second World War, thousands of Cossacks in British hands, for example, were "repatriated" back to Soviet Russia. Once home they were sent straight off to the Soviet gulag.[4] Because of such concerns, the neutral International Committee of the Red Cross interpreted international law as requiring that any prisoner due for repatriation had the right to appeal if they faced persecution in their homeland. The ICRC told me:

"In the event that the person expresses concern that s/he may risk ill-treatment after transfer, the well-foundedness of such fears must be reviewed by a body that is independent of the one that took the transfer decision. The transfer must be suspended pending this body's review."[5]

As explained before, after 9/11, the Bush administration opened a new legal chapter by announcing that in the War on Terror the Geneva Conventions would not apply. In law, the key to whether Geneva would apply would normally be whether a state of "international armed conflict" existed, and whether prisoners were taken as part of that conflict.

Before 9/11, when the rendition programme was launched under President Clinton in the mid 1990s, Geneva was rightly not a consideration. No kind of war had been declared against Al Qaeda and the territory of no sovereign country was invaded. So no one would argue that the state of "international armed conflict" existed.

After 9/11, when Afghanistan was invaded it was clear that an "international armed conflict" certainly did now exist. Normally, many of both the CIA and the military's new prisoners would be fully recognised as Prisoners of War (PoWs).

In the event, though, Bush declared that Geneva did not apply to Al Qaeda. As stated before, Alberto Gonzales had revealed in his memo to the President on 25 January 2002 that the *motive* for abandoning Geneva was the need to "quickly obtain information from captured prisoners and their sponsors."[6]

But the legal *justification* needed something more. Gonzales and Bush argued that the Taliban and its Al Qaeda allies were not lawful combatants and therefore did not qualify for PoW status. Both, they said, did not wear proper uniforms; nor did they represent a country that was internationally recognised.[7] It was a very thin argument. At the very least, according to the ICRC, the US needed to hold tribunals, as required under Geneva, to determine a prisoner's status before declaring he was not a PoW. No such tribunals were held in Afghanistan.[8] Moreover, soon after making these declarations, the Pentagon released a snapshot of members of US Special Forces deployed to Afghanistan. They were riding horses, and none showed any visible sign of a uniform. The principle effort in the early days was led, moreover, by CIA paramilitaries. They wore purely civilian clothes.[9]

Yet, beyond who wore uniforms or berets, the more important point was the spirit and purpose of the Convention. The reason why the United States signed Geneva and had applied its provisions during all previous armed conflicts, regardless of whether Geneva strictly applied, was to avoid mistreatment of its own prisoners. If it decided to treat its enemies as "unlawful combatants" with no legal rights, then its enemies would retaliate. Just how painful this might be for America was illustrated after Vietnam. For years, families had struggled to find out what happened to those US servicemen Missing in Action (MIAs). Yet after 9/11 the US judged it acceptable to make large numbers go missing — "disappearing" many prisoners who were captured by the CIA or US military. Abandoning the law that prohibited coercive interrogations of prisoners would also prove to be a propaganda own goal. Poor treatment of prisoners serves to harden the attitude of an army's fighters and garners it support for an enemy. Among the prisoners' families there would be strong demands too for reprisal — particularly in the Arab world where tribal and clan loyalties remain strong. Too many people were thrown into the enemy camp.

While Bush had said that Geneva did not apply in the conflict against Al Qaeda, he did at least order the military, through the Secretary of Defense, to treat prisoners humanely, even if only to the "extent necessary and appropriate with military necessity." But this was rarely a meaningful constraint. For example a Pentagon investigation reported the treatment of one prisoner, Muhammed al Qahtani, had been "abusive" and "degrading" but was said not to be "not inhumane." While held at Guantánamo, al Qahtani was, among things:

— stripped naked while interrogators, male and female, watched
— told his mother and sister were whores
— deprived of sleep when interrogated for 18-20 hours, for 48 out of 54 days
— tied to a leash, led around the room and forced to perform a series of dog tricks
— held down while a female interrogator straddled him
— forced to wear a bra and have a thong placed on his head during interrogation
— doused with water 17 times.[10]

If all those acts were officially considered "humane," then the US government's assurances about its treatment of prisoners had to be taken with great skepticism.

And the order for humane treatment was not intended for the CIA. In a written testimony to the Senate, Gonzales said this policy was intended only "to provide guidance to the United States armed services." Asked by Senator Leahy whether the directive applied to CIA and other non-military personnel, Gonzales replied, "No."[11] Later, on 5 October 2005, by an overwhelming majority vote of 90-9, the Senate passed an amendment proposed by Senator John McCain that required all US personnel, including the CIA, to use only approved and humane interrogation techniques.[12] But it did not define clearly what inhumane treatment was, allowing considerable scope for selective interpretation.

Even if prisoners captured in the War on Terror did not enjoy their rights under the Geneva Conventions, the CIA's lawyers were however always concerned about another strict piece of international law, the UN Convention Against Torture (CAT).[13] In implementing the rendition programme, this was their biggest worry.

Ratified by Congress in 1994, Article 3 of the Convention (known in full as the UN Convention Against Torture and Other Cruel, Inhuman or Degrading Treatment or Punishment), stated that:

1. No State party shall expel, return, or extradite a person to another state where there are substantial grounds for believing that he would be in danger of being subjected to torture.

2. For the purpose of determining whether there are such grounds, the competent authorities shall take into account all relevant considerations including, where applicable, the existence in the State concerned of a consistent pattern of gross, flagrant or mass violations of human rights.[14]

The Convention further stated that the ban on torture was absolute, with no exceptions, for example, on national security grounds. Specifically, CAT Article 2(2) declares that "[n]o exceptional circumstances whatsoever, whether a state of war or a threat of war, internal political instability or any other public emergency, may be invoked as a justification of torture." When the Convention was submitted to Congress for ratification in 1988, the accompanying presidential memo specified that such an absolute prohibition was seen as necessary by the authors of the Convention "if the Convention is to have significant effect, as public emergencies are commonly invoked as a source of extraordinary powers or as a justification for limiting fundamental rights and freedoms." In its 1988 analysis of the Convention, however, the State Department specified that certain police brutality did "not amount to torture". The term "torture" was, according to the same memo, "usually reserved for extreme, deliberate, and unusually cruel practices...[such as] sustained systematic beating, application of electric currents to sensitive parts of the body, and tying up or hanging in positions that cause extreme pain."[15]

To become US law, the treaty needed to be ratified by Congress, which clarified that under the US definition the phrase "substantial grounds for believing that he would be in danger of being subject to torture" would be taken to mean "if it is more likely than not that he would be tortured."[16]

Precisely how the CIA would legally defend its practice of rendition under the Convention was, at the time of writing, still officially a classified matter. One key memo after 9/11 that defined this defence was drawn up on 13 March 2002, and entitled "The President's Power as Commander in Chief to Transfer Captured Terrorists to the Control and Custody of Foreign Nations."[17] But it was not published. When Maher Arar tried to sue the US government for his rendition to torture in Syria, a New York judge refused to hear the matter. He said it was not his job to challenge the right of the President to make decisions about national security. "Arar's claim that he faced a likelihood of torture in Syria is supported by US State Department reports on Syria's human rights practices," said the judge, but security and foreign policy issues raised by the government were "compelling" and were not for the courts; "the need for secrecy can hardly be doubted."[18]

Despite the wall of secrecy, many officials involved did make clear in interviews with me the outlines of how CIA would propose to defend itself.[19] The defences amounted to the following propositions:

"We are just the taxi drivers"

One of the earliest ideas in the CIA was to keep US involvement to a minimum so they would function, in effect, only as a travel agency. In December 2001, when the Gulfstream took the two Egyptians from Stockholm to Cairo, it had called first in Cairo to collect an Egyptian security official. The same process was used when the Gulfstream was used to pick up Iqbal from Jakarta and also take him to Cairo. In theory, then, the CIA could claim that the prisoners were never in their custody. The idea, said Michael Scheuer, was one of insulating the CIA, to make sure the prisoners were in American hands for "as little time as possible". If the CIA was picking up a Namibian suspect it made sense to have a Namibian team on board to take custody on the CIA plane "without us being anything but the taxi driver."[20] In practice, all concerned knew the defence was paper thin, particularly since the renditions had been organised almost entirely by the CIA. As things got busy in the years after 9/11, the CIA stopped bothering to pick up these foreign agents. No Moroccan agent, for example, was on board Binyam Mohamed's flight from Pakistan to Rabat.

"The law doesn't really apply to us"

This second defence was invented by John Yoo, who worked as deputy assist-ant attorney general between 2001 and 2003,[21] and who drafted most of the key memos that were concerned with the definitions of torture. It was based on the argument that the Senate had ratified parts of the Convention Against Torture subject to some limitations. And so, while the full convention might in theory protect everyone from transfer to torture, US Law, a sort of "Convention Lite", was not so sweeping. Yoo first argued that Article 3, as implemented in US law, had "no extraterritorial effect (except in the case of extradition)" and did not ap-ply to prisoners transferred from Guantánamo Bay, Afghanistan or elsewhere to other countries.[22]

Crucially for the CIA's rendition programme, the drafters of the Conven-tion thought otherwise and intended the treaty not to apply just to people ex-pelled from the United States. In other words, a case such as Maher Arar's. Instead it was meant to apply to any form of transfer of individuals, namely everyone in the rendition programme. Two of the main drafters of the Con-vention clarified that:

a State is not only responsible for what happens in its own territory, but it must also refrain from exposing an individual to serious risks outside its territory by handing him or her over to another State from which treatment contrary to the *Convention* might be expected. . . . As it now reads, *the article is intended to cover all measures by which a person is physically transferred to another state.*[23]

Congress had later endorsed this point, passing a law in 1998 that stated it was not the policy of the United States to send anyone to face torture "regardless of whether the person is physically present in the United States."[24] Government agencies were ordered to make regulations to enact this law. Although Yoo might argue this was policy not law, the legal consensus was that acts like rendition, to be lawful, would need to meet the full requirements of the Convention Against Torture.[25]

One law that most certainly applied to all US officers, in the CIA or any agency, was the Anti-Torture Statute that in 1994 had put the UN Convention Against Torture into the US Criminal Code. It defined torture as an act "specifically intended to inflict severe physical or mental pain or suffering (other than pain or suffering incidental to lawful sanctions) upon another person within his custody or physical control."[26] The maximum sentence was to be twenty years in jail — or the death penalty if the torture victim died.[27] The Statute had particular relevance for the CIA as it was aimed specifically at what US officials did overseas. (Congress decided that torture within US domestic borders was already adequately covered by existing legislation.)

The statute prohibited not only torture by the CIA itself but also banned any form of *conspiracy to torture*. Conspiring to torture would be "subject to the same penalties" as torture itself, except for the death penalty.[28] Under wider US criminal law, the conspiracy "need not be an express or formal agreement; a tacit understanding is sufficient."[29] This point was raised at the end of November 2002, in a memo from a FBI special agent based in Guantánamo. The agent first analysed and objected to some approved Pentagon techniques for interviewing senior Al Qaeda detainees, such as exploiting "phobias" like "the fear of dogs" or dripping water "to induce the misperception of drowning". He went on to consider renditions and discussed a plan to send a detainee "to Jordan, Egypt or another third country to allow those countries to employ interrogation techniques that will enable them to obtain the requisite information."[30] The FBI agent stated that an intent like this, to facilitate the use outside the US of techniques that were banned within the country would be a "per se violation of the US Torture Statute." He added that anyone discussing such a plan could be seen as conspiring to violate the law. "Any person who takes any action in furtherance of implementing such a plan would inculpate all persons who were involved in creating this plan. This technique cannot be utilised without violating US Federal law."[31]

When considering some of the CIA's own interrogation techniques, administration lawyers drew a distinction between the legal definition of torture and the lesser (but also illegal) category of "cruel, inhuman and degrading" treatment. Yoo argued that while, under the anti-Torture Statute, US agents were prohibited from engaging in torture worldwide, there was no specific ban in this statute on using such lesser techniques abroad. Although this was never described in detail, these arguments appeared to be designed to allow the use of some of the CIA's extended methods, like sleep deprivation or even simulated drowning of prisoners, in its secret prisons. In his confirmation hearings before the Senate, Gonzales endorsed this argument when he stated that "there is no legal prohibition under the CAT [Convention Against Torture] on cruel, inhuman or degrading treatment with respect to aliens overseas."[32] But his arguments horrified many senators. Senator John McCain's anti-torture amendment made clear there was no such loophole for interrogators abroad. And so, once again, it became clear that the CIA's practices were fully regulated by US law.

"They promised us they wouldn't torture"

However weak it sounds, this defence was the CIA's ace card, revealed by President Bush at his April 2005 press conference. Ever since the renditions began a decade earlier, the hope was that, legally speaking, the agency could use a series of "diplomatic assurances" from countries like Egypt that would protect all concerned from an accusation of breaking the law. The point was stated by Alberto Gonzales when he said to the Senate that "assurances from a country that it will not engage in torture… can provide a basis for concluding that a person is not likely to be tortured if returned to another country."[33]

The idea of using these sorts of promises was an old and well-worn concept used by many countries, but with mixed success. Nothing in the UN Convention made any mention of such assurances. But in deportation cases, US law had already incorporated the idea, and had given the Attorney General and his deputy the power to accept promises not to torture. But, whether promises had been obtained or not, the law still required the government to examine the facts, including the cases of others who had been deported to a country before, and oppose any transfer of prisoners if there were "substantial grounds" for believing he would be tortured, defined in US law as more than a 50 per cent chance.

When it came to CIA renditions, whatever promises were made, the likelihood of torture in many countries was close to 100 per cent. The law stated that "all evidence relevant to the possibility of future torture shall be considered." The fact that almost all prisoners in the rendition programme subsequently protested about being tortured was a matter that the US government, in law, was dutybound to consider. But in reality, when it came to CIA renditions, the promises were never serious, amounting in some cases to a mere verbal assurance given by the head of local intelligence to the chief of the local CIA station. Everyone involved knew it was a sham. When the CIA's rendition process was founded in Egypt, it was supervised by Edward Walker Jr., then US Ambassador to Cairo. He supported the process and years later still defended it. But he described the assurance process as highly informal. "I can't say to you with any candour that there was anything more than the verbal assurance, or even a written assurance.

There was very little effort to follow up on that."[34] At headquarters, the CIA's Michael Scheuer was equally dismissive. "No-one was kidding anyone here," says Scheuer. "We knew exactly what that kind of promise was worth."[35]

The point was that, as everyone knew, in a country like Egypt the use of torture was endemic. It was highly unlikely that it would not be used. Someone caught just for stealing fifty cents in Cairo was bound to be beaten by police, said Walker, so imagine the fate of alleged terrorists: "If you're having that kind of behaviour on the criminal level, certainly you've got to expect that behaviour at the terrorism [level]." There was an explanation for this endemic ill-treatment of prisoners. The primary basis of the Egyptian legal system was the confession. The police and intelligence services had almost no idea of how else to extract admissions of guilt. "So there is a huge emphasis on getting confessions and people get promoted for it," he said. Walker continued:

I cannot believe that anybody that was involved in this didn't in his heart of hearts, if he was halfway intelligent, think that they [the prisoners rendered by the US] were getting abusive, aggressive interrogation techniques that were tantamount to torture or that they would be tried in a fair and US-style trial.[36]

Burton Gerber, a former CIA Chief of Station and specialist in the ethics of intelligence, said while in principle he could see the logic of sending a captured and dangerous prisoner back to their home country, to avoid having to release him, he was troubled by the notion of sending them back for "further purposes" like interrogation. "It seems to me a little disingenuous to say yes we sent these people there and that we don't want them to be tortured," he said. "If you send someone to somewhere like Syria or Egypt then what are you really expecting to happen to them there? If they are being sent to torture, then it is wrong: it's a corruption of the human soul *as much as if we did it ourselves.*"[37]

In response to such criticisms, the Bush administration insisted that the promises not to torture were verified. In March 2005, an anonymous US official told the *New York Times* that "we check on those assurances, and we double-check on these assurances," that US officials are assigned to verify that promises not to torture were kept, and that compliance was "very high."[38] On 16 February 2005, the CIA director, Porter Goss, testified to the Senate Intelligence Committee that "of course, once [prisoners are] out of our control, there's only so much we can do. But we do have an accountability programme for those situations."[39] Asked what Goss meant by an "accountability programme," an anonymous intelligence official told the *Washington Post* that "in some cases, the US government is allowed access and can verify treatment of detainees."[40] But most in the intelligence community doubted Goss's unsubstantiated promises. "The truth is we could not get access to most of these prisoners once they have been rendered even if we tried," one CIA source told me. "Once you've lost control of a prisoner, it is almost impossible to check what is done with him," he said.[41]

What then of the government's claim that the CIA carried out no torture by itself? Before 9/11, the emphasis was on out-sourcing. The CIA was not trained as jailers and they had no plans to run their own prisons. But after 9/11, things changed. The priority was to obtain intelligence and the most important prisoners would be kept in-house.

These "high value detainees" disappeared into what came to be known as "black sites". These were true ghost prisoners, undeclared to the Red Cross and held, in some cases, for years without all communication with even their families.

Among those captured and held exclusively within the CIA's own custody were:

• Khalid Sheikh Mohammed, captured in March 2003
• Abu Zubaydah, captured in March 2002
• Ramzi Binalshibh, captured in September 2002
• Hambali (real name: Riduan Isamuddin), Indonesian Islamic militant; captured in August 2003.[42]

Under pressure to glean information, the CIA chose to apply some of the most severe methods, as seen for example at the CIA wing at Abu Ghraib. The methods, based on techniques refined over many decades, were referred to not as those of torture but of "enhanced interrogation". Having been told by President Bush that the Geneva Conventions did not apply after 9/11, the CIA needed advice on what thresholds were appropriate. And this gave rise to the first defence against the charge that they were perpetrating torture.

"It may have been rough, but it wasn't strictly torture"

In the spring of 2002, after the capture in Pakistan of Abu Zubaydah, the CIA sought further advice on what methods could legally be used to interrogate him. It was this that resulted in the infamous torture memos, described in Chapter 7, in which Department of Justice and White House lawyers sought not to advise on what was established law, but to try to re-invent the law. After Abu Ghraib, and after the outrage at the torture memo's contents, the advice was withdrawn. A new policy was issued in December 2004.[43] But by then the damage was done. CIA officers had been told their backs were covered. They were operating legally. But now they began checking with their personal lawyers. Could they face prosecution for participating in torture?

The point is, there were fine distinctions and grey areas. If the CIA went beyond the Geneva Convention it did not necessarily imply actual torture. Geneva effectively prohibited any "coercive questioning" — but did all such questioning imply torture or inhumane treatment?

Among the darkest stories of US conduct after 9/11 was the decision to cross the line — to move not only beyond the Geneva Convention but to include what, to most reasonable people, would be considered torture. Among such methods widely described by former CIA officers, including those involved at the time, was the deployment, albeit in only a handful of cases, of techniques creating the sensation of suffocation or near-drowning ("water-boarding"), the use of physical stress positions that caused excruciating pain and severe psychological threats.

According to Burton Gerber, who has continued to advise the government on the ethics of intelligence-gathering, Geneva would "hardly allow any kind of questioning at all." And in some cases it was right to go beyond it. Acceptable techniques might include, he said, "shouting at people, solitary confinement, disruption of daily routine, of sleep patterns." But when these became physical or involved a mortal threat, then the line was crossed. "Torture, to my mind, begins long before the line the Attorney General drew *at the point of real danger of physical harm*. ... Torture includes any kind of physical assault on someone's person; I also think it's not proper, practically nor morally, to attack someone's religion or their close family."[44]

Other former US government officials, who, unlike Gerber, had access to information about the CIA's practices after 9/11, told me that, in some "carefully-supervised" cases, this line had indeed been crossed after 9/11. Many defended such practices as necessary given the extreme threat posed by Al Qaeda and the need to extract secrets from the most important detainees as rapidly as possible. Yet, as one put it to me, to pretend such methods were not torture was just "pure politics". It was one thing to write memos in Washington and another to be the CIA officers required to carry out the instructions. For those who used methods like waterboarding, the distinction between a "torture" and an "enhanced method" of interrogation was a mere nicety. The point was to force, shock, or scare someone to talk. As one former CIA official, once a senior figure in the Directorate of Operations, told me: "Of course it was torture. Try it and you'll see."

Another former high-up in the Directorate of Operations, also told me: "Yes, it's torture and that's why a lot of people involved, not only the people who were in the room, but all the people who gave the orders, are looking around for personal lawyers. Because I know these things are going to become enormous." He added: "The authorities came from Gonzales down. But ultimately people are worried about whether these authorities will really stand the test."[45]

"In War, the President is the Law"

In the weeks after 9/11, one of the most extraordinary arguments developed was that, when it came to the law, the President ultimately, in time of war, could have the final say. It was first detailed in a memo on 25 September 2001 by John Yoo, who described the "broad constitutional power" of the president that prohibited any limits on the president's "determinations as to any terrorist threat, the amount of military force to be used in response, or the method, timing, and nature of the response." Yoo later claimed: "Why is it so hard for people to understand that there is a category of behaviour not covered by the legal system?" Expanding these war powers to the methods of interrogation, Yoo argued that Congress did not have the power to "tie the President's hands in regard to torture as an interrogation technique." He continued: "It's the core of the Commander-in-Chief function. They can't prevent the President from ordering torture."[46]

Later Gonzales, in a Senate testimony, refused repeatedly to refute this argument. The point was mute, he said, because as a matter of policy the President had declared that he abhorred all forms of torture.

But when Bush signed into law the McCain amendment that banned US officials from using any form of inhumane treatment, he again implied his war powers were intact and he could, if he wished, merely over-ride any Congressional limits on interrogation practices, stating the amendment would be interpreted consistent with the "constitutional authority of the President to supervise the unitary executive branch and as Commander in Chief". The implications angered the Senate. In response, Senators John McCain and John Warner, both Republicans, issued a statement that insisted that the Congress had rejected administration demands for any kind of presidential waiver. "Our Committee intends through strict oversight to monitor the Administration's implementation of the new law."[47] Whether the President would ignore the law passed by Congress and how the McCain amendment would impact on CIA interrogation methods was still, at the time of writing, un-tested ground.

"Let's keep it secret"

As a tactic of defence, this was probably the CIA's best. As details of the CIA's "black sites" emerged, the Agency went to enormous efforts to persuade both its current and former agents to stay silent. Porter Goss, the new head of the CIA, then railed against those who damaged national security by leaking secrets and the Agency's office of security started putting pressure on many of those who had recently retired. Anyone with a security clearance, including the thousands of contractors who worked alongside the Agency, were told that all public comments and contacts with journalists needed to be vetted in advance. Ultimately, though, it was the King Canute defence. Enough people involved were determined to speak out — if only because of anger with the White House. "The Executive ordered us to carry out these things, and now they will pretend they never knew about these matters. It's an old story — leave the Agency's foot soldiers hanging out to dry," said one retired official.

In both their outsourcing of interrogation and the use of their own enhanced methods then, CIA officers knew that torture was involved. Many in fact believed that, in a state of war, these methods were necessary. But, ultimately, most said, the decision of necessity was a matter for political leaders — for those at the White House who gave them their orders. And, from the beginning, the White House was made fully aware of *everything* that was happening. In its leaks to journalists, the CIA leadership itself was careful to make this very clear. Citing remarks by anonymous "current and former" officials, provided on the eve of the CBS *60 Minutes* programme that I assisted, the *New York Times* reported how the CIA had been authorised after 9/11 by the White House "to transfer prisoners to other countries solely for the purpose of detention and interrogation."[48]

The involvement of the White House in all decisions about rendition policy was emphasised by all those I interviewed. As Scheuer wrote more generally:

For now, the beginning of wisdom is to acknowledge that the non-C.I.A. staff members... knew that taking detainees to Egypt or elsewhere might yield treatment not consonant with United States legal practice. How did they know? Well, several senior C.I.A. officers, myself included, were confident that common sense would elude that bunch, and so we told them — again and again and again. Each time a decision to do a rendition was made, we reminded the lawyers and policy makers that Egypt was Egypt, and that Jimmy Stewart never starred in a movie called "Mr. Smith Goes to Cairo."[49]

On 5 December 2005, Condoleezza Rice, now Secretary of State, arrived at Andrews Air Force Base. Before she boarded her plane to Europe she called a press conference to discuss rendition. "Rendition is a vital tool in combating transnational terrorism," she said. "Its use is not unique to the United States, or to the current administration." Rendition had been used for years, she said, including by the French. She cited the case of Carlos the Jackal, who in 1994 was seized in Sudan and rendered back to Paris. A rendition by the French government brought him to justice in France, where he is now imprisoned. "Renditions take terrorists out of action, and save lives. In conducting such renditions, it is the policy of the United States, and I presume of any other democracies who use this procedure, to comply with its laws and comply with its treaty obligations, including those under the Convention Against Torture."

But a storm was already raging. Europe was not opposed to a rendition of a prisoner like the Jackal to face a proper court trial in a place like Paris. But it was angered about renditions to countries that tortured and held no fair trials. It was angered too about reports of the CIA's secret jails, and of the CIA's air fleet crisscrossing the Continent. Rice was off to Berlin where politicians were clamouring for answers about the case of their citizen, Khaled el-Masri. Would Rice finally issue an apology for his kidnap from Macedonia?

Although much of the CIA's rendition programme, both to foreign-controlled and CIA-controlled jails, appeared to be illegal, it was a fair bet that most of these legal arguments would not be tested in any US criminal court for many years. In the middle of a war, what federal prosecutor would wish to take up the case? But in Europe, among all of America's most vital allies in the War on

Terror, the picture was different. There, the Convention Against Torture is in-corporated into the European Convention on Human Rights (ECHR) and had been enshrined in national laws. As a matter of national policy too, the policy of renditions left the United States uniquely at odds with all its key Western allies, including Great Britain and Germany. All of them said they would play no part in the rendition programme.

Britain, for instance, had been down the road of torture many times before. Its own record was hardly gleaming. Torture was used in the British Army's Ma-laya, Kenya, and Northern Ireland campaigns. In World War Two, according to recently disclosed files, British intelligence operated an interrogation centre in London and later in northern Germany that used a series of severe torture tech-niques, including forcing prisoners to kneel while they were beaten on the head, making them stand for twenty-six hours and threatening executions.[50]

As a result, in the mind of most members of Britain's Army and security serv-ices, lessons had been learned. For example, torture had produced damaging results in Northern Ireland. The information obtained had been poor, and the publicity caused by the revelation of these methods had hardened support for the IRA's terrorist campaign. Moreover, these methods of interrogation had also been judged illegal by a January 1978 ruling from the European Court on Human Rights. It considered five techniques used by the Army, including wall-standing (also known as a "stress position"), hooding and sleep deprivation. After 9/11, *all* were being used again by the CIA and US military, and had been judged legal by White House and Department of Justice lawyers. But the European Court had judged that it all amounted to an illegal practice of "inhuman and degrad-ing treatment." So, in effect, Britain was bound to oppose the methods that the United States had now judged necessary in its conflict against terrorism. It was still bound by an "unqualified" promise made by Britain's Attorney General in 1977, that the "five techniques" would not "in any circumstances be reintro-duced as an aid to interrogation."[51]

In the spring of 2005, after complaints of British complicity with US tor-ture, an inquiry by the UK's Intelligence and Security Committee, a watchdog appointed by the Prime Minister, issued a low key report. It found that Brit-ish intelligence agents, while not participating in abuse of detainees, had been present on some key occasions. As a result of this report, instructions were now issued to all British personnel, both in the military and intelligence servic-es, that no British official could have any contact whatsoever with any detainee who might be likely to be transferred without legal process or face any kind of mistreatment.[52] It put British personnel in a difficult position. Among those difficult cases was that of Binyam Mohamed, who had been questioned by Brit-ish officers in Pakistan, prior to his rendition to Morocco. In a parliamentary answer, Jack Straw, the Foreign Secretary, confirmed that an interview had taken place, but he said the British had no involvement in what happened next.

"The Security Service had no role in his capture or in his transfer from Pakistan," he insisted.[53]

Meanwhile, in both Italy and Germany, criminal investigations were underway into whether CIA agents had committed serious crimes by their abduction of Islamic suspects. Italy was investigating the Abu Omar case, described earlier, while in Germany, a prosecutor close to Ramstein airbase asked whether the transfer of Abu Omar on his way to Egypt constituted kidnap under German law. Prosecutors in Munich, meanwhile, continued to investigate the abduction of Khaled el-Masri from Macedonia, as the kidnap of a German citizen.

The exposure of US interrogation methods and the rendition system had embarrassed America's allies. While they themselves had carried out no renditions, the publicity over these methods exposed their own degrees of complicity. *Former and current intelligence officers in Britain, France, Germany, and Italy all confirmed to me that their governments had been fully aware of the rendition programme*, even if their own officers had taken no direct part in the matter. One senior British security source, for example, acknowledged to me that Britain had been "involved at the periphery" of some rendition operations.[54]

What became utterly clear was that the CIA's fleet of aircraft I had tracked had made widespread use of both civilian and military European airports. A survey I carried out for the *New York Times* of a small sample of just over 300 CIA flights in Europe (between November 2001 and the summer of 2005) showed the following number of landings by country:[55]

Germany	94	Poland	6	Croatia	1
UK	76	Italy	5	France	1
Ireland	33	Romania	4	Sweden	1
Portugal	16	Iceland	4	Hungary	1
Spain	15	Switzerland	2	Macedonia	1
Czech R	15	Malta	2	Estonia	1
Cyprus	13	Turkey	2	Netherlands	1
Greece	13			**TOTAL**	307

Most of these flights had nothing to do with renditions; the CIA had many purposes for its fleet. CIA critics alleged they were indications of prisoners transported wholesale through European airspace. There was little proof of that. But what was apparent was that several rendition operations had used Europe as a base for both their planning and execution.

Flightlogs of the CIA planes showed, for example, that British and German bases were widely used staging posts in rendition operations after 9/11. In addition to the case of Abu Omar's rendition from Milan to Egypt via Germany, at least the following known renditions were staged out of Frankfurt:

Jamil Qasim Mohammed, Pakistan to Jordan on 23 October 2001
Martin Mubanga (a British citizen), Zambia to Guantánamo on 19 April 2002
Abu al-Kassem Britel (an Italian citizen) from Pakistan to Morocco on 25 May 2002
Mohammed Slahi, Jordan to Kabul on 19 July 2002
Binyam Mohamed, Pakistan to Morocco on 21 July 2002
Abdul Shaqawi and Hassan bin Attash, Jordan to Afghanistan on 8 January, 2004.

A series of rendition operations saw the use of Prestwick airport in Scotland as a refuelling stop as the planes returned to Washington, DC, after the transfers of:

Jamil Qasim Mohammed (mentioned above).
Ahmed Agiza and Mohammed al-Zery, Sweden to Cairo on 18 December 2001.
Muhammad Saad Iqbal Madni, Jakarta to Cairo on 11 January 2002.

One CIA pilot told me Prestwick was a popular destination for refuelling stops and layovers. "It's an 'ask no questions' type of place and you don't need to give them any advance warning you're coming," he said.

Did the use of these bases for rendition operations make countries like Britain and Germany complicit? According to experts in international law, the important thing was whether the governments concerned had knowledge that their air space and bases were being used for these activities. When American planes in April 1986 staged a raid on Tripoli, Libya, from British soil, there was no doubt that Britain was legally co-responsible. The only debate at the time was whether the raid itself was legally justified. (The justification given was of self-defence.) According to Dr Georg Nolte, a law professor at the University of Munich, the position was clear-cut. He told me that if they knew, they were co-responsible. And if they did not know, but concrete facts emerged that established this knowledge, then they had a clear duty to investigate the matter.[56]

Britain had little excuse for its pleas of ignorance on rendition. Because of its close intelligence relationship with the US, it was kept informed of most of what was happening in the War on Terror — even if not the exact location of the most secret prisons. More to the point, given the many arrests of British citizens and residents by the US, the Foreign Office had specific cause and duty to investigate and discover the facts about how they were being treated. When the Briton, Martin Mubanga, for example, was snatched in Zambia, accused of having fought in Afghanistan, the Foreign Office said at the time that Mubanga, a 29-year-old from north London, had dual UK-Zambian nationality and so demands for UK consular access had been refused. But, on his release, Mubanga, claimed he had been questioned by a UK intelligence officer in Zambia, implying the UK was involved and had closely monitored his fate. What is certain is that from Zambia he was rendered illegally on to Guantánamo without any extradition proceedings. My flight records showed that on 18 April 2002, just before his departure, the Gulfstream V CIA jet used in so many renditions departed from Frankfurt with a flight plan for Entebbe, Uganda, just a short hop from Zambia. From there, the plane disappeared off the radar, resurfacing only in Washington, DC on 20 April by which time Mubanga had already arrived in Cuba. This plane and its regular pilots, which on the available evidence had organised his rendition, were frequent visitors to British airspace and airports. Yet there was no attempt to question anyone involved — even after Mubanga, who said he condemned the September 11 attacks and had no connection with Al Qaeda, was released from Cuba without any charges.

Another close potential connection between the UK and the US system of secret detentions was the British sovereign base of Diego Garcia in the Indian Ocean. Leased to the United States as a strategic air and naval base, it was widely reported to have been used to detain terror suspects. In statements to parliament, ministers assured MPs that these reports were wrong. For example, Ian Pearson, a Foreign Office minister, told the Foreign Affairs Select Committee on 23 November 2005:

I can say that the US authorities have repeatedly assured us that assertions in the press that there are or have ever been suspected terrorists and/or Iraqi prisoners under interrogation at Diego Garcia, or on any other vessels in British territorial waters, are unfounded. The British representative on Diego Garcia has also confirmed this to be the case.

Again, evidence from CIA flight plans raised doubts about how thoroughly those US assurances had been investigated. On 11 September 2002, at 11.40 p.m. local time, the CIA Gulfstream V set off from Washington, DC for Athens. After re-fuelling, it took off again with a flight plan for the Diego Garcia base. This flight took off from the US the same day as the most important capture to that date in the War on Terror — the arrest in Pakistan of Ramzi Binalshibh, the 9/11 plotter. Binalshibh was reportedly transferred directly to a secret CIA facility. The flight to Diego Garcia that followed straight afterwards was clear, if circumstantial, evidence of a link between the British base and the interrogation of CIA prisoners.

What further angered Europeans was the suggestion not only of CIA overflights but that European soil itself might have been used for the CIA's secret prisons. I had first noticed a strong pattern of movements of CIA planes to many cities in Eastern Europe. Some included flights from Afghanistan, Jordan or Morocco that might have involved the transfer of prisoners. But I never thought that on its own this flight data really proved anything.

But then, in an article of 2 November 2005, the *Washington Post*'s Dana Priest made a specific allegation that secret jails had been set up in Eastern Europe. The article did not name which countries were involved. But then Human Rights Watch, referring to copies of various flight logs, alleged that the countries involved were Romania and Poland. Both countries vehemently denied the allegation, and, at the time of writing, while the existence of CIA secret jails was confirmed by President Bush, their location in Europe had not been confirmed by any official or on-the-record source. But the political damage was done. Europe demanded answers and, with the movement of CIA planes confirmed, there was an impetus to set in motion further inquiries.

As a result, both the European Parliament and the Council of Europe began their own investigations. The latter, as the agency that effectively policed the European Convention on Human Rights, had real powers to demand answers from governments and it had particular influence over former Soviet governments that knew that concern over their human rights record would damage their attempts to join European institutions.

The Council's investigators, led by a Swiss former prosecutor, Dick Marty, obtained a full copy from Eurocontrol, the Brussels-based European air traffic agency, of the movements of alleged CIA planes through its airspace. In his first report, published in June 2006, he concluded:

It is now clear — although we are far from having established the whole truth — that authorities in several European countries actively participated with the CIA in these unlawful activities. Other countries ignored them knowingly, or did not want to know.

Another European involvement in the rendition programme was in the actual arrests of terrorists. Special Forces from Great Britain had been integrated with the US Delta Forces and took part in the arrest of terror suspects in both Iraq and Afghanistan. Some of those, said British security sources, had ended up in the US prison network. In a memo leaked from the Foreign Office addressed to Tony Blair's Downing Street office in early December 2005, an official said the issue of whether such prisoners "have subsequently been sent to interrogation centres" was under research, but "the basic answer is that we have no mechanism for establishing this."[57] The memo also recorded that extraordinary rendition, as defined by a transfer to a country where torture was likely, was "almost certainly illegal", and if the US was to break international law by organising an extraordinary rendition without human rights assurances then "cooperation with such an act would also be illegal if we knew of the circumstances." As the same memo revealed, the increasing attention on rendition was particularly embarrassing to Britain, which was then negotiating agreements with countries like Algeria that would allow the deportation of terror suspects from London with "no torture" promises in place. The reporting on rendition was showing that such promises might hold little water.

To my mind Europe's greatest involvement with the rendition programme was through the exchange and use of intelligence data. Since 9/11, there was a premium on "working together to fight terrorism", yet few explored what that really meant. What happened was an exchange of information on a vast scale about all kinds of people, including European citizens and residents, who might present a possible link to terrorist groups. The trouble, as we saw with Maher Arar and many other cases, was that mere association with someone accused of terrorist involvement might be no indication at all of an actual terrorist connection. And the Europeans began to notice that some of those mentioned in their intelligence reports began to "disappear" once they travelled beyond Europe's borders. As one British source explained to me, for example, it was no surprise to them because they had full knowledge that the rendition programme existed. An obvious example of UK intelligence exchange that led to US renditions was that of the British citizen Wahab al-Rawi, and two long-term British residents, Bisher al-Rawi (Wahab's brother and an Iraqi citizen), and Jamil al-Banna, a Jordanian. All three were arrested in the Gambia at the behest of the United States in 8 November 2002 after Britain's Security Service (MI5) exchanged intelligence reports about the trio's alleged connections to Islamic militant groups. Wahab was released after a month of questioning in Gambia by US agents, but the other two were rendered in the CIA's Gulfstream V to a CIA prison in Afghanistan and later onwards to Guantánamo.[58]

On 1 November, after the three were initially held at Gatwick Airport by MI5, Britain circulated a telegram (to an un-specified foreign agency) describing them as "three individuals associated with the prominent spiritual cleric Omar Othman [Abu Qatada]". The telegram stated that the information was being communicated in confidence for research purposes only and "MAY NOT BE USED AS THE BASIS FOR OVERT, COVERT OR EXECUTIVE ACTION." One of the trio was said to be carrying what preliminary inquiries suggested might be "a timing device or could possibly be used as some part of a car-based Improvised Explosive Device." It was a serious allegation, but although the device was later determined to be an innocent battery charger, the allegation, according to the men's lawyers, was never withdrawn. On 11 November, after the men were arrested, MI5 circulated another telegram that described al-Banna as "Abu Qatada's financier" and Bisher al-Rawi as an "Iraqi Islamic extremist". There was no mention of how, as later disclosed to the High Court in London in March 2006, Bisher had been assisting MI5.

Britain argued that, under treaties of cooperation, it was obliged to share intelligence about terrorist threats. But, under the international law of co-responsibility outlined by Professor Nolte, it had a duty also to find out how the information was used. In a statement to me, the Foreign Office said the UK "did not request the detention of the claimants in the Gambia and did not play any role in their transfer to Afghanistan and Guantánamo Bay." But the telegrams did suggest the UK's role was not entirely benign. A final telegram, sent on 6 December, just before Bisher and al-Banna were rendered to Afghanistan, confirmed that "in relation to Islamists currently in detention in the Gambia, the UK would not seek to extend consular protection to non-British nationals." The UK had washed its hands of the case — and the men were left to their fate.

These then were the issues that Secretary Rice faced as she flew into Europe to confront the controversy of rendition and CIA flights. In a statement issued from Andrews Air Force Base on 5 December, Rice claimed that "the United States has not transported anyone, and will not transport anyone, to a country when we believe he will be tortured. Where appropriate, the United States seeks assurances that transferred persons will not be tortured. ... the United States does not transport, and has not transported, detainees from one country to another for the purpose of interrogation using torture." Again and again the legality of US practice was underlined. "Torture is a term defined by law," said the Secretary of State; "we rely on law to govern our operations."

On her way to Berlin, and once there, Rice clarified: "All agencies of the United States are operating under our obligations concerning the CAT [Convention Against Torture]. ...We are going to be best at fighting the war on terrorism and protecting our citizens if we cooperate. And we have been cooperating." Rice's party line did not stretch to admitting a specific error in the case of Khaled el-Masri: "What I did say is that while I could not talk about the specifics of the el-Masri case, that we recognize that the Chancellor will be reviewing this in a committee of the Bundestag. We also recognize that any policy will sometimes result in errors, and when it happens we will do everything we can to rectify it."[59]

Later others repeated the message. Tony Blair said he was satisfied with American assurances they opposed the use of torture and he knew nothing about renditions. "I have absolutely no evidence to suggest that anything illegal has been happening here at all," he told Parliament, "and I am not going to start ordering inquiries into this, that and the next thing, when I have got no evidence to show whether this is right or not."[60] But, privately, the British noted, for example in the secret memo from the Foreign Office, that Rice was emphasising that the US did not "torture", rather than denying the use of "cruel, inhuman or degrading treatment."[61] Coercive measures in this category, such as sleep deprivation and use of constant exposure to loud noise, were outlawed in Europe under the European Convention on Human Rights.

Porter Goss, then head of the CIA, was also quick to deny US accountability for torture. *USA Today* reported him as saying in November 2005 that "This agency does not do torture. Torture does not work... we use lawful capabilities to collect vital information, and we do it in a variety of unique and innovative ways, all of which are legal and none of which are torture." But undoubtedly, foreign sources of intelligence were useful: "[W]e have to, within the law and within all the requirements of our professional ethics in this profession, develop agility. And that means putting a lot of judgment in the hands of individuals overseas. ... For the record, I will state again, and assert with eyeball-to-eyeball frankness, this agency does not do torture." Goss also stated "the CIA remains officially neutral on the proposal by Sen. John McCain."[62]

Attorney General Alberto Gonzales stated in a speech given in London on 20 March 2006 that "the US abhors torture and categorically rejects its use." Gonzales had suggested in a leaked White House memo of 2002 that torturing Al Qaeda operatives abroad "may be justified".[63]

But were Rice and the President and Porter Goss telling the truth?

On the matter of rendering people to foreign countries, was it correct that the US knew nothing of the torture that followed? I put this question to Ambassador Walker: "When Condoleezza Rice and the president now stand in front of people and say we don't send people to countries where they torture, are they telling the truth?"

"No, they're not telling the truth," he replied.

Was Walker arguing that rendition was a correct response to terrorism but it was dishonest to say that the assurances of non-torture were credible?

"That's correct," he replied. "I think everybody involved in that did a wink, wink and (thought) 'Yeah, they've given us assurances, that's what they want in Washington.' But they all know what it means."[64]

And what of the point that the CIA itself practised no torture? Here was what one former CIA official told me:

Coming out and saying "we don't do torture" is as bad as President Clinton saying "I didn't have sex with that woman." It's in the same league. It's a bare-faced lie. Of course we do torture. Imagine putting President Bush's head under water and telling him to raise his hand when he thinks he's being tortured. Give him the water-board treatment and he'd be raising his hand straight away. My view is that we need to be honest about what we are doing.[65]

There were those then who denied everything, and those from the CIA like Scheuer who spoke honestly, who acknowledged that torture, of course, took place. Others confirmed the torture at the CIA's own hands. Most of those who acknowledged torture also defended it too. It is this form of *Realpolitik* defence of rendition that we examine in the next chapter.

11

THE REALPOLITIK OF TORTURE

AT A PRISON IN A FAR-OFF PLACE

An interrogator faces his prisoner, shackled to the floor, alone inside a closed room. His mission is to wrestle from his prisoner whatever information he may hold. The interrogator feels a long way from home. Yet he fears this prisoner may hold knowledge that, if divulged, could save the lives of innocent civilians, or bring a killer to justice.

In his mission to save lives, this interrogator may know that certain harsh tactics — physical pressure that may legally constitute torture — could produce the information that will help him succeed in his mission. The temptations are obvious. Some interrogators will choose to apply such torture. Others will choose not to. Some may consult their superiors. This is the well-known torture question.

The dilemmas faced in this room are vital to the interests of a nation. Terrorism is a crime whose victim may be any citizen, living at home or abroad. If the interrogator chooses to employ torture, or a lesser method also judged illegal, he may later be prosecuted and punished by his peers. But his motives can be well understood and even sometimes praised. If asked why he employed torture, the interrogator may state that "no other option" was available to him. He may be right.

At the policy level, in the White House, it all looks different. A President may be aware that the employment of torture by those under his command, if discovered, may damage his reputation and the reputation of the nation as a whole. As commander in chief and master, with Congress, of the foreign policy of an entire nation and a budget of over 2,700 billion dollars,[1] he cannot argue he had "no other option" but to sanction these tactics.

As we've seen, the policy of rendition of Islamist terrorist suspects, created in the mid 1990s, was implemented by those in the CIA who believed too that they had no other option in order to save lives and disrupt Islamist terrorism. All involved knew that those militants would face torture. They knew there were

213

better ways to win, for example by taking military action in Afghanistan or by confronting Pakistan or Saudi Arabia. Michael Scheuer said it might have been possible to detain all prisoners in the United States, under American law. But yet the politicians did not want to take this route. "We're in a lot of positions around the world where we don't have a lot of options, and sometimes you have to work with the devil," he said. As long as American policymakers did not deal with prisoners under the American legal system, the CIA had no choice but "do what you can with what you have." So like the interrogator in his interrogation room, men like Scheuer felt their political masters had given them only limited means to carry out their orders.

Again, the options for the presidents involved, Clinton and Bush, were much wider. To them, and to those in Congress with oversight of these operations, could be asked the broader question: were the tactics of rendition actually effective? Were they necessary? And, given all the means at the US government's disposal, could they have sanctioned a better way?

In this chapter I descend then into *Realpolitik,* and try to assess whether rendition and more widely the toleration or direct use of torture as tactics really made sense, and what they achieved. As the last chapter discussed, there was much about rendition that could be considered a violation of both domestic and international law. Many might argue it was also immoral. But, ignoring all these legal and ethical points for now, did it work anyway? The broader alternatives are considered separately in the next, concluding chapter.

Many would after all consider that, faced with the danger of Islamist *jihad,* in a time of war, moral niceties would have to be set aside.

Danielle Pletka, a vice president of the American Enterprise Institute, and a former senior staffer on the Senate Foreign Relations Committee, made just such a point to me. "I'm not a big fan of torture," she said, nor did she endorse the way countries like Syria or Egypt ran their prisons or security system. But she added:

Unfortunately, there are times in war when it is necessary to do things in a way that is absolutely and completely abhorrent to most good, decent people. And while again I don't want to say that the United States has engaged routinely in such practices, because I don't think that it is routine by any standard, but that said, if it is absolutely imperative to find something out at that moment, then it is imperative to find something out at that moment, and Club Med is not the place to do it.[2]

Rendition as a tactic

To judge rendition fairly, the first step is to examine its real objectives. Was it a torture programme, designed for the purpose of gathering intelligence by outsourcing interrogation? Or was it a policy that simply resulted in torture? All those with knowledge of the rendition programme, apart from senior policy-makers, as I discussed, acknowledged that torture did result from rendition, so the point may be seen as rather academic. Yet, tracing its real purpose is not only vital to judging its success, but also to seeing how it evolved over time.

With some exceptions, most of those involved in the early rendition programme insisted its primary objective was the disruption of terrorist cells, not to glean intelligence. Operations like the rendition of five people from Albania in the summer of 1998 effectively consisted of two components: the arrest of a cell of individuals suspected of plotting terrorism, and second their transfer from the field to a jail in Egypt. Under this scheme, the CIA organised the arrest, with some local help, and then Egypt arranged the next step. Precisely what happened in Egypt's jails afterwards, those involved said, was secondary. The important thing was that they disappeared from the scene. "Getting anyone off the street who you're confident has been involved or is planning to be involved in operations...is a worthwhile activity," said Michael Scheuer.[3] Not everyone described it to me in quite so clear cut a way: Ambassador Walker, then US Ambassador to Egypt, remembered the rendition policy as one of bringing people "for further interrogation in Egypt."[4] But, despite the qualification, most others involved told me the renditions were principally about a disappearance, not about interrogation.

It is important here to spell out that many people confuse the initial success of arrest operations with the outcome of the renditions that followed. As a simple tactic of disruption, rendition did achieve some success before 9/11. It did nibble away at Al Qaeda's structure. When Scheuer told me that rendition was a "brilliant tactical success," he was correct in so far as he meant that the arrests had disrupted the plans of several key militant figures. As he pointed out, the most important intelligence was often gathered at the arrest stage, not later in some Cairo torture cell after rendition. Often such information came from the documents and computers seized from the militants. "It was amazing what sort of things these people wrote down," he said.

After 9/11, the CIA and the US military (who took custody of more than 10,500 prisoners in Afghanistan and Pakistan alone)[5] again achieved some striking tactical success with their capture programme. The US invaded Afghanistan with a mission of apprehending bin Laden. Tracked by the CIA to Tora Bora, he escaped when the US military refused to commit troops to surround him.[6] But, despite this failure, the swift collapse of the Taliban and the destruction of Al Qaeda's training camps was a significant victory that surprised bin Laden's associates.[7] Through dogged intelligence work, the CIA went on to capture some of the most important members of bin Laden's circle — not only the main architects of 9/11, mentioned above, but key operatives such as Abd al-Rahim al-Nashiri, the leader of Al Qaeda in the Gulf, and Ahmed Khalfan Ghailani, who was wanted for the 1998 embassy bombings.[8] The arrests caused profound disruption to the Al Qaeda network. They isolated bin Laden and required the group to re-organise completely.

The real problems came in the next stage after arrest, when the CIA and the US military began to render these new prisoners across the world. It put the Agency at the centre of a large global prison network. From the end of 2001, the purpose of these renditions was widened. Rendition now was not just used to incarcerate (or "disappear") a captured prisoner; it was used also to find out what they knew. This was how a programme aimed at supporting arrest and disruptions became one that out-sourced torture.

The prisoners of the War on Terror were divided according to their importance, and faced three types of rendition: The most important prisoners, people like Khalid Sheikh Mohammed, were to be kept within the CIA's own custody. They were seen as holding knowledge of Al Qaeda's innermost secrets. The conduct of their interrogation was vital. So they were to be rendered to the CIA's own secret facilities, to what was called its "black sites." There they remained entirely in American hands. A second category of prisoners was to be held by the US military as "unlawful combatants." Most were eventually transshipped to the US base at Bagram, north of Kabul, or rendered across to Guantánamo. Finally, a third and largest category were rendered to the prisons of America's oldest and newest allies in the Muslim world — to Egypt, Jordan, Morocco, Syria, Uzbekistan and even Libya.

The function of all these renditions was now twofold. As before, there was still an objective of simply removing people, as President Bush described it, "from harm's way" (or more accurately put "from causing harm"). But in each category of rendition, in all corners of this crowded new prison network, a top priority was also to gather more intelligence.

Some of those I interviewed with the most reliable sources in the CIA would disagree. One told me that transfers to places like Egypt were still primarily for the purpose of detention, not so they could be interrogated. "They may well have been tortured, but we didn't ask for it," one told me. "Do you really think we would rely on what the Egyptians told us? Their priorities were to find out what threat these people might pose to Cairo, not to ask questions about threats to the United States."[9]

But however unreliable the Egyptians or Syrians were, the evidence described here supported the contradictory accounts of other CIA sources I interviewed. Outsourcing of interrogation, according to my evidence, did become routine — out of a practical and a political necessity. The CIA just could not cope alone with the sheer volume of prisoners to interrogate. "The US had a log jam of prisoners from Afghanistan and it had to do something with then," recounted one British intelligence official, who was officially in the loop on these matters.[10] Before 9/11, few CIA officers were actually trained in interrogation. Burton Gerber, who retired after thirty-nine years in the CIA, latterly as assistant director of covert operations, explained to me: "I was never trained in interrogation; to induce you, seduce you, but not to interrogate you." He added that this was not something that covert operatives were trained to do. It was a not a skill taught at training school.[11] As others explained, good interrogation also needed fluent speakers of Arabic and other key languages. These were in short supply. The CIA knew too that once it took full custody of key prisoners, they could be stuck with them almost indefinitely. The methods of interrogation they would have to use would be rigorous. And no political leader would ever want those methods described in a court room, whether military or civil, and want to risk their release by a judge. So there were limits to how many prisoners the CIA would want to hold itself. Out of hundreds of captives, at most less than three dozen were retained in the CIA's secret sites.

Faced with so many prisoners to interrogate, and a need for them to be questioned by men who knew their language and customs, hundreds of them were passed on to be questioned by foreign powers. If rendition had not started as a programme to outsource interrogation, after 9/11 it became one. Prisoners could face transfer not only to their country of origin or to where they were wanted on criminal charges, as had applied before 9/11, but now to any country that would help in their interrogation.

One prisoner after another, when describing their treatment, has recounted how they arrived in a foreign jail to face questions provided by the US or its Allies. In the mid 1990s, rendition was sending back Egyptian dissidents, who were tortured in Egypt to confess to their plots to attack the Egyptian state. But after 9/11, rendition transferred prisoners to Arab jails to be questioned about their plots to attack the West.

As described before, Maher Arar, Abdullah Almalki, Ahmed al-Maati, and Mohammed Zammar all were questioned in Syria at the request of the United States or Canadian governments. Their questioning was outsourced.

Binyam Mohamed was an Ethiopian. He was sent to Morocco, although he had no connection at all with that country. He was questioned about his alleged involvement with militant groups in Britain and a possible plot to commit a terrorist act in the United States. His questioning was outsourced.

Khaled el-Masri was sent to Afghanistan, though no one has ever accused him of visiting that country before or plotting to commit a terrorist crime there. He was questioned by US interrogators. His imprisonment was outsourced.

So while the most important prisoners — most of the key 9/11 plotters, for example — remained in US hands, hundreds of other prisoners were held by foreign countries and interrogated about questions of importance to the United States and its Western allies.

The prisoners then began arriving in Cairo, in Amman, Damascus, Tashkent and Rabat. Many times, as we've seen, they arrived with their questions attached.

And the interrogations began. Could useful information emerge from their torture? Moral and legal factors aside, could this torture be justified?

The effectiveness of torture

It is easy to be trite about torture, or to sit, from a comfortable vantage point, on the moral high ground. Torture, say many liberal commentators, is not something that works. It is not only immoral but produces, they claim, a stream of inaccurate information. "People will say anything under torture!" is the refrain. This is too easy an answer.

Judging the success of torture depends on what exactly the torturer is actually trying to achieve.

If the object is to obtain a confession, then torture can be highly effective, for the very same reason that physical or psychological coercion, if applied expertly, will indeed finally persuade anyone to say anything. In *1984*, George Orwell wrote of Room 101, in which the agents of Big Brother would always find the one weakness that everyone has that would persuade him to submit to his torturers. Some people, who might have lived ordinary comfortable lives, require only mild physical pressure to sign a confession.

As described earlier in this book, Syria's Palestine Branch was a highly effective "confession factory" that induced one person after another to sign a statement stating what was required, regardless of its truthfulness. Stalin's torturers in the NKVD, and then KGB, were equally efficient. And yet their principal objective was not to gather intelligence but to obtain those confessions required for their dictator's show trials. The object of a confession was to legitimise before the public the victimisation of those arrested and imprisoned. "Thus it was," wrote Solzhenitsyn in *The Gulag Archipelago*, "that the conclusions of advanced Soviet jurisprudence, proceeding in a spiral, returned to barbaric or medieval standards. Like medieval torturers, our interrogators, prosecutors, and judges agreed to accept the confession of the accused as chief proof of guilt."[12] But such a process of legitimisation by confession was not just a refuge of the Communists. Many legal systems, particularly in the Middle East, function almost entirely by confession. Sceptics might also wonder if in Guantánamo too, a confession, regardless if true or false, would help to justify to the world's eyes why a particular prisoner had been incarcerated in grim conditions for years after 9/11.

What though of the objective of acquiring useful intelligence? Here too it is particularly trite to dismiss torture and coercive interrogation as an ineffective tool. While many could and do provide a stream of false information to interrogators, many others are also prepared to confess to the truth. Not every extremist is so wedded to the cause that they can endure too much pain.

In the War on Terror, there are the examples of those who provided false or misleading information and those whose torture or coercive interrogation proved effective. Among the examples of effective interrogation were:

Khalid Sheikh Mohammed was said to have talked almost immediately after the application of physical pressure, reported to have included simulated drowning.[13] He provided a stream of detailed information about the Al Qaeda network, detailed in the annexes of the 9/11 Commission report.

Abu Zubaydah, believed to have been Al Qaeda's top military strategist since late 2001, also began talking,[14] implicating José Padilla in the dirty bomb plot. Yet, when it came to using his testimony in the Padilla case, the US government refused because his evidence might have been obtained under duress.[15]

Others, however, provided misleading evidence:

Ahmed al-Maati confessed to a plot to bomb the Canadian parliament. His torture caused untold misery to those who were implicated, like Maher Arar and Abdullah Almalki, both of whom were arrested and then tortured.

Ibn al-Sheikh al-Libi As discussed, Colin Powell's claims on the links between Saddam Hussein and Al Qaeda were based on a false confession from al-Libi after he was rendered to Egypt.

Uzbek militants According to Craig Murray, citing MI6 intelligence reports, information passed by Uzbek intelligence via the CIA contained false claims made by Uzbek prisoners. For example, they suggested the existence of a training camp above the hills of Samarkand. Murray's military attaché, he said, knew the area well and knew the claim to be absurd.[16]

Three British detainees at Guantánamo, who, after intense questioning by the US military, confessed to appearing on an Al Qaeda video in Afghanistan. But the police found clear evidence that all three were living in Britain at the time the video was shot.[17]

With both true and false information emerging from confessions, one of the key problems then was assessing which of those confessions were useful, particularly when carried out by third parties, without monitoring by US agents. The former would frequently use such intelligence reports for their own purposes, for example to implicate dissidents living abroad who threatened their regimes. And here was the heart of the problem with all such "liaison relationships". As witnessed in the debacle of false intelligence that helped justify the 2003 invasion of Iraq, the problem for intelligence analysts is rarely the *volume* of intelligence. Their challenge is to look through all the thousands of sources of information — be it open source, communication intercepts or interrogation reports — and then determine what, to a high degree of confidence, is true. In this process of *verification*, evidence obtained coercively can muddy the water.

Confronted with conflicting information on terrorist networks from hundreds of sources, the *credibility* of any piece of intelligence is paramount. As former CIA operatives, some of whom have held among the most senior positions in the Agency, warned me, the policy of out-sourcing has created a critical weakness at the heart of counter-terrorist work. "The quality of information you get back from these sort of countries, from the interrogations, from Morocco and the Egyptians, is pretty low," a veteran CIA official told me.[18]

Ticking bombs

There are, of course, the famous "ticking bomb" scenarios where the problem of verification is less of an issue. If you torture a suspect, and he tells you where a bomb is and you find that bomb, then you know he has told the truth. Yet, even here, and even accepting that such scenarios may really occur, there is a broader issue that is problematic for those advocating torture or coercion.

A government that controls an agency like the CIA must look beyond the circumstances of one particular case. In the end, what happens in the torture room becomes public and must be judged not only by the information produced but upon the wider reaction to what occurred. As shown in the events at Abu Ghraib, our societies are judged by the actions of those who fight on our behalf. And torture, or a policy of harsh interrogations, helps shape how the rest of the world sees us and how others will, in future, treat our soldiers and citizens. In the longer term, the interests of democratic societies like the United States and Britain are served by the global spread of democracy and values of tolerance. A controversial policy of tolerating torture, which offends many who share our broader values and goals, can be deeply divisive.

The Battle of Algiers — a case study of realpolitik failure

When the 1966 film *The Battle of Algiers,* by Gillo Pontecorvo, was re-released at the end of 2003, it caused a stir among young Washington conservative thinkers, particularly as the Pentagon had held a screening of it that August, just as the insurgency in Iraq was getting established. The flyer announced:

How to win a battle against terrorism and lose the war of ideas. ... Children shoot soldiers at point blank range. Women plant bombs in cafes. Soon the entire Arab population builds to a mad fervor. Sound familiar? The French have a plan. It succeeds tactically, but fails strategically. To understand why, come to a rare showing of this film.

Here was a case study of how brutal tactics employed by French paratroopers, including both torture and execution, had succeeded in rounding up and defeating almost the entire urban leadership of the terrorist organisation, the FLN

(National Liberation Front) of Algeria and in winning the Battle of Algiers for the French authorities.

But the point that appeared to be lost by many viewers in Washington, despite the Pentagon brochure's clear warning, was that the victory over the FLN was only temporary. France was soon to lose the entire war. As one former soldier commented: "In Algeria, torture won the battle but lost the war."[19]

As the world's most successful insurgent movements have found (from the IRA in Northern Ireland, to the KLA in Kosovo, to the Vietcong in south Vietnam, to Sunni insurgents in Iraq today), the way to turn a minority terrorist movement into a broad movement with popular support would be to provoke repression, preferably of the worst kind. The Brazilian communist, Carlos Marighella, even put this cynical strategy down in writing in his 1969 *Mini-Manual for Urban Guerrillas*, which described the strategy thus:

The rebellion of the urban guerrilla and his persistence in intervening in political questions is the best way of ensuring popular support for the cause which we defend. ... The government has no alternative except to intensify its repression. The police networks, house searches, the arrest of suspects and innocent persons, and the closing off of streets make life in the city unbearable. ... The political situation is transformed into a military situation, in which the militarists appear more and more responsible for errors and violence.[20]

These tactical ideas, developed among left-wing rebels, found their way in the 1970s to Arab nationalists, and then to Islamist militants, who followed closely the lessons of communist insurgency in Central and South America. As Michael Sheehan, the former US counter-terrorism ambassador, commented after the film's release, the lessons of Algeria were "quite well known to modern insurgents", and particularly the lesson to provoke the heavy-handed response that "further legitimizes their movement and de-legitimizes those that they're fighting against." The key lesson for the West was the need to respond effectively to terrorism with a political strategy that helped to isolate the terrorists, not make them more powerful.

In France's case, the use of torture and repression not only bolstered popular support for the FLN; it also sapped the moral strength of France as exposure of the brutal tactics of their own country's military helped turn the abandonment of Algeria from a political taboo (supported by no mainstream political party) into a majority demand.

The lesson of these conflicts was that however great the atrocity committed by terrorists, the way to fight insurgency is by calculated restraint, however "weak" or "liberal" it may seem. As Senator John McCain said, in an impassioned rejection of torture, what helped him and his fellow soldiers through captivity and torture in Vietnam was that "every one of us—every single one of us—knew and took great strength from the belief that we were different from our enemies, that we were better than them, that we, if the roles were reversed, would not disgrace ourselves by committing or approving such mistreatment of them."[21]

The blunt razor

Whatever the rights or wrongs of particular cases, or the details of any torture that might follow, none of those involved in rendition ever doubted it was a repressive measure involving the removal of a human being's legal rights. It was justified, to those who ordered rendition's execution, in the belief that the prisoners involved presented a "clear and present" danger to Western interests. The defense of rendition, by this logic, required that the threat be real — in other words, that it was founded on the existence of solid intelligence.

Any kind of repressive measure results in a negative reaction. It might cause public outrage, like the response of world public opinion to abuses at Abu Ghraib and Guantánamo; or it might result in a reprisal, such as the threatened response of Dr Ayman al-Zawahiri to the renditions from Albania. If viewed purely tactically, the positive success of any repressive tactic like rendition (or assassination or even just longer prison sentences) would have to be balanced against its side-effects. This is what Alastair Crooke, a former senior officer in Britain's MI6, calls the "Jenin Paradox". For years, during his MI6 career, Crooke acted as an intermediary with militant groups, including in Afghanistan, southern Africa, and, on behalf of the European Union, in Israel and Palestine. He explained that when speaking to Israeli officers after military raids on the town of Jenin, in the West Bank, they would say something like this:

"There were ten terrorists in Jenin; we took out six of them and now there are only four left."

Crooke would then go into Jenin and ask the Palestinians what had happened and they would say:

"There used to be ten terrorists in the city. The Israeli Army came in and killed six, and now there are twenty-four."[22]

A violent strategy had served to recruit more extremists. Applied to the policy of rendition, Crooke's Jenin Paradox is a reminder of a simple truth: that whatever tactical benefit might be achieved by removing one terrorist suspect might be outweighed by the broader costs of the policy.

Rendition then, as a successful tactic, if ethics and legality are set aside, might have used a sharp razor — a repressive means of eliminating those most bent upon killing innocent people. The evidence from its recent application by the United States, however, was that a blunt razor had been employed. Both innocents and some very minor figures were all among those dispatched both to America's own Guantánamo prison and into the jails of repressive regimes. Intelligence used to select targets was often poor. On occasions there was also a sense, as seen with the rendition of Khaled el-Masri, that proof or even just hard evidence was really not that important. The CIA, in his case, seemed too busy to check his details: they left him abandoned in his cell for days. As the former CIA officer, Reuel Marc Gerecht, pointed out, rendition came to be targeted not at the most guilty figures (who would be held in the CIA's own custody), but at those against whom evidence was often simply too thin. "Rendition … solves the problem of how to deal with minor-league would-be Islamic terrorists or guerrillas who may or may not have the United States in their sights." He claimed that "rendition appeals to the CIA because it is easy."[23] Here lay the problem. If rendition was used to remove people who just might become terrorists, it was only a short-term solution. Every rendition operation risked causing a reaction or a reprisal. The larger the rendition programme, the bigger that reaction, and the more counter-productive the whole strategy became.

WINNING THE WAR

Flightlog

Registration: **N312ME**;
Type: **Beech Super King 200**;
Operator: Aero Contractors Ltd;
Date: **13 March 2006**

Flight plan:
Johnston County, NC
  (dep. 1.00 p.m. EST)
Jackson-Evers International, MS
  (arr. 03.17 p.m. CST)

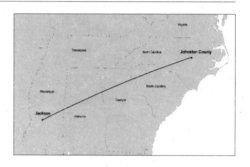

JOHNSTON COUNTY, NORTH CAROLINA
13 March 2006

On a sleepy Sunday afternoon, I paid a visit to the home of CIA aviation. It was a sunny day, and I stood in the public car park by the runway and watched as a little twin-prop plane taxied and then took off to the north. I recognised the plane's tail number N312ME — one of the fleet of CIA planes we had identified nearly a year before. Later, I checked on the computer and there was the flight plan of the plane — heading over to Mississippi. Behind a screen of pine trees, I saw the blue hangar of Aero Contractors, the CIA front company that handled the Agency's fleet of planes. Inside would usually be the company's World War Two-era DC3, a plane that, according to pilots, was still fitted with mountings for machine guns that had been attached when the plane deployed in the early 1990s for agency missions in the Sudan and Somalia.

As I drove around Johnston County, it struck me how open America was. More than four years earlier, when I first heard of the CIA's rendition programme, I had wondered how I could unlock the mystery it represented. Yet I've been astonished by how willing many of those with close knowledge of these US secret agencies had been to share their concerns. None of what I wrote would be possible without those who felt there were certain stories that simply needed telling. It was not because they were squeamish, far from it. But among them were those who felt some of the US policies and tactics being used in the War on Terror were wrong — and needed to be corrected if the West had a chance to avoid being drawn into a prolonged conflict.

Of course, much remains to be revealed. Many of the US tactics deployed against this terrorist threat remained national secrets, and some rightly so. Many insiders are still summoning up the courage to share what they know. On the other side, of the thousands of terrorist suspects arrested since 9/11, just a few have been released. Many others would either die in prison or not tell their stories for many years.

Although some facts about the policy of extraordinary rendition remain undisclosed, its role as a key tactic in the War on Terror is now apparent. Some will argue that its details should remain in the dark, that to reveal the CIA's activities helps undermine the potency of their operations, and even puts lives in danger.

Yet, the programme of using rendition against Islamic militants began more than ten years ago. In that time, the conflict between the Western world and those forces has expanded in leaps and bounds.

From meeting the Taliban in Afghanistan, to witnessing the smouldering embers of the World Trade Center, to talking to insurgents and seeing the blood and gore of suicide bombs in Baghdad and Basra, not to mention the devastation wrought in my home city of London, I've had glimpses of the ongoing war from close at hand. I do not see it ending quickly.

In late 2004, President Bush announced that three-quarters of Al Qaeda's senior leadership had been killed or captured.[1] It seemed an exaggerated figure, but there is no doubt the CIA and the US military have together eliminated much of the former top echelon of Osama bin Laden's former network, even as the leader himself and his deputy, Dr Ayman al-Zawahiri, remained at large as of September 2006. Globally, however, terrorism has continued unabated.[2] In 2005, official US figures showed there were over 5,000 terrorist incidents around the world, up from some 3,000 in 2004. These attacks resulted in the deaths of 6,728 people and 11,877 injured.[3]

It is true that by mid-2006 there has not been a second attack within the United States, but then the last one took at least six years for Khalid Sheikh Mohammed to plan.[4] There was now an easier battleground too for the *jihadists* to strike America. In Iraq, soon after the invasion, Bush had declared "mission accomplished". Later he declared "bring 'em on"[5] to those who wanted to fight America. They answered his call and found a welcoming environment to stage their *jihad*. Of the people killed in terrorist attacks worldwide in 2005, over 50 per cent were died in Iraq.[6] There too, new leaders of the Sunni *jihad* have emerged, those like the late al-Zarqawi. And, when bin Laden is killed or captured, his and al-Zarqawi's successors will take up the wider banner of confrontation with the West, both in Iraq and closer to our homes.

After more than a decade of broadly *unsuccessful* struggle against Al Qaeda, its protégés and its offshoots, it is imperative that an informed debate begins on whether the West's approach, conducted largely in the shadows, is the right one.

In this account of one aspect of the War on Terror, I've spoken both to those who have waged this war — those closely connected to the CIA and US government — and to the people caught up in its operations, including many former prisoners. Despite describing things from different poles, I've found that most have outlined a similar story. Few on either side doubt, for instance, the scale of torture implemented within many of the jails where America has sent its prisoners. Or indeed the many tactical successes scored by both sides.

Although the tradecraft employed in renditions since 9/11 has often seemed awry, I have levelled few criticisms against those in the CIA who invented these tactics or employed them, even if those tactics might ultimately be judged as illegal or wrong. As we've seen, the CIA took its orders from the White House. The men involved were handcuffed from deploying other options through political and legal restrictions.

Instead, the only conclusions I would seek to offer are *positive* in nature, tentatively answering the question: "If mistakes have been made, *what should then be done instead*?" Having described in this account one aspect of what has happened so far in this war, I have sought the advice both of those who have followed this conflict most closely and those who, through their past experience of covert and overt warfare, seem to me to offer the wisest counsel about how the West should proceed. Many of these individuals, unwilling to lose their security clearances, are not named here. Many of them will agree with one part of what I say and not other parts. But what follows is a distillation of sound advice. The mistakes, of course, are my own.

Who are we fighting?

Consider first the nature of the enemy, those who believe it is right to wage a war against the West and justify the tactics of bombing civilians. The focus of the declared "War on Terror" has been the Al Qaeda network headed by Osama bin Laden that mounted the attacks of 9/11. But the United States and its allies have also expanded this battle to include almost all militant Islamist groups that use the weapons of terrorism to achieve their ends: the Palestinian militants of

Hamas, the Hezb'allah party of Lebanon, the Chechen rebels who confront the Russian army, and a long list of other groups across the world.

One common misconception, gleaned from those who speak of a "clash of civilizations," is to imagine that these groups share broadly the same aims and policies.[7] Both Tony Blair and George W. Bush often refer to terrorists who "hate our way of life."[8] In that they are referring to statements of both the Taliban and bin Laden when they describe their objective of recreating the old idea of the Islamic Caliphate — a holy state governed by the early principles of Islam that were followed by the companions of the Prophet Mohamed. Such ideas, both Western leaders and bin Laden would agree, are incompatible with some of the basic principles of modern Western democracies, for example the toleration of diverse opinions and of different lifestyles. This religious fundamentalism has influenced many of those responsible for attacks on Western targets. The Madrid bombers, for instance, left literature about the Caliphate at their flat in Madrid.

Yet, many Islamist militant groups, while often adopting the language of Islamic revolt, have an agenda that is far more secular and political. The objective of Hamas is primarily to eject Israel from what it regards as occupied territories. The Chechens want an independent Chechen Republic. Many Egyptian militants primarily want the overthrow of the Mubarak dictatorship. While many religious extremists have joined the Iraq insurgency, the majority of those fighting American forces are confronting not the "Western way of life" but are above all fighting the presence of US troops and are against the establishment of a new Shia-dominated state.

Once in Baghdad, I was talking to someone linked to the insurgency who was drinking a can of Coca-Cola, just as he described how much he hated America. "Why are you drinking Coke, then?" I asked. He didn't really have an answer. But the point was that he disliked nothing about the Western lifestyle. He simply wanted the Americans out of Baghdad. So you might, in jest, call this second, more secular, warfare the "Coca-Cola *jihad*".

Alastair Crooke, the former senior MI6 officer, was based in the 1980s on the North-West Frontier between Pakistan and Afghanistan as part of Western efforts to support the Afghan mujahideen. At the time, he came into close contact with some of the Arab fighters who became key figures in Al Qaeda's leadership. He ended his career in 2004 after being seconded from MI6 to be the lead European negotiator with Palestinian militants. He argues that our perception of the terrorism threat is radically wrong: the overall threat from Al Qaeda is over-rated, but the overall threat from Islamist militancy and insurgency is *underestimated*.

Crooke argues that these distinctions mean that what the West is facing is far broader a threat than that posed simply by Al Qaeda. Much of what we face is better called an *insurgency* not a *terrorist* campaign. Terrorism is just one weapon in the armoury. Indeed most of the camps in pre-9/11 Afghanistan were training people not for terrorist operations in the West but for much more conventional warfare against their home regimes.[9]

This desire to overthrow home regimes remains a fundamental part of both bin Laden's and al-Zawahiri's messages. In a response to President Bush's 2005 State of the Union address, l-Zawahiri issued a broadcast in which he explained his version of "freedom". He explained that the Ummah [pan-Is-lamic nation] "must forcibly seize its right to choose the ruler, hold him ac-countable, criticize him and depose him. [The pan-Islamic nation] should resist oppression, tyranny, thievery, forgery, corruption and hereditary rule, a process that our rulers use with America's blessing and support."[10]

To confront every one of these groups as an enemy of the West is to ignore what many of these groups are fighting for and creates the danger of driving these organisations into a common front against us. When looking at pictures of the devastation caused by the Russian Army in Grozny, it is quite hard to determine which side of that conflict would be most in line with Western val-ues. Ultimately, though many of the tactics might be condemned, some of these groups have leaders who, says Crooke rightly, might ultimately be prepared for an accommodation with the West — by embracing democracy and a plural society, for instance.

The nature of Al Qaeda itself has been changing radically. Before 9/11, there was a leadership based in Afghanistan who prepared and approved detailed plans for the series of operations launched against the United States. Bin Laden approved the 1998 Embassy bombings, the attack on the USS *Cole*, and the at-tacks of 9/11. With this leadership structure in place, the CIA's failed attempts to penetrate bin Laden's circle, or its more successful efforts to arrest and render key leaders, made a great deal more sense. Now, with much of the former top echelon of Al Qaeda either killed or in custody, these tactics seem respectively less of a priority and much less efficient.

With many of its leaders removed, the power of Al Qaeda has become far more a matter of influence and propaganda and far less a question of operational involvement. Some US intelligence analysts have reached this conclusion after studying why, since 9/11, there had by mid-2006 been no significant attack by Al Qaeda on American soil; in fact, latest assessments appear to indicate, as one senior serving US counter-terrorism official told me: "There really was no sec-ond wave planned. September 11 really was their biggest move."[11]

Abroad, there have been a series of terrorist atrocities — most notably the Bali bomb and the Madrid train bombs. But investigation into each of these attacks has shown that while certainly *inspired* by Osama bin Laden, they were not in any sense *organised* by him.

The ricin plot in Britain was portrayed (most notably by Colin Powell in his Iraq war speech to the United Nations) as an attempt by Al Qaeda to deploy chemical weapons in Britain. But what emerged from the trial of those responsible was a self-starting and bungling group of 'clean skins' with only the thinnest connection with the main Al Qaeda leadership.[12]

Likewise, initial investigation of the July 2005 bombings in London showed few if any links between the Al Qaeda leadership and the terrorists. The ringleaders of the cell based in Leeds who blew themselves up on 7 July 2005 had indeed travelled to Pakistan and attended a training camp where they learned how to manufacture explosives. But they had not *needed* instructions or approval from bin Laden either to devise or to implement their mission.

"What we are seeing is that the biggest threat from Al Qaeda is from the *inspiration* they provide, rather than from the activities of the network itself," the US counter-terrorism source continued.

Alastair Crooke likens it to Howard Dean's 2004 presidential campaign.

Howard Dean was a governor from a minor state who had no mechanism, had no structure, had very few finances, so he got together a small core of bright internet people called Echo Ditto and they put up websites, and they started trying to mobilise people through the internet. The people at the other end of the internet, the members of the campaign for Howard Dean, started raising money, collecting money from people locally, sending it back to the headquarters; they started sending political intelligence back about what to do. But at the end of this, would you say that the people who were organising street parties for Howard Dean were under his command, were obeying his orders? Clearly that's fatuous. They were not. These were people who broadly thought that Howard Dean was important, that he was saying things that they supported and he was in the right direction. And they felt that he was an idealist that they wanted to support. They couldn't be said to be his army or that they were obeying orders or that they were part of an organisational structure. And I think Al Qaeda was much closer to the campaign model of Howard Dean than it was to the westernised, Cold War type of model, with hierarchies, and battalions of people out to destroy the West.[13]

If inspiration is the key to how the terrorist network now functions, then an attempt to destroy terrorism by killing or capturing key leaders (and rendering those survivors off to forgotten jails) may head off some particular attacks but it is doomed to be strategically unsuccessful. New leaders and new cells will simply emerge. While torture may persuade one of these leaders to talk and talk, the likelihood is they have no idea what is being planned, even in their name, around the world. They have no idea where the ticking bomb lies.

The lesson from this analysis is not defeatist. It does not suggest the War on Terror is un-winnable, even if labelling it a "war" may in itself be counter-productive. Rather, it implies that the key battleground is the realm of ideas; that the effort to win the hearts and minds of the Arab world, and counter Muslim militant thinking, may outweigh the illusory short-term advantages of resorting to the tactics of repression. Just as Soviet communism foundered when even its own leaders realised that its basic principles were bankrupt, so the most violent ideas of the Islamist jihad must also be shown to be ineffective and unrewarding. Winning this war of ideas is not just about propaganda. It also means getting the policies right. Western policies and ideas must be those that inspire people in the Middle East; they must be far more potent than anything Osama bin Laden could ever tell Al Jazeera from his cave.

The damage caused by failed western policies has been underlined by Sir Richard Dearlove, the former head of MI6 from 1999 to 2004 and a man who played a pivotal role in the Anglo-American alliance after 9/11. In some rare public comments, he declared that Western strategy against extremism was doomed unless it reclaimed "the moral high ground." Speaking to James Fallows of the *Atlantic* magazine and others during a July 2006 seminar in Colorado, he suggested that during the Cold War the supremacy of western ideas was much clearer-cut. And this made the primary task of a spymaster — the recruitment of agents — that much easier then. People would volunteer to assist agencies like MI6 because they believed in the cause. Now, however, the West was "building a wall of rejection" through morally compromising policies. Some of these US responses to 9/11, he said, would have been "illegal in Great Britain as a matter of common law." By that, recounted Fallows, Dearlove was "thinking, especially, of 'renditions' — sending prisoners to other countries in the full knowledge that they would be tortured — and the entire Guantánamo operation." Dearlove was rightly not downplaying the threat of conflict with Islamic extremists; he was addressing how it should be understood.

Western thinking as it encounters terrorists and insurgents seems sometimes to have progressed little since General Paul Harkins, one of the US commanders in Vietnam and a former aide to the wartime military genius, General George Patton, spoke of "the common man of the Orient," who was ever respectful of the strong. Ruled by dictators, and populated by under-employed, restless and humiliated peoples, the solution to Middle East terrorism requires a far-sighted strategy that requires not only military but moral leadership.[14]

At the heart of the Western message must be the promotion of what the West does best — democracy and a pluralistic society.

Defending democracy

Much of the Middle East contains a rich pool of recruits for Islamic militancy and one of the key reasons for this is the absence of democracy. With political opposition banned, only religion stands in the way of the state. So the mosques become the natural channel for any form of protest.

The history of the Arab world since the Second World War is one of stalled development and failed states. There is not one functioning democracy— and none that has exploited its natural wealth to create a modern functioning economy and civil society. Instead, each regime has one form or another of dictatorship. Saudi Arabia, Jordan, Kuwait and Morocco all have hereditary monarchies with no or limited elections. Algeria, Egypt, Syria, Tunisia and Yemen are all officially republics, though in reality they are either authoritarian, military-backed regimes or one-party states.[15]

Yet democracy and respect for civil rights still provide the only real hope of future development. Dictatorship engenders a pervasive corruption, an access to wealth and property based on connections to the elite in power. Those outside the elite are denied opportunities for employment and self-betterment. Despite the strong support for Islamic militant groups, many youngsters in the Arab world look to the West and admire its freedom, even if they don't wish to replicate the exact same model. A survey by the Pew Global Attitudes Project showed that in 2005, 80 per cent of Jordanians believed that democracy could work in their country, as did 83 per cent of Moroccans.[16]

In his 2005 State of the Union address, President Bush committed the US to a strategic goal of establishing democracy in the Middle East. In doing so, he correctly focussed on the role of Arab dictatorships in fomenting political violence through their repression.

Yet, as we've seen in this account, the tactics of rendition employed in the War on Terror have involved close co-operation with among the worst aspects of the regimes that stand against democracy. When talking of fighting terrorism, the West refers to its partners as "liaison services" or "local intelligence services." But when talking of spreading liberty, we refer rightly to the same partners as the "secret police" that stifle democracy and dissent.

It is a counter-productive strategy.[17] When the State Department in 2002 accused Uzbek police and security services of "routinely" torturing prisoners, including by rape and suffocation,[18] yet in the same year the US provided the regime with an *additional* $180.2 million in aid,[19] it is not difficult to see how these relationships foster the impression that our concern for human rights and democracy is merely shallow rhetoric.[20]

The likes of Michael Scheuer recognise the dilemma. He believes that dictatorial regimes such as Egypt and Syria are part of the reason that Islamic militancy exists. So it makes little sense, strategically, to be working so closely with them. "Any kind of a detainee capture is a technical success, but in the strategic sense we are losing, and one of the main reasons is because of our support for dictatorships in the Muslim world."[21]

In Egypt, the US wants to encourage democracy and yet most of the nearly $2 to $3 billion in annual economic aid[22] from the US comes in the form of military assistance, which goes to support the regime's military structures.[23] In the 1990s, when Ambassador Walker chose to raise the issues of human rights with President Mubarak, "he just basically ignored me", recalled Walker. Egypt knew the US depended on it: depended on its cooperation in the Arab-Israeli peace process, depended on its permission for military overflights and the passage of nuclear warships through the Suez Canal. Increasingly, the US has relied on Egypt too for some of the most secretive aspects of the War on Terror.

But, as Reuel Marc Gerecht points out, "eventually, the contradictions be-tween the practice of prisoner transfer… and the Bush administration's intent to work for the democratic transformation of the Middle East could paralyze the administration's foreign policy."[24]

As America has enlisted these regimes to become "allies" in the War on Ter-ror, its silken words of praise to the "progress" of Arab dictatorships amount to the same kind of appeasement that many on the Left were guilty of in their glo-rification of "progress" in the Soviet bloc. As Craig Murray recalled: "I sat listen-ing to the American ambassador praising to high heaven the progress towards democracy of the Uzbek government, and I realised I couldn't stomach it."[25]

Beyond promoting democracy, there is much more that is required to combat the successful propaganda of Islamist militancy. Much of the Arab world's an-ger against the United States, an anger that recruits young men to violence and is exploited by Arab regimes to divert attention from their own failings, is directed at elementary US foreign policies. Rightly or wrongly, the US is perceived as con-stantly ignoring the plight of the Palestinian people and of showing a consistent bias towards Israel. Many also feel deep anger over the US treatment of Iraq — not just President Bush's 2003 invasion, but the suffering caused by years of UN sanc-tions before. As Scheuer told me: "I really think that if this so-called war on terror-ism is going to continue, it's going to be continued because we don't change our policies." There is no space here to discuss these issues in-depth, but confronting a wider Islamist insurgency against the West requires a radical re-think of many public stances in the Middle East and not just relations with Israel.

Here, for instance, is an example of how intelligence analysts view the effect of these policies. A secret assessment by Britain's Joint Intelligence Committee of the impact of the Iraq invasion, written in April 2005, stated:

We judge that the conflict in Iraq has exacerbated the threat from international terrorism and will continue to have an impact in the long term. It has reinforced the determination of terror-ists who were already committed to attacking the West and motivated others who were not.

The document said the war provided an "additional motivation for attacks" against Britain; was "increasing Al Qaeda's potential"; and "energising" terrorist networks engaged in holy war. Equally worrying, Iraq was being used as a "training ground and base" for terrorists to return to carry out attacks in Britain and elsewhere.[26]

Defending the alliance against terrorism

In the days after 9/11, the world stood behind the United States. When Tony Blair declared that Britain would "stand shoulder to shoulder" with the US, 76 per cent of Britons agreed with him.[27] The French newspaper, Le Monde, declared on its front page "We are all Americans."[28] The French public, traditionally quite critical of America, revealed a 24 per cent increase in sympathy for America following the attacks.[29] Polling in Muslim countries after 9/11 apparently showed that 50 per cent of respondents had a favourable view of the US.[30] Even the Libyan leader Qadhafi called on Muslim aid groups to offer help to America, saying that "it is a human duty to show sympathy with the American people, and be with them at these horrifying and awesome events which are bound to awaken human conscience."[31] The Presidents of Syria and Iran offered their condolences and denounced terrorism.[32] In the weeks that followed, seventeen countries, from Britain to Japan, pledged troops or operational support for the US attacks on Afghanistan in response to 9/11.[33]

Many in the US administration, however, seemed to care little for the offers of support. Right after 9/11, then deputy Defense Secretary Paul Wolfowitz implied that America was capable of going it alone. "If we need collective action we'll ask for it," he said.[34] By March 2004, only 58 per cent of Britons, 38 per cent of Germans and 37 per cent of French had a favourable view of the United States. In the Middle East, the plummeting support was even more obvious, with only 5 per cent of surveyed Jordanians and 27 per cent of Moroccans holding a favourable view of the US.[35]

The policies of rendition and the support for methods of interrogation that in many allied countries would be legally prohibited were an important factor that helped erode support for America around the world. The exchange of intelligence information by Britain with America had led, for example, to the arrest and rendition of some of its own citizens and residents in a manner to which the UK government was completely opposed.[36] In this way, such tactics eroded confidence in the exchange of information.

The nature of global terrorism is that it transcends national boundaries. However large the US fleet and however many satellites are hanging in the skies above the earth, the US simply cannot hope to wage war on terrorism without the consistent support of its allies (just as European countries cannot hope to defeat domestic terrorist threats without the help of the United States). The kidnap of Abu Omar in Milan and his rendition to Egypt, including his transfer through German sovereign territory without obtaining proper legal authority, was an example of the sort of operation that damages this alliance. European governments might have known a lot more than what they have admitted, but the public revelation of these operations, and the reality of condoning torture, has helped to weaken the position of those in Britain and Europe who argue for ever closer relationships with the United States. As two former senior officials at the National Security Council, Steven Simon and Daniel Benjamin, after highlighting the cost of abuses at Guantánamo and Abu Ghraib, wrote: "Through uncritical support of autocratic regimes, we have undermined our own campaign for democratization. America has become unrecognizable to many of its oldest, most devoted friends abroad." They added:

We need to reacquaint ourselves with some of the hard lessons of the Cold War, where we at times undercut our own long-term interests by making common cause with the wrong side simply because it was vocally anti-communist. ... When we make it easy to hate us, we are also hastening the next attack.[37]

Putting the past behind, however, there are simple ways to restore confidence and to strengthen the bonds with allies. Most of all, the Western alliance must commit itself to a common set of values and of tactics against terrorism that reflect those values.

An end to out-sourcing and the extra-legal world

If the US believes that a method of interrogation is necessary and justified then it should be prepared to employ that method itself — under proper controls. Sheltering behind the secrecy of roguish allies like Egypt or Uzbekistan, when exposed, will never be a tactic that commands public support or creates confidence in the Western way of life.

Sir David Omand, a former director of GCHQ, the UK signal intelligence agency and Tony Blair's Security and Intelligence Coordinator from 2002 to 2005, believes that, whatever the rights or wrongs of tactics used in the aftermath of 9/11, the time has come to draw a line in the sand and develop a more sophisticated long-term strategy, one that has a chance of actually succeeding in combatting terrorism.

He told me: "There are tactics that may have appeared justified in the context of the post 9/11 emergency and the clear immediate threat posed both by the Al Qaeda leadership and the network of camps in Afghanistan." Over time, though, the importance of two strategic challenges had become clearer – the need to defeat the "ideological content of the terrorist message" and secondly the need to shape foreign and domestic policy to build "inclusive communities" that respected the law. "Some of the tactics employed so far may no longer therefore be justified when set against these strategic goals," he said.

Rendition, for example, he asserted, was an important and legitimate tactic against terrorism if it meant returning individuals to face justice in countries where they were suspected of serious crimes. "But renditions," he said, "must be carried out within the framework of the rule of law and with oversight. There needs to be a safety net that provides someone threatened with a rendition the opportunity to appeal against that rendition, for example to a court or tribunal, before it happens." Likewise, guarantees of fair treatment provided by countries needed to be credible.

As we've seen earlier, the rendition programme was devised not as a best-case policy but in response to a political weakness that prohibited the US finding its own solutions to dealing with terror networks. But, by handing over the critical gathering of information to a "liaison service" (the secret police of the Middle East), a great deal of the intelligence was rendered useless.

Even among those who believe that torture, or at least harsh interrogation, *can* be effective occasionally, there are those, such as the CIA's Reuel Marc Gerecht, who argue persuasively that it would be better done by the US itself, rather than through proxies. "A cardinal rule of the intelligence business... is to maintain control of the individuals you are debriefing or interrogating," he says. Therefore if the United States were using rendition as an outsourcing of interrogation, "it would amount to the United States willfully diminishing the flow of reliable information."[38]

One former military interrogator in Afghanistan, Chris Mackey, similarly argued to me that repatriation of terrorist suspects to their home countries was one thing, but the line was crossed when the US made use of information subsequently gathered there. "It is a sort of cowards way out. ... I think that if a prisoner is from that country, you could repatriate him and have a clean conscience, but I don't think that you can go and use somebody else as your stooge to collect information." If tough treatment of a prisoner was really required, then America interrogators should go ahead — and then stand properly accountable for what they did.[39]

After 9/11, when President Bush authorised the transfers of prisoners to the CIA's own secret facilities and into the hands of countries like Egypt and Jordan, one of the principle objectives was said to be to keep them out of the hands of domestic agencies like the FBI. "The feeling was they would simply read them their rights," one former CIA officer told me.[40] After 9/11, the US was faced with a logjam of prisoners and made a series of snap judgements. Some of those judgements were wrong and can be corrected. If US law is too tight to allow terrorist suspects to be imprisoned in US territory, then those laws need to be amended.

European countries face exactly the same challenge. One of the reasons the CIA adopted the rendition policy was because none of its allies, even close ones like Britain, could find a proper legal basis for detaining those with a clear association with terrorist networks. A tightening of British law has finally corrected some of these measures. But further measures are needed, such as the admissability of phone tap evidence into court trials. The more effective methods that are introduced to tackle terrorism legally, the less temptation there is to employ covert extra-legal tactics. Human rights activists who criticise US methods like rendition should recognise the importance of finding legal alternatives.

European policy-makers need to respond to the challenges that terrorism poses. Instead of protesting about the existence of CIA detention centres in Europe, they should welcome them, even invite their creation. But they should insist at the same time that those centres should be acknowledged publicly, be subject to outside inspection and exist under the rule of law.

An answer to the torture question

What then of torture itself? Of all the more pragmatic questions these insiders raise, the most critical is whether torture actually works. I've interviewed former military officers who have carried out torture in various forms and on one thing they almost always agree — it can work, but it is rarely useful.

Yes, torture makes people talk. The threat and application of pain causes most people to crack. It worked during the Spanish Inquisition, when used by the British Army in the combatting Colonial insurrections, by the French Army in Algeria and in the Soviet Gulag. Yet the principle output from this torture are confessions, rarely (but not never) good information. There is often just too much suspicion over the quality of torture evidence to give it credibility — and, without credibility, intelligence is useless.

Torture also recruits prisoners to support greater extremism. This account has described an investigation of a secret world of prisons, planes and torture cells, but it is a secret only from the public, from ordinary citizens. For the inmates of these dungeons, their prison experiences will the most formative of their lives. Innocent or guilty when captured, few will emerge without a burning hostility to the United States and the West.

Sayid Qutb, the philosopher-terrorist whose ideas inspired Osama bin Laden and the worldwide *jihad*, wrote his treatise inside Cairo's Torah prison.[41] Ayman al-Zawahiri too declared war on the United States after his own experience of torture in Egypt. Speaking at his trial in 1982, as a sort of appointed leader for the three hundred or so militants arrested in connection with the assassination of President Anwar Sadat, al-Zawahiri decried the torture in practisedEgyptian jails.

There they kicked us, they beat us, they whipped us with electric cables, they shocked us with electricity! They shocked us with electricity! And they used the wild dogs! And they used the wild dogs! And they hung us over the edges of the doors with our hands tied at the back!

He continued:

So where is democracy? Where is freedom? Where is human rights? Where is justice? Where is justice? We will never forget! We will never forget![42]

So when some rogue Americans use similar practices, tying prisoners to walls with their hands behind their backs, or terrorising them with dogs, how are they not to be seen in the same light as those from other oppressive regimes? Simply referring to these methods as "enhanced interrogation techniques", rather than "torture" does not change their impact on the subjects of such abuse, and how they are perceived.

After their release from Guantánamo and from jails across the world, what new *jihad* will the new generation of tortured prisoners inspire?

To my own mind, the *reason* it is wrong to employ torture is not for the pain or anger it causes, nor for its poor intelligence value. It is wrong because it degrades our own societies. It must be concealed with a corroding and hypocritical secrecy, and it undermines the rule of law and our own morality.

This point was best expressed by a veteran CIA officer, Jack Devine, a former acting head of global operations, and a veteran of covert action in both Latin America and Afghanistan. Devine, who retired in 1999 as London station chief, had no knowledge of any kind of torture sanctioned by the CIA in the War on Terror. His words, though, serve as a warning. "Torture is like a cancer," he said. "It eats you up and puts you on the same level as those you might oppose." Psychologically, it could leave those involved as "walking wounded." As he once put it to me: "My worry is what happens to our people.... After the execution, what do you do with the executioner?"[43]

EPILOGUE

SANAA, YEMEN
7 May 2006

By the gates of the Old City, Mohamed Bashmilah was walking, talking, and laughing in the crowd — behaving like a man without a care in the world. Bargaining with the spice traders and chatting to passers-by, at last he was a free man.

A thirty-three-year-old businessman, Bashmilah has an impish sense of humour; his eyes sparkled as he chatted about his country and the *qat* leaves that all young men were chewing. But when I began my interview, and I asked the story of his last three years, his mood shifted. His face narrowed; his eyes calmed; and he stared beyond me — as if looking directly into the dark netherworld from which he had so recently emerged.

For eleven months, Bashmilah was held in one of the CIA's most secret prisons — so secret that he had no idea in which country, or even on which continent, he was being held. He was flown there, in chains and wearing a blindfold, from another jail in Afghanistan; his guards wore masks; and he was held in a ten by thirteen foot cell with two video cameras that watched his every move. He was shackled to the floor with a chain of 110 links. From the times of evening prayer given to him by the guards, the cold winter temperatures, and the number of hours spent flying to this secret jail, he suspected he was held somewhere in eastern Europe — but he could not be sure.

When he arrived at the secret prison, said Bashmilah, he was greeted by an interrogator who told him: "Welcome to your new home." He implied he would never be released. "I had gone there without any reason, without any proof, without any accusation," he said. His mental state collapsed and he went on hunger strike for ten days — till he was force-fed food through his nostrils.

Arrested in Jordan in August 2003, Bashmilah was transferred to Afghanistan and held by the US until May 2005. *Throughout he was never brought before any court or accused of a concrete crime.* Even when returned to Yemen, the government there said the US had demanded he should be detained as a terrorist — even though a promised file of accusations never arrived. He was finally

Mohamed Bashmilah

released in March 2006. His mother told me it was like her son had died. "He came back from a prison as if arising from a tomb; and yet he was changed; he was a different man."[44]

As I've completed this account, more and more prisoners like Bashmilah have come forward to give their accounts of rendition and torture — and more evidence has emerged to corroborate what they say. There is no space to give justice to everyone's story.

Terrorists, of course, are said to be trained to invent stories of torture and mistreatment. A so-called Jihad manual told Al Qaeda brothers to "insist on proving that torture was inflicted on them by State Security." Yet, as we've seen, there has been little need in recent years to concoct such accounts.

Instead, many of those interviewed have been careful not to exaggerate. When he first arrived in Afghanistan, Bashmilah said there was no physical torture — nothing compared to the beatings he had endured when first arrested in Jordan. Like many others, his torture at American hands was psychological.

It was mental torture, and some of the causes were that I was kept in solitary confinement ... and there was music 24 hours a day so you couldn't sleep, read or pray. And secondly, when we tried to relax or sleep, the guards would look in at you and knock on the door so you had to wake up and raise your hands to show you were alive and not dead. This is enough to bring about a very awful mental state.

Like Bashmilah, Khaled el-Masri, who was still campaigning to find out why he was sent to Afghanistan, suffered deep emotional scars. As he recounted his story again and again, he has always resisted embellishment. He has never said he was physically tortured, even as he recounted the worst horrors that some of his fellow prisoners endured and described his own hunger strikes. His emotional scars run deep. I watched from the public gallery as he gave evidence before the German Parliament on 22 June and broke down as Khaled relived the anguish of returning home at last from CIA custody — only to find his wife and children gone and his home ransacked.

Later, after keeping his cool under hostile questioning by German MPs, I met him for dinner. He looked drained. His pony-tailed hair had now turned grey, and the effort of battling and battling for justice was wearing him out, even as more evidence emerged that challenged the German government's claim that it had not been involved in his rendition. Earlier that month, the German intelligence service (BND) revealed that one of its officers had admitted hearing of el-Masri's kidnap while he was on a trip to Macedonia; but the BND said he had never informed his bosses.[45]

As it defends its position on torture, the American government promised justice and compensation to torture victims. Speaking on 5 May in Geneva to the UN Committee Against Torture, John Bellinger, the State Department legal adviser, said Congress had passed laws providing for "severe federal sanctions, both civil and criminal, against those who engage in torture outside the territory of the United States." There was also legislation "that enables citizens and non-citizens of the United States who are victims of torture to bring claims for damages against foreign government officials in US federal courts."[46]

Yet, as prisoners who tried to take their cases to court were to discover, this promise of legal remedy was hollow. Time and again, fellow members of the Bush administration would tell the courts that cases like rendition were not a matter for judicial review — there were too many national secrets at stake.

Just as Maher Arar's lawsuit against the US government for sending him to Syria was dismissed on "state secrets" grounds because "the need for secrecy can hardly be doubted," Khaled el-Masri's lawsuit against the CIA was also dismissed by a federal judge on 18 May because "any admission or denial of these allegations by defendants in this case would reveal the means and methods employed pursuant to this clandestine programme and such a revelation would present a grave risk of injury to national security."

The US torture statute — described by Bellinger in Geneva — was in principle a powerful one. As the anonymous FBI special agent at Guantánamo had written, a plan to render a prisoner to a country where he would face torture, might amount to a criminal conspiracy. "Any person who takes any action in furtherance of implementing such a plan would inculpate all persons who were involved in creating this plan," he said. At the time of writing, however, the US attorney general has shown no inclination and faced almost no political pressure to investigate such potential crimes.

"This whole rendition process has been conducted under the guillotine. You just wait for the blade to fall," Michael Scheuer had told me.[47] No one in Washington, however, wanted to release the blade. But in Europe things were different. The process of shedding light on the rendition system has continued to gather pace. In July 2006, the Milan prosecutors at last discovered what they believed was their missing link in their investigation — a trail pointing to the illegal involvement of Italian military intelligence (SISMI) in the abduction of Abu Omar.

Tracing more cell phones that were at the scene of Abu Omar's February 2003 snatch, Armando Spataro was led to a Carabinieri officer named Luciano Pironi. According to court papers, Pironi confessed to being involved: "I was convinced that I was participating in an intelligence operation," he said. He had been recruited by the CIA station chief Bob Lady, he said, to help stop Abu Omar on the road. But he had also checked with SISMI that the CIA operation had Italian approval. The trail from here led to two senior SISMI officers — the then head of all operations in northern Italy, Marco Mancini, and his then boss in Rome, Gustavo Pignero. Both were arrested in a co-ordinated operation on 5 July. The alleged former head of the CIA in Rome, Jeff Castelli, was also added to those publicly accused of involvement in the kidnapping.[48]

As this book went to press, the accusations against all those charged with involvement in the Milan rendition had still to be tried in a court of law, but the investigators' trail was leading higher and higher. If Pignero and Mancini were involved in the kidnap, as Spataro claimed, then would they really have acted without the approval of their bosses — the head of Italian intelligence, Nicolo Pollari, and the now former Prime Minister, Silvio Berlusconi? Both had vehemently denied any advance knowledge of the operation.

In Washington the ease with which journalists had discovered details of the CIA's air operations and cover identities had angered Congress, and as a new head of the CIA was appointed, Air Force General Michael Hayden, there was evidence of new caution being applied. The movements of CIA jets were proving increasingly hard to follow, and new measures were put in place to protect those involved from unwelcome attention.

As for the Ghost Plane, the Gulfstream involved in so many rendition operations, it took on a new lease of life. In early 2006, it was sold by the CIA and transferred, under a new registration, to a wealthy group of condominium developers. After four years of strange movements around the world, a total of 1,117 recorded landings, it was now to be used for the purpose it was built: the transport of Very Important People in high luxury.[49]

I sat in a bar with a former CIA officer who used to ride in the back of the Agency's executive planes. He was describing a rendition to a country I cannot name. "We had captured a group of terrorists," he said, "all equipped with all the tools necessary to cause a great loss of life. And then I was faced with a dilemma. If I handed them over to the local authorities, I knew from experience they would be released in weeks. So the alternative I chose, with approval, was to render them to another country, to a place from which they would certainly not be released."

Then he turned the tables on me. "What would *you* do in these circumstances? Would you release the terrorists to carry out their crime?"

In all honesty, I understand the man's dilemma — even if his decision may have led to prisoners being ill-treated. What was wrong here was not so much the actions of this officer, who has served his country with great distinction, but the system within which he worked. His own country and its political masters have chosen to find no place where these men could be lawfully tried for their conspiracy and had put in place no realistic safeguards to ensure that, once rendered, the prisoners were protected from torture.

In the years after 9/11, the administration had tried to create a system that was outside the rule of law, and yet such an attempt was utterly at odds with the very founding principles of the United States.

On 29 June 2006, the US Supreme Court declared that, even in war, no president was outside the law. Ruling on charges before a military commission of a prisoner at Guantánamo, Salim Ahmed Hamdan, Osama bin Laden's former driver, the justices voted five to three to declare the entire system illegal — also thereby suspending the forthcoming trial of Binyam Mohamed. They ruled:

Even assuming that Hamdan is a dangerous individual who would cause great harm or death to innocent civilians given the opportunity, the Executive nevertheless must comply with the prevailing rule of law in undertaking to try him and subject him to criminal punishment.

Most importantly — in a far-reaching verdict — the justices ruled that the Geneva Conventions *did* apply to the war against Al Qaeda, thereby rejecting the most crucial legal assumption made by President Bush soon after 9/11. Although Al Qaeda followers might not count as prisoners of war, the justices made clear that Geneva gave a further basic protection in the article (3) common to all four Geneva Conventions that demanded humane treatment for *all* prisoners. It protected them from "cruel treatment or torture" and banned the passing of any sentences without the judgment of a "regularly constituted court affording all the judicial guarantees ... recognised as indispensable by civilized people."[50]

On 6 September President Bush responded to the Supreme Court and declared henceforth all prisoners would be protected by Geneva and all would have their day in court. He finally admitted that the CIA did indeed have secret prisons. The fourteen remaining prisoners in these jails were being transferred on to Guantánamo Bay. But the President repeated his torture mantra: "The United States does not torture. It's against our laws and it's against our values. I have not authorized it and I will not authorize it."

As Martin Lederman, a Georgetown law professor, pointed out, Bush's supposed concessions were a "Jekyll and Hyde routine." Bush effectively proposed to Congress a two-track system. The Pentagon would abide by new, restrictive rules. But the CIA could continue with what Bush called its "alternative set of procedures" – tactics that officials said included water-boarding, sleep deprivation, and bombardment with sounds. Bush also proposed a set of "get out of jail free" cards for the CIA. All its practices since 9/11 were to be declared fully legal and all its operatives were to be indemnified from prosecution. Bush also listed a series of intelligence gleaned as a result of the CIA's aggressive procedures — but provided no evidence that similar high quality evidence could have been gathered by normal means.

Among the biggest untruths from the White House was the claim there were now "no terrorists in the CIA program." It implied CIA jails were empty, and beyond those in Guantánamo the US had no further responsibilities. Yet, as I have outlined, the alleged terrorists arrested since 9/11 numbered in the many thousands. And Guantánamo and the CIA's "black sites" were only ever one small part of a global network of prisons. Rendition had outsourced interrogation and detention by sending hundreds of people to an uncertain fate at the hands of foreign jails and in the certain knowledge of their torture. Bush still offered no apology, nor compensation for the innocents caught up in the system.

Sixty years ago, the Allied powers constituted the Nuremberg Tribunals to pass judgement on the most heinous of Nazi crimes. And they did so despite granting rights to prisoners, like the right to hear the evidence against them, that went far beyond those offered to today's terrorist suspects. The crimes of Al Qaeda were great — but they were nothing compared to those of Hitler and his murder squads.

The risks of ensnaring the innocent in a system of rendition that is managed without legal supervision or court trials was always apparent in the case of the Canadian, Maher Arar. Soon after Bush's announcement, the final report of the Canadian public inquiry into Arar's account of his rendition to Syria was published. Justice Dennis O'Connor declared, despite weeks of *incamera* hearings, that he had heard no evidence against Arar. "I am able to say categorically that there is no evidence to indicate that Arar has committed any offense or that his activities constituted a threat to the security of Canada." O'Connor's report confirmed suspicions that Canadian officials had placed Arar on a watchlist and sent inaccurate information to the United States, wrongly indicating that he was a suspected terrorist and linked to Al Qaeda. But, the inquiry affirmed, the decision to send Arar to Syria and to share information on Arar with the Syrians, information that was put to him during torture, was entirely that of the United States.

As I write, politicians in Washington are still considering Bush's proposals, none of which offer any means of redress for those detained and tortured since 9/11 and later found innocent, or make any attempt to restrict CIA renditions or the "disappearance" of other key suspects around the world. Many in Congress share Bush's desire for a political fix to "work around" both the Supreme Court and the Geneva Conventions. They are seeking ways to keep Guantánamo open and to maintain unfettered powers to interrogate, transport and imprison alleged terrorists. Many are seeking to strip the rights of prisoners to make any challenge against their detention in US courts — arguing that the threat of indefinite detention is a useful interrogation tool. But these politicians are missing the point. America's programme of extraordinary rendition and its harsh treatment of prisoners have not, when considered strategically, been successful weapons against terrorism. Osama bin Laden must cheer every time a new repressive measure is approved by Congress or the President. Ignoring human rights helps to recruit terrorists, to justify terrorism and defeats the best thing we have going for us — the fact we stand for something better: for freedom, tolerance and laws that protect all.

Stephen Grey   *London, September 2006*

APPENDIX
CHRONOLOGY OF RENDITIONS
BEFORE AND AFTER 9/11

A selected list of renditions to the United States and of "extraordinary renditions": the transfer involving US agents to foreign or military jurisdictions outside the effective control of American civilian courts of law. Twenty rendition flights have been matched so far with CIA flightlogs.

DATE	NAME	RENDITION

1987

17 SEPTEMBER — **Fawaz Yunis** — **Cyprus to USA**

Accused of a 1985 Royal Jordanian Airlines hijacking.[1]

1993

15 JULY — **Omar Mohammed Ali Rezaq** — **Nigeria to USA**

Accused of a 1985 EgyptAir hijacking.[2]

1995

12 APRIL — **Abdul Hakim Murad** — **Philippines to USA**

Accused of plotting to hijack US airlines.[3]

22 SEPTEMBER — **Abu Talal al-Qasimi** — **Croatia to Egypt**

Also known as Talat Fouad Qassem, an Egyptian accused of involvement in the assassination of Egyptian president Anwar Sadat.[4]

12 DECEMBER — **Wali Khan Amin Shah** — **Malaysia to USA**

Accused of plotting to hijack a US airline.[5]

1996

21 SEPTEMBER — **Tsutomu Shirosaki** — **Nepal to USA**

Accused of a 1986 attack on the US Embassy in Jakarta, Indonesia.[6]

1997
JUNE   **Mir Aimal Kansi**   **Pakistan to USA**
Accused of a 1983 shooting at CIA headquarters.[7]

1998
3 JUNE   **Mohammed Rashid**   **Egypt to USA**
Accused of an August 1982 bombing of a Pan Am flight.[8]

JULY   **Ahmed al-Naggar**   **Albania to Egypt**
                              Mohamed Hassan Tita
                              Shawki Salama Attiya

AUGUST   **Ahmed Ismail Osman Saleh**   **Albania to Egypt**
                              Essam Abdel Tawwab
                              Abdel Halim   **Bulgaria to Egypt**
All Egyptians suspected of plotting to attack US targets; four were arrested in
Tirana and a fifth in Sofia. They were shipped by the CIA to Egypt.[9]

20 AUGUST   **Mohamed Sadeek Odeh**   **Kenya to USA**

26 AUGUST   **Mohamed Rashed**
                              Daoud al-'Owhali   **Kenya to USA**
Both Odeh and al-'Owhali were accused of the August 1998 bombing of the US
Embassy in Nairobi.[10]

AUTUMN   **Ihab Mohammed Saqr**   **Azerbaijan to Egypt**
                              Ahmed Salama Mabrouk
                              Essam Mohammed Hafez Marzouq
The three had travelled to take part in the conflict in Nagorno-Karabakh in Ar-
menia; they were put on trial in the same "returnees from Albania" case as those
returned to Cairo in July and August 1998 described above.[11]

1999
MARCH/APRIL   **Mohammed al-Zawahiri**   **United Arab**
                                                             Emirates to Egypt
Brother of Ayman al-Zawahiri and suspected leader of the Egyptian Islamic Ji-
had's military arm. He has been in prison since his rendition to Egypt.[12]

| 7 OCTOBER | **Khalfan Khamis Mohammed** | **South Africa to USA** |

A Tanzanian accused of involvement in the August 1998 bombing of the US Embassy in Dar es Salaam, Tanzania.[13]

| 10 OCTOBER | **Hani al-Sayegh** | **USA to Saudi Arabia** |

A Saudi Arabian national and suspect in the 1996 attack on Khobar Towers. He was deported to the US from Canada and then on to Saudi Arabia after losing a court battle to prevent his transfer.[14]

| NOVEMBER/DECEMBER | **Hussein al-Zawahiri** | **Malaysia to Egypt** |

Brother of Ayman al-Zawahiri and an engineer, arrested in Malaysia and flown by private jet to Cairo. Released in 2000.[15]

2001

| | **Rifa Ahmed Taha** | **Syria to Egypt** |

Leader of Egypt's Gama'a al-Islamiyya who rejected the 1997 ceasefire and signed Osama bin Laden's 1998 fatwah; tracked to Damascus by US, Italians, and Egyptians; arrested in late spring, final date of transfer to Egypt put variously as just after and just before 9/11. Also known as "Abu Yasser".[16]

SEPTEMBER 11, 2001

| 28 SEPTEMBER | **Zayd Hassan Abd al-Latif Masud al-Safarini** | **Pakistan to USA** |

Accused of the hijacking of Pan Am flight 73 in Karachi, Pakistan in 1986.[17]

| END SEPTEMBER | **Jamal Mohamed Alawi Mar'i** | **Pakistan to Jordan** |

A Yemeni, he was arrested on 23 Sept. in Karachi and handed over to US officers who flew him to Jordan. Accused of working for Al-Wafa Islamic charity in Kandahar. Held for four months in Jordan, before being transferred to Guantánamo.[18]

| 23 OCTOBER | **Jamil Qasim Saeed Mohammed** | **Pakistan to Jordan** |

Flightlog N379P. A Yemeni microbiology student, Mohammed was wanted in connection with the attack against USS *Cole*; flown by US to Jordan from Karachi.[19]

| 29 OCTOBER | **Mamdouh Habib** | **Pakistan to Egypt** |

An Australian, he was captured in Pakistan, sent to Afghanistan, sent to Egypt for six months; then transferred back to Afghanistan.[20] See also April 9, 2002.

28 NOVEMBER	**Mohamedou Ould Slahi**	**Mauritania to Jordan**

Arrested in his home country, Mauritania, Slahi was flown into US custody in Jordan. He was accused in the 9/11 Commission Report of being a link between bin Laden and the Hamburg cell that carried out the 9/11 attacks.[21] See also July 19, 2002.

NOVEMBER/DECEMBER	**Multiple prisoners**	**Pakistan to Afghanistan**

Transfer of large number of prisoners from Kohat jail, Pakistan, by bus to US detention in Kandahar, Afghanistan.

10 DECEMBER	**Abdullah Eidah al-Matrafi**	**Pakistan or UAE to Afghanistan**

A Saudi director of the Al-Wafa charity, Kabul, al-Matrafi was last seen boarding a plane from Lahore to Dubai. He was later transferred to Guantánamo.[22]

18 DECEMBER	**Mohammed al-Zery Ahmed Agiza**	**Sweden to Egypt**

Flightlog N379P. Two Egyptian asylum-seekers. Extradited from Sweden back to Egypt. They later alleged they were tortured on arrival.[23]

27 DECEMBER	**Mohammed Haydar Zammar**	**Morocco to Syria**

A German of Syrian origin and allegedly a member of the Hamburg cell. Arrested in Morocco around December 8; questioned by US officers then flown to Syria and held at the Palestine Branch.[24]

2002

JANUARY	**Walid al-Qadasi**	**Iran to Afghanistan**

Yemeni. He was arrested in late 2001 and held for four months in Iran. He was transferred across the border and held in the CIA's Dark Prison in Kabul, before later being transferred to Guantánamo. In 2004 he was sent to Yemen. Released in Feb. 2006.[25]

JANUARY	**Shaker Aamer**	**Pakistan to Afghanistan**

A former British resident and Saudi citizen, also known as Shakir Abdurahim Mohamed Ami, he was captured in Pakistan in January 2002 and claims he was sold to US forces. He claims he was held in the Dark Prison in Kabul.[26]

| 3 JANUARY | **Mullah Abdul Salam Zaeef** | **Pakistan to Afghanistan to USS *Bataan*** |

Taliban's former ambassador; handed over to US agents by Pakistan; he was questioned aboard the USS *Bataan* in the Arabian Sea before being flown to Guantánamo. Released in September 2005.[27]

| 4 JANUARY | **Ibn al-Sheikh al-Libi** | **Pakistan to Afghanistan Afghanistan to Egypt Egypt to Afghanistan** |

Libyan. Considered a senior Al Qaeda figure and military camp trainer, arrested by Pakistani authorities as he crossed over the border from Afghanistan. He was sent to Egypt for questioning, returned to Afghanistan, and then sent to a secret CIA location.[28]

| 11 JANUARY | **First detainees arrive at Guantánamo Bay** | **Afghanistan to Cuba** |

In total more than 750 prisoners will be rendered to Cuba by the US military – all without formal legal procedures and all without status as prisoners of war. The majority were first arrested outside the Afghan combat zone.[29]

| | **Muhammad Saad Iqbal Madni** | **Indonesia to Egypt** |

Flightlog N379P. Egyptian-Pakistani, arrested in Jakarta, Indonesia, after arriving from Pakistan, mid November 2001. Then hustled aboard a US-registered Gulfstream jet and flown to Egypt. See also April 16, 2002. Later sent to Guantánamo.[30]

| 19 JANUARY | **Boumediene Lakhdar** **Saber Lahmar** **Mustafa Ait Idir** **Boudella Haj** **Bensayah Belkacem** **Mohammed Nechle** | **Bosnia to Cuba** |

Six Algerians flown to Guantánamo from Bosnia despite an order for their release from the Bosnian supreme court. As of May 2006, they were all still at Guantánamo.[31]

FEBRUARY   **Abduh Ali Shaqawi**   **Pakistan to Jordan**

A Yemeni; possibly the suspect identified in press reports at the time of his arrest in Karachi in February 2002 as Abdul Rahim al-Shaqawi or "Riyadh the facilitator," an alleged terrorist financier. [32] See also January 7, 2004.

Moazzam Begg   **Pakistan to Afghanistan**

British national. Arrested in Islamabad, Pakistan and driven off in the trunk of a car. Held by the US in Bagram until February 2003, when he was sent to Guantánamo. [33] Released January 2005.

Richard Belmar   **Pakistan to Afghanistan**

British national. Arrested in Karachi, Pakistan, then sent to Guantánamo. [34] Released January 2005.

MARCH   **Jabarah Mohamed Mansour**   **Oman to USA**

A Kuwait-born Canadian citizen, he is alleged to have been involved in an attempt to bomb the US and Israeli embassies in Singapore. He was arrested in Oman, and handed over to US agents. According to US officials he consented to his transfer to the US and has provided detailed statements to the FBI. [35]

1 MARCH   **Wesam Abdul Rahman**   **Iran to Afghanistan**

A Jordanian, he was arrested in Iran, transferred to Afghanistan, and says he was held in a CIA facility in Kabul for 14 months, transferred to the Bagram airbase, and then onwards to Guantánamo. [36] Released in March 2004.

19 MARCH   **"Issa"**   **Somalia to Kenya**
                 (aka Suleiman Abdalla Salim Hemed)

A Yemeni, he was arrested by US agents in a hospital in Mogadishu; questioned over links to the 1998 embassy bombings and flown to Kenya. [37]

28 MARCH   **Abu Zubaydah**   **Pakistan to CIA custody**

Flightlog N379P out to Dubai; returned via Anchorage. A Palestinian and alleged senior Al Qaeda leader, he was among twenty Arabs arrested in Pakistani/FBI raids on March 28-29 in Faisalabad, Multan and Lahore. [38]

| **APRIL** | **Omar Deghayes** | **Pakistan to Afghanistan** |

British resident; Libyan national. He was transferred to Guantánamo in Sept. 2004. He has reportedly been interrogated at Guantánamo by Libyan officials (flight logs N379P) and threatened with being sent to Libya.[39]

| **9-16 APRIL** | **Mamdouh Habib** **Muhammad Saad Iqbal Madni** | **Egypt to Afghanistan** |

Both men are later transferred to Guantánamo. Habib was released in Jan. 2005 and returned to Australia.[40]

| **20 APRIL** | **Martin Mubanga** | **Zambia to Guantánamo** |

Flightlog N379P. Dual British-Zambian citizen. Picked up in Zambia, he was questioned by US and UK officials, and flown to Guantánamo.[41] Released January 2005.

| **MAY** | **Barah Abdul Latif** **Bahaa Mustafa Jaghel** | **Pakistan to Syria** |

Syrian students in Pakistan, both were arrested, questioned by US agents and handed over to Syrian officials in Pakistan before being flown back for questioning at the Palestine Branch, Damascus.[42]

| **14 MAY** | **Abdul Halim Dalak** **Omar Ghramesh** **An unnamed teenager** | **Pakistan to Syria** |

Transferred in a US plane, possibly N379P via Jordan; Dalak was a student arrested in November 2001; Ghramesh and the teenager were arrested with Abu Zubaydah.[43]

| **24 MAY** | **Abu al-Kassem Britel** | **Pakistan to Morocco** |

Flightlog N379P. Dual Italian-Moroccan national, he was captured in Pakistan and flown in an executive jet to Rabat, Morocco.[44]

| **6 JUNE** | **Omar al-Faruq** | **Indonesia to Afghanistan** |

Flightlog N379P. Arrested in West Java, and taken by CIA officers to Afghanistan. Escaped from Bagram on July 11, 2005, with three other prisoners.[45]

17 JULY   **Yasser Tinawi**   **Somalia to**
                               Omar bin Hassan   **Ethiopia**

A Syrian and a Palestinian national. Arrested and flown to Ethiopia by US agents, who interrogated Tinawi for one hundred days. Tinawi was later flown to Cairo and on to Syria. (See 26 October and 29 October 2002). Hassan was released after questioning.[46]

19 JULY   **Mohamedou Ould Slahi**   **Jordan to**
                                                                   Afghanistan

Flightlog N379P. Transferred to Guantánamo on 4 August 2002.[47]

21 JULY   **Binyam Mohamed**   **Pakistan to**
                               Unknown   **Morocco**
                               Unknown

Flightlog N379P. Ethiopian accused of Al Qaeda links and alleged accomplice of José Padilla, the so-called "dirty bomber." He remembered two others on board this flight.[48] See also 22 January 2004.

AUGUST   **Muhammed al-Darbi**   **Yemen to CIA**
                                                                   custody

Allegedly an important member of Al Qaeda, he was arrested in Yemen and then questioned in US detention.[49]

SEPTEMBER   **Hassan bin Attash**   **Pakistan to Jordan**

Aged seventeen when he was arrested, bin Attash spent four days in a US-run facility in Afghanistan before being flown to Jordan, where he alleges he was held for 16 months and was beaten and hung upside down. Brother of Waleed bin Attash(q.v.).[50] See also 7 January 2004.

11 SEPTEMBER   **Ramzi Binalshibh**   **Pakistan to**
                                                                   CIA custody

Flightlog N379P to Diego Garcia on 13 September. An alleged planner of the 9/11 attacks, he was arrested in Pakistan and transferred for interrogation by the CIA.[51]

LATE SEPTEMBER   **Abdulsalam al-Hela**   **Egypt to**
                                                                   Azerbaijan

Flightlog N379P from Egypt to Azerbaijan. A Yemeni businessman and alleged intelligence operative, he was arrested in Cairo on a business trip. His family was told he was sent to Azerbaijan, though other reports suggest he may have been transferred direct to Afghanistan. See also June 2003 and 20 September 2004.[52]

8 OCTOBER   **Maher Arar**   **USA to Syria**

Flightlog N828MG. A Canadian citizen, arrested after changing planes at JFK, New York, and then sent to Syria where he was held for a year. [53] Released and returned to Canada in October 2003.

26 OCTOBER   **Yasser Tinawi**   **Ethiopia to Egypt**
29 OCTOBER   **Yasser Tinawi**   **Egypt to Syria**

Held in Sednaya prison for two years and four months. He was released in February 2005. [54]

8 NOVEMBER   **Abd al-Rahim al-Nashiri**   **UAE to**
                                                        CIA custody

Possibly taken first to Jordan, he was captured after travelling from Yemen to Dubai. Alleged Al Qaeda commander in the Gulf region. [55]

8 DECEMBER   **Bisher al-Rawi**   **Gambia to**
                           Jamil al Banna   **Afghanistan**

Flightlog N379P. Two British residents of Iraqi and Jordanian nationality, they were arrested on 8 November in Gambia. Later transferred to Guantánamo. [56]

2003

                           Abdullah al-Sadek   **Thailand to Libya**
                           (aka al-Amir)

Libyan national. Picked up by Thai Police, who handed him over to US agents.

                           Abu Monzer al-Saidi   **Hong Kong**
                                                        to Libya

Libyan national. Detained in Hong Kong and handed over to US agents. They interrogated him, and then handed him over to Libyan authorities, who rendered him back to Libya. [57]

17 FEBRUARY   **Abu Omar**   **Italy to Germany**
                                                        to Egypt

Flightlogs of N85VM and US airforce "Spar-92." An Egyptian refugee, he was captured in Milan, driven to Aviano airforce base, flown to Ramstein, Germany, and then onwards to Cairo. [58]

1 MARCH   **Khalid Sheikh Mohammed**   **Pakistan to**
                                                        CIA custody

The self-confessed architect of the 9/11 attacks, he was arrested in Rawalpindi, Pakistan. Handed over to US interrogators and transferred to a secret CIA facility.[59]

	Mustafa al-Hawsawi	**Pakistan to CIA custody**

An alleged Al Qaeda financier, arrested at the same time as Khalid Sheikh Mohammed in Pakistan.[60]

15 MARCH	**Yassir al-Jaziri**	**Pakistan to CIA custody**

A Moroccan-Algerian national, al-Jaziri was alleged to be an Al Qaeda financier. He was arrested in Karachi and transferred to an unknown location.[61]

MAY	**Laid Saidi**	**Malawi to Afghanistan**

Algerian national. He was expelled from Tanzania to Malawi for being a local director of Al-Haramain, a Saudi charity. Held in Malawi for a week, he was handed over to US agents and flown to the Dark Prison. He was held there for sixteen months, then flown to Algeria where he was released in August 2004 wihout charge.[62]

1 MAY	**Waleed Mohammed bin Attash**	**Pakistan to CIA custody**

A suspect in the USS *Cole* attack, Attash (also known as Tawfiq bin Attash) was arrested on 29 April in Karachi, and held until at least 1 May in Pakistan, before being transferred into CIA custody. Fellow prisoners testified to his presence at a CIA facility in Afghanistan and also another secret facility, possibly in Europe.[63]

	Ali Abdul Aziz Ali (aka Ammar al-Baluchi) Majid Khan	**Pakistan to CIA custody**

Accused in 9/11 Commission report of assisting the 9/11 pilot, Hani Hanjour, Ali is a suspected Al Qaeda financier. He was captured on 29 April 2003, in Pakistan along with Waleed bin Attash, see above, and handed into US custody. Also captured at the time and taken into US custody was Majid Khan, an alleged associate.[64]

24 JUNE	**Mahmoud Sardar Issa (Sudanese) Fahad al-Bahli (Saudi)**	**Malawi to Zimbabwe**

Arif Ulusam (Turkish)	Zimbabwe to
Ibrahim Itabaci (Turkish)	Sudan
Khalifa Abdi Hassan (Saudi)	

Members of an Islamic charity, rendered despite court order for their release. All finally released on 25 July 2003 in Sudan.[65]

| JULY | Abu Naseem | Pakistan to Unknown |

Tunisian national arrested in Peshawar in June 2003. Suspected of providing forged documents to Al Qaeda. No information on where he was transferred.[66]

| 13 JULY | Adil al-Jazeeri | Pakistan to Afghanistan |

Algerian national and alleged Al Qaeda operative, arrested 17 June 2003 in Peshawar, and transferred to Bagram airbase by US agents.[67]

| 22 JULY | Saifulla Paracha | Thailand to Afghanistan |

Flightlog N379P to Tashkent, disappearing east and then returning from Kabul. Pakistani businessman arrested in Bangkok after he was lured to a meeting in a US operation. Transferred to Bagram, Afghanistan and then to Guantánamo, 20 September 2004. His son, Uzair, was found guilty in a New York federal court in November 2005 of conspiring to help Majid Khan (see March/April 2003) to enter the US with false documents.[68]

11 AUGUST	Hambali (Riduan Isamuddin)	Thailand to
	Mohamad Nazir bin Lep	CIA custody
	Mohamad Farik Amin	

Hambali, an Indonesian arrested in Ayutthaya, central Thailand, was the leader of Jemaah Islamiah (JI), a south-east Asian militant group. Bin Lep (also known as bin Lap) and Amin, both Malaysians, were suspected of being his aides.[69]

| 26 OCTOBER | Salah Nasser Salim 'Ali | Jordan to |
| | Muhammad Bashmilah | Afghanistan |

Flightlog N379P. Yemeni nationals both arrested in Jordan and transferred to US custody.[70] See also 24 April 2004 and 5 May 2005.

| 27 DECEMBER | Mohamed al-Assad | Tanzania to Djibouti |

Yemeni national, was arrested on 26 December and flown out before dawn the next day in a US plane.[71] See also 3 March 2004, 24 April 2004 and 5 May 2005.

2004

JANUARY   **Hassan Ghul**   **Iraq to**
                                                                        CIA custody

An alleged associate of Khalid Sheikh Mohammed, his arrest in Iraq was announced on 26 January 2004 by President Bush.[72]

7 JANUARY   **Abduh Ali Shaqawi**   **Jordan to**
                                Hassan bin Attash   **Afghanistan**
                                                                        (possibly on the
                                                                        same flight)

Flightlog N313P. Both were transferred to Guantánamo on 20 September 2004.[73]

22 JANUARY   **Binyam Mohamed**   **Morocco to**
                                                                        Afghanistan

Flightlog N313P. Ethiopian national, British resident.[74] He was transferred to Guantánamo on 20 September 2004.

23 JANUARY   **Khaled el-Masri**   **Macedonia to**
                                                                        Afghanistan

Flightlog N313P. German used car salesman. Held for three weeks by Macedonian authorities, before his transfer to US custody in Afghanistan.[75] Released in Albania, 28 May 2004.

3 MARCH   **Mohamed al-Assad**   **Djibouti to**
                                                                        Afghanistan

Flightlog N379P. After questioning by agents describing themselves as from the FBI, al-Assad was placed on a plane to Kabul.[76]

24 APRIL   **Mohamed al-Assad**   **Afghanistan to**
                                Muhammad Bashmilah   **CIA custody**
                                Salah Nasser Salim 'Ali

All three prisoners describe transfer around the same date from Bagram air base in Afghanistan to a secret detention facility, possibly in Europe.[77] See also 5 May 2005.

15 JUNE   **Musaad Aruchi**   **Pakistan to**
                                (aka Musab al-Baluchi,   **CIA custody**
                                al-Balochi, al-Baloshi)

Described as a nephew of Khalid Sheikh Mohammed, Aruchi was said by Pakistan officials to have been arrested in Karachi, questioned for three days, and then flown into secret US custody.[78]

AUGUST	Ahmed Khalfan Ghailani	Pakistan to CIA custody

Tanzanian. Arrested on 25 July 2004. Indicted in the US for his involvement in the 1998 embassy bombings in Kenya and Tanzania. Pakistani officials said he was handed over to the CIA in early August.[79]

20 SEPTEMBER	Adel Hamlily Ahmad Ghulam Rabbani Abdul al-Rahim Ghulam Rabbani Hassan bin Attash Mohammed (unknown full name) Sanad Khasim Unknown Unknown Abduh Ali Shaqawi Abdulsalam al-Hela Unknown Unknown Binyam Mohamed Saifulla Paracha	Afghanistan to Guantánamo

A special flight took fourteen prisoners from Afghanistan. According to those among them identified and interviewed by lawyers at Guantánamo, all had previously been transported to Afghanistan in the CIA rendition programme.[80]

2005

2 MAY	Abu Faraj al-Libi	Pakistan to CIA custody

Libyan national. Arrested in Mardan, thirty miles north of Peshawar, and described by Pakistan officials as the "number three" in Al Qaeda, though others doubted this description.[81]

5 MAY	Mohamed al-Assad Muhammad Bashmilah Salah Nasser Salim 'Ali	CIA custody to Yemen

Transferred to Yemen and held "awaiting charges" to be sent by the US; the accusations were never forthcoming, and the men were released in March 2006.[82]

2006

3 SEPTEMBER   **Khalid Sheikh Mohammed**   **CIA custody to**
                     Abu Zubaydah   **Guantánamo**
                     Ramzi Binalshibh
                     Hambali
                     Mustafa al-Hawsawi
                     Abu Faraj al-Libi
                     Mohamad Nazir bin Lep
                     Ali Abdul Aziz Ali
                     Waleed Mohammed bin Attash
                     Majid Khan
                     Abd al-Rahim al-Nashiri
                     Ahmed Khalfan Ghailani
                     Gouled Hassan Dourad
                     Mohammed Farik Amin

Transferred by order of President Bush, who announced the CIA's secret jails were now empty.

NOTES

Research for this account came from interviews conducted in the United States, Great Britain, Canada, France, Italy, Germany, Sweden, Yemen, Egypt, Syria, Iraq, and Saudi Arabia. All interviews, unless otherwise indicated, were by the author. Interviews marked "JG" were conducted on my behalf by John Goetz, who assisted with research in Germany. No CIA official has been named unless previously identified publicly.

PROLOGUE

1   Description from a visit to Damascus, including the Sheraton Hotel and Palestine Branch, 28 May –1 June 2006.
2   Interviews with Maher Arar in Ottawa on 10 December 2003, Abdullah Almalki in London on 21 November 2005, and Nizar Nayouf in Paris on 9 June 2006, all former residents of the Palestine Branch.
3   Interview with Maher Arar, 10 December 2003.
4   Interview with Abdullah Almalki by phone on 20 April 2006.
5   As described in Chapter 3, Syria brought no charges against him. In Canada, Arar has never been accused of any crime. Nor was he charged with any by the United States. "His Year in Hell," *Sixty Minutes II*, CBS broadcast 21 January 2004. Imad Moustapha, Syria's highest-ranking diplomat in Washington, told CBS, "We could not substantiate any of the allegations against him."
6   "By 1984, one branch of the *mukhabarrat* had acquired a machine known as the 'German chair,' which slowly broke the vertebrae of the victim strapped into it. It had allegedly been manufactured in East Germany, although there was later a less refined instrument which was locally produced and thus called the 'Syrian chair.' This broke backbones more quickly." See Robert Fisk's *Pity the Nation* (Oxford University Press, 1990), p. 179.
7   Arar was held at the Palestine Branch from 9 October 2002 to 19 August 2003. His account of torture was examined by Professor Stephen J. Toope, in an official fact-finding report for Canada's Commission of Inquiry into the Actions of Canadian Officials in relation to Maher Arar. In July 2005, Toope was instructed to "investigate and report on Mr Arar's treatment during his detention in Jordan and Syria" (p. 3). Toope's report, delivered 14 October 2005, concluded that "Mr. Arar was subjected to torture in Syria. The effects of that experience, and of consequent events and experiences in Canada, have been profoundly negative for Mr. Arar and his family" (p. 25).
8   Interviews with Abdullah Almalki on 20 April 2006, Maher Arar on 10 December 2003; and chronology prepared by Almalki.
9   A former prisoner, Driss bin Lakoul, first recounted Zammar's treatment in "Al Qaeda Recruiter Reportedly Tortured", Peter Finn, *Washington Post*, 31 January 2003. I obtained more details in interviews with Abdullah Almalki, in London on 20 April 2006, and with

Maher Arar on 10 December 2003, both of whom were held nearby Zammar in the Palestine Branch.

10 Detailed in a report to the German parliament, "Federal Government Report Responding to the 25 January 2006, Request of the Parliamentary Oversight Committee on Events Connected to the Iraq War and the Fight Against International Terrorism," including annexes and additions classified as secret, issued on 15 February 2006; hereafter, called "Classified report to German Parliament." According to the report, the CIA told German foreign intelligence, the Bundesnachrichtendienst (BND), in July 2002 that "Zammar, following a US request, was arrested in Morocco and deported to Syria." In return for its cooperation, the report said, the CIA urged Germany to "avert pressure [on Morocco] from the EU side because of human rights abuses in connection with the arrest because Morocco was a valuable partner in the fight against terrorism." The CIA also "offered to ask written questions provided by the BND to be used in the interrogations of Zammar and that the respective results would be provided to the German side." Syria also offered to provide access to Zammar, but only in return for the lifting of charges against Syrian intelligence agents in Germany accused of threatening Syrian dissidents. These charges were then dropped, and a team from Germany went to Damascus. His interrogation (21 - 23 November 2002) by German agens in Damascus was first reported in an article in *Der Spiegel* ("The Forgotten Prisoner," Holger Stark, 21 November 2005). After posing their last questions, the German delegation went out for a celebratory dinner with Asef Shawqat, then head of Syrian military intelligence, reported Stark.

11 Full names: Abdel Halim Dalak and Omar Ghramesh; the name of the teenager in cell 12 is unknown. Source: interviews with Abdullah Almalki in London, 21 November 2005 and by telephone, 20 April 2006.

12 Flightlogs of N379P indicate the plane's presence in Amman, Jordan, on the date when the prisoners were transferred; prisoners transferred to Syria were generally sent through Amman, according to former inmates of Palestine Branch (interviews 2004-2006).

13 Interview with Abdullah Almalki in London, 21 November 2005. Details of raid described in "How the Perfect Terrorist Plotted the Ultimate Crime," Jason Burke, *The Observer*, 7 April 2002; "Anatomy of a Raid," Tim McGirk, *Time Asia*, 15 April 2002.

14 Full names: Barah Abdul Latif (cell 17) and Bahaa Mustafa Jaghel (cell 7). Sources: interview with Abdullah Almalki, 21 November 2005; interview with Walid Saffour of the Syrian Human Rights Committee, London, 6 April 2006.

15 "State Sponsors of Terrorism," US State Department report (www.state.gov/s/ct/c14151. htm; accessed on 25 May 2006).

16 White House press release, 6 November 2003; Bush was referring to both Iraq and Syria.

17 US Department of State, *"Country Reports on Human Rights Practices: Syria, 2002"* (Published March 2003) (www.state.gov/g/drl/rls/hrrpt/2002/18289.htm).

18 In "Beyond the Axis of Evil: Additional Threats from Weapons of Mass Destruction," a speech by John Bolton, under secretary of state for arms control and international security, to the Heritage Foundation, 6 May 2002, he said: "Beyond the axis of evil, there are other rogue states intent on acquiring weapons of mass destruction. ... I want to discuss three other state sponsors of terrorism that are pursuing or who have the potential to pursue weapons of mass destruction or have the capability to do so in violation of their treaty obligations. ... Syria, which has signed but not ratified the Biological Weapons Convention (BWS), is pursuing the development of biological weapons and is able to produce at least small amounts of biological warfare agents." The three "rogues" he discussed were Libya, Syria and Cuba (www.state.gov/t/us/rm/9962.htm). In May 2006, the United States resumed full diplomatic relations with Libya. See "US Restores Full Diplomatic Ties with Libya," Glenn Kessler, *Washington Post*, 16 May 2006.

19 "Consul Visits Canadian Detained in Native Syria After US Deportation," Stephen Thorne, *Canadian Press*, 23 October 2002 (www.cp.org).

20 Born 11 September 1965. "The Shy Young Doctor at Syria's Helm; Bashar al-Assad," *New York Times*, Susan Sachs, 14 June 2000.

21 Transcript of press conference with Prime Minister Tony Blair and President al-Assad, 16 December 2002. (www.number10.gov.uk/output/Page1744.asp). "Of course we don't have in Syria what are called organisations supporting terrorism. We have press offices," said Bashar. Also see "Britain to Host Arab Summit on Middle East'" Ewen MacAskill, Michael White, and Chris McGreal, *The Guardian Weekly*, 19 December 2002.

22 Summary of press briefing by Alastair Campbell, the prime minister's official spokesman (PMOS), on 16 December 2002: "Asked to comment on reports at the weekend that the CIA was willing to engage in the torture and assassination of Al Qaida members, Campbell said that we never commented on the security policies of other countries. This was a question that should be directed to the American authorities. We had always made clear that the British authorities acted in accordance with British and international law. In answer to repeated questions on the subject, the PMOS declined to elaborate further" (www.pm.gov.uk/output/Page1503.asp).

23 Menu for the Syrian president's banquet provided by the City of London, under a Freedom of Information request, 13 January 2006.

24 Interview with Maher Arar, October 2003.

25 William Burns, Assistant Secretary, Bureau of Near Eastern Affairs, US State Department, told the House Subcommittee on the Middle East and South Asia on 18 June 2002: "It is true that the cooperation the Syrians have provided in their own self-interest on Al Qaeda has saved American lives, and that is a fact, but our agenda goes well beyond that." (commdocs.house.gov/committees/intlrel/hfa80287.000/hfa80287_0f.htm). "The Government of Syria has cooperated significantly with the United States and other foreign governments against Al Qaeda, the Taliban, and other terrorist organizations and individuals." US State Department, "Patterns of Global Terrorism Report 2002, Overview of State-Sponsored Terrorism" (www.state.gov/documents/organization/20117.pdf).

INTRODUCTION — NOT FOR THE SQUEAMISH

1 Philip Agee, *Inside the Company: CIA Diary* (New York: Penguin Books, 1975), p. 456. The description in the first two paragraphs is based on pp. 455-6.

2 Agee resigned from the CIA in 1969 and went to live in the UK, where his book was first published. He was later expelled from the UK and a number of other European countries. He eventually settled in Cuba, where he still lives.

3 In remarks to veterans of the OSS, 23 October 1991, President George H.W. Bush said Agee's publication of the name of Richard Welch, and Welch's position as a CIA station chief, had led to his murder by left-wing terrorists. "I don't care how long I live; I will never forgive Philip Agee and those like him who wantonly sacrifice the lives of intelligence officers who loyally serve their country," he added.

4 NSC 10/2 (18 June 1948) directed the CIA to conduct "covert" rather than merely "psychological" operations, defining them as all activities "which are conducted or sponsored by this Government against hostile foreign states or groups or in support of friendly foreign states or groups but which are so planned and executed that any US Government responsibility for them is not evident to unauthorized persons and that if uncovered the US Government can plausibly disclaim any responsibility for them." US State Department, "Foreign Relations 1964-1968, Volume XXVI, Indonesia; Malaysia-Singapore; Philippines,

Note on US Covert Action Programs"(www.state.gov/r/pa/ho/frus/johnsonlb/xxvi/4440. htm).

5   Horton resigned in 1984 over his refusal to bring a report on Mexico into line with administration policy. He wrote an article: "Why I Quit the CIA," *Washington Post*, 2 January 1985. He also participated in a Discovery Channel documentary in 1997 marking the fiftieth anniversary of the CIA, entitled, *CIA: America's Secret Warriors*.

6   "His Legacy: Realism and Allure," by Jerrold Schecter, *Time*, 24 January 1977.

7   This was Operation Mongoose, described in a CIA Inspector-General's report on "Plots to Assassinate Fidel Castro," p. 77, delivered 22 May 1967, and finally declassified in 1993.

8   Over twenty thousand people were killed, according to the Church Committee Report which calculated that the Phoenix program took at least 20,000 lives in South Vietnam. See "Church Committee Report, Book I, Section II (Foreign and Military Intelligence Operations of the United States: An Overview")," by US Senate Select Committee to Study Governmental Operations with Respect to Intelligence Activities, aka the Church Committee, p. 27 (www.aarclibrary.org/publib/church/reports/book1/html/ChurchB1_0018a.htm).

9   Christopher Robbins, *Air America* (New York: Avon, 1979), p. 5: "At its zenith Air America was, in terms of the number of planes it either owned or had at its disposal, the largest airline in the world."

10 Ibid., Alfred McCoy, in *The Politics of Heroin in Southeast Asia* (New York: Harper & Row, 1972), reported: "In Laos the CIA created a Meo mercenary army whose commander manufactured heroin for sale to American GIs in South Vietnam," and concluded that "the CIA's role in the heroin traffic was simply an inadvertent but inevitable consequence of its cold war tactics" (p. 8).

11 "A Study of Assassination," National Security Archive, George Washington University, Washington, DC. Available at www.gwu.edu.

12 "Church Committee Reports 1975-1976." Available at: www.aarchlibrary.org/publib/church/reports/contents.htm.

13 Gerald Ford signed executive order 11905 on 18 February 1976. Section 5: Restrictions of Intelligence Activities reads: "No employee of the United States Government shall engage in, or conspire to engage in, political assassination."

14 Interview with Jack Devine, former CIA deputy director of operations, New York, 19 April 2006.

15 See remarks to members of the National Press Club on arms reduction and nuclear weapons by President Ronald Reagan, 18 November 1981.

16 The story was told in June 2000 by David Gergen, a former adviser to President Clinton, in an interview with Chris Bury for PBS's Frontline show. In an interview with James Woolsey (10 December 2001), he told me: "I had two semi-private meetings with the president in two years."

17 Details of Clinton's "scrub" described in Chapter 6.

18 *Meet the Press with Tim Russert*, 16 September 2001.

19 He said in full: "All I want to say is that there was 'before' 9/11 and 'after' 9/11. After 9/11 the gloves came off." From Cofer Black's testimony to the Joint Committee Investigation into September 11: Fourth Public Hearing, 26 September 2002.

20 Quoted in "Special Operations Soldiers Expected to Be on Leading Edge," by Anne Griffin and Raleigh Bureau, *Charlotte Observer*, 21 September 2001.

21 This phrase is cited in "Preparing for Role in War on Terror; Navy Base in Cuba to House Taliban, Al Qaeda Detainees," Sue Anne Pressley, *Washington Post*, 10 January 2002. Vice President Dick Cheney also called the detainees "the very worst of a bad lot. They are very dangerous," quoted in "Debate Continues on Legal Status of Detainees," John Mintz,

Washington Post, 28 January 2002.

22　He was chairman from 1997 until August 2004.

23　Transcript of interview with Porter Goss, 14 December 2001, conducted by author and Richard Miniter, for the *Sunday Times*.

24　Interview with CIA contractor, spring 2002.

25　Early reports of rendition will be dealt with in Chapter 5. Among the earliest references to rendition were from the London-based Egyptian dissident Yasser al-Sirri, who issued statements about the capture and transfer of terrorist suspects as early as 1998. In the Western media the first mentions appeared after 9/11; the first seems to be an article in the *Boston Globe* by Anthony Shadid ("America Prepares the War on Terror; US, Egypt Raids Caught Militants'" 7 October 2001) and Barton Gellman's series in the *Washington Post* (including "Broad Effort Launched After '98 Attacks," 19 December 2001). The first reference to the use of executive jets appears to be a report in a Pakistan newspaper by Masood Anwar (*The News*, Islamabad, 26 October 2001), followed by the *Washington Post*'s piece about the rendition of Mohamad Iqbal Madni, "US Behind Secret Transfer of Terror Suspects," by Rajiv Chandrasekaran and Peter Finn, 11 March 2002.

26　Alexander Solzhenitsyn, *The Gulag Archipelago*, vol. 1 (1974), vol. 2 (1975), vol. 3 (London: Fontana, 1978).

27　Anne Applebaum admits in *Gulag* that it is impossible to state accurately the numbers of dead. Official "archival" sources have given a figure of almost three million, although Applebaum speculates the true figure must be much higher. As for the total number of inmates, she writes: "Adding the numbers together, the total numbers of forced labourers in the USSR comes to 28.7 million. I realize, of course, that this figure will not satisfy everybody." Anne Applebaum, *Gulag* (New York: Penguin Books, 2003) p. 520.

28　Alexander Solzhenitsyn, *The Gulag Archipelago*, vol. 1, p. x. "Zek" is the term for an inmate of the gulag.

29　The apparatus of the gulag was camouflaged in day-to-day banality. "From the outside, the 'Black Ravens' [transport trucks], as they were nicknamed, appeared to be regular heavy-goods trucks. In the 1930s, they often had the word 'bread' painted on the sides, but later more elaborate ruses were used. One prisoner, arrested in 1948, remembered traveling in one truck marked 'Moscow Cutlets' and another labeled 'Vegetables/Fruits.'" Applebaum, *Gulag*, p. 160.

30　*The Lion, The Witch, and The Wardrobe*, C. S. Lewis (Collins, 2001); *Harry Potter and the Sorcerer's Stone*, J. K. Rowling (Scholastic, 1999).

31　Author visit to Egypt, September/October 2003.

32　Chapter 2 describes the case of Binyam Mohamed, an Ethiopian arrested in Pakistan and transferred to Rabat by the Americans on 21 July 2002; an Italian citizen named Abu al-Kassem Britel was also brought by "a small American plane" from Pakistan to Morocco on 24 May 2002.

1. THE MEN IN BLACK

1　The detailed chronology of the events that evening are laid out in the *Swedish Chief Parliamentary Ombudsman's Report* of 22 March 2005: "A Review of the Enforcement by the Security Police of a Government Decision to Expel Two Egyptian Citizens." Hereafter the *Swedish Chief Parliamentary Ombudsman Report*. The weather at Bromma on 18 December 2001 is from Weather Underground: Web site www.wunderground.com/NA

2　Telephone interview with Paul Forell, 3 January 2005.

3　Paul Forell, 3 January 2005.

4   Ibid.

5   *Swedish Chief Parliamentary Ombudsman's Report*, 22 March 2005.

6   Paul Forell, 3 January 2005.

7   "The Broken Promise, Part 2," *Kalla Fakta*, 24 May 2004.

8   Flightlog of N379P.

9   "Mystery Man Handed Over to US Troops in Karachi," Masood Anwar, *The News International*, Pakistan, 26 October 2001.

10 Testimony of Bisher al-Rawi to Clive Stafford Smith at Guantánamo Bay; sent to author by e-mail 22 March 2006.

11 Testimony of Binyam Mohamed to CSS at Guantánamo Bay; recorded in memo dated 10 June 2005, referred to from now on as "CSS Memo 10 June 2005."

12 See Chapter 4.

13 Weather at Johnston County airport on 17 December 2001: overcast, 53-57 °F, from Weather Underground.

14 Interviews with former CIA pilot, 2005/2006.

15 Sherman announced Lee's surrender from the steps of the Johnston County Courthouse in Smithfield in April 1865.

16 Visit to Smithfield, March 2006.

17 "The Broken Promise, Part 1," *Kalla Fakta*, 17 May 2004.

18 *Sweden's Chief Parliamentary Ombudsman's Report*, 22 March 2005, Section 2.4.3.

19 Account based on Swedish government sources interviewed for *Kalla Fakta's* investigation.

20 Timings, officer's testimony, details of search operation and flight are from *Swedish Chief Parliamentary Ombudsman's Report*, 22 March 2005.

21 On 17 November 1997, fifty-eight tourists and four Egyptians were massacred by members of Gama'a al-Islamiyya at Deir el-Bahri in Luxor, Egypt. Statistics from State Dept. Report, *Patterns of Global Terrorism: 1997*.

22 Interview with Montasser Al-Zayat, Cairo, Egypt, 5 October 2003.

23 See Gilles Kepel, *The Prophet and Pharaoh: Muslim Extremism in Egypt*, trans. by J. Rothschild (London: Al Saqi Books, 1985), pp. 28, 41-3.

24 "Pharaohs in Waiting," by Mary Anne Weaver, *Atlantic* (October 2003).

25 Interview with Kjell Jönsson, 12 January 2005, for *File on Four*, BBC Radio 4, 8 February 2005.

26 Interviewed in January 2005 in Cairo by Hossam al-Hamalawy, who collaborated in researching this book. He now works for the *Los Angeles Times* and was a co-author of the Human Rights Watch report, *The Fate of Islamists Rendered to Egypt*, May 2005.

27 "Swedish Government Repatriates Two Suspected Terrorists in Egypt'" Karl Ritter, Associated Press, 20 December 2001.

28 "In Shift, Sweden Extradites Militants to Egypt," Anthony Shadid, *Boston Globe*, 31 December 2001.

29 An article in *Jane's Intelligence Review* explains: "Other al-Jihad leaders disagreed with al-Zawahiri's alliance with bin Laden, fearing it would incur the wrath of the world's superpower—as indeed now seems to be case. They broke away from al-Zawahiri." From "Ayman al-Zawahiri: Attention Turns to the Other Prime Suspect," Ed Blanche, 3 October 2001.

30 Al-Sirri was on Egypt's most wanted list, and was accused by the United States of being an Al Qaeda financier. He runs the Islamic Observation Centre in London.

31 Massoud's killers had introduced themselves to him with a letter apparently printed on the stationery of al-Sirri's organisation. But it was discovered that the letter had been faked on the computer of Ayman al-Zawahiri, later recovered in a Kabul auction by a journalist from

the *Wall Street Journal*, Alan Cullison. "British Court Frees a Muslim Arrested After 9/11," by Alan Cowell, *New York Times*, 10 August 2002.

32 Interview in January 2005 in London for *File on Four*, BBC Radio 4, 8 February 2005; and subsequent telephone conservations.

33 Amnesty issued a press release on 20 December 2001 that read: "Muhammad Suleiman Ibrahim el-Zari and Ahmed Hussein Mustafa Kamil Agiza were forcibly returned to Egypt by the Swedish authorities on 18 December. In Egypt both men are at grave risk of torture and unfair trial." From: "Sweden: Deportations Leave Men at Risk of Torture in Egypt," AI Index EUR 42/003/2001.

34 Interview with Kjell Jönsson, Brussels, 23 March 2006.

35 *Agiza v.* Sweden, United Nations Committee Against Torture (UNCAT) decision CAT/ C/34/D/233/2003, par 12.11, 20 May 2005.

36 Comments by the Swedish government to the UN Human Rights Committee: "It is the opinion of the Swedish Government that the assurances obtained from the receiving State are satisfactory and irrevocable and that they are and will be respected in their full content. The Government has not received any information which would cast doubt at this conclusion." Comments by the Government of Sweden on the Concluding Observations of the Human Rights Committee, CCPR/CO/74/SWE, par. 16, 6 May 2003.

37 UNCAT decision 199/2002, par 4.8, 24 November 2003, concerning expulsion of Agiza's wife and children.

38 UNICAT decision 233/2003, par 13.10.

39 A speech given to the International Commission of Jurists by a member of the Egyptian Organization for Human Rights states: "The Swedish Consulate was prevented from attending the first two hearings of Agiza's trial held on the 15th and 13th April 2004. The Swedish Secondary at the Swedish Consulate Asa Pousard was unexpectedly allowed to attend the third hearing without being informed why she was banned from attending the previous hearings." Speech delivered by Hafez Abu Saeda at the International Commission of Jurists (ICJ) Biennial Conference, Berlin, 27 August 2004. Also in *Kalla Fakta*, "The Broken Promise: Part I," 17 May 2004.

40 Interview with Swedish diplomat in Cairo, 4 October 2003, on condition of anonymity.

41 *Kalla Fakta*, "The Broken Promise, Part I," 17 May 2004.

42 "America's Gulag," Stephen Grey, *New Statesman*, 17 May 2004.

43 "A Secret Deportation of Terror Suspects," Craig Whitlock, *Washington Post*, 25 July 2004.

44 For example, these figures quoted by George Tenet, in oral teestimony before the 9/11 Commission, Wednesday, 24 March 2004.

45 "Rule Change Lets CIA Freely Send Suspects Abroad to Jails," Douglas Jehl and David Johnston, *New York Times*, 6 March 2005.

46 BBC news monitoring service translation of report by Iranian Students News Agency of a press conference given by Iranian intelligence minister Ali Yunesi on 17 July 2005: "[S]o far over 1,000 Al-Qa'idah members have been identified, detained, deported or tried. Currently, about 200 of them are in jail." Figures for Egypt from the Egyptian prime minister, Ahmed Nazif, speaking on NBC News' *Meet the Press*, 15 May 2005. Figures for Sudan from a speech by the Sudan expert, Janet McElligott, at the Former Members of Congress Annual Meeting, 15 May 2003. She refers to them as "extraditions".

47 Figure quoted by President Bush in a statement at Crawford, Texas, 28 December 2001.

48 According to *The New York Times*, "an intelligence official estimated that the number of terrorism suspects sent by the United States to Tashkent was in the dozens." Don Van Natta, "US Recruits a Rough Ally to Be a Jailer," *New York Times*, 1 May 2005. Routine memos from the FBI's Criminal Justice Information Services (CJIS) to Counter-terrorism

Department show repatriations listed for prisoners from Bagram, although no destinations are visible. Available at: www.aclu.org/torturefoia/released/FBI_3910_3927.pdf

49 Written statement to the author from the legal division of the International Committee of the Red Cross, Geneva, 28 April 2006. Referred to from now as the "Red Cross comments." See further detail on this point in Chapter 7.

50 Third Geneva Convention on Prisoners of War, Article 17; the Third Geneva Convention covering civilians captured also stated in Article 31 that "no physical or moral coercion shall be exercised against protected persons, in particular to obtain information from them."

51 According to the Red Cross comments, the current situation in Afghanistan, after the holding of *Loya Jirga* (council of elders) and the establishment of a new lawful government on 19 June 2002, was defined as a "non-international armed conflict." It added: "The ICRC no longer views the ongoing armed conflict as international but as non-international, since it no longer involves opposing states." Prisoners captured in such a conflict would not be POWs but their rights, in addition to customary international humanitarian law, were defined in a common Article 3 of the Geneva Conventions, which stated that anyone no longer taking part in a conflict-for example, after their detention-should "in all circumstances be treated humanely" and not be subject, among other things, to "cruel treatment and torture" or "outrages upon personal dignity, in particular, humiliating and degrading treatment."

52 According to the Red Cross comments, the term "global war on terror," was a political description. The law depended on whether a prisoner was seized within what the law clearly defined as international armed conflict or non-international armed conflict. It said: "The designation 'global war on terror' does not extend the applicability of humanitarian law to all events included in this notion, but only to those that involve armed conflict. ... When armed violence is used outside the context of an armed conflict in the legal sense or when a person suspected of terrorist activities is not detained in connection with any armed conflict, humanitarian law does not apply. Instead, domestic laws, as well as international criminal law and human rights, govern."

53 A White House fact sheet on the status of detainees at Guantánamo, issued 7 February 2002, states: "The United States is treating and will continue to treat all of the individuals detained at Guantánamo humanely and consistent with military necessity, to the extent appropriate and in a manner consistent with the principles of the Third Geneva Convention of 1949."

54 Between 1990 and 2000, there were 56 terrorist incidents in Egypt, resulting in 142 fatalities and 212 injuries. Data from the National Memorial Institute for the Prevention of Terrorism (MIPT) Terrorism Knowledge Base, accessed 31 March 2006 (www.tkb.org).

55 Interview with Robert Baer by phone, 17 January 2005, for *File on Four*, BBC Radio 4, 8 February 2005.

56 Baer, 17 January 2005.

57 President Jimmy Carter brokered a peace treaty between President Anwar Sadat of Egypt and Prime Minister Menachem Begin of Israel; it was signed on 17 September 1978 at the White House.

58 Since 2001, the amount of FMF to Egypt has represented over 50 per cent of US aid to the country. In 2003 total aid to Egypt was $1.75 billion ($1.29 billion as FMF); in 2004, these figures were $1.95 and $1.29 billion respectively. Figures from the *Greenbook*, compiled and updated by the US Agency for International Development (USAID) to give "a complete historical record of US foreign aid to the rest of the world." Available at: qesdb.cdie.org/gbk/index.html.

59 Office of Management and Budget (OMB), "Budget of the United States Government, Fiscal Year 2007, Budget Appendix, International Security Assistance, Foreign Military Financing Program" (US GPO, 2006). Of a budgeted $4.5 billion in FMF, Israel is to receive

$2.8 billion and Egypt "not less than $1.3 billion." Available from GPO Access, the US Government Printing Office.

60 The most extensive research on renditions to Egypt was carried out by Hossam al-Hamalawy.

61 Flightlogs: N379P (fifteen visits), N85VM (four visits) N313P (one visit).

62 Interview with Jack Cloonan, New York, 19 April 2006.

63 "Detainee Says He Was Tortured in US Custody," Raymond Bonner, *New York Times*, 13 February 2005.

64 Telephone interview with Professor Joe Margulies, for *File on Four*, BBC, 14 January 2005.

65 Bonner, New York Times, 13 February 2005.

66 Statement by Ian Kemish to the Australian Senate Foreign Affairs Committee on 2 June 2004. Kemish was then first assistant secretary for public diplomacy at the consular and passports division of the Australian Department of Foreign Affairs and Trade.

67 *Dateline: The Trials of Mamdouh Habib*, SBS Television, Australia, broadcast on 7 July 2004.

68 Ibid.

2. THE FOG OF WAR — THE "CONFESSIONS" OF A BRITISH "DIRTY BOMBER"

1 Attorney General John Ashcroft Regarding the Transfer of Abdullah al-Muhajir (Born José Padilla) to the Department of Defence as an Enemy Combatant," 10 June 2002, Department of Justice. Available at www.usdoj.gov; and see "US Authorities Capture 'Dirty Bomb' Suspect," CNN, 10 June 2002.

2 "Traces of Terror: The Congressional Hearings; Whistle-Blower Recounts Faults Inside the F.B.I.," by David Johnston and Neil A. Lewis, *New York Times*, 7 June 2002.

3 According to Gary Berntsen, who took part in the earliest CIA mission into Afghanistan, bin Laden escaped to Pakistan with 200 "Yemenis and Saudis" while 135 others took another less direct route into Pakistan. Gary Berntsen and Ralph Pezzullo, *Jawbreaker* (New York: Crown, 2005), p.307.

4 Abu Zubaydah was thought by some to have been Al Qaeda's top miliary commander since late 2001, following the death of Mohammed Atef, and to have been behind plots to bomb Los Angeles International Airport, as well as plots to attack hotels in Jordan. He was sentenced to death in absentia in Jordan for his involvement in the foiled plot. According to the *9/11 Commission Report* (p. 500) he helped run the Khaldan terrorist training camp in Afghanistan. He has been in US custody since his arrest in Pakistan in March 2002.

5 Quoted in Memo from Matthew Rycroft to David Manning (Downing Street officials), 23 July 2002, and published as "The Secret Downing Street Memo," *Sunday Times* , 1 May 2005.

6 "John Ashcroft, Minister of Fear," CBSNews.com, 12 June 2002.

7 The front page of the *New York Times* carried the headline "Traces of Terror: The Investigation; US Says It Halted Al Qaeda Plot to Use Radioactive Bomb," with a photograph of Padilla. He was *Time* magazine's Person of the Week, 14 June 2002: "For incarnating the sum of our fears, the former Chicago thug-turned-terror suspect is our person of the week."

8 CSS Memo, 10 June 2005.

9 Ibid.

10 Ibid.

[11] Information supplied by Binyam Mohamed's sister to Clive Stafford Smith, June 2005.

[12] CSS Memo, 10 June 2005.

[13] He obtained grades C, D, and E in physics, biology and chemistry respectively. Source: E-mail from Edexcel examining board 7 July 2005

[14] CSS Memo, 10 June 2005.

[15] Binyam Mohamed's sister to CSS, June 2005.

[16] Tyrone Forbes interview in "Suspect's Tale of Travel and Torture," Stephen Grey and Ian Cobain, *The Guardian*, 2 August 2005.

[17] *Guardian* interview with Abdulkarim Khalil. From "Suspect's Tale of Travel and Torture," 2 August 2005.

[18] E-mail from Abdul S., a friend of Mohamed's, to the author, 23 July 2005.

[19] E-mail from Abdul S., 23 July 2005.

[20] "As Justice Weigh Military Tribunals, A Guantánamo Tale," Jess Bravin, *Wall Street Journal*, 28 March 2006: "He [Clive Stafford Smith] says Mr. Mohamed 'dabbled with the idea of going to Chechnya' to join Islamic rebels fighting Russian rule but denies any tie to a terrorist plot against the US-or knowing Mr. Padilla."

[21] Michael Scheuer explained: "And so we are bedeviled again... by what too many individuals more intelligent and influential than I consider an inconsequential semantical difference between the terms 'terrorist' and 'insurgent.' " *Imperial Hubris*, by Anonymous (Michael Scheuer) (London: Brassey's, 2004), p. 221. Former senior MI6 officer Alastair Crooke also believes this point has hardly been grasped by anyone, least of all the interrogators and tribunals at Guantánamo. Interviewed in London, on 4 April 2006, he said: "I spoke to someone from Guantánamo who kept saying the interrogators kept saying to him, 'Oh, so you were at the Jamaat al-Qaeda camp, that's where you were at, Jamaat al-Qaeda camp?' Jamaat was Massoud's group. And they didn't even understand that this was a seperate party. And they kept calling it as if it was the name of an Al Qaeda camp. So you mean, how good is rendition if you haven't got the basic tools of understanding of the groups and the background to be able to distinguish and understand these sorts of complex areas?"

[22] The US Supreme Court ruling in the case Rasul *v.* Bush no. 03-334 (524 US), 28 June 2004, states that the district court "has jurisdiction to hear petitioners' habeas corpus challenges to the legality of their detention at the Guantánamo Bay Naval Base," pp. 15-16.

[23] Interview with Benhur Mohamed, 25 July 2005.

[24] Sufyian Barhoumi, Jabran Said bin al Qahtani, and Ghassan al Sharbi.

[25] *United States of America v. Binyam Ahmed Muhammad* [sic], 29 June 2005.

[26] *United States of America vs. Binyam Ahmed Muhammad* [sic], conspiracy charge 14 (j).

[27] CSS Memo, 10 June 2005, p.1.

[28] "*Top Secret* with Yosri Fouda", aired on Al Jazeera 12 September 2002. The story of Fouda's visit was told in *Masterminds of Terror* by Yosri Fouda and Nick Fielding (Edinburgh: Mainstream Publishing, 2003). Page 36 records: " 'They say that you are terrorists.' Fouda surprised himself by throwing in this line so early as he took his place on the floor between them. ... It was Khalid who answered: "They are right. That is what we do for a living.' "

[29] Remarks of US Deputy Attorney General James Comey regarding José Padilla, Tuesday, 1 June 2004.

[30] CSS Memo, 10 June 2005.

[31] Reading a prepared statement, Straw told the parliament that Mr Habashi (Binyam's clan name: it literally means "the Ethiopian") had indeed been "interviewed once in Karachi by the security services." Straw continued: "The security services had no role in his capture or transfer from Pakistan. The security service officer did not observe any abuse and no incidents of abuse were reported to him by Mr Habashi." "Former UK Student Was Interrogated by MI6 in Pakistan," *The Independent*, 14 December 2005.

32 Author's interview with Yosri Fouda, London, 10 January 2006.

33 According to the *9/11 Commission Report*, interrogations of Abu Zubaydah are listed as having taken place on the following dates: 10 July 2002, 29 August 2002, 29 October 2002, 7 November 2002, 16 May 2003, 24 June 2003, 13 December 2003, 18 February 2004, and 19 February 2004 (pp. 466, 490, 491, 500, 507, 524, and 527).

34 See Chapter 11.

35 Remarks of Deputy Attorney General James Comey regarding José Padilla, Tuesday 1 June 2004.

36 "Ashcroft on Dirty Bomb," CBS News, 10 June 2002.

37 Interview with Abdullah Almalki, London, 20 April 2006, see Chapter 3.

38 Flightlogs of Gulfstream V Registration N379P.

39 "Spanish Armada Sounds Retreat," Matthew Campbell, *Sunday Times*, 22 July 2002.

40 CSS Memo, 10 June 2005.

41 Ibid.

42 Ibid.

43 Flightlog of Boeing Business Jet N313P, 21 January 2004, GMME (Rabat) to OAKB (Kabul).

44 Amnesty International report, "*Torture in the 'Anti-Terrorism' campaign — The Case of Temara Detention Centre*," 24 June 2004, Amnesty International reference: MDE 29/004/2004, describes Temara as "located in a forested area...some 15 km south of the capital" (p. 6).

45 E-mail to author from Abderrahim Mouhtad, head of Ennassir: Pour Le Soutien des Détenus Islamistes au Maroc (Association in Support of Islamist Detainees).

46 Flightlogs of plane N379P.

47 Fédération Internationale des Ligues des Droits de l'Homme (International Federation for Human Rights) Report 379/2, *Morocco: Human Rights Abuse in the Fight Against Terrorism*, July 2004, p. 15; referred hereafter as *FIDH report* (www.fidh.org/IMG/pdf/maroc379-2.pdf).

48 Amnesty International report, *Torture in the 'Anti-Terrorism' campaign — The Case of Temara Detention Centre*, 24 June 2004, Amnesty International reference: MDE 29/004/2004, p. 5.

49 FIDH report, p.11.

50 Ibid., pp. 11-12.

3. MAHER ARAR

1 Interview, with Maher Arar, Ottawa, 10 December 2003.

2 Maher Arar, Ottawa, 10 December 2003.

3 See below, Abdullah Almalki and Ahmed al-Maati.

4 Interview with Maher Arar, 10 December 2003; this was confirmed in a later public inquiry into the actions of Canadian officials. Established on 4 February 2004, it was headed by judge, Dennis R. O'Connor (hereafter the "Arar inquiry.")

5 Imad Moustapha, the Syrian ambassador to the United States, told CBS News that Arar was released as a gesture of goodwill toward Canada ("His year in Hell," reporter Vicki Mabrey, *60 Minutes II*, 21 January 2004).

6 Interview with Maher Arar in Brussels, 23 March 2006.

7 In February 1997.

8 "A Modified Constant Modulus Algorithm Enters the Scene," by Maher Arar, *Wireless Systems Design*, April 2003 (www.wsdmag.com/Articles/ArticleID/6540/6540.html).

9 Public statement of Maher Arar to a press conference in Ottawa, 4 November 2003.

10 A census taken in 2001 revealed that the total Syrian population in Canada was 22,065. Those resident in Ottawa represented 1,055 out of a total 827,854 inhabitants of that city. Source: telephone interview with agent from Statistics Canada.

11 Transcript of the Arar inquiry, p. 7768. Transcript available at: www.commissionarar.ca.

12 "Arrest at US Border Reverberates in France," John F. Burns, et al., New York Times, 22 December 1999.

13 Al-Maati's chronology prepared with his lawyer, Barbara Jackman. Available on Amnesty International Canada's Web site at: www.amnesty.ca/english/main_article_home/elmaatichronology.pdf. Hereafter referred to as Al-Maati's Chronology.

14 Al-Maati's Chronology.

15 Author's file.

16 "Who is Abdullah Almalki", Andrew Duffy, Ottawa Citizen, 30 October 2005.

17 Kadr was first identified and charged with aiding and financing terrorism in 1996. See: "Canadian Faces Charges of Terrorism," Rosemary Spiers, Toronto Star, 16 January 1996.

18 Interview with Abdullah Almalki, London, 21 November 2004; details of his observation emerged at the Arar inquiry.

19 Testimony of Michael Cabana, leading RCMP officer in the investigation into Arar, to the Arar inquiry. See: Transcript of the Arar inquiry, p. 7757.

20 Interview with Maher Arar in Brussels, 23 March 2006.

21 The very same day the Los Angeles Times broke the news of the suspicions against Ahmed al-Maati, reporting how, in a reference to the map seized at the Buffalo checkpoint in August, US agents had been briefed on a thirty-six-year-old Kuwaiti man in whose belongings were discovered "documents that identified specific buildings in an Ottawa government complex — notably the atomic energy building and the virus and disease control labs". "Dragnet Yields the Chilling, Alarming," Patrick McDonnell and William Remple, Los Angeles Times, 12 October 2001.

22 Maher Arar's removal order, signed by Immigration and Naturalization Service (INS) regional director J. Scott Blackman, 7 October 2002. According to Babana, this was the day Arar first became a "person who was either an associate or a person of interest in respect of the invastigation of AO-CANADA." See Transcript of the Arar inquiry, p. 8236.

23 Interview with Maher Arar, 23 March 2006.

24 Interview with Maher Arar, 10 December 2003.

25 A letter from State Department official Nancy J. Powell, then/Acting Assistant Secretary, Legislative Affairs, to Congressman Edward J. Markey, dated 11 February 2005, states: "Mr Arar's name was placed on a United States terrorist lookout list based on information received as part of an ongoing general sharing of information between the Governments of the United States and Canada."

26 "Supplemental Report on 11 September Detainees Allegations of Abuse at the Metropolitan Detention Centre in Brooklyn, New York," Office of the Inspector General for the US Department of Justice, December 2003.

27 Copy of Arar's removal order and "notice of inadmissibility," both dated 7 October 2002, and signed by Blackman were obtained by the Center of Constitutional Rights in New York. Thompson's role was first reported in "His Year in Hell," 60 Minutes II, CBS News, 21 January 2004: "60 Minutes II has learned that the decision to deport Arar was made at the highest levels of the US Justice Department, with a special removal order signed by John Ashcroft's former deputy, Lary [sic]Thompson" (www.cbsnews.com/stories/2004/01/21/48hours/main594974.shtml). This allegation that Arar was a member of Al Qaeda was reiterated by the DoJ in a written statement to the same television program: "We have information indicating that Mr. Arar is a member of al Qaeda and, therefore, remains a

threat to US national security."

28 Country Report on Human Rights Practices 2001, US Department of State, 4 March 2002, Available at www.state.gov.

29 Interview, 10 December 2003.

30 Yale-Loehr teaches immigration law at Cornell Law school and is the co-author of the leading twenty-volume US immigration law treatise: *Immigration Law and Procedure*. O'Neill is a 2005 graduate of the School.

31 "The Legality of Maher Arar's Treatment Under US Immigration Law," Stephen W. Yale-Loehr and Jeffrey C. O'Neill, p. 14. Submitted on 16 May 2005 to the Commission of Inquiry into the Actions of Canadian Officials in Relation to Maher Arar (www.ararcommission. ca/eng/Yale-Loehr_may16.pdf).

32 Weather report from Weather Underground Web site: www.wunderground.com.

33 Records of Maher Arar's flight; first published by Stephen Grey and Scott Shane in the *New York Times*, "Detainee's Suit Gains Support from Jet's Log," 30 March 2005.

34 As evidenced by the widespread use of another Gulfstream jet (then registration: N85VM) belonging to the owner of Red Sox baseball team, for example, in the rendition of Abu Omar (see Chapter 9).

35 *The International Directory of Civil Aircraft* confirms that the jet's maximum range with eight passengers and reserves is 4,100 nautical miles (4,718 miles).

36 Interview with Maher Arar, 17 January 2005.

37 Flightlogs of N829MG.

38 Report of Professor Stephen J. Toope, Fact Finder, to the Arar inquiry, 14 October 2005, pp 13-14. Available at: www.commissionarar.ca/Toope Report_final.pdf.

39 "Syria's Top Man in Lebanon to Head 'Political Security Agency,' " Agence France-Press (AFP), Beirut, 9 October 2002.

40 Syria continues to support the Islamic militant group Hezb'allah.

41 William Buckley was CIA chief of station in Beirut when he was kidnapped in March 1984. After fifteen months of captivity, torture, and illness, Buckley died. His body was returned to US officials in 1991, and he was buried in Arlington National Cemetery with full military honours.

42 Interview with former MI6 officer, summer 2004. "Syria has far more WMD than Iraq," he told me.

43 *The Independent* reported at the time that the United States suspected the Syrian Ahmed Jibril of the Popular Front for the Liberation of Palestine of organising the bombing. Jibril was a Damascus-based former Syrian Army captain, and would have needed Assad's approval for his activities. "The Lockerbie Disaster," John Bulloch, *The Independent*, 7 January 1989. See also Cofer Black's 2003 speech to the Senate Foreign Relations Committee entitled "Syria and Terrorism" at www.state.gov/s/ct/rls/rm/2003/25778.htm.

44 Amnesty International, "Torture, Despair and Dehumanisation in Tadmur Military Prison," Amnesty International reference: MDE 24/014/2001, 19 September 2001.

45 No official figure was ever disclosed. Robert Fisk recalls in *Pity the Nation* (Oxford: London, 1990), p.186: "The Syrians would claim that fatalities were only in the hundreds. We later estimated them to be as high as 10,000". A number of contemporary reports suggest the figure may be as high as 20,000. See BBC News, "Profile: Rifaat al-Assad," 12 June 2000: news.bbc.co.uk/1/hi/world/middle_east/788021.stm.

46 William Burns of the US State Department said in Congress: "It is true that the cooperation the Syrians have provided in their own self-interest on Al Qaeda has saved American lives, and that is a fact, but our agenda goes well beyond that." William Burns, Assistant Secretary, Bureau of Near Eastern Affairs, State Department. Statement made on 18 June 2002, in hearings before the House Subcommittee on the Middle East and South Asia (commdocs.

house.gov/committees/intlrel/hfa80287.000/hfa80287_0f.htm).

[47] "UN nears Agreement on Iraq as US lawmakers debate force," Agence France- Press, 10 October 2002.

[48] Interview with former CIA officer, 2003.

[49] "Syria Denies Deadly Intelligence War Is Gripping Damascus," An Nahar news agency, 4 September 2003. Syrian dissident sources: journalist Nizar Nayouf and Syrian Human Rights Committee both claim to have independent sources that Tajer was the key link between the CIA and the Syrian regime. He died mysteriously at the end of 2004. Nayouf claims Tajer had got too close to the CIA for the regime's liking.

[50] Interview with Maher Arar, Brussels, 23 March 2006; Ottawa, 10 December 2003 and 17 Janurary 2005.

[51] White House press conference, 28 April 2005; see Chapter 10.

[52] Interview with Maher Arar, 10 December 2003.

[53] Evidence of Ward Elcock, former CSIS Director, to the Arar Inquiry. Original transcript of hearing, 21 June 2004, p. 161.

[54] Al-Maati's chronology states that: "In the end Ahmed said what he thought they wanted him to — that he had seen them both in Afghanistan" (page 9). Abdullah Almalki, in an interview on 20 April 2006, said it appeared al-Maati had seen him when he was working for an aid agency, he had visited Afghanistan; but Abdullah had not seen or recognised al-Maati there.

[55] Arar's lawyer, Marlys Edward, cited a *Boston Globe* article to the Arar inquiry that stated: "There was nothing secret about the map. ... Moreover [the nuclear facilities] were gone from the location long before the map aroused the suspicions of US customs agents" (Transcript of the Arar inquiry, p. 12441. The original article, "It Was Hyped as a Terrorist Map, It Was Cited by Egyptian Torturers, It Is a Visitor's Guide to Ottawa," is by Jeff Sallot and Colin Freeze, *Canada Globe and Mail*, 6 September 2005).

[56] Arar inquiry, Exhibit P-257, quoted in "Evidence Grows That Canada Aided in Having Terrorism Suspects Interrogated in Syria," Clifford Krauss, *New York Times*, 17 September 2005.

[57] Telephone Interview with Abdullah Almalki, 20 April 2006.

[58] Interview with Maher Arar, 17 Janurary 2005, for *File on Four*, BBC Radio 4, 8 February 2005.

[59] Interview with Maher Arar, Ottawa, 10 December 2003.

[60] Ambassador Pillarella's report of a conversation on 22 October between himself and General Hassan Khalil, head of Syrian Military Intelligence, reads: "In a 45-minute meeting with General Hassan Khalil, Head of Military Intelligence, he confirmed the information I had received the night before from (redacted) that Arar is now in Syria and he is being interrogated. ... According to General Khalil, Arar has already admitted that he has connections with terrorist organisations." Source: Transcript of Arar inquiry, pp. 6647-6653.

[61] Pillarella's report of the meeting, which came out during the Inquiry hearings, recorded that: "A meeting with (redacted) to review the Arar case proved to be extremely positive. ... When I asked (redacted) whether I could get a resume of information obtained so far from Arar that I could take to Canada with me, he agreed to do so." From the Testimony of Ambassador Pillarella to the Arar inquiry; transcript pp. 6842-6851.

[62] Cabana's comments recounted by Jim Gould, deputy to Dan Livermore. Both citations from "Evidence Grows That Canada Aided in Having Terrorism Suspects Interrogated in Syria," Clifford Krauss, *New York Times*, 17 September 2005.

[63] Abdullah Almalki speaking to Anna Maria Tremonti on *The Current*, Canadian Broadcasting Company, Radio 1, 18 October 2005.

4. MISTAKEN IDENTITY — A GERMAN CITIZEN'S JOURNEY TO AN AFGHAN HELL

[1] Interview with Khaled el-Masri, 22 January 2005, on *Frontal 21* programme, ZDF Television (Germany). Hereafter referred to as ZDF Interview, 22 January 2005.

[2] Report to the Majorca prosecutor entitled, "Trial Court no. 7, Summary Proceeding, Law 7/88, no. 2630 Incident of Illegal Detention," hereafter referred to as the "Guardia Report".

[3] Interview with Francisco José, at Palma de Majorca, 13 January 2005.

[4] It was too large, in fact, to land at the Johnston County Airport, the headquarters of the plane's operators, Aero Contractors, and the home base of much of the CIA aviation fleet. The 737's home base was nearby Kinston Airport, where in 2003 a special hangar was constructed to accommodate this larger plane. "TransPark Expects New Charter Plane Hangar," *Kinston Free Press*, 27 July 2003.

[5] CSS Memo, 10 June 2005.

[6] Brochure from Marriott Son Antem resort.

[7] Author's interview with barman, 12 January 2005.

[8] Interview published in "They Beat Me From All Sides," James Meek, *The Guardian*, 14 January 2005 (hereafter, *Guardian* interview).

[9] Interview published in "German's Claim of Kidnapping Brings Investigation of US Link," Don Van Natta, Jr., and Souad Mekhennet, *New York Times*, 9 January 2005 (hereafter, *New York Times* interview).

[10] Interview published in "Man's Claims May Be a Look at Dark Side of War on Terror," *Los Angeles Times,* Jeffrey Fleishman, 12 April 2005. (hereafter *LA Times* interview).

[11] ZDF interview.

[12] *LA Times* interview.

[13] Cost: €120 (or £80) for the round trip.

[14] *LA Times* interview.

[15] Witnesses on the bus confirmed el-Masri's story about the events on the Macedonian border. The Macedonian authorities later asserted, in a diplomatic note given to German foreign minister Steinmeier in December 2005 during a NATO foreign ministers conference, that el-Masri had entered Macedonia from Serbia-Macedonia at the Tabanovce crossing on 31 December 2003, and that (incorrectly) he left the country via Blace (into Kosovo) on 23 January 2004." See "Classified Report to German Parliament," p. 113.

[16] *New York Times* interview.

[17] The hotel was located by ZDF; el-Masri confirmed the identification from photographs and videos of the place.

[18] Interview with Khaled el-Masri, 22 April 2006 (JG).

[19] Interview with Reda Seyam, 19 April 2006 (JG).

[20] ZDF interview.

[21] When applying for asylum in Germany in October 1985, he told the German authorities that he had been a member of the Al Tawhid Group. The group had fought against the Alawite minority in Lebanon, and was later repressed by the Syrian security forces. Source: *Classified Report to German Parliament,* p. 86.

[22] ZDF interview.

[23] *Classified Report to German Parliament,* p. 89.

[24] Interview with Reda Seyam, 19 April 2006. (JG)

[25] Ibid.; and interview with el-Masri, 22 April 2006.

[26] Abduh Ali Al Hajj Sharqawi. This is according to testimony he gave at Guantánamo that was passed to the lawyer, Clive Stafford Smith, and declassified.

[27] Table of transfers from Bagram Air Base disclosed in a FOIA request by the Associated

Press.

28 Food and drink invoice from Sky Chefs Barcelona for aeroplane N313P, dated 23 January 2004. Reproduced in annex to *Guardia Report*, p. 274.

29 *LA Times* interview.

30 *Rasul vs Bush* (524 US), No. 03-334, 28 June 2004. (See Chapter 2).

31 The first reference to the name Salt Pit appears in "CIA Avoids Scrutiny of Detainee Treatment" Dana Priest, *Washington Post*, 3 March 2005. It is also referred to in the ACLU lawsuit. According to el-Masri (interview with Khaled el-Masri, 1 May 2006), the prisoners had no name for it, though they had heard that it was in the Sherika district of Kabul, close to the home of the Afghan president Karzai, and had been the scene of much fighting.

32 ZDF interview.

33 ZDF interview.

34 Khaled el-Masri video statement 30, May 2004.

35 ZDF interview.

36 A section called "Prisons and Detention Centres" advises: "If an indictment is issued and the trial begins, the brother has to pay attention to the following: At the beginning of the trial, once more the brothers must insist on proving that torture was inflicted on them by State Security [investigators] before the judge; complain [to the court] of mistreatment while in prison."

37 ZDF interview.

38 Interview with Khaled el-Masri, 22 April 2006 (JG).

39 ZDF interview.

40 "Rice Ordered Release of German Sent to Afghan Prison in Error," David Johnston, *New York Times*, 22 April 2005.

41 *Guardian* interview.

42 ZDF interview.

43 He even picked out a federal policeman from a police line-up in Munich whom he was convinced was the Sam in question. But the policeman provided a convincing alibi that he was not in Afghanistan. As reported in "Germany Weighs If It Played Role In Seizure by US," Don Van Natta, Jr., Souad Mekhennet and Nicholas Wood, *New York Times*, 21 February 2006.

44 *Classified Report to German Parliament*, p. 97. The German government insisted that no member its intelligence services was Sam. The report said there was no means of verifying wheather one of the German-speaking Americans identified by the BND was Sam.

45 "Sind Sie Sam" (Are you Sam?) *Stern* magazine, 19 April 2006.

46 ZDF interview.

47 *Classified Report to German Parliament*, p. 88.

48 ZDF interview.

49 Interview with Khaled el-Masri, 22 April 2006, Khaled el-Masri video statement, 30 May 2004.

50 Khaled el-Masri video statement, 30 May 2004; further details from interview with Reda Seyam, 19 April 2006 (JG).

51 Khaled el-Masri video statement, 30 May 2004.

52 Interview with Reda Seyam, 19 April 2006 (JG).

53 *Classified Report to German Parliament*, p. 90. The letters were sent 8 June 2004.

54 In 2005, a medical team at Munich University ran tests on Khaled el-Masri's hair , an analysis that can indicate through trace elements where someone has lived, and came to the conclusion that "it is very probable that the observed changes in the test isotope signatures correspond in fact with the testimony of K.E.M [Khaled el-Masri]," according to the *Classified Report to German Parliament*, p. 100.

55 *LA Times* interview.

56 White House press release of a statement by President George W. Bush, on the United Nations International Day in Support of Victims of Torture, 26 June 2003.

57 "Rice Ordered Release of German Sent to Afghanistan in Error," David Johnston, *New York Times*, 23 April 2005.

58 "Wrongful Imprisonment: Anatomy of a CIA Mistake," Dana Priest, *Washington Post*, 4 December 2005.

59 The *9/11 Commission Report* contains a reference to one Khalid al-Masri. "The available evidence indicates that in 1999, Atta, Binalshibh, Shehhi, and Jarrah decided to fight in Chechnya against the Russians. According to Binalshibh, a chance meeting on a train in Germany caused the group to travel to Afghanistan instead. An individual named Khalid al-Masri approached Binalshibh and Shehhi (because they were Arabs with beards, Binalshibh thinks) and struck up a conversation about jihad in Chechnya." Section 5.3 (The Hamburg Contingent), *9/11 Commission Report*, p. 165.

60 Interview with Scott Pelley for CBS report: "CIA Use of Rendering to Get Information from Suspects," 6 March 2005.

61 ZDF Interview.

62 Interview with Khaled el-Masri, 22 April 2006. (JG)

63 "Classified Report to German Parliament," p. 87.

64 Interview with Khaled el-Masri, 1 May 2006. (JG)

65 Interview with Khaled el-Masri, 22 April 2006. (JG)

66 Ibid.

67 Moreover, the *Classified Report to German Parliament* emphasises how important the cooperation is between the German and American security services: "The close cooperation of the international community is primarily focused on the prevention of further attacks. A close and complete exchange of information between security authorities is essential in this context. It is a completely normal and essential thing that German security authorities exchange information and findings with US security authorities. (pp. 98-9).

68 Both the German television (ARD) news magazine programme *Panorama* and the *New York Times* reported that the German foreign intelligence service provided vital military information to the US Central Command in Doha in the months leading up to the war, and during the war. "Bombs on Baghdad — German Agents Involved in Iraq War" by John Goetz, ARD-TV, 12 January 2006; "German Intelligence Gave US Iraqi Defense Plan, Report Says," by Michael R. Gordon, *New York Times*, 26 February 2006.

69 First reported in "Anatomy of a CIA Mistake," *Washington Post*.

70 *Classified Report to German Parliament*, p. 91.

71 Speaking to the German parliament on 14 December 2005, the interior minister, Wolfgang Schäuble, also described how Coats had told Schily that the United States had both apologised to el-Masri and "paid him an amount of money." But, after inquiries by el-Masri's lawyer, Manfred Gnjidic, the German government withdrew the allegation. Writing to Gnjidic on 21 December that year, an official confirmed "the foreign ministry has no documentation to show that your client received money or payments from US authorities."

72 Interview with Khaled el-Masri, 1 May 2006. (JG)

73 Interviews with former officials of the DIA. (JG)

5. COVERT ACTION — UNMASKING THE NEW AIR AMERICA

1 Interviews by phone (May 2005) with journalists who were in the Panschir in November 2001, including Stefan Smith (AFP, now in Teheran), Elizabeth Rubin (*New Republic/*

New York Times Magazine), Tim Lambon (ITN cameraman), Chris Stephens (freelance British journalist, now in Moscow), and Peter Jouvenal (veteran BBC cameraman). The arrival of the plane was reported most notably in *Agence France Press*, 4 November 2001, "New Opposition Airstrip Opens Up Anti-Taliban Supply Link," Stefan Smith, from Gulbohar, Afghanistan; and "US Warms to Rebels, Slowly," Scott Peterson, *Christian Science Monitor*, Bagram Front, 4 November 2001. References to use of the airstrip in 1919 from Bob Woodward, *Bush at War* (New York: Simon and Schuster, 2002), pp. 190-91.

2 *Bush at War*, pp. 190-1, 293-5; Gary Schroen describes the Jawbreaker mission in detail in *First In* (New York: Presidio Press, 2005) as does Gary Berntsen (with Ralph Pezzullo) in *Jawbreaker* (New York: Crown, 2005).

3 *Air Forces Monthly* (January 2002), Afghanistan Diary, "Day 29 — Sunday 4th November," (p. 75). The registration had been misread by the journalists in the Panschir as N6160, leading them on a false trail.

4 Flightlogs of N6161Q.

5 The actual budget is classified. In the most recent disclosure, the Director of Central Intelligence revealed the total intelligence budget for 1998 was $26.7 billion. Mary Margaret Graham, the deputy director of National Intelligence for Collection, revealed an overall post-9/11 figure of $44 billion in a speech given in November 2005. "Official Reveals Budget for US Intelligence," Scott Shane, *New York Times*, 8 November 2005.

6 This claim is made by Christopher Robbins, *Air America*, (1979), as cited above.

7 "CIA Air Operations in Laos, 1955-1974," by William M. Leary (www.cia.gov/csi/studies/winter99-00/art7.html#rft0).

8 The involvement of the Meo in the opium trade was well documented by correspondents in Laos at the time, and most notably in Alfred McCoy's *The Politics of Heroin in South East Asia* (New York: Harper and Row, 1972). But although the Meo were at the center of the opium trade, and the CIA knew this, no concrete evidence emerged that the CIA was deliberately involved in its trafficking. One former pilot, Jim Parrish, was quoted by Robbins as saying: "We knew we hauled a lot of dope, although we didn't haul it intentionally." The Senate's Church Committee later endorsed the conclusion that "the CIA air proprietaries did not participate in illicit drug trafficking." But as a later CIA inspector general's report noted, "Opium was as much part of the agricultural infrastructure of this area as rice." More significantly, Robbins found that by supplying villagers with a regular supply of food, the CIA effectively freed them to use their fields to grow opium instead. As he summarised: "While the Meo fought the war for the CIA, the Agency turned a blind eye to their generals' profitable sideline in opium" *(Air America*, pp. 226, 233, 237).

9 The United States Senate Select Committee to Study Governmental Operations with Respect to Intelligence Activities, a.k.a the Church Committee, delivered its final report to Congress on 26 April 1976. (www.aarclibrary.org/public/church/reports/book1/pdf/ChurchB1_11_Propreitaries.pdf).

10 Ibid.

11 Interview with Brian Martin, 26 May 2005. For example, his flight on 1 October 1982, went first from Basle to Berlin (Schönfeld Airport) to Lisbon. Once outside communist airspace, the final destination was then switched from Angola to Washington, DC.

12 "Airline 'Carrying CIA Guns to Unita' ", Alan George, *Independent*, 18 February 1989.

13 "Angolan CIA Hercules Air Crash Killed Tepper Aviation Chief," *Flight International*, 13 December 1989.

14 The CIA's direct role in the mining operation was first disclosed in the *Wall Street Journal* in "US Role in Mining Nicaraguan Harbors Reportedly is Larger Than First Thought," Dana Rogers, 6 April 1984, and disclosed in Congress in remarks by Senator Barry Goldwater (R-Arizona) the same month.

[15] For how the trail developed, see for example *Miami Herald*, 13 June 2004, "Iran Contra Scandal Marred Presidency" Alfonso Chardy. Hasenfus's operation was traced back to Colonel Oliver North, who was running the Iran-Contra programme from the National Security Council. Shortly after the crash a weekly magazine in the Lebanon reported the Iran connection, disclosing a trip by Colonel North to Teheran in May 1986.

[16] Journalists like Dana Priest of the *Washington Post* and Jane Mayer of the *New Yorker* exposed stunning details of the rendition programme. For example: "CIA Holds Terror Suspects in Secret Prisons," Dana Priest, *Washington Post*, 2 November 2005; and: "Outsourcing Torture," Jane Mayer, *New Yorker*, 14 February 2005. Mayer's articles are largely based on on-the-record interviews. The most notable early references of the rendition programme were by Anthony Shadid in "US, Egypt Raids Caught Militants," *Boston Globe*, 7 October 2001; the *Wall Street Journal* investigation into a case involving Albania ("Cloak and Dagger: A CIA-Backed Team Used Brutal Means to Crack Terror Cell," by Andrew Higgins and Christopher Cooper, *Wall Street Journal*, 20 November 2001); and the *Washington Post* investigation into the road to 9/11 published in December 2001 (e.g. "Broad Effort Launched After '98 Attacks," by Gellman, 19 December 2001).

[17] "Mystery Man Handed over to US Troops in Karachi," Masood Anwar, *The News International*, 26 October 2001.

[18] The suspect was reportedly from Tai'z, Yemen. His location remains unknown to me.

[19] "US Behind Secret Transfer of Terror Suspects," Rajiv Chandrasekaran and Peter Finn, *Washington Post*, 11 March 2002.

[20] Sources at *Washington Post*.

[21] Transcript from *Kalla Fakta*, "The Broken Promise: Part 1", which aired on Swedish TV, 17 May 2004.

[22] Ibid.

[23] Telephone interview with Joachim Dyfvermark, 17 April 2006.

[24] "America's Gulag," Stephen Grey, *New Statesman*, 14 May 2004.

[25] See for example www.acarsonline.co.uk. I have not used such a system.

[26] Flightlogs of plane N379P; the date of the rendition is from Chandrasekaran and Petr Finn, *Washington Post*, 11 March 2002.

[27] Flightlogs of plane N379P; also see "MI5 enabled UK pair's rendition", author's report for BBC *Newsnight*, 27 March 2006.

[28] Telephone interview with Jack M., Aero Contractors, October 2004.

[29] "US Accused of 'Torture Flights,' " Stephen Grey, *The Sunday Times*, 14 November 2004.

[30] The Gulfstream V (registration N379P, then N8068V) was sold to Bayard Foreign Marketing in Portland, Oregon; the Boeing 737 (registration N313P then N4476S) was sold to Keeler and Tate Management in Reno, Nevada.

[31] I have records of this plane's movements from 22 November 2002, with a flight from Andrews Air Force Base to Frankfurt.

[32] Flightlogs of plane N313P, later renumbered N4476S.

[33] "CIA Flying Suspects to Torture?" reported by Scott Pelley, *60 Minutes*, CBS, 6 March 2005.

[34] First reported in "German's Claim of Kidnapping Brings Investigation of US Link," Don Van Natta, Jr., and Souad Mekhennet, *New York Times*, 9 January 2005.

[35] "Aboard Air CIA," by Michael Hirsh, Mark Hosenball and John Barry, with Stephen Grey in London and Stefan Theil in Berlin, *Newsweek*, 28 February 2005.

[36] Interview with the *New York Times* in January 2005. ("Bush Says Iraqis will want G.I.'s to stay to help," by Elizabeth Bumiller, David E. Sangar and Richard W. Stevenson, 27 January 2005); he later changed this to countries that "*say* they won't torture" (emphasis added). President George W. Bush, White House press conference, 17 March 2005. See also Chapter 10.

[37] I later obtained further flightlogs that confirmed the plane's leg onward to Amman and then its return flight via Athens.

[38] Interview by telephone with Maher Arar, 25 March 2005.

[39] An official US government Web site listed the names of aviation companies that had permits to land at US air bases (www.usaasa.belvoir.army.mil/CALP/CALPDec05.htm).

[40] I was beaten to publication on this one by the *Chicago Tribune* ("Italy Probes Possible CIA Role in Abduction," John Crewdson, 25 February 2005).

[41] "CIA Uses Jet, Red Sox Partner Confirms," Gordon Edes, *Boston Globe,* 21 March 2005.

[42] "Jet Is an Open Secret in Terror War," Dana Priest with Margot Williams, Julie Tate, *Washington Post*, 27 December 2004.

[43] "CIA Expanding Terror Battle Under Guise of Charter Flights, " Scott Shane, Stephen Grey and Margot Williams, *New York Times*, 31 May 2005.

[44] Ibid.

[45] Interviews with former CIA pilots, 2005-2006.

[46] Dun and Bradstreet Business Information database, accessed May 2005.

[47] Interview with former CIA pilot, 2005-2006.

[48] Email from US Embassy in Austria, 14 May 2005, from an embassy spokesperson.

[49] Interview with former senior officer, CIA directorate of operations.

[50] I tracked many trips to Venezuela: 9 November 2004 (N259SK); 13 March 2002 (N368CE); 4 March 2002, 6 December 2003, 3 January 2004 (N829MG); 3 September 2003; 4 September 2003 (N970SJ); 19 November 2002 (N982RK). These were all private charter jets, not planes we had proven were being used by the US government, so it offers no proof of a CIA operation. The first appearance of the planes was on 4 March 2002. On 5 March 2002, opposition leader Carlos Ortega signed a pact to remove (peacefully) controversial president Hugo Chavez. Another plane came in 13 March to take whoever back to JFK.

[51] "Let's Dare Call it Treason," Phil Brennan, NewsMax.com, 1 June 2005 (newsmax.com/archives/articles/2005/5/31/224326.shtml).

[52] "Why would the *Times* publish this story?" by Frederick Turner, Tech Central Station, 6 June 2005 (www.tcsdaily.com//article.aspx?id=060605B).

[53] "Shane, Grey and Williams: Are They Human?," posted by anonymous author "Demosophist" on 7 June 2005, at Anticipatory Retaliation (anticipatoryretaliation.mu.nu/archives/086071. php).

[54] See "The Public Editor: The Thinking Behind a Close Look at a CIA Operation," Byron Calame, *New York Times*, 19 June 2005.

[55] Flightlogs of N379P and N313P.

6. COVERT ACTION — THE SECRET WAR AGAINST AL QAEDA

[1] Interview with Michael Sheehan, 25 April 2006.

[2] He was a National Security Council (NSC) aide to both presidents George H. W. Bush and Clinton until his retirement from the Army in 1997; he was appointed counter-terrorism ambassador at the State Department after the embassy bombings of August 1998.

[3] Interviews with former Clinton officials, September 2001 - January 2002.

[4] Ibid., *9/11 Commission Report* (pp. 189-90) says there were fifteen flights in total, beginning 7 September, during which a "man in white" was spotted at Tarnak Farms. During another sighting, on 28 September, analysts, "determined that he was probably bin Laden."

[5] *9/11 Commission Report*, p. 221.

[6] Interview with Michael Sheehan, 25 April 2006. Sheehan had had knowledge of other surveillance assets deployed in the Balkans as part of a programme to capture wanted

Serbian war criminals; he argued they could be redeployed to Afghanistan.

7 O'Neill was chief of the FBI counterterrorism section at FBI headquarters, 1995-7, and then a director of national security and counterterrorism at the New York field office 1997-August 2001. He then became director of security at the World Trade Centre, where he died on 11 September.

8 *9/11 Commission Report*, p. 120, interviews with former Clinton officials, December 2001 - January 2002.

9 "Road to Ground Zero" series, *Sunday Times*, "Clinton's Secret War," by Stephen Grey, Jon Ungoed-Thomas, Nicholas Hellen, Gareth Walsh and Joe Lauria, 20 January 2002.

10 Interviews with former senior Clinton officials, November-December 2001.

11 Quoted in "How the CIA Lost Its Bearings in the 'Scrub' of 1995," Stephen Grey, Jon Ungoed-Thomas, Nicholas Hellen, Gareth Walsh and Joe Lauria, "Road to Ground Zero" series, *Sunday Times*, 13 January 2002.

12 Interview with Senior former Clinton official, December 2001; Berger's use of this phrase was first reported in "Broad Effort Launched After '98 Attacks," Barton Gellman, *Washington Post*, 19 December 2001.

13 Detailed in his book *A Spy for All Seasons* (New York: Scribner, 1997), pp. 349-59. Also interview with Duane "Dewey" Clarridge in Baghdad, 25 February 2004.

14 *A Spy for All Seasons*, p. 359.

15 "Foreign Policy Leads Us into an Odd Wordscape," William Safire, *New York Times*, 20 June 2004.

16 "Kidnapping or Extradition? Overseas Drug Arrests Prompt Debate," Henry Gottlieb, Associated Press, 7 April 1988.

17 "*Larry King Live*", CNN, 8 Febuary 2001.

18 *A Spy for All Seasons*, pp. 349-59.

19 "Administration Alters Assassination Ban," David B. Ottaway and Don Oberdorfer, *Washington Post*, 4 November 1989.

20 Text at www.cia.gov/cia/information/eo12333.html#2.6.

21 *A Spy for All Seasons*, p.351.

22 Interview with Duane "Dewey" Clarridge in Baghdad, 25 February 2004; also detailed in his book *A Spy for All Seasons*, pp. 334-35.

23 Association of the Bar of the City of New York & Centre for Human Rights and Global Justice, *Torture by Proxy: International and Domestic Law Applicable to Extraordinary Renditions*, Section C. (2) (New York: ABCNY & NYU School of Law, 2004), p. 31.

24 "This Court has never departed from the rule announced in Ker v. Illinois, 119 US 436, 444 , that the power of a court to try a person for crime is not impaired by the fact that he had been brought within the court's jurisdiction by reason of a 'forcible abduction,' " US Supreme Court, *Frisbie v. Collins*, 342 US 519 (1952), Decided 10 March 1952.

25 *Frisbie v. Collins*, 342 US 519 (1952).

26 Interview with Barbara Olshansky, New York, 18 January 2005.

27 Text of PDD-39 available at www.fas.org/irp/offdocs/pdd39.htm.

28 *The 9/11 Commission Report*, Staff Statement No.5, p. 2, 23 March 2004, (emphasis added).

29 A number of the suspects found guilty of the WTC bombing in 1993 were followers of Sheikh Omar Abdul Rahman, an Egyptian cleric living and preaching in New York and in New Jersey. Abdul Rahman had previously been the spiritual leader of the "Arab-Afghans," Arabs who had joined the mujahideen fight against the Soviets. Mahmud Abouhalima, a principal actor in the WTC attack, was an Egyptian member of Gama'al-Islamiyya. Allegedly trained in Afghanistan and Pakistan with the mujahideen, he also raised money for the Afghan fighters while living in Brooklyn, NY. In the Philippines, Ramzi Youssef,

probably the architect of the WTC attack, had been involved in recruiting volunteers to fight with the mujahideen.

30 Interview with then congressman Porter Goss, Washington, DC, 14 December 2001.

31 Interview with Jim Woolsey, 10 December 2001.

32 Interview with former senior CIA officers.

33 Interview by author and Richard Miniter with Richard Shelby, December 2001. Figures from *9/11 Commission Report*, page 90.

34 Interview with Michael Scheuer, 14 March 2006.

35 The term "extraordinary rendition" was wrongly ascribed to the agency, including by me. As described, it was previously used almost interchangeably with the simple term "rendition". Since 9/11, the term "extraordinary rendition" has been subject to multiple definitions.

36 Interview by author for *File on Four*, BBC Radio 4, 8 February 2005; "A Fine Rendition," by Michael Scheuer, *New York Times*, 11 March 2005.

37 Interview on 13 March 2006, with former Ambassador Edward S. Walker, Jr., US ambassador to Egypt, 1994-7. (Hereafter, Walker interview.) He could not recall the date of his first briefing on the rendition programme.

38 The Terrorism Knowledge Base at www.tkb.org.

39 Walker interview.

40 "Outsourcing Torture" Jane Mayer, *The New Yorker*, 14 February 2005.

41 Presidential Decision Directive, PDD-39, June 1995; see: *9/11 Commission Report*, Staff Statement No. 5, p. 2 (www.9-11commission.gov/staff_statements/staff_statement_5.pdf).

42 *File on Four*, BBC Radio 4, 8 February 2005. Interview with Michael Scheuer, 21 January 2005.

43 Ibid.

44 Walker interview.

45 Walker interview. El-Alfi was interior minister, 1993-7.

46 Walker interview.

47 Interviews with senior Italian security source, Milan, May 2005. Italian authorities were informed of the operation.

48 "The CIA's Secret Army," by Douglas Waller, *Time*, 26 January 2003; and "Inside the CIA's Covert Forces," Douglas Waller, *Time*, 10 December 2001.

49 *9/11 Commission Report*, Staff Statement No.5, p. 2.

50 *9/11 Commission Report*, p. 173.

51 "Cloak and Dagger", Higgins and Cooper.

52 Ibid.; and "US, Egypt Raids Caught Militants," Anthony Shadid, *Boston Globe*, 7 October 2001.

53 Interviews in Cairo, 26 September to 8 October, 2003; and "Cloak and Dagger," by Higgins and Cooper; records of the trial examined at Egyptian Organisation for Human Rights.

54 Montasser al-Zayat, *Ayman al-Zawahiri kama Araftoh* (Ayman al-Zawahiri As I Knew Him), (Cairo: Dar al-Mahroussa; 2002), p. 135.

55 Oral testimony before 9/11 Commission, Wednesday, 24 March 2004.

56 Statement of Director of Central Intelligence George J. Tenet before the Senate Select Committee on Intelligence (SSCI), "The Worldwide Threat in 2000: Global Realities of Our National Security" (2 February 2000).

57 US State Department, "Patterns of Global Terrorism," 1998 and 1999 reports; FBI Report, "Terrorism in the United States, 1999," p. 52 (www.fbi.gov/publications/terror/terror99.pdf).

58 "Two Yemenis Held Abroad Are to Face Trial in a US Court on Conspiracy Charges," Eric Lichtblau, *New York Times*, 17 November 2003.

59 "Death Toll Rises in Blast That Tore into US Destroyer," Jamie McIntyre, Kelly Wallace, Gary

Tuchman, and Carl Rochelle, CNN.com, 13 October 2000.

60 *9/11 Commission Report*, p. 214.

61 US airspace was locked down to all but official and military planes — and to departing members of Osama bin Laden's family.

62 "Time to Think About Torture," Jonathan Alter, *Newsweek*, 5 November 2001.

63 "Torture Seeps Into Discussion By News Media," by Jim Rutenberg, *New York Times*, 5 November 2001.

64 Mark Bowden, "The Dark Art of Interrogation", *Atlantic Monthly*, Oct. 2003

65 "Is There a Torturous Road to Justice?", Alan Dershowitz, *Los Angeles Times*, 8 November 2001.

66 Dershowitz interview with Wolf Blitzer, CNN, 4 March 2003.

67 Interviews with former CIA officials. The date of the memorandum was reported first in Shaun Waterman, "Ex-CIA Lawyer Calls for Law on Rendition," United Press International, 8 March 2005.

68 "Rule Change Lets CIA Freely Send Suspects Abroad to Jails," Douglas Jehl and David Johnston, *New York Times*, 6 March 2005.

69 "Against Rendition," Reuel Marc Gerecht, *The Weekly Standard*, 16 May 2005.

70 Described in detail in Gary Berntsen's *Jawbreaker*.

71 "The agency initially had few interrogators and no facilities to house the top detainees." James Risen, David Johnston, and Neil A. Lewis reported in "Harsh C.I.A. Methods Cited in Top Qaeda Interrogations," *New York Times*, 13 May 2004. The General Accounting Office published a report in January 2002 warning, "Lack of staff with foreign language skills has weakened the fight against international terrorism and drug trafficking and resulted in less effective representation of US interests overseas" — "Foreign Language Report to Congressional Requesters," GAO-02,375, January 2002. One CIA source remarked to Reuel Gerecht that the standard of living in the Middle East for an undercover agent put a lot of people off: "Operations that include diarrhea as a way of life don't happen". Quoted from "The Counterterrorist Myth," by Reuel Marc Gerecht, *Atlantic Monthly*, July/August 2001.

72 Interviews with former case officers and former senior officials, CIA directorate of operations; with CIA contractor; with senior serving US government official — all 2005/6.

73 Interview with Chris Mackey, 12 January 2005, by the author for BBC radio. His book with Greg Miller, *The Interrogators: Inside the Secret War Against Al Qaeda* (Boston: Little, Brown, 2004) refers on page 221 to three options for the prisoners at Bagram: repatriation, release, or transfer to Guantánamo Bay. (Mackey uses a pseudonym.)

74 Michael Scheuer, 21 January 2005.

7. THE ICE MAN

1 The autopsy was performed five days later — 9 November 2003, by the US military, according to an account in "A Deadly Interrogation," Jane Mayer, *New Yorker*, 14 November 2005. And his body was kept by the US military until February 2004, and then released to the International Committee of the Red Cross (ICRC), according to Human Rights First and the *Guardian* copy of the autopsy in authors's file.

2 Photographs were first shown in CBS's *60 Minutes II*, 28 April 2004: "Abuse of Iraqi POWs By GIs Probed" (www.cbsnews.com/stories/2004/04/27/60II/main614063.shtml). Other articles: "Torture At Abu Ghraib," Seymour Hersh, *New Yorker*, 10 May 2004; "The Struggle for Iraq: Treatment of Prisoners; G.I.'s Are Accused of Abusing Iraqi Captives," *New York Times*, 29 April 2004; "Resign, Rumsfeld," accompanied by one of the Abu Ghraib torture photographs, was the front page of *The Economist* on 8 May 2004; "Blair 'Appalled' by Iraq

Prison Torture," *The Guardian*, 30 April 2004.

[3] Transcript of President Bush's interview with Alhurra Television, 5 May 2004; available at www.whitehouse.gov.

[4] "Article 15-6 Investigation of the 800 Military Police Brigade, Part One (Detainee Abuse) Findings, Section 6 (a) to (m) and Section 8 (a) to (h)," by US Army Major General Antonio M. Taguba. Hereafter, *Taguba Report*.

[5] As revealed at the court-martial hearings. A CIA official had insisted to the *New York Times* that abuse of prisoners at Abu Ghraib was "not something to the best of our knowledge my agency has any involvement in." The report continued: "Altogether, the official said, the agency was involved in the interrogation of no more than two dozen individuals at Abu Ghraib between September and December." Quoted in: "Army Punishes 7 With Reprimands For Prison Abuse," Tom Shanker and Dexter Filkins, *New York Times*, 4 May 2004.

[6] *Larry King Live*, CNN, 3 February 2005.

[7] From transcript of interview for *Charlie Rose*, 17 February 2006 (released on www. defenselink.mil).

[8] Pentagon operational update briefing, 4 May 2004; available at www.defense link.mil.

[9] *Taguba Report*, Section 10.

[10] "AR 15-6 Investigation of the Abu Ghraib Detention Facility and 205 MI Brigade," by Major General George R. Fay, p. 87 (www4.army.mil/ocpa/reports/ar15-6/AR15-6.pdf). Hereafter, *Fay Report*.

[11] See "Who Should We Believe?" Stephen Grey, *New Statesman*, 10 May 2004.

[12] Clive Stafford Smith, from testimony collected from his clients in Guantánamo, identified a flight on 20 September 2004 that took fourteen prisoners from Afghanistan to Cuba. Among these were: Adel Hamlily, "Sanad," Hassan bin Attash, Abduh Ali Shaqawi, Binyam Mohamed, Saifulla Paracha, and Abdulsalam al-Hela. Five were unidentified. (E-Mail to author from Stafford Smith, 13 February 2006.)

[13] Testimony of Secretary Rumsfeld to the Senate Armed Services Committee on 7 May 2004. "We've released 31,000 out of 43,000 that were detained" (www.defenselink.mil/speeches/2004/sp20040507-secdef0421.html). On 28 November 2005, over 14,000 detainees were still in custody in Iraq, according to figures released on the military's "Operation Iraqi Freedom" Web site (www.mnf-iraq.com/TF134/Numbers.htm).

[14] Task Force 121 combined CIA, Army Delta Force, and Navy SEALS troops and was the result of a merger between TF 5, a Special Forces unit hunting Osama bin Laden in Afghanistan, and TF 20, an Iraq-based Special Forces unit hunting Saddam Hussein. According to "In Secret Unit's Black Room," Eric Schmitt and Carolyn Marshall, *New York Times*, 19 March 2006, it was renamed TF 6-26, then TF 145.

[15] Interview with former Brigadier General (Army Reserve) Janis Karpinski, interviewed on 5 August 2005, for *The Torture Question*, by FRONTLINE, Public Broadcasting Service, and also with a British officer attached to US intelligence in Baghdad, interviewed late 2005.

[16] As described in the *Taguba Reprort*.

[17] Telephone interview with Karpinski, 31 August 2005.

[18] Flightlogs of N379P and N313P.

[19] "The Death of an Iraqi Prisoner," reported by John McChesney, *All Things Considered*, NPR, 27 October 2005.

[20] "Navy SEAL Officer Found Not Guilty In Iraqi Detainee Beating Death" William J. Brown, All Headline News wire agency, 28 May 2005 (available at www.allheadlinenews.com).

[21] Account of al-Jamadi's interrogation from "Death of an Iraqi Prisoner," NPR.

[22] Swanner is not undercover, according to Mayer, 14 November 2005.

[23] Ibid.

[24] "Kenner told CIA investigators, 'the prisoner did not appear to be in distress. He was walking fine, and his speech was normal.' From Ibid.

[25] "Iraqi Died While Hanging by His Wrists," by Seth Hettena, *Associated Press*, 18 February 2005.

[26] "A Deadly Interrogation", Mayer.

[27] Ibid., and in "Iraqi Died While Hanging by His Wrists," Hettena.

[28] "A Deadly Interrogation," Mayer.

[29] Telephone interview with Department of Justice spokeswoman, 26 July 2006.

[30] Donald Rumsfeld told a Pentagon press conference on 4 May 2004, that "the actions of the soldiers in those photographs are totally unacceptable and un-American" and promised that "as the senior official responsible for this department, I intend to take any and all actions as may be needed to find out what happened and to see that appropriate steps are taken." (Defense Department operational update briefing, Tuesday 4 May 2004.)

[31] The existence of the first memo was first reported in "Memo Offered Justification for Use of Torture," Dana Priest and R. Jeffrey Smith, *Washington Post*, 8 June 2004.

[32] The Third Geneva Convention on Prisoners of War covers POWs and defines the limits on interrogation in Articles 17 and 99. Afghan citizens, if not judged to be combatants in international armed conflict, were covered by the Fourth Geneva Convention on the protection of civilians in time of war, which defined the ban on coercive treatment in Article 31.

[33] "Memorandum for the President from Alberto R. Gonzales, re: Decision re: application of the Geneva convention on prisoners of war to the conflict with al Qaeda and the Taliban," 25 January 2002. In *The Torture Papers*, Karen Greenberg and Joshua Dratel (eds), (Cambridge University Press, 2005), p. 118.

[34] "Memorandum from George Bush to the Vice President et al., re: Humane treatment of Al Qaeda and Taliban detainees," 7 February 2002. In Ibid., p. 134.

[35] First reported in "Memo Offered Justification for Use of Torture," Dana Priest and R. Jeffrey Smith, *Washington Post*, 8 June 2004.

[36] Footnote 8 of memorandum from Daniel Levin, assistant attorney general, to James Comey, deputy attorney general, titled "Legal Standards Applicable under 18 USC 2340-2340A," 30 December 2004, states: "While we have identified various disagreements with the August 2002 Memorandum, we have reviewed this Office's prior opinions addressing issues involving the treatment of detainees and do not believe that any of their conclusions would be different under the standards set forth in this memorandum."(Full text available at www.usdoj.gov/olc/dagmemo.pdf.)

[37] "Memorandum for the Chairman of the Joint Chiefs of Staff from Donald Rumsfeld, Subject: Status of the Taliban and Al Qaeda", 19 January 2002. *Torture Papers*, p.80.

[38] Fact Sheet, Status of Detainees at Guantánamo, Office of the Press Secretary, The White House, 7 Febrary 2002 (available at www.whitehouse.gov).

[39] As outlined in Appendix H of the US Army's Field Manual 34-52, titled "Intelligence Interrogation," and issued in May 1987, authorised techniques include such methods as those named Fear Up (Harsh), Fear Up (Mild), Pride and Ego Up, Futility Technique, and Rapid Fire. During Fear Up (Harsh), for example, "the interrogator behaves in an overpowering manner with a loud and threatening voice. The interrogator may even feel the need to throw objects across the room to heighten the source's implanted feelings of fear" (http://www.globalsecurity.org/intell/library/policy/army/fm/fm34-52/app-h.htm).

[40] Ranging from "Incentive" and "Yelling at detainee" to "20-hour interrogations," "forced grooming (e.g. shaving)," "removal of clothing," and "inducing stress by use of detainee's fears (e.g. with dogs)," *Torture Papers*, p. 1239.

[41] "Memorandum from Secretary of Defense Rumsfeld to the General Counsel of the

Department of Defense," 15 January 2003. The provision for inducing stress were limited to use of a female interrogator, and an allowance for "stress positions for a maximum of four hours" was rescinded. *Torture Papers*, p. 238.

42 Quoted in "The Bagram File — Revisiting the Case," Tim Golden, *New York Times*, 13 February 2006.

43 Ibid.

44 Report by Vice Admiral Albert T. Church III into Department of Defense (DoD) interrogation operations, unclassified executive summary, 2 March 2005, p. 7. There is more here on the "migration" of approved techniques; however, the report insists that no detainee deaths can be linked to approved techniques. (www.defenselink.mil/news/ Mar2005/d20050310exe.pdf).

45 From annex (titled "Status of Legal Discussions re Application of Geneva Conventions to Taliban and Al Qaeda") attached to memo from William H. Taft IV, a legal adviser to the State Department, to the Counsel to the President (Alberto Gonzales), dated 2 February 2002. (*The Torture Papers*, p. 133). Moreover, the CIA was not subject to the Uniform Code of Military Justice (UCMJ) used to prosecute such abuses. In his confirmation hearing as attorney general on 6 January 2005, Gonzales confirmed that "the UCMJ, for example, would be — would be a limitation on military forces that may not be applicable — that would be not be applicable to the CIA."

46 Reported in Mayer "A Deadly Interrogation".

47 "A list of 10 techniques authorised early in 2002 for use against terror suspects included one known as waterboarding, and went well beyond those authorized by the military for use on prisoners of war," reported Douglas Jehl in "Report Warned CIA on Tactics In Interrogation," *New York Times*, 9 November 2005.

48 Mayer, "A Deadly Interrogation".

49 Telephone interview with Brigadier General Janis Karpinski, 31 August 2004; interviews in Iraq with senior US military and other coalition officers stationed in Baghdad, summer 2004.

50 "A Tortured Debate," Michael Hirsh, John Barry, and Daniel Klaidman, *Newsweek*, 21 June 2004.

51 For example, see "Harsh CIA Methods Cited in Top Qaeda Interrogations," James Risen, David Johnston, and Neil A. Lewis, *New York Times*, 13 May 2004.

52 Memorandum to Commander Joint Task Force 170, titled "Legal Brief on Proposed Counter-Resistance Strategies," Lieutenant Colonel Diane E. Beaver, 11 October 2002. (Reproduced in *The Torture Papers*, p. 229-35.)

53 Among those who came forward was Chris Mackey, who had worked in Bagram prison, and described his experiences in *The Interrogator's War* (Little, Brown, 2004); see also Erik Saar (a Military Intelligence officer) and Viveca Novak's book, *Inside the Wire: A Military Intelligence Soldier's Eyewitness Account of Life at Guantánamo Bay* (New York: Penguin Press, 2005).

54 The rulings were made in *Rasul et al. v. Bush et al.* and *Hamdi v. Rumsfeld*. Detailed in "Justices Back Detainee Access to US Courts; President's Powers Are Limited," Charles Lane, *Washington Post*, 29 June 2004.

55 Interview with Clive Stafford Smith, who represented many prisoners at Guantánamo. He said this was the *main effect* of the ruling.

56 At Guantánamo, on 20 September 2004, Habib's case was heard by a Combatant Status Review Tribunal convened by the US military. He was determined by the tribunal to be an enemy combatant as "a member or affiliated with Al Qaeda forces." According to a summary of the hearing, declassified and released under the Freedom of Information Act to the Associated Press, the tribunal was told he admitted, among other things, to training

the 11 September hijackers in martial arts. Habib declined to appear at the hearings but, through a representative, declared that all his confessions had been obtained under torture.

8. THE SPECIAL RELATIONSHIP — OUR MAN IN TASHKENT

1   Interview with Craig Murray, 9 January 2006.
2   James Bamford, in his account of the National Security Agency, *Body of Secrets* (New York: Anchor Books, 2002), describes how the United Kingdom-USA (UKUSA) Communications Intelligence Agreement signed on 5 March 1946, by the United States with Britain, Canada, Australia and New Zealand divided the world into spheres of interest, with signal intelligence pooled (pp. 40, 394). Other agreements, defined by a series of classified exchanged letters and memoranda, define broader intelligence cooperation between the UK and US. According to both British and US security sources interviewed by the author, a key component of these agreements is the so-called "third party rule," whereby intelligence received from a partner cannot under any circumstances be disclosed, without approval of the partner, to any third party.
3   Forty-nine flights into Tashkent, per flightlogs of N2189M, N8183J, N379P, and N313P.
4   "Unfortunately," Karimov continued, "the British were never able to make any progress towards Central Asia, and their efforts to do so met with some very great historic defeats." Quoted in *Murder in Samarkand*, Craig Murray (London: Mainstream, 2006),Chap. 4.
5   Agency operatives trained for the operation in San Antonio, Texas. Interview with former FBI agent Jack Cloonan, 19 April 2006.
6   Described in "Clinton's Secret War," *Sunday Times*, 20 January 2002.
7   Described in *Jawbreaker*, by Berntsen and Pezzullo, and *First In*, by Schroen, pp. 73-8; and *Bush at War*, Woodward, pp. 141-2.
8   In "Crackdown Muddies US-Uzbek Relations," *Washington Post*, 4 June 2005, Ann Scott Tyson and Robin Wright quoted Pentagon spokesman Bryan Whitman as saying: "Access to this airfield is undeniably critical in supporting our combat operations" as well as humanitarian deliveries. Whitman "said the United States has paid $15 million to Uzbek authorities for use of the airfield since 2001." Official USAID figures, quoted in "US Overseas Loans and Grants, Obligations and Loan Authorizations" (also known as the "Greenbook" and available at: qesdb.cdie.org/gbk/index.html), show that in 2001 Uzbekistan received a total of $62.3 million in economic and military aid, rising to $167.3 million in 2002, $75 million in 2003, and $42.3 million in 2004. A further payment of $23 million in base-leasing fees was frozen in October 2005, as described below.
9   Interview with Craig Murray, 9 January 2006; also quoted in *Murder in Samarkand*.
10   Spelled differently by Murray as "Khuderbegainoy" in his book.
11   "Uzbekistan: Alleged Torture Victim Sentenced to Death," *Human Rights Watch Report*, 4 December 2002.
12   Interview with Craig Murray, 9 January 2006.
13   "Diplomatic Service Appointments," *The Times*, 26 April 2002.
14   "President Karimov Wins Landslide Election Victory," BBC news monitoring service translation of Uzbek Television, 11 January 2000.
15   Quoted in "Uzbekistan Shaken by Unrest, Violence and Uncertainty," by C. J. Chivers, *New York Times*, 16 May 2005.
16   "Base Motives," Michael Andersen, *The Spectator*, 26 May 2005.
17   Quoted in report by Amnesty International, "Uzbekistan: Appeal Cases," published 18 November 2003.

[18] While falling short of designating Hizb-ut-Tahrir a terrorist organisation, the US State Department said the group's European headquarters, for example, "transmits a hateful, anti-Semitic and anti-American call for the overthrow, albeit nonviolent, of existing governments and the reestablishment of a single Islamist theocracy." (Testimony of Daniel Fried, assistant secretary for European Affairs, to the subcommittee on European Affairs of the Senate Foreign Relations Committee, 5 April 2006.)

[19] "Uzbek Mother Who Publicised 'Boiling' Torture of Son Gets Hard Labour," Nick Paton Walsh, *The Guardian*, 13 February 2004.

[20] Letter of findings to Mr. Alistair Walker, an official at the Foreign and Commonwealth Office (FCO), from Dr. Peter Vanezis OBE, 25 November 2002.

[21] US Ambassador John Herbst, speaking at the Opening of Freedom House in Tashkent, 17 October 2002. (Transcript provided by the US Embassy, Tashkent.)

[22] This remark was made by local human rights campaigner Talib Jakubov to BBC reporter Sanchia Berg in Tashkent on 17 October 2002, quoted on *The Today Programme*, BBC Radio 4, 11 November 2003.

[23] Craig Murray's speech at Freedom House opening, 17 October 2002.

[24] Letter from "FCO official" to Craig Murray, 15 October 2002. All correspondence referred to here and below was seen by the author.

[25] E-Mail from "FCO official", 16 October 2002.

[26] Letter from Craig Murray to "FCO official", 17 October 2002.

[27] Letter from "FCO official" to Craig Murray, 17 October 2002.

[28] Telegram (TELNO 285) from Jack Straw to Tashkent Embassy, "Reaction to Human Rights Speech," dated 25 October 2002.

[29] Murray's later July 2004 telegram wrongly stated that Moran met the CIA chief of station, a meeting that was denied by the CIA to *The New York Times*. In *Murder in Samarkand*, Murray wrote that with Moran then back in the UK, he had misrecollected whom she had met with; he was later informed it had been a US embassy political officer.

[30] "FCO official" memo to FCO legal adviser, 13 March 2003.

[31] Interview with Craig Murray, 9 January 2006.

[32] Later appointed Uzbekistan's prime minister in December 2003.

[33] Craig Murray's speech to the Royal Institute of International Affairs at Chatham House, London, 8 November 2004.

[34] Open Letter of 2 January 2006, Craig Murray to Brian Barber, weblog of Sir Brain Barder, a former UK diplomat (www.barder.com/ephems/2006/01/01/torture-and-the-diplomats-role/).

[35] Source: Letter from "FCO official" re "British Embassy Tashkent," 6 August 2003.

[36] E-Mail from "FCO official" to unspecified recipient, 7 August 2003.

[37] E-Mail from "FCO official" London, 7 August 2003.

[38] E-mail from "FCO official" 7 August 2003.

[39] Record of 21 August 2003, meeting dated 27 August 2003.

[40] Interview with Craig Murray, 9 January 2006.

[41] Statement by "FCO official" at the Tashkent embassy, 10 September 2003, describing what Murray told staff on his return to the embassy.

[42] Letter to Craig Murray from "FCO official" 28 August 2003.

[43] James McGrory to *The Times*, 7 September 2003 (238.pdf).

[44] Edward Chaplin memo, 2 December 2003.

[45] Interview with Craig Murray, 9 January 2006.

[46] E-Mail and then letter from "FCO official", 13 October 2004, and 15 October 2004.

[47] "Diplomat in Torture Claims to Sue Straw," *Scottish Daily Record*, 16 February 16 2005.

[48] Testimony of Galima Bukharbaeva to the Commission on Security and Co-Operation in

Europe, on the Andijan massacre (available at www.csce.gov).

49 State Department spokesman, Richard Boucher, said on 16 May 2005 the US was "deeply disturbed by the reports that the Uzbek authorities fired on demonstrators last Friday. We certainly condemn the indiscriminate use of force against unarmed civilians and deeply regret any loss of life." (Transcript of State Department daily press briefing.) A US State Department profile of Uzbekistan released in July 2005 on the department's website (www. state.gov) stated "in June 2005, Karimov refused US demands for a formal investigation of the Andijan massacre, exacerbating the divide between the two nations."

50 An Associated Press report on 5 October 2005 reported: "In a move meant to send a message to Uzbekistan, the Senate voted Wednesday [30 September] to block the payment of $23 million for past use of an air base that the Uzbek government recently said will no longer host US aircraft and troops." The report quoted Senator John McCain, R-Arizona, as telling the Senate: "Paying our bills is important. But more important is America's standing for itself, avoiding the misimpression that we overlook massacres and avoiding cash transfers to the treasury of a dictator." A State Department fact sheet dated 17 August 2005, states that "funding for two components of security assistance, Foreign Military Financing (FMF) and International Military Education and Training (IMET), was cut off in 2004 and 2005, and remain so, due to Uzbekistan's failure to meet its framework commitments to human rights and democratization." But the outstanding bill for the K2 base was eventually paid by the United States.

51 See "Uzbekistan's Closure of the Airbase at Karshi-Khanabad: Context and Implications," Congressional Research Service report to Congress (www.opencrs.com/rpts/RS22295_20051007.pdf).

52 Steve Crawshaw, statement to the author, 11 April 2004.

9. THE ITALIAN JOB

1 Nabila was born in Egypt on 25 June 1968.

2 Born in early 1996, while Nasr sought asylum in Munich, as reported in "Wife Was Left Behind With the Children" Tom Hundley and John Crewdson, *Chicago Tribune*, 3 July 2005.

3 From intercepted conversation between Abu Omar's wife, Nabila Ghali, and his family in Egypt. Official English translation of the Italian warrant for the arrest of Monica Adler et al. n. 10838/05 R.G.N.R, including attached police report, issued by Judge Chiara Nobili (hereafter referred to as *Italian first warrant*) p. 35, 22 June 2005.

4 *Italian first warrant*, p. 37.

5 According to Milan prosecution sources, the anti-terrorism branch of the Carabinieri has a special office in via Lamarmora; DIGOS (*Divisione Investigazioni Generali e Operazioni Speciali*) has a tapping center in via Fatebenefratelli.

6 Interview with Milan prosecution source, May 2005.

7 As described later in the chapter, Roberts Castelli, then justice minister, denounced Armando Spataro as a "left-wing militant" and declared: "The interests of the state are on the line." See "Italian Resists Pressure on CIA case", by Frances D'Emilio, Associated Press, 2 March 2006.

8 Interview with Armando Spataro, 6 March 2006.

9 Email from Armando Spataro, dated 11 April 2006.

10 Spataro, 6 March 2006.

11 DIGOS deals with terrorism and other serious crime.

12 *Italian first warrant*, pp. 24-5.

[13] Ibid., p. 4.

[14] Jeffrey Castelli was named as a former CIA station chief under investigation for his potential role in the Milan kidnapping in an article by Carlo Bonini, entitled "The Chief of American 007s in Italy behind the Kidnapping of Abu Omar," *La Repubblica*, 8 June 2006, as well as other Italian press reports. He was also named in public evidence to the European Parliament by Armando Spataro on 23 February 2006. An arrest warrant for him was issued on 3 July 2006. Another CIA officer involved in distributing the message, also passed to Italian intelligence agencies, was Ralph Russomando, according to Armando Spataro in an interview, 4 May 2006.

[15] Central Directorate of Preventative Policing, headquarters in Rome of Italy's anti-terrorist police.

[16] Italian first warrant, p. 5.

[17] "5 More Arrested in Spain for Bombings," by Michael Martinez, *Chicago Tribune*, 19 March 2004: and "Italy Arrests Two as Terrorist Suspects," by Al Baker, *New York Times*, 9 June 2004.

[18] Italian first warrant p. 66. According to prosecution sources he was born 1 October 1958 in Gharbia, Egypt.

[19] On 31 March 2003, Abu Omar's successor as leader of the militant community in Milan, Radi Abd el-Samie Abu el-Yazid el-Ayashi, alias Mera'i, was jailed after confessing, according to the Italian press, to having recruited mujahiddeen for the Iraq war but "only to fight against the American soldiers [and] not to make terrorist attacks against the civilians." (Source: Email from Paolo Biondani, journalist, *Corriere della Sera*, 11 April 2006.) According to prosecution documents (author's file) dated 9 December 2005, both Mera'i and Abu Omar were under investigation for the "formation of an Islamic army" and the attempted reorganisation of Al Qaeda cells in continental Europe after important cells in Italy and Germany had been broken up. Police operations began on 31 March 2003, when a number of alleged terrorists where arrested; the prosecution contended that those Islamic militants were responsible for the procurement of forged papers, fund-raising for jihad, and the recruitment of "brothers" to be sent to Iraq to fight in fledgling guerilla warfare waged by the insurgency. Abu Omar, it was alleged, was a key personality in this operation, and was in contact with other groups ready for jihad, including associates of Abu Musab al-Zarqawi. A prosecutor's warrant describes how wiretaps on mobile phones belonging to Islamic radicals in Parma had picked up traffic with several telephone numbers belonging to a commercial satellite telephone network, Thuraya, and operating from a training camp for Islamic militants in Iraq belonging to al-Zarqawi's network. In the summer of 2002 the Parma-based radicals provided hospitality to Abu Omar when he visited Parma to consider whether to take a job at the local mosque, after more moderate members at Milan's Via Quaranta mosque, where he presided, had urged him to step down. Although his voice was amply recorded, Abu Omar was never questioned on his involvement, as he had disappeared a month and a half before the start of the operation that led to the arrest and imprisonment of his associates. Police found the same Thuraya satellite numbers of al-Zaqarwi's network had been written in a notebook belonging to Omar's successor at the Milan mosque, el-Ayashi.

[20] Meeting described in an e-mail from Armando Spataro, 11 April 2006. Elbadry's statement is transcribed in the *Italian first warrant*, pp. 7-9.

[21] "Madrid Suspect Arrested in Italy," Keith B. Richburg, *Washington Post*, 9 June 2004.

[22] The operation had targeted links between Milan militants and Gama'a al-Islamiyya

[23] Italian police sources; interview with Yasser al-Sirri, London, 14 April 2006, interview with the former FBI agent, Jack Cloonan, New York, 19 April 2006.

[24] *Italian first warrant*, p. 60. Expanded and explained by Spataro, 6 March 2006.

25 "During the First Kidnap in 1995 the Hostage Was Killed in Egypt," *Corriere Della Sera*, 2 July 2005.

26 Italian first warrant p. 26.

27 Interview with Michael Scheuer, 14 March 2006.

28 DIGOS report, 19 July 2004; cited in Italian first warrant, p.60.

29 Profile of Lady and reference to bugging devices in report by Guido Olimpio, "Chi ha coperto Bob, 007 senza limiti?" *Corriere della Serra*, 24 June 2005. Confirmed by interviews with Italian police sources.

30 Interview with Milan police source, 2005.

31 Interviews with Milan police sources, 2005-2006.

32 Interview with Milan police source, 2006.

33 Interview with Armando Spataro, 6 March 2006.

34 E-mail from Armando Spataro, 11 April 2006.

35 Interview with Armando Spataro, 6 March 2006.

36 Only 3 July 2006, a warrant was issued for Russomando's arrest.

37 Nineteen were named in the Italian first warrant; of whom thirteen were charged with the alleged kidnapping. A second warrant issued on 20 July 2005, charged the remaining six. A third warrant, issued on 27 September 2005, charged a further three.

38 *Italian first warrant*, p. 103. Barbara was not accused by the Italians of involvement in any crime or wrongdoing.

39 *Italian first warrant*, p.104.

40 The *Italian first warrant* also notes: "An additional element is that one of the telephone subscriptions implicated most in the operations, transfers, and communication exchanges related to the kidnapping was officially assigned to a CIA agent appointed to the American Consulate in Milan: for his part, as pointed out before, Robert Seldon Lady, was an intelligence attaché to the American Consulate in Milan, operating as CIA superintendent" (p. 23). The CIA agent was not accused of doing anything wrong.

41 When he first disappeared, even the fact of his kidnapping was treated as unproven; for example, "Imam disappears from Milan," *Corriere della Sera*, 1 March 2003, reported that there was no concrete proof of his abduction, but did mention there were accusations from the Islamic community it might be the Egyptian secret service or even the Americans who were responsible.

42 Flightlogs of N379P.

43 Coverage included "Investigation in Milan into Missing Islamic Radicals," Paolo Biondini, Guido Olimpio, *Corriere Della Sera*, 2 December 2004. The article suggested Abu Omar's disappearance might have been a rendition, and details of Abu Omar's reappearance, phone calls, and disappearance again are reported, along with his accusations of US involvement. "The missing Islamists: Covert Interrogations in a US Base in Italy," Paolo Biondani and Guido Olimpio, *Corriere della Sera*, 3 December 2004, said intercepts convinced the investigators of the existence of a covert operation with "Italian and American secret agents."

44 Czaska was a registered staff member at the US consulate in Milan, according to prosecution sources. She was not charged with any offence.

45 The names "Maura" and "Torya" were not known to the Italian investigation; the "Sabrina" was assumed to be Sabrina de Souza, registered as a second secretary at the US Embassy in Rome but based in Milan. She was named but not charged in the first Italian warrant.

46 Interview with Armando Spataro, 25 January 2005, Milan.

47 "US Agents 'Kidnapped Militant' for Torture in Egypt," Stephen Grey, *Sunday Times*, 6 February 2005, was followed by "CIA Under Investigation in Italy," Carlo Bonini, Giuseppe D'Avanzo and Ferruccio Sansa, *Corriere della Sera*, 14 February 2005.

[48] Duffin spent €7,591.00, Adler €6,540.00. Totaling €14,131, or £9,950. Source: Italian first warrant, pp. 135-6. Duffin and Adler's cover, and that of the other alleged kidnappers named in this chapter, was blown with the issuing of the Italian first warrant and the publication of their names in evidence submitted to the European Parliament and on numerous Internet sites.

[49] *Italian first warrant*, p. 16.

[50] From 23 March to 22 June, 2005.

[51] As mentioned in Chapter 5, I was "scooped" on the publication of this story by the *Chicago Tribune* on 25 February, 2005.

[52] According to Georg Nolte, a law professor of the University of Munich (in an interview on 20 July 2006), all US personnel stationed in Germany were obligated to respect German laws, subject to certain exceptions. These laws included the crime of kidnapping. In addition, Article 2.2 together with Article 104 of the German constitution requires that no one should be deprived of their liberty except by a lawful arrest warrant and requires the German government to take all necessary stepts to ensure this right is not violated.

[53] Another vital piece of evidence found at the villa were flight bookings for a Zurich to Cairo round-trip (24 February 2003 to 7 March 2003), according to prosecution sources. This appeared to confirm that Robert Lady stayed in Egypt for two weeks. In her report, Judge Chiara Nobili said the cellphone records showed, inaccurately, that Lady was in Egypt from 22 February to 15 March, noting that those were likely the first days Omar was being tortured during interrogations.

[54] *Italian first warrant*, p. 208.

[55] This detail was first published by the *Washington Post* on 25 June, 2005: "Italy Seeks Arrest of 13 in Alleged Rendition," by Craig Whitlock and Dafna Linzer; research by Julie Tate.

[56] "Italy Knew about Plan to Grab Suspect," Dana Priest, *Washington Post*, 30 June 2005.

[57] "The Triangle of Anger," by Yosri Fouda, first shown on Al Jazeera TV in 5 January 2006.

[58] "Intelligence Source Alleges Initial Italian Involvement in Milan Kidnapping," BBC news monitoring service, translation of *La Stampa* newspaper Website, 3 July 2006, as cited above.

[59] D'Emilio, 2 March 2006, as cited above.

10. THE TORTURE LIE — RENDITION AND THE LAW

[1] Transcript available at www.whitehouse.gov/news/releases/2005/04/20050428-9.html.

[2] Bush Says Iraqis Will Want G.I.'s to Stay to Help," Elisabeth Bumiller; David E. Sanger, and Richard W. Stevenson, *New York Times*, 28 January 2005.

[3] Many of the legal references here are drawn from Katherine Hawkins, "The Promises of Torturers: Diplomatic Assurances and the Legality of 'Rendition," *Georgetown Immigration Law Journal*, vol. 20, issue 2 (winter 2006) p. 213.

[4] There were over twenty thousand anti-Bolshevik partisans who sided with Hitler in order to oppose Stalin. The British invited the Cossack officers to a "conference," handed them over to the USSR, then sent on the women and children (Applebaum, *Gulag*, p. 395).

[5] Source: Red Cross comments of 28 April 2006. The ICRC continued: "The person must be given the opportunity to make representations to the said body in this regard and should be granted the opportunity to appeal the decision of this body. Should a risk be determined to exist, s/he must not be transferred."

[6] Also referred to in Chapter 7: "Memorandum for the President from Alberto R. Gonzales, re: Decision re application of the Geneva Convention on Prisoners of War to the Conflict with Al Qaeda and the Taliban," 25 January 2002. In *The Torture Papers*, p.118.

7   Bush's Memorandum of 7 February 2002, states that Geneva "assumes the existence of 'regular' armed forces fighting on behalf of States. Also none of the provisions of Geneva apply to our conflict with Al Qaeda in Afghanistan or elsewhere in the world because, among other reasons, Al Qaeda is not a high contracting party to Geneva." In *The Torture Papers*, pp.134-5.

8   The requirement to hold a "competent tribunal" was specified in Article 4 of the POW Convention. The Red Cross's comments of 28 April 2006 stated that it never argued that all prisoners captured in a conflict such as in Afghanistan should be given POW status — "contrary to some assertions, the ICRC has never stated that all persons who have taken part in hostilities in an international armed conflict are entitled to POW status." The ICRC's position was simply that such a decision on status could not be decided in advance in Washington. It had to be determined on a case-by-case basis. Foreign fighters in Afghanistan, such as alleged members of Al Qaeda, were unlikely to be covered by the POW Convention, it believed. However, the laws of war and basic humanitarian law continued to provide them with equivalent protection against abusive treatment, for example, in the 1977 First Additional Protocol to the Geneva Conventions. Although this was never ratified by the United States, it contained an article 75 listing "fundamental guarantees" that have been taken by US government to be a definition of customary international law. (For example, William Taft, then deputy legal adviser of the State Department wrote in the *Yale Journal of International Law* in the summer of 2003 that: "While the US has major objections to parts of First Additional Protocol, it does regard the provisions of article 75 as an articulation of safeguards to which all persons in the hands of an enemy are entitled.") This Article 75 provides that anyone not protected by other conventions, would, under the laws of war, be guaranteed, at minimum to "be treated humanely in all circumstance" and not subject to "torture of all kinds, whether physical or mental … outrages upon personal dignity, in particular humiliating and degrading treatment … threats to commit any of the foregoing acts." Anyone arrested and charged with an offence related to the armed conflict "shall be informed promptly, in a language he understands, of the reasons why these measures have been taken. Except in cases of arrest or detention for penal offences, such persons shall be released with the minimum delay possible and in any event as soon as the circumstances justifying the arrest, detention or internment have ceased to exist." In addition, "no sentence may be passed and no penalty may be executed on a person found guilty of a penal offence related to the armed conflict except pursuant to a conviction pronounced by an impartial and regularly constituted court respecting the generally recognized principles of regular judicial procedure," which were elaborated in detail.

9   Clothing issue referred to in Schroen, *First In*, pp. 129-32. Most of the military did wear uniforms.

10   "Investigation into FBI Allegations of Detainee Abuse at Guantánamo Bay," Lieutenant General Randall M. Schmidt, 1 April 2005. Executive summary was published on www.defenselink.mil; the full report was not released. Al-Qahtani's name emerged in media accounts.

11   "Gonzales Says Humane-Policy Order Doesn't Bind C.I.A.," Eric Lichtblau, *New York Times*, 19 January 2005.

12   The McCain amendment (attached to the Department of Defense Appropriations Act, 2006) stated that: "No individual in the custody or under the physical control of the United States Government, regardless of nationality or physical location, shall be subject to cruel, inhuman, or degrading treatment or punishment." This ban was to be applied without "any geographic limitation." Although the term "cruel, inhuman, or degrading treatment or punishment" was defined in the amendment as meaning the same treatments or punishments already prohibited within the United States by the US Constitution (Fifth,

Eighth, and Fourteenth Amendments) as further described by the US reservations to the United Nations Convention Against Torture, none of the above provides a specific definition of the term "inhuman,"apart from making clear that the death penalty is not prohibited.

[13] See Memorandum from Jay S. Bybee for Alberto R. Gonzales, 1 August 2002, Sec. II: "U.N. Convention Against Torture and Other Cruel Inhuman or Degrading Treatment or Punishment," in *The Torture Papers*, pp. 184-6.

[14] "UN Convention Against Torture and Other Cruel, Inhuman or Degrading Treatment or Punishment, S. Treaty Doc. No. 100-20, 1465 U.N.T.S. 85, 10 December 1984. It was finally ratified by the United States in 1994.

[15] Senate Executive Report, no. 101-30 at Sections 13-14.

[16] The Senate's reservations to the Treaty can be found at www.ohchr.org/english/countries/ratification/9.htm#N11.

[17] Memo, Bybee to Gonzales, p. 38.

[18] Memorandum and Order from US District Judge David G. Trager, 16 February 2006.

[19] Interviews with former CIA officials 2005-6, including those cited below.

[20] Interview with Michael Scheuer, 14 March 2006.

[21] Yoo was a former clerk for US Supreme Court justice Clarence Thomas; he also served as general counsel of the US Senate Judiciary Committee 1995-6. As deputy assistant attorney general in the Office of legal counsel at the Department of Justice from 2001 to 2003, he worked on issues involving foreign affairs, national security, and the separation of powers. He is professor of law at the University of California, Berkeley Boalt Hall School of Law.

[22] John Yoo, "Symposium: The Changing Laws of War: Do We Need a New Legal Regime After Sept. 11?: Transferring Terrorists", *Notre Dame Law Review*, 1229 (2004)

[23] J. Herman Burgers and Hans Danelius, *The United Nations Convention Against Torture: A Handbook on the Convention Against Torture and Other Cruel, Inhuman or Degrading Treatment or Punishment*, (Dordrecht: Martinus Nijhoff, 1988), pp.125-6. According to Katherine Hawkins, "Interestingly, Burgers and Danelius say that the original draft of Article 3 referred only to expulsion and extradition, and that it was the addition of the prohibition on 'return ('refoulement')' that made Article 3 applicable to all transfers of persons. *Id.* at 126. So insofar as we are interested in the actual subjective intent of the CAT drafters, it appears that using the same phrasing as Article 33 of the Refugee Convention was intended to do exactly the opposite of what Yoo claims it was intended to do."

[24] Foreign Affairs Reform and Reconstruction Act of 1998, Section 2242(a)

[25] Hawkins, in the cited article, quotes Burgers and Danelius as pointing out "that the original draft of Article 3 referred only to expulsion and extradition, and that it was the addition of the prohibition on "return ('refoulement')" that made Article 3 applicable to all transfers of persons."

[26] 18 USC § 2340 (2005)

[27] 18 USC § 2340-340A

[28] 18 USC § 2340A (2005) (c) states: "A person who conspires to commit an offense under this section shall be subject to the same penalties (other than the penalty of death) as the penalties prescribed for the offense, the commission of which was the object of the conspiracy."

[29] *United States v. Huynh*, 246 F.3d at 745 (quoting *United States v. Burns*, 162 F.3d 840, 849 (5th Cir. 1998)).

[30] Memo by anonymous FBI official entitled "Legal Analysis of Interrogation Techniques", (27 Novemeber 2002) p.1, available at balkin.blogspot.com/rendition.fbi.memo.pdf. First reported in "Memo Probes US Policy on Terror Suspects" Michael Isikoff, *Newsweek*, 8 August 2005.

31 FBI, "Legal Analysis".
32 Responses of Alberto Gonzales, nominee to be attorney general, to the written supplemental questions of Senator Dianne Feinstein (D-California), January 2005.
33 Responses to Alberto Conzales, nominee to be attorney general, to the written supplemental questions of Senator Richard Durbin (D-Illinois), January 2005.
34 Interview with Edward S. Walker Jr., 13 March 2006.
35 Interview with Michael Scheuer, 14 March 2006. A report in the *Washington Post* also described the procedure for obtaining assurances as brief and informal: The CIA station chief of the country where the prisoner was being rendered requests a verbal assurance from the foreign intelligence service, and then cables the assurance back to CIA headquarters,". From "CIA's Assurances on Transferred Suspects Doubted," Dana Priest, *Washington Post*, 17 March 2005.
36 Interview with Edward S. Walker Jr., 13 March 2006.
37 Interview with Burton Gerber, 9 March 2006.
38 "Rule Change Lets CIA Freely Send Suspects Abroad to Jails", Douglas Jehl and David Johnston, *New York Times*, 6 March 2005.
39 Ibid.
40 "CIA's Assurances on Transferred Suspects Doubted", Dana Priest, *Washington Post*, 17 March 2005.
41 Interview with former senior official, CIA directorate of operations, 2005.
42 Alleged head of operations for Jemaah Islamiyya in Asia.
43 "This memorandum supersedes the August 2002 Memorandum in its entirety," stated the memorandum for James B. Comey, deputy attorney general, US Department of Justice, Office of Legal Counsel, 30 December 2004 (www.usdoj.gov/olc/dagmemo.pdf).
44 Interview with Burton Gerber, 9 March 2006.
45 Interviews with two former officials in the CIA's directorate of operations, 2006.
46 Yoo telephone interview with the *New Yorker's* Jane Mayer, cited in her piece "Outsourcing Torture", 14 February 2005.
47 Senator John McCain press release entitled "Senator John W. Warner and Senator John McCain. Statement on Presidential Signing Detainee Provisions", 4 January 2006.
48 "Rule Change Lets CIA Freely Send Suspects Abroad to Jails", Douglas Jehl and David Johnston, *New York Times*, 6 March 2005.
49 "A Fine Rendition", Michael Scheuer, *New York Times*, 11 March 2005.
50 "Secrets of the London Cage", Ian Cobain, *The Guardian*, 14 November 2005.
51 The case was *Ireland v. The United Kingdom* (ECHR 1, 5310/71) and the then attorney general was Samuel Silkin, Q.C., M.P.
52 These new regulations emerged from a report presented to Parliament by Prime Minister Blair in April 2005, entitled: "Government Response to the Intelligence and Security Committee's Report on the Handling of Detainees by UK Intelligence Personnel in Afghanistan, Guantánamo Bay and Iraq." Blair accepted the recommendation of the Intelligence and Security Committee (the UK parliament's intelligence oversight body) that "prior to their deployment, UK intelligence personnel are clearly instructed as to their duties and responsibilities in respect of the treatment of detainees and of the reporting procedures in the event of concerns." The precise scope of those "duties and responsibities" was not disclosed although a Foreign Office official, speaking on terms of anonymity, told me they included instructions not to be involved in any US rendition operations.
53 Jack Straw was speaking before the House of Commons' Foreign Affairs Committee, 13 December 2005. Transcript from www.publications.parliament.uk
54 Interview with senior British security source, 2005.
55 These figures were quoted in "Reports of Secret US Prisons in Europe Draw Ire and

Otherwise Red Faces", Ian Fisher, *New York Times*, 1 December 2005, to which the author contributed reporting.

[56] Telephone interview with Dr Georg Nolte, April 2005; quoted in "CIA Expanding Terror Battle Under Guise of Charter Flights", Scott Shane, Stephen Grey and Margot Williams, *New York Times*, 31 May 2005.

[57] First reported in "Rendition: The cover-up", Martin Bright, *New Statesman*, London, 23 January 2006. Copy of memo at www.newstatesman.com/pdf/rendition/rendition.pdf.

[58] Flightlogs of N379P; British government telegrams released in High Court hearing in London, author's file.

[59] Condoleezza Rice, in a press briefing with German Chancellor Angela Merkel, 6 December 2005. Transcript at www. state.gov.

[60] Transcript of British Prime Minister's press conference, 22 December 2005; quoted on news.bbc.co.uk/1/hi/uk_politics/4627360.stm.

[61] "Rendition: the cover-up", *New Statesman*.

[62] From interview by Porter Goss with *USA Today*, November 2005: "Lawmakers: Interrogators not using techniques to full benefit", John Diamond, *USA Today*, 21 November 2005; see also "CIA Chief: Methods 'Unique' but Legal", John Diamond, *USA Today*, 21 November 2005.

[63] Quoted in 'Memo on Torture Draws Focus to Bush', Mike Allen and Dana Priest, *Washington Post*, 9 June 2004.

[64] Walker interview.

[65] Interview with former senior offical in CIA directorate of operations, 2006.

11. THE REALPOLITIK OF TORTURE

[1] The Official Budget of the US government, financial year 2007, projects the spending of $2,770 billion (www.whitehouse.gov/omb/budget/fy2007/tables.html).

[2] Interview with Danielle Pletka, 21 January 2005, for BBC Radio 4.

[3] Interview with Michael Scheuer, 21 January 2005.

[4] Interview with Edward Walker Jr., 13 March 2006.

[5] Ten thousand in Afghanistan, from Deptartment of Defense news briefing, 13 February 2004 (www.defenselink.mil) and five hunded detained in Pakistan immediately following 9/11, according to the *9/11 Commission Report*, p. 368.

[6] Detailed in the account of the Tora Bora episode in Gary Berntsen's *Jawbreaker*.

[7] One Al Qaeda website recorded that "when retreat followed retreat in Afghanistan ... despair began to creep among many... and feelings of impending defeat and the end of the mujahideen there began to overtake them." Quoted in *The Next Attack*, Daniel Benjamin and Steven Simon (New York: Times Books, 2005), p. 23.

[8] Al-Nashiri, the presumed leader of Al Qaeda in the Gulf, was wanted in connection with the attack on the USS *Cole*; he was arrested in 2002. Ghailani (aka Ahmed the Tanzanian) was wanted in connection with the 1998 US Embassy bombings in Africa; he had been on the FBI's Most Wanted list since then; he was arrested in Pakistan in August 2004.

[9] Interviews with CIA contractor, 2005-6.

[10] Interview with British security source, 2005.

[11] Interview with Burton Gerber, 9 March 2006.

[12] Solzhenitsyn, *Gulag Archipelago*, vol. I, p 101.

[13] "Shift On Suspect Is Linked To Role Of Qaeda Figures" Douglas Jehl and Eric Lichtblau, *New York Times*, 24 November 2005.

[14] According to the *9/11 Commission Report* (pp. 446, 490, 491, 500, 507, 524, 527),

interrogations of Abu Zubaydah were listed as having taken place on the following dates: 10 July 2002; 29 August 2002; 29 October 2002; 7 November 2002; 16 May 2003; 24 June 2003; 13 December 2003; 18 February 2004 and 19 February 2004.

15 "Shift on Suspect Is Linked To Role Of Qaeda Figures", Douglas Jehl and Eric Lichtblau, *New York Times*, 24 November 2005.

16 Interview with Craig Murray, 9 January 2006.

17 Known as the "Tipton Three" because they were all from Tipton, in the English Midlands, Shafiq Rasul, Ruhal Ahmed and Asif Iqbal, underwent over 200 interrogations by both American and British military and security services. By checking police, employment and passport records, British police finally proved that the three men were in the UK at the time they were accused of appearing in an Al Qaeda video. Reported in "Revealed: the full story of the Guantánamo Britons", David Rose, *The Observer*, 14 March 2004.

18 Interview with former official in the CIA's directorate of intelligence.

19 Ted Morgan, a draftee in Algeria in 1956-57, in a speech to the National Press Club Book Rap on 14 March 2006. As reported in the National Press Club newsletter, *The Record*, 23 March 2006. Morgan is the author of *My Battle of Algiers: A Memoir* (New York: Harper Collins, 2006).

20 The tactic of inciting repression dates back to nineteenth-century anarchism. It was rejected by many early communists, including the Russian revolutionary leader Vladimir Lenin, who argued that terrorism was only justified at the critical moment of revolution to help seize power. See also "The Nature of Modern Terrorism", Dr John Gearson (Senior Lecturer in Terrorism Studies at King's College, London), *The Political Quarterly*, (August 2002). Translation of the manual from Website: http://www.baader-meinhof.com/students/resources/print/minimanual/manualtext.html

21 "Torture's Terrible Toll", John McCain, *Newsweek*, 21 November 2005.

22 Interview with Alastair Crooke, 4 April 2006.

23 "Against Rendition", Reuel Marc Gerecht, *The Weekly Standard*, 16 May 2005.

CONCLUSION — WINNING THE WAR

1 Presidential nomination acceptance speech to the 2004 Republican National Convenion, New York City, 2 September 2004 (www.whitehouse.gov/news/releases/2004/09/20040902 -2html).

2 Daniel Benjamin and Steven Simon, in *The Next Attack: The Failure of the War on Terror and a Strategy for Getting it Right* (New York: Times Books, 2005), cite senior analysts at the CIA, FBI and the Terrorist Threat Integration Centre, who all poured scorn on the figure as a "White House number". They conclude: "The claim is hard to comprehend. No intelligence agency is known to have fully mapped Al Qaeda's leadership then or now, and many terrorism analysts would question whether that was even possible or meaningful given the fluidity of the group and its impressive ability to replace its losses by promoting from within." (p. 25).

3 Data from the National Counterterrorism Centre, a multi-agency organisation that works closely with the CIA's Counter-Terrorist Center (CTC) and was established in 2004 as part of US intelligence reforms following the 9/11 Commission. Worldwide Incidents Tracking System (WITS) (www.nctc.gov. and wits.nctc.gov./Incidents.do).

4 The "planes operation" was originally conceived by Khaled Sheik Mohammed in 1995. But it did not receive interest or approval from bin Laden until 1999. See: *9/11 Commission Report*, Chapter 5, Section 5.2, pp. 153-4.

5 "There are some who feel like — that the conditions are such that they can attack us there.

My answer is, bring them on. We've got the force necessary to deal with the security situation.", White House transcript, 2 July 2003 (www.whitehouse.gv/news/releases/2003/07/20030702-3.html).

6   Data from the National Counterterrorism Centre's (NCTC), Worldwide Incidents Tracking System (WITS) (www.nctc.gov and wits.nctc.gov/Incidents.do).

7   *The Clash of Civilizations and the Remaking of World Order* Samuel P. Huntington (New York: Simon & Schuster, 1996).

8   Prime Minister Tony Blair said in an address to the nation on 20 March 2003, "But this new world faces a new threat: of disorder and chaos born either of brutal states like Iraq, armed with weapons of mass destruction; or of extreme terrorist groups. Both hate our way of life, our freedom, our democracy." (www.number10gov.uk/output/Page33322.asp). President Bush said on 13 September 2001: "These people can't stand freedom; they hate our values; they hate what America stands for." (www.whitehouse.gov/news/releases/2001/09/200109 13-4.html).

9   This point is also made by Michael Scheuer in *Imperial Hubris*, p. 217.

10 Originally broadcast on Al Jazeera television on 10 February 2005; transcript from BBC news monitoring service.

11 Interview with senior US counter-terrorism officer, January 2005.

12 "The Ricin Ring that Never Was" Duncan Campbell, *The Guardian*, 14 April 2005.

13 Interview with Alastair Crooke, 4 April 2006.

14 *A Bright Shining Lie,* Neil Sheehan (New York: Vintage, 1988), p.697.

15 All data from the *CIA World Factbook*: http://www.cia.gov/cia/publications/factbook/index.html.

   Algeria: When the Islamic Salvation Front looked set to win the country's first round of elections in 1991, the army intervened and cancelled the elections. In 1991, the military appointed Abdelaziz Bouteflika president and he was re-elected in 2004 with 85 per cent of the vote.

   Egypt: The first multi-candidate elections were held in 2005. Marred by violence and allegations of fraud, and with a low voter turnout (30 per cent), President Mubarak was re-elected with 88.6 per cent of votes. The main opposition candidate, Ayman Nour, has since been sentenced to a five-year prison term for alleged forgery.

   Syria: It has had a secular authoritarian government since 1970. Despite holding parliamentary elections, there is a constitutional guarantee that 50 per cent of the seats go to the ruling Ba'ath party. President Bashar al Assad was re-elected with 67 per cent of the vote in 2003.

   Tunisia: President Bourguiba ruled in a one-party system from 1956 to 1987. Since then the president has been Zine el Abidine Ben Ali, who was re-elected in 2004 with 94.5 per cent of the vote.

   Yemen: President Salih has ruled since the country was officially unified in 1990. He was last re-elected in 1999 with 96.3 pr cent of the vote.

16 "How the United States is Perceived in the Arab and Muslim Worlds", Testimony of Andrew Kohut to the US House of Representatives, International Relations Committee, Subcommittee on Oversight and Investigations, 10 November 2005.

17 Since the 1980s, every US budget has included a clause stipulating that Egypt should receive no less than $1.3 billion in foreign military aid, yet it took until 2005 for the country to hold semi-democratic elections and in April 2006 Egypt approved an extension of its 1982 emergency law allowing the indefinite detention of suspects without charge. The US continues to buy oil from and sell arms to countries like Saudi Arabia, despite the fact that they (and many Arab countries) boycott Israeli goods and ban Israelis from travelling to their country.

[18] US State Department report on Human Rights Practices, 2002, Uzbekistan. Available at www.state.gov.

[19] Figures from USAID, the US Overseas Loans and Grants, Obligations and Loan Authorisations, known as the "Greenbook" (qesdb.cdie.org/gbk/index.html).

[20] The US has since reduced the amount of aid to Uzbekistan because of the continued abuses there. In 2002, the US gave Uzbekistan $167.3 million in aid; in 2004 that figure was $42.3 million

[21] Interview with Michael Scheuer, 21 January 2005.

[22] In 2002: $2.2 billion; 2003: $1.75 billion; 2004: $1.96 billion. Figures from USAID "Greenbook".

[23] In 2002: $1.3 billion; 2003: $1.29 billion; 2004: $1.29 billion. Ibid.

[24] "Against Rendition", Reuel Marc Gerecht.

[25] Since 9/11, praise has been lavished on the progress made by dictatorial regimes. "I don't accept the fact that [Egypt] is stagnating, and I don't accept the fact that the government of Egypt doesn't want to change, commented Ken Ellis, head of USAID Egypt in 2004, (as quoted in "$50 billion later, taking stock of US aid to Egypt", Charles Levinson, *The Christian Science Monitor*, 12 April 2004.

Paul Wolfowitz, former US deputy defense secretary, said on 16 January 2005: "The real way ahead is through what I think is an impressive movement throughout the Arab world toward political reform. You read in places like Egypt and Saudi Arabia about people talking openly about democracy in a way they never did before. In places like Morocco, they actually have made real political reforms". (Interview in *Tempo* magazine, Jakarta).

White House Press Statement announcing the visit of Uzbek president Karimov to Washington on 21 February 2002: "The President's discussion will reflect the new relationship that is evolving between the United States and Uzbekistan. The countries' unprecedented level of cooperation first became evident in the fight against terrorists in Afghanistan." (Statement on www.whitehouse.gov.)

President Bush's statement welcoming King Mohamed VI of Morocco to Washington declared: "Countries like Morocco are leaders in advancing the cause of peace and prosperity, and deserve our full support. America is lucky to have a friend such as Morocco, and thanks His Majesty King Mohamed VI for his leadership." (8 July 2004 statement on www.whitehouse.gov.).

[26] "Iraq terror backlash in UK 'for years'" David Leppard, *Sunday Times*, 2 April 2006.

[27] ICM Research/Panorama Terrorist Poll, 28-9 Sept. 2001 (www.icmresearch.co.uk/reviews/2001/terrorist-poll-sept-2001.htm).

[28] "Nous sommes tous Américains", *Le Monde*, 13 September 2001.

[29] Poll by *Sofres/Nouvel Observateur*, Nov. 2-3 2001 showed 65 per cent with sympathy for the US, compared with 41 per cent in May 2000 (www.tns-sofres.com/etudes/pol/141201_usa_r.htm).

[30] *The 9/11 Commission Report*, p. 375.

[31] "Global Outrage At Terror Attacks", CBS News, 12 September 2001 (www.cbsnews.com/stories/2001/09/11/archive/main310763.shtml).

[32] Various news sources, including CNN.com (archives.cnn.com/2001/WORLD/europe/09/12/world.reaction/index.html).

[33] Figures from White House press release, "President thanks world coalition for anti-terrorism efforts", 11 March 2002.

[34] Deputy Defense Secretary Wolfowitz press conference in Brussels, 26 September 2001 (transcript available at www.defenselink.mil).

[35] *Global Opinion: The Spread of Anti-Americanism*, Pew Global Attitudes Project, 21 January 2005 (pewglobal.org/commentary/pdf/104.pdf).

[36] For example, in November 2002, a British citizen Wahab al-Rawi and two British residents, Jamil al Banna, and Wahab's brother, Bisher al-Rawi, were arrested in the Gambia after the UK supplied intelligence indicating they were close to the militant British-based cleric Abu Qatada. The US arranged for the arrest of all three. Wahab was released after a month, during which period he was denied access to British consular officials; the other two were rendered to a CIA jail in Afghanistan in the agency's Gulfstream V and then subsequently to Guantánamo. Another British citizen, Martin Mubanga, was also picked up in Zambia in 2002, and rendered to Guantánamo. In both cases, UK government sources insisted they did not approve of the CIA's use of extra-legal methods, though it was not clear if they were informed at the time or had made any protests.

[37] *The Next Attack*, p. 201.

[38] "Against Rendition", by Reuel Marc Gerecht, *The Weekly Standard*, 16 May 2005.

[39] Interview with Chris Mackey, 12 January 2005.

[40] Interview with former case officer, CIA directorate of operations, 2006

[41] *The Prophet and Pharaoh: Muslim Extremism in Egypt*, Gilles Kepel, pp. 28, 41-3.

[42] From footage of the trial, described in "The Man Behind Bin Laden", Lawrence Wright, *New Yorker*, 16 September 2002.

[43] Interview with Jack Devine, New York, 21 April 2006.

Epilogue

[44] Interview with Mohamed Bashmilah and his mother, Yemen, 6/7 May 2006.

[45] "German spy knew about el-Masri kidnapping," UPI wire report, 1 June 2006.

[46] "Opening Remarks at the US Meeting With the UN Committee Against Torture Geneva, Switzerland", by John B. Bellinger III, 5 May 2006. Transcript from State Department Web site.

[47] Interview with Michael Scheuer, 14 March 2006.

[48] Fourth warrant issued in the investigation into kidnapping of Abu Omar in Milan, signed 3 July 2006 by Judge Enrico Manzi. Also see "Inquiry in 2003 Abduction Rivets Italy," Stephen Grey and Elisabetta Povoledo, *New York Times*, 8 July 2006.

[49] The Gulfstream was offered for sale, with full details of its history, on a Web site www.usaircraftsales.com. Its sale was confirmed by the FAA's aircraft registry on www.faa.gov which listed its new owner as a Florida company, N126CH Inc, whose officers were the owners of a major property development company. There is no suggestion the company or the owners have any relationship with the US government.

[50] *Hamdan v. Rumsfeld*, Secretary of Defense, et al., decided by the Supreme Court on 29 June 2006.

APPENDIX

[1] *A Spy for All Seasons* Duane R. Clarridge, with Digby Diehl (New York, Scribner, 1997).

[2] FBI Report, *Terrorism in the United States 1999*, published January 1999, p.52.

[3] Ibid.

[4] Described in Chapter 6, first reported by Yasser al-Sirri, Islamic Observation Centre in London. Al-Sirri is quoted, citing the date of the handover, in Anthony Shadid, "America Prepares the War on Terror; US, Egypt Raids Caught Militants," *Boston Globe*, 7 October 2001.

[5] *Terrorism in the United States 1999*, p.52

[6] Ibid.

7 US State Department, *Patterns of Global Terrorism*, 1999, Appendix D, published April 2000.

8 *Terrorism in the United States 1999*, p.52

9 First reported by Islamic Observation Center, London, and described by Andrew Higgins and Christopher Cooper, in "CIA-Backed Team Used Brutal Means To Break Up Terrorist Cell in Albania," *Wall Street Journal*, 20 November 2001.

10 *Terrorism in the United States 1999*, p.52

11 Reported by Shadid, 7 October 2001

12 Interview in December 2004 in Cairo with Mahfuz 'Azzam, an uncle of the al-Zawahiri brothers, cited in "Black Hole: The Fate of Islamists Rendered to Egypt," Tom Kellogg and Hossam el-Hamalawy, Human Rights Watch, May 2005; interview with senior former CIA officer, 2006, confirming US involvement.

13 *Terrorism in the United States 1999*, p.52.

14 Press reports including "Bomb suspect loses bid for deportation," Michael J Sniffen, *Chicago Sun-Times*, 8 October 1999.

15 Interview with Mahfuz Azzam, op. cit.

16 Yasser al-Sirri, Islamic Observation Centre, London; Italian security sources in May 2006; interview with former FBI official, Jack Cloonan, 19 April 2006.

17 Source: FBI/State Department.

18 Statement from Ma'ri's brother to a Combatant Status Review Tribunal at Guantánamo, October 2004, de-classified and released by the Pentagon. The statement disclosed a letter from Ma'ri, sent via the International Committee of the Red Cross, when he was held in Jordan.

19 "Mystery man handed over to US troops in Karachi", Masood Anwar, *The News International*, Pakistan, 26 October 2001.

20 Email to author, 7 December 2004, from Habib's former lawyer, Stephen Hopper, based on testimony by Habib at Guantánamo.

21 Details of transfer from Sylvia Royce, a member of Slahi's legal team, in emails, July/August, 2005.

22 "Saudi Family to Sue US for Kidnapping Its Member", *Pakistan News Service*, 17 January 2002.

23 See Chapter 1 for details of case.

24 Detailed in "Classified Report to German Parliament", see Prologue and Chapter 4.

25 Amnesty International Action Sheet: "Walid Muhammad Shahir Muhammad al-Qadasi," August 2005. Amnesty International index number AMR 51/127/2005.

26 Interview with Clive Stafford Smith, his lawyer at Guantánamo, May 2006.

27 "US Takes Custody Of a Qaeda Trainer Seized by Pakistan," Eric Schmitt with Erik Eckholm, *New York Times*, 6 January 2002.

28 Schmitt and Eckholm, 6 January 2002 (his initial capture); interview with Jack Cloonan, 19 April 2006; and interview, on condition of anonymity, in 2006 with a former prisoner held with him at Bagram (on his transfer to Egypt and return), hereafter "Bagram prisoner interview."

29 In their "Report on Guantánamo Detainees: A Profile of 517 Detainees through Analysis of Department of Defense Data," published February 2006 as Seton Hall Public Law Research Paper No. 46, Mark Denbeaux, a professor at Seton Hall University School of Law and Joshua Denbeaux, an attorney, studied the profile of detainees at Guantánamo, using de-classified documents, and found that: "Only 5% of the detainees were captured by United States forces. 86% of the detainees were arrested by either Pakistan or the Northern Alliance and turned over to United States custody." Among those captured in Pakistan, and named in a detailed list published on www.cageprisoners.com, a British Web site that has

monitored all the residents of Guantánamo Bay, were: Abdullah al Noaimi from Bahrain, Ahmed Errachidi from Morocco, Karama Khamis of Yemen, Nizar Sassi of France, Mohammed al-Daihani of Kuwait, Omar Rajab Amin of Kuwait, Issa Ali Abdullah Al-Murbati, Fawzi al-Odah of Kuwait, Adil Kamil Abdullah Haji of Bahrain, Abd Al Aziz Sayer Uwain Al Shammari of Kuwait, Mehdi Muhammad Ghezali of Sweden, Abdullah Saleh Ali al-Ajmi of Kuwait, Abdullah Kamal al-Kandari of Kuwait, Adel al-Zamel of Kuwait, Abdul Hakeem Bukhari, Jamal Abdullah Kiyemba of Uganda.

30 "US Behind Secret Transfer of Terror Suspects", Rajiv Chandrasekaran and Peter Finn, *Washington Post*, 11 March 2002

31 Memo from Mark C. Fleming, attorney to the Bosnia rendition prisoners, to Claudio Fava, rapporteur of the European Parliament inquiry into CIA renditions, 10 February 2006.

32 Shaqawi's transfers were reported in un-dated written testimony by him at Guantánamo obtained by the author. The arrest of "Riyadh the facilitator" described, among other reports, in "US believes it has senior Al-Qaeda leader in custody," John J Lumpkin, Associated Press, 31 March 2002.

33 Testimony of released detainees, see for example "At-a-glance: Guantánamo Bay Britons," BBC News website, January 27, 2005 (news.bbc.co.uk/1/hi/uk/4163911.stm).

34 Ibid.

35 "Al Qaeda recruit consented to go to US", Stewart Bell, *National Post*, Canada, 15 February 2006.

36 Interview with Rahman in "Ex-Gitmo Jordanian Describes Hell in US Prisons," Tareq Delawani, *IslamOnline.net*, 5 July 5 2004.

37 "5-Year Hunt Fails to Net Qaeda Suspect in Africa," Desmond Butler, *New York Times*, 14 June 2003, and "American Operation in Mogadishu," *Indian Ocean Newsletter*, 22 March 2003.

38 Abu Zubaydah's interrogation in US custody recorded in the 9/11 Commission report. pp. 466, 490, 491, 500, 507, 524, 527

39 Testimony to Clive Stafford Smith at Guantánamo, described at www.reprieve.org.uk/casework_omardeghayes.htm

40 Email from Hopper, 7 December 2004, cited above. After his release, Habib told one reporter, who asked to remain anonymous, that he was on the same flight as Madni.

41 Interview with Martin Mubanga, 20 November 2005.

42 Interview with Abdullah Almalki, 21 November 2005 and interview with Walid Saffour of the Syrian Human Rights Committee, London, 6 April 2006.

43 Almalki, 21 November 2005.

44 Britel was interviewed during a brief period of release by the International Federation for Human Rights, Paris, and cited in the organisation's, "*Morocco: Human Rights Abuse in the Fight Against Terrorism*", Report 379/2, July 2004, p.18.

45 Report of his transfer in "Terrorism: Indonesia Getting Its Act Together", Yang Razali Kassim, *The Business Times*, Singapore, 22 October 2002.

46 Interview with Tinawi, 31 May 2006.

47 Royce emails, July/August 2005.

48 CSS Memo, 10 June 2005, as cited in Chapter 2.

49 "Al Qaeda Threat Has Increased, Tenet Says," Dana Priest and Susan Schmidt, *Washington Post*, 18 October 2002, and "US Decries Abuse but Defends Interrogations," Dana Priest and Barton Gellman, *Washington Post*, 26 December 2002.

50 Testimony cited in "Seven Detainees Report Transfer to Nations That Use Torture," Farah Stockman, *Boston Globe*, 26 April 2006, and other testimony to his lawyers at Guantánamo.

51 His arrest was announced publicly and he is one of ten high-value detainees confirmed officially in the *9/11 Commission Report* (pp. 146, 488) as in US custody.

52 "Cairo to Kabul to Guantánamo: the Abd al-Salam Ali al-Hela case," *Human Rights Watch* briefing paper, issued 30 March 2005, citing interviews with al-Hela's brother and reports by an Egyptian state-run news agency that confirmed his transfer to Azerbaijan. Also "Case Sheet 15: Abdulsalem al-Hela," Amnesty International, 11 January 2005, also citing interview with his family. Some reports however suggest he was transferred from Egypt directly to Afghanistan. In a letter smuggled out of Afghanistan, where he was by June 2003, al-Hela appears to be unaware that he may have been held in Azerbaijan.

53 See multiple sources cited in chapter 3.

54 Interview with Tinawi, 31 May 2006.

55 One of ten high-value detainees confirmed officially in the *9/11 Commission Report* (pp. 146, 488) as in US custody.

56 Testimony to Clive Stafford Smith at Guantánamo, detailed in email to author, March 22, 2006.

57 Al-Hayat, 8 December 2004.

58 *Italian first warrant*, and other multiple sources cited in Chapter 9.

59 One of ten high-value detainees confirmed officially in the *9/11 Commission Report* (pp. 146, 488) as in US custody.

60 Al-Hawsawi's detention in US custody was confirmed during the 2006 trial in Virginia of Zacarias Moussaoui, in which selected interrogation reports from al-Hawsawi were disclosed; reported in "Defense Tries to Undo Damage Moussaoui Did," Neil A Lewis, *New York Times*, 29 March 2006.

61 "Terror funding hurt by Al Qaeda arrest in Pakistan", Scott Baldauf, *Christian Science Monitor*, 17 March 2003.

62 "Algerian Tells of Dark Odyssey in US Hands", Craig S. Smith and Souad Mekhennet, *New York Times*, 7 July 2006.

63 "Bagram prisoner interview." Arrest Described in "Al Qaeda Agent's 9/11 Role Comes Into Focus," Richard A Serrano, *Los Angeles Times*, 21 May 2006

64 Their presence in US detention was confirmed after a federal judge in the New York trial of Uzair Paracha allowed defence lawyers to introduce evidence from Ali and Khan's interrogations, described in Serrano, 21 May 2006.

65 "USA/Malawi: Another Unlawful Transfer to US Custody?," *Amnesty International* press release (reference AMR 51/092/2003), 25 June 2003.

66 Source: "Alleged Qaeda Big Goes to Bagram," *CBS News*, 14 July 2003.

67 Ibid.

68 Statement from Paracha dictated 8 December 2004, and admitted as evidence in his Combatant Status Review Tribunal held the same month at Guantánamo and de-classified by the Pentagon. In the statement, Paracha says he was arrested at Bangkok airport on 6 July and held "for a few days" at an unknown place before being flown to Afghanistan.

69 Hambali is one of ten high-value detainees confirmed officially in the *9/11 Commission Report* (pp. 146, 488) as in US custody. Details of the arrest of bin Lep and Amin in "Bali: Could It Happen Again?", Simon Elegant and Andrew Perrin, *Time* magazine, 13 October 2003.

70 Testimony by prisoners to Amnesty International, described in "Below the Radar: Secret Flights to Torture and 'Ddisappearance'," *Amnesty International*, 5 April 2006; interview with Bashmilah by the author in Sanaa, 6/7 May, 2006.

71 "Below the Radar," 5 April 2006

72 Bush's reference to Ghul in "President Bush Calls for Medical Liability Reform," White House news release, 26 January 2004. Ghul was also of ten high-value detainees confirmed officially in the *9/11 Commission Report* (pp. 146, 488) as in US custody.

73 Bin Attash's transfer reported in Stockman, 26 April 2006; Shaqawi's transfers reported in undated written testimony made by him at Guantánamo, obtained by author.

74 CSS Memo, 10 June 2005.

75 His journey was described in his testimony after release, detailed in "Classified Report to German Parliament," see Chapter 4.

76 "Below the Radar," 5 April 2006.

77 Ibid.; Bashmilah interview, 6/7 May 2006.

78 "Al Qaeda Arrest in June Opened Valuable Leads," Kamran Khan, *Washington Post*, 3 August 2004.

79 "Pakistan Hands Over 1998 Bomber to US," Anwar Iqbal, *United Press International*, 3 August 2004, and other wire reports.

80 Multiple testimony of detainees at Guantánamo, described in memo to author from Clive Stafford Smith, 13 January 2006.

81 "US military says Al Qaeda suspect taken to USA," (no byline), *USA Today*, 8 June 2005, re-printing an Associated Press report that quoted a US military spokesman saying al-Libi was flown directly into US custody from Pakistan, and not to Afghanistan.

82 "Below the Radar," 5 April 2006; Bashmilah interview, 6/7 May 2006.

INDEX